T0265781

EMPIRE'S SON, EMPIRE'S ORPHAN

EMPIRE'S SON, EMPIRE'S ORPHAN

✦✦✦✦✦

The Fantastical Lives of Ikbal and Idries Shah

Nile Green

W. W. NORTON & COMPANY
Independent Publishers Since 1923

For information about permission to reproduce selections
from this book, write to Permissions, W. W. Norton & Company, Inc.,
500 Fifth Avenue, New York, NY 10110

For information about special discounts for bulk purchases, please
contact W. W. Norton Special Sales at specialsales@wwnorton.com
or 800-233-4830

Manufacturing by Lake Book Manufacturing
Book design by Lovedog Studio
Production managers: Louise Mattarelliano and Julia Druskin

ISBN: 978-1-324-00241-3

W. W. Norton & Company, Inc.
500 Fifth Avenue, New York, N.Y. 10110
www.wwnorton.com

W. W. Norton & Company Ltd.
15 Carlisle Street, London W1D 3BS

1 2 3 4 5 6 7 8 9 0

For Nushin
for whom truth knows no country

This book is a record of a struggle between
two temperaments, two consciences and
almost two epochs. It ended, as was
inevitable, in disruption.

—Edmund Gosse, *Father and Son* (1907)

CONTENTS

EMPIRE'S SON, EMPIRE'S ORPHAN

PREFACE

THE BEARDED FIGURE IN THE ROBE AND RAY-BANS SITS cross-legged on a leopard skin, reading from a bookstand of the kind used for the Quran.[1] As heir to a mystical lineage in the Hindu Kush, he is expounding the cryptic tales of a trickster called Nasrudin, whose riddles encapsulate the wisdom of the East. Pausing to provide commentary, he looks over his shoulder to where seated women wear long skirts and caftans. Three young men stand to attention, brandishing swords and clad in Moroccan djellabahs. They look hot, and perhaps feel a little foolish, in the bright sunshine. One of them sports a turban; another, the same sunglasses as his cross-legged teacher, who says he is from Afghanistan. But everyone in this country house garden is dressing up today. No one realizes the teacher was raised in the London suburbs, the son of a father from India and a mother from Scotland.

The teacher has inherited his talk of "the East" from his father, who wrote countless works on Islam and Afghanistan for readers in the West. By the time the son's followers gather round him that summer afternoon in 1965, he has written several books of his own. Not on Islam—everyone knows religion's days are numbered—but on the occult and magic. Recently, though, he has published a book on the Sufis, and it's selling well—the most celebrated poet in the English-speaking world has even penned a preface for it. The 1960s are well underway, and for young bohemians, the mystical East is where it's at. In England, the great political game of empire is over, so empire's orphans now have to find other games to play in the harmless realm of culture. And since the British Empire has dissolved, the man on the leopard skin has found his mission in guiding his fellow orphans.

✦

ALTHOUGH THE TEACHER—his name was Idries—had a great sense for the dramatic, he usually preferred to hide behind a type-writer rather than a beard and sunglasses. Words offered many more possibilities of self-reinvention, of reaching others far and wide, of literary play with high stakes. His father, Ikbal, was also a prolific author. One in the age of empire, the other in its aftermath, both father and son were raised on legends of heroic Afghan ancestors, whom both men pursued in a quest for authenticity—that modern chimera that haunted their contemporaries. Together they helped shape how Afghanistan and the entire Muslim world were perceived on both sides of the Atlantic.

With their gift for literary gamesmanship, Ikbal and Idries wrote works that appealed to everyone from readers of middlebrow potboilers to public intellectuals and politicians. For all their idiosyncrasies and inventions, they both sought to harmonize Islam with the West in ways that echoed the ideals of other Muslim liberals of their day. Their rise to prominence involved literary agents and book publishers, newspaper editors and spymasters, publicists and poets. Yet their struggle to enter the Anglo-Saxon networks of publishing and politics involved a series of masquerades that incrementally created a make-believe world. And as publishing and politics converged through their shared concerns with the Muslim world, the East that Ikbal and Idries depicted increasingly diverged from the changing facts on the ground. Invented by empire, then cultivated in the nostalgic soil of exile, theirs was the myth of an Afghan Shangri-La that emerged, as it ended, in conflict.

Their story began long before and far away from that summer day of dressing up in an English garden. It began instead on the bloody frontiers of the British Empire where the need for local allies initiated the convergence of unfamiliar worlds. One of those allies was Ikbal and Idries's ancestor: a wily Afghan warrior called Jan Fishan Khan.

Way back in 1839, British officers led an army of largely Indian soldiers that crossed the Khyber Pass to successfully conquer Afghanistan. But three years later the British found themselves unable to win the peace, prompting what they hoped would be a dignified withdrawal. It soon descended into a massacre. For decades afterward along the winding road from Kabul to Jalalabad, the unburied bones of sixteen thousand foot soldiers and camp followers lay scattered with those of their pack animals. Forty years later in London, the memory of those events was frozen forever in a painting of an exhausted Scotsman riding a sagging horse to a mudbrick garrison. In the distance, a party of British officers gallops out to greet him, the heroic lone survivor. Yet like primer beneath paint, the true picture of events had a murkier texture, made of collusion and compromise. And when Kabul had first fallen within Britain's widening imperial horizon, one man symbolized the blurred hues of mixed loyalties and merged identities that made empire possible. His name was Sayyid Muhammad Shah; or to use the bellicose title by which he was better known, he was Jan Fishan Khan, the "Scatterer of Souls."

A hereditary landlord from the village of Paghman, near Kabul, Jan Fishan had found himself drawn into the fighting as his highland orchards gained strategic value in the battle for the capital. Rather than join the growing rebellion, though, he sided with the invaders during their triumphant early years of occupation. Then, as the capital and countryside began to fall to the rebels, he escaped to exile in India with the first rounds of evacuees who left ahead of the great massacre. Even so, much danger still lay on the long road to Delhi, and in defense of his Christian companions, Jan Fishan lived up to his martial sobriquet. He, too, was later painted. Two hawkish eyes stare out of the portrait from beneath eyebrows defiant as an archer's bow; above them, a broad turban magnifies the size of his skull, while below, a black beard hangs into a point that draws down the gaze to the dagger in his belt. He was one of Britain's best allies in Afghanistan. But unlike the image of the heroic Scotsman, his painting wouldn't be reproduced on patriotic tins of shortbread.

Yet, the expansion of the British Empire would never have been possible without the alliance of such men; and the lands the British conquered in India provided rich revenues to reward such allies as Jan Fishan. So they granted him a little palace on a large estate in fertile agricultural land at Sardhana, just fifty miles north of Delhi.[2] It was a good exchange for the pomegranate groves he had left behind in Afghanistan, and he was happy with the new empire he had entered. Fifteen years later, when rumors of a potential uprising spread across northern India, Jan Fishan dashed off to convene a discreet meeting with the British commander at Kanpur, warning him of the coming danger.[3] When in 1857 Indian soldiers did indeed rebel in their barracks at Kanpur, Jan Fishan assembled an irregular cavalry to suppress them. After joining the British—and the Indian soldiers who remained loyal to them—in the consequent recapture of Delhi, he was officially commended for "gallant service."[4] The Scatterer of Souls was still in business, and a remunerative business it was. The British not only expanded his estate but also endowed him with a pension and the title Nawwab of Sardhana. A Persian word, *nawwab* originally referred to a deputy or viceroy of the Mughal emperors. But as their empire was replaced by the British, the latter maintained such old titles to tie India's aristocrats to their new dispensation. So attached did Jan Fishan become to his British allies that a report on the recapture of Delhi recounted that, "flushed with excitement of the battle, the Afghan chief is said to have declared that another such day would make him a Christian."[5]

When Jan Fishan died in 1864, his lands and title as Nawwab of Sardhana passed down to his heirs. As the empire reached its peak in the long reign of Victoria, the Nawwabs of Sardhana lived quiet lives in their palace. Their status was as secure as the empire itself: they were, after all, a small section of its bedrock. Modest though it was in size, the palace was elegant in form, entered through an arched gateway, above which was a five-arched balcony, or *naqqara-khana*, where musicians would announce the nawwabs' coming and going. Meanwhile, as the tales of Jan Fishan were embellished with each telling, the passing of time turned Afghanistan into a place of romance in the family's imagination.

But as a new century drew nigh, there were calls to look to the future, as modernizing ideas began to spread among India's Muslim elites. When in 1894 one of the subsequent nawwabs' wives gave birth to a boy called Ikbal, his counselors suggested he should receive a different education from his hunting and hawking forebears. He was an aristocrat, certainly; even as a boy he inherited the noble title of *sirdar*. Yet the nawwab's counselors advised that the boy should not be raised by traditional tutors in the palace at Sardhana. Instead, he should be sent to the Muhammadan Anglo-Oriental College, a British-style school three hours south of Sardhana by train. Designed as a blend of Mughal madrassa and Oxford college, the school had been founded twenty years earlier to rear a new generation of Indian Muslims in the loyalty and skills to serve the imperial bureaucracy. There, alongside the sons of other Muslim gentry, the young sirdar would learn the English language of the wide world that reached far beyond India. And later, were the nawwab to agree, his son might even be sent to university in Britain.

The nawwab followed his counselors' advice. In July 1913, after graduating from the Muhammadan Anglo-Oriental College, Ikbal sailed from Bombay aboard the P&O steamship *Salsette* to commence his studies in distant Edinburgh.[6] From the mountains that surrounded Kabul to the rural reaches of Sardhana and the industrial cities of Scotland, empire was drawing different worlds together. Somehow they would have to come to terms with each other. Ikbal, and his own son in turn, would try to help them. Entangled in the larger contests of empire and its unraveling, their own great games were about to begin as father and son played what chips they had in their new adoptive homeland.

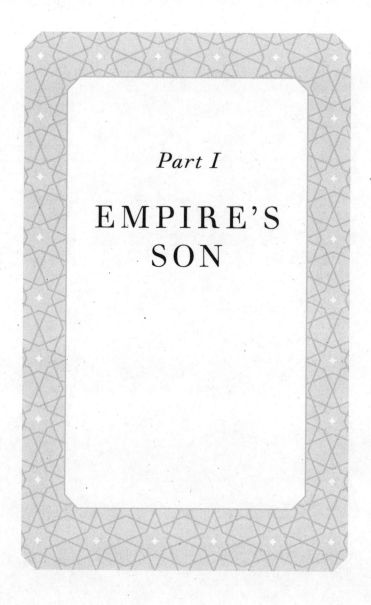

Part I

EMPIRE'S SON

Chapter One

STUDENT

The system on which I was being educated deprived all
things, human life among the rest, of their mystery.

—Edmund Gosse, *Father and Son*

HOW SMALL AND GRAY THIS COUNTRY SEEMED COMPARED
to its empire! The nineteen-year-old sirdar Ikbal Ali Shah had
crossed the whole of England, from its southern capital all the way
into Scotland, and it had scarcely taken a day: the train had left London's King's Cross station at only ten that morning.[1] By the time it
arrived in Edinburgh, the clock had just struck six-thirty. Back in
India, eight hours on a train would scarcely carry one across Punjab,
let alone the length of the country. Though it was the famous Flying Scotsman, this train seemed hardly any faster than the Imperial
Indian Mail. Still, it was finally pulling into its destination, where
the Gothic lettering on a platform sign spelled out "Waverley Station" in reference to the novels of Sir Walter Scott. Widely read at
the Anglo-Oriental College that Ikbal had recently left, the novels presented Scotland as a land of magnificent mountains, but the
uplands Ikbal had passed along the way would scarcely be called
hills in India. They were nowhere near as high as the Hindu Kush
that once enclosed his ancestors behind stone walls that nudged the
clouds from the sky. Surely Sir Walter hadn't lied.

Stepping outside, the sun had already disappeared. It was early

October, and here in the empire's northern reaches, the night came quickly. Outside the station it was cold—not the alpine chill of Indian hill stations, but a different sensation, like wind but wet and immobile, as though the weather were actually touching you. The streets were almost as busy as those Ikbal had briefly seen in London, but the pavements were much narrower. How could everything be so small in "Great" Britain? Two years earlier in 1911, when George V had laid the foundation stone for his new Indian capital, New Delhi, locals were awed at the scale of the grand avenues being laid out, thinking Britain's own cities must be even larger. But they were not.

Ikbal likely asked someone for directions to the Edinburgh Indian Association on St. George's Square. Surely it was famous: India was the jewel in the colonial crown. In reply, something would have been said about a bridge. And Ikbal would have pressed on till one came into view, just about, shrouded in smoke from the passing trains below.

Halfway across North Bridge, a lofty assembly emerged from the fumes: a statue of four soldiers, scrambling out of the rock from which they were carved. Beneath them, the inscription was perhaps just legible by gaslight: "In memory of officers, non-commissioned officers and men who served with the King's Own Scottish Borderers." Then there was a list of campaigns, one of which was Afghanistan, 1878–80. The Second Anglo-Afghan War. Forty years earlier Ikbal's ancestor Jan Fishan Khan had fought in the First Anglo-Afghan War, siding with the British and helping deliver the few survivors to safety. Survivors like the military surgeon William Brydon, the man in the painting *The Remnants of an Army*, made famous by printed copies displayed all over India. Brave Dr. Brydon was both a son of Scotland and a graduate of its famous medical school, where Ikbal was enrolled to study. Surely his name must still be known there, perchance remembered together with that of Jan Fishan Khan.[2]

✦

SCOTLAND WAS NOT ONLY the home of Ikbal's first literary hero, Sir Walter Scott. It was also one of the birthplaces of modern science, engineering (all those vast Indian railway bridges), and medicine. In the days after his arrival, Ikbal began his studies at the Edinburgh Medical School, whose buildings recreated the harmonious order of a Renaissance palace. According to the world-famous Edinburgh Model, Ikbal was to spend his first years studying, not medicine in its narrowly applied sense, but the sciences in their encyclopedic glory.

During that first Michaelmas term of 1913, Ikbal was constantly informed of new discoveries that were changing everything in the world around him. It was not clear whether all this fulfilled or questioned the Quranic motto of his former school, *ʿalama al-insana ma lam yaʿlam*, or "He taught man what he knew not," as he would have said in English. (Unlike his Urdu, Ikbal's Arabic was quite basic.) The words had been chosen to encapsulate the ideals of the school's founder, Sir Sayyid Ahmad Khan, a rationalist Muslim reformer who believed in the harmony of scripture and science. If the Quran seemed to contradict modern science, Sir Sayyid had taught, then Muslims weren't reading it correctly. That spirit of combining the best of Eastern and Western learning had given the school its long and peculiar name: the Muhammadan Anglo-Oriental College. In the forty years since its foundation in 1875, the school had enabled scores of English-speaking Indian Muslims to enter the professions and the ballooning imperial bureaucracy, as well as elite universities like Edinburgh.

By contrast, none of Ikbal's ancestors had even attended school. They were born to rule, in the old days over their minor domains at Paghman north of Kabul, and for the past few generations over their estate at Sardhana north of Delhi. As far as his forebears were concerned, schools were for *munshis*, clerks paid to keep their accounts and record their rulings. But times were changing in India, and so

Ikbal's father, the nawwab, had sent his son to the school that Sir Sayyid established. After all, being located at Aligarh, it was only a hundred miles south of Sardhana. Ikbal, the young "lord" or sirdar, could return home regularly; he could still learn the nobler arts of rule and recreation at his father's palace.

And so back in April 1905, Ikbal had entered the Muhammadan Anglo-Oriental College.[3] The following year a distinguished alumnus came to lecture the schoolboys about the countless possibilities that could open to them by studying in Britain.[4] Having graduated from Oxford, the guest lecturer, Syed Mahdi Hussain Bilgrami, moved at such high levels himself, and would later be knighted for his services to the empire. Boosted by such encouragement, Ikbal spent seven years at the Anglo-Oriental College pursuing an education that promoted the compatibility of empire, Islam, and science. Though he never learned the arts of war at which his forefathers had excelled, he was taught to respect the Prophet Muhammad and Sir Isaac Newton alike.

As the weeks turned into months, and that first Michaelmas term rolled into the Martinmas term of 1914, Ikbal was expected to spend a good deal of time on his preparatory studies at the medical school and its adjoining museum of anatomy. There, stripped to the bone, every one of God's creatures displayed the rational design that lay hidden under feathers and fur. As Sir Sayyid had taught—high school assemblies were often laced with homilies from the founder's writings—the new findings of science would reveal to humankind the same lofty truths as the old revelations of religion.

Yet it was now sixty years or more since Sir Sayyid Ahmad Khan had made those high promises, and little by little it became clear that Ikbal's Edinburgh professors did not necessarily share the same views. Some of them seemed positively irreligious, and more than one of the younger faculty openly declared himself an atheist. The most famous professor at the medical school, Sir William Turner, had similar views, and he was the principal of the university as a whole.[5] Consequently, the intellectual atmosphere there was a marked contrast to Ikbal's school back in India, where faith was taken for granted. As eminent an Edwardian as he had been a Victorian, Sir William was the last survivor of the heady age of Darwin and Huxley, when scientists had first thrown off the shackles of faith. In his laboratory on campus, Sir William had spent decades examining the skulls of whales, seals, and apes. Eventually, his focus had settled on *Homo sapiens*—and on the brains that made them human. His reputation had spread widely, leading to a knighthood from Queen Victoria and the prestigious Keith Prize for his *Memoir on the Craniology of the Peoples of India and Scotland.*[6] While Darwin's breakthroughs had come through observations of earthworms and barnacles, Sir William's had been made via the crania of the colonized. His Edinburgh lectures on the anatomy of the brain were legendary affairs, though, with five hundred students crammed into the lecture hall to hear him arguing that there was no evidence in the brain for a soul. Ikbal and his fellow medical students were taught to think of man as a biological machine.

Sir William placed Darwinism at the center of the medical syllabus. After all, it had been in Edinburgh that Darwin himself had studied medicine and begun his own anatomical researches. Sir William's greatest triumph, though, was founding the Museum of Anatomy, where the skeletons and skulls of every class of mammal were laid out in evolutionary order. For medical students, there were regular tours of the museum, where they were confronted with unassailable ossuary arguments for evolution. Far from being proof of God's elegant design of his creation, the skeletons were given godless meaning as anatomical reactions to cruel nature. Students raised as religious believers like Ikbal must have found it an immense challenge, both moral and mental. In India, Muslim intellectuals had for a generation been struggling with Darwinism in doctrinal abstraction. But in the Museum of Anatomy, Ikbal confronted its vivid physical evidence.

Yet as a university administrator, Sir William also showed the more attractive face of social Darwinism. He was convinced that effort combined with education could change the destiny of both individual lives and societies as a whole, whether in Britain or across its empire. So under his stewardship, the medical school steadily increased the number of Indians it admitted. By 1913, when Ikbal arrived, 101 Indian students were already studying there.[7] Many more were at Oxford and Cambridge, as well as at the medical and law schools of London. The earliest had arrived back in the 1860s, so by Ikbal's time several generations of Indian elites had taken degrees in Britain.

It was not all studying for Ikbal, though. As well as taking country drives in the car paid for by his father, he spent much of his time at the Edinburgh Indian Association, which in the years since its foundation back in 1883 had acquired a splendid mansion on stately George Square.[8] Its donors included Sir William Turner; Lord Ripon, the former viceroy of India; and Syed Ameer Ali, a leading liberal Muslim lawyer who resided in London.[9] Other fundraising activities further raised the profile of the Indian presence in Edinburgh, including an "Indian Fair" at a music hall.[10] When the association's new premises on George Square had opened in 1908, they housed elegant clubrooms, a well-stocked library, a billiard room, a dining hall, and a spacious debating chamber. For Ikbal, it was a bit like being back in the Anglo-Oriental College, only with far fewer Muslims.

When he had first stayed at the association on his arrival in Scotland, the place must have been truly inspiring. Never before would he have seen so many educated and confident Indians gathered in one place. Having been in Edinburgh longer, other members would have seemed more assured of their place in Britain. Some of them sported the hairstyles and spectacles worn by fashionable British students. As those first weeks turned into months, Ikbal perhaps retired to the association's clubroom after lectures for the purpose of speaking to someone in Hindustani (known also as Urdu). Not that everyone spoke the language at the association. There were many students from Bombay and Calcutta, who spoke among themselves in Gujarati and Bangla; nearly all were Hindus. When they talked together, Ikbal must have realized that he could understand the local people in this foreign city better than many of the people from the country where he had lived his whole life.

He responded to the linguistic disunity among his fellow expatriates by offering lessons in Hindustani, the spoken vernacular language of northern India, to members of the association from other parts of the subcontinent. The association's board of directors eagerly agreed, since this was a means of fulfilling the pledge in its constitution to offer "courses of instruction in Indian Languages."[11] Although Ikbal was one of a small number of Muslims among the Indian student body, his teaching helped him establish himself as one of the association's key members. When the board members heard him mention his status as an aristocratic sirdar, they further arranged for him to assume the position of honorary secretary.[12] On top of his language teaching, it was another distraction from his studies. But in his new environment, where no one may have heard of his family estate at Sardhana, it offered a reassuring recognition of status.

His duties as secretary were to conduct the association's correspondence, keep minutes at its meetings, bring motions to its governing committee, and vet new members.[13] After all, not every Indian might pass muster, and Ikbal was raised to be a stickler for social standards. Proud of his title as sirdar, he could be confident that even the more politically progressive Indian students saw some good in the old aristocracy, because a few years earlier the Maharaja of Cooch Behar had given the association a handsome donation (though they perhaps thought differently when they saw Ikbal driving his smart motorcar to class).[14]

Outside his secretarial duties, teaching, and studies, Ikbal quietly nurtured his love of English literature. The association's clubhouse faced the former home of Sir Walter Scott. On the other side of George Square stood the house of the Edinburgh doctor-turned-celebrity-author Sir Arthur Conan Doyle, whose Dr. Watson had served in the Second Anglo-Afghan War, and whose *The Sign of the Four* featured the 1857 rebellion in which Jan Fishan had fought so heroically for the British (though Watson neglected to mention this). It occurred to Ikbal that he might try to become a writer himself. Not in Urdu but in the English that was by this time also an Indian language, not least since it was the only language that all the association's members had in common.

Ikbal's first literary efforts were not exactly stories, nor poems for that matter. They were evocations of a romantic India summoned by the nostalgic (and sometimes nationalist) conversations at the association. His homeland looked all the more alluring from the empire's cold and distant north. Influenced by the overwhelmingly Hindu companionship he found at the clubhouse, he called his first poetic effort "The Marble Temple."[15] It was a two-page paean to a nameless Indian goddess, an idol of idols whose statues were displayed in the white niches of an immaculate temple. Such visions served to distract him from the worrying headlines of the Great War that had broken out during his second year in Edinburgh. Though his prose-poems made no direct mention of the escalating conflict, there were hints of anxiety. One opened with a cry for the Goddess of Peace, before moving quickly to homesick pangs and images of withered roses.

Soon it was not only prose-poems that Ikbal was writing. The war, as it took hold, prompted him to leverage his position as honorary secretary of the association to pen a speech, which he delivered in its large lecture hall.[16] More truly a sermon, the speech urged listeners to "follow the spiritual truths contained in your Books or given by your spiritual leaders."[17] Echoing the rhetoric of the eager first phase of the war, Ikbal quoted the muscular Victorian churchman Frederic Farrar: "To be good requires an effort; it requires the girded loin and the burning lamp; it requires the soldier's armour and the athlete's nerve."[18] It was all stirring stuff, patriotic but also vaguely spiritual. Afterward he posted a copy to Britain's first purpose-built mosque at Woking, outside London, suggesting it could be published in the mosque's journal, *Islamic Review and Muslim India*. With a circulation of around three thousand, it became his first publication.[19]

Writing to the mosque marked a shift in Ikbal's sense of identity, as his encounters at the association were teaching him that India was different than he had formerly thought. Based on his experiences before Edinburgh, he could easily assume that all of India was like his family estate in Sardhana: a land owned by Muslim nobles with martial Britishers gazing paternalistically over their shoulders. Whether at home or at high school, almost all the Hindus in his circle had been servants or peasants, at best shopkeepers or clerical staff. The Edinburgh Indian Association had turned that social hierarchy on its head. Not only were most of its members confident and commanding Hindus, so was everyone on its governing board, except for Ikbal in his lesser post of honorary secretary. The association also celebrated far more Hindu festivals than Muslim ones. Though Ikbal had previously had no reason to carefully consider the abstract idea of "India," it was now easy to suspect that, like the association, his homeland was under Hindu domination—or would be if ever the Indian National Congress came to power. Like Muslim members of the Congress at the same time, Ikbal was an outvoted minority, and he would gradually become more wary of Hindus, not least when they were in a majority. Such wariness had already caused many Muslim elites to abandon the Indian National Congress and join the All-India Muslim League, founded in 1906 as a counterweight to Hindu majoritarianism. Ikbal had still been a boy when the League was founded, but he was a young adult when Muhammed Ali Jinnah became its president in 1913. Perhaps Mr. Jinnah was right that, in an independent and democratic India, Muslims would always be outvoted by Hindus, and that the only way for Muslims to be in charge was to separate themselves, and run their own show.

By the time Ikbal wrote his next prose-poem, he had dropped his imagery of Hindu temples and goddesses to instead evoke his homeland through the more abstract beauty of nature.[20] After almost three years in Scotland, he voiced his longing to see the gardens of his family estate with their bamboo twigs, honeybirds, and sunshine (especially the sunshine). And yet the homeland he invoked was somehow insubstantial, as though its memory were slipping away to become vague and thereby malleable.

As the Great War approached its grim second birthday in the summer of 1916, the question of loyalty—to the empire or to the Congress—came up again and again during debates at the Edinburgh Indian Association. Increasingly, discussions turned around Mr. Gandhi and his proposals for Home Rule, a euphemism for independence. The motions put forward in the association's debating hall now all seemed to be of the same kind: "Is Mr Gandhi Justified in his Recent Statement?" and "Should Indians Cease Volunteering to Fight in this War?"[21] For Ikbal, such talk bordered on treason! His ancestors, like Jan Fishan, had been loyal fighting men. Till now the war in Europe had been only a minor distraction to his studies, but as more and more of his British classmates either volunteered or were conscripted, the lecture halls seemed emptier by the week. As the debates at the association made clear, a comparably large number of Indian volunteers was also heading into battle. As early as September 1914, over 28,000 Indian soldiers had arrived in France, and during the next couple of years, hundreds of thousands would follow them, mostly as volunteers. Ikbal was stirred to do something too, just as Jan Fishan had in the empire's earlier hours of need. But it was out of the question that he join the Indian lower ranks in the trenches. True, a few Indian princes had volunteered, including Bhupinder Singh, the Maharaja of Patiala, who early in the war had set off to command his own troops in France before falling sick along the way. But despite his fighting ancestry, Ikbal was no warrior.

At the association in Edinburgh, there had been many a discussion about the treatment of the Indian volunteers. Back in December 1914, around three hundred wounded Indians had been ferried from France for treatment in Brighton, a famous resort on England's south coast. Local officials had quickly seized on the idea of turning the

Brighton Pavilion into a hospital. There were multiple advantages to lodging the Indians in the Pavilion: it was large and airy, and as council property, also cheaper than Brighton's grand hotels. Moreover, having been originally designed as a baroque echo of Mughal architecture, its bulbous domes and pointed arches might even make the soldiers feel at home.

It was large enough to accommodate over seven hundred injured men. But as the wounded kept pouring in, space at the Pavilion soon ran short. Special arrangements were made for those who died (though remarkably, only thirty-two out of more than four thousand patients succumbed).[22] The Muslim dead were taken to the Shah Jahan Mosque, Britain's first purpose-built place of Islamic worship that had recently published Ikbal's speech. There beneath the mosque's little cupola and within earshot of church bells, the Muslim soldiers who died fighting for their Christian emperor received full Islamic funeral rites before being interred in nearby Horsell Common, in a cemetery laid out like a Persian garden.

In the autumn of 1915, at the height of the crisis, Ikbal found his opportunity to do something for the war effort. Earlier that year a fellow Indian Muslim medical student called Abdul Hamid Shaikh had left Edinburgh to join the Indian Field Ambulance and by September was serving in France.[23] Though Ikbal's medical training was limited as yet—he was only six terms into his studies—he would offer what skills he had. Many of the injured soldiers had lost limbs, making orthopedics the most crucial branch of medicine, so even his basic understanding of anatomy might aid their recovery. Two years after arriving in Edinburgh, he took the Flying Scotsman back to London and, after crossing the city, boarded a train from Victoria Station for the seventy-minute journey to Brighton, where the architectural folly of the Brighton Pavilion had been turned into a hospital for wounded Indians. In that single short hour, his sheltered life was shattered. Row upon row, in room after room, empty faces stared at him above blood-soaked bandages and stumps where once there were limbs. Many of the injured were fellow Muslims. Punjabi

Mussulmans made up the largest section of the British Indian Army, which also included thousands of Pathans, ethnic Afghans from the Indian side of the border with Afghanistan. A Pathan soldier called Mir Dast had even been awarded the Victoria Cross, the empire's highest military honor, at the Brighton Pavilion just a month before Ikbal arrived there.[24]

The Royal Brighton Pavilion Indian Hospital was at once a place of horror and beauty. By the time Ikbal came, all sorts of entertainments were being held for the Indian soldiers. There were musical performances, book readings, music hall matinées, magic lantern shows. Those who were agile again could take day trips to London; those who were crippled were pushed in bath chairs through seafront gardens. Brighton seemed like paradise compared to the fields of war the soldiers had come from. Many of them were also from the poor rural sections of Indian society: to be allowed into, let alone be looked after in, a princely palace was beyond their wildest dreams. But then there were those other dreams, of the pandemonium into which that paternalist empire had thrown them. Each night the Pavilion echoed with screams and calls for mother in every language from Peshawar to Madras, followed by sobs that ended in the cough of lungs corrupted by poison gas. And then the silence of the night swallowed the horrors that none of those languages had words to describe. Every morning the nurses in their dawn routine wrapped a padding of cheer around those damaged souls, like a bandage bloodied anew every night.

Ikbal was given work as a dresser, treating the awful gashes caused by machine guns and landmines.[25] Carefully and up close, he had to peel off bandages, inspect raw flesh, then re-dress it. Over and again, every hour of the day. As one Indian soldier wrote home from Brighton, "This is not war. It is the ending of the world."[26] The trauma of the hospital apparently filled Ikbal's nights with images of horror that transmogrified his duties into apocalyptic dreamscapes. For like hundreds of university men caught up in the war, in his spare hours Ikbal sought solace in literature. But his outlet was not poetry like that of Rupert Brooke, nor the embellished prose of his first two pieces on India's temples and gardens. It was not nostalgia but dread that now moved him; not memories of tranquil landscapes but imagined scenes of gore.

He wrote of a lonely poet sitting in an empty room as an old woman enters to recount her "mournful" tale.[27] The poet-narrator lies down on his bed and feels the "balm of amaranth" pour over his eyes, summoning a vision of an angel who leads led him to a pedestal carved from jasper, on which stands a single vessel, cut from sapphire. Its contents are the sacred liquid of a single tear. From this morose paradise, the angel then takes the poet through celestial cities of diamond, from where they gaze down on an earth peopled by skeletons, who march through the land wielding "stained swords."[28]

Ikbal's next prose-poem described another such vision. As though spellbound, he watches a macabre scene where skeletons' hands hold rusted sabres, and ships are loaded with broken bodies.[29] Shifting without volition, his gaze turns to a lonely man—the last man—standing solitary on the horizon. He is speaking to the fading sun, awaiting his own impending death. It is was a vision of resignation, yet also of survival. For the last man is not loaded onto the ship of death.[30]

More than psychological (and perhaps pharmacological) forces were at work here, for Ikbal's visionary pieces reflected several literary influences. Many Anglophone Indians, including his fellow students at the Edinburgh Indian Association, were reading the symbolist and occultist poetry of W. B. Yeats, and Ikbal echoed this style. His prose-poem "A Tear in a Sapphire Vessel" had a more direct influence, though. Not only specific phrases like "balm of amaranth" and "pedestal of jasper" but the entire visionary narrative of an angel leading the dreamer to a sapphire vessel containing a single tear were lifted wholesale from the nineteenth-century prose-poem "The Tear," penned by an anonymous "modern Pythagorean."[31] The original had appeared back in 1832 in a literary journal Ikbal happened upon. (Various issues of the journal included poems by

Sir Walter Scott, while its editor, Frederic Shoberl, had also written books on Persia and India.) When Ikbal decided to publish "A Tear in a Sapphire Vessel" under his own name, it marked his first small step toward literary subterfuge, a little game of letters that went unnoticed amid the vast deadly game being played out around him.

Ikbal spent ten months working at the Royal Brighton Pavilion Indian Hospital. Like hundreds of thousands of other young men from India, he had volunteered to serve the empire that he, as a student of the Muhammadan Anglo-Oriental College, then of the Edinburgh Medical School, associated with lofty science and reason. Yet every conversation with a new patient carried in from the Somme made that image of empire seem more threadbare. What was chemistry but a means of making gases to poison lungs still not fully grown? What was engineering but a means of making trenches where youths were mortared into muddy graves? At the end of the summer of 1916, when the Indian Army was redeployed from France to Iraq and Egypt, Ikbal returned to his studies in Edinburgh. He had given almost a year of his life to tending the wounds of ordinary men from across the subcontinent. But he would never practice medicine again.

There remained other ways to help with the war effort, though. The war years were witnessing a colossal increase in charity work, and one of the great fundraising drives were Flag Days, based on selling small flags or lapel pins bearing the insignia of allied nations and colonies. For the Edinburgh Indian Association, they provided a way of raising funds for injured fellow Indians. One of Ikbal's teachers, Dr. James Miller, who supervised the Indian medical students' education, introduced him to such an event.[32] Building on the momentum of a high-profile Flag Day for Indian soldiers organized by the Red Cross in September 1916, all through that autumn Ikbal helped the association set up a rolling campaign.[33]

Returning to the solitude of his studies after almost a year in Brighton had left him feeling isolated, though. Even if he knew how to speak of his experiences, there seemed no one whom he could talk to about them. Certainly, plenty of invalid soldiers could be seen around Edinburgh, but unlike them, he had no direct experience of battle. The horrors he had seen were vicarious, visible only in the marks they had left on other men's bodies. Yet they continued to haunt him as he rented rooms at Thirlestane Road in Edinburgh's Marchmont district, a good distance from the association's clubhouse where he had previously spent so much time.[34]

Sitting in his room, he turned again to his pen to write more prose-poems. Though no longer than a couple of pages, they gave voice to the loneliness of his evenings and the dark sway of his mind. In one of them, a dying man sits in a solitary garret, writing a letter by candlelight on a wet and thundery night.[35] As though in a tale by Edgar Allan Poe, a voice comes from nowhere and says simply, "Yes!" The same lonesome scene appeared in his next piece, in which, on another "distinctly chilly" night, a nameless man sits alone in his chamber when Lady Moon moves past his window.[36] The man feels an ecstasy of "sublime stillness," before realizing it is nothing less than the silence of death. With its nods to John Keats's *Endymion*, about a lonely shepherd loved by the moon goddess, it was very much a young man's poem, albeit one tinged with trauma.

Ikbal's dark night of the soul was to end before autumn was out, though, since he was about to happen upon his own Lady Moon. The twenty-two-year-old Elizabeth Mackenzie, like most women of her age across Britain, was doing her bit for the war effort.[37] A friend had suggested she might help with collecting sphagnum moss, a rare antiseptic fungus that grew abundantly in the Scottish Highlands—the vast demand for dressings was bringing former folk custom into medical use. When Elizabeth hesitated at the thought of gathering moss in the freezing hills, her friend suggested another option: preparing boxes of flag pins to be sold by volunteers on Flag Days. It was still hard work: she found herself not only filling boxes but also spending twelve-hour days selling their contents on the streets whenever a Flag Day was announced. She had been nineteen when the war broke out and Edinburgh's young men had marched out to war, so when the woman who ran the flag depot invited her to a charity reception at the university to thank the volunteers, Elizabeth leaped at the chance of an evening out. Her parents agreed on condition that she return home no later than ten.

The chance of escaping the women's world of the flag depot was sufficiently rare that Elizabeth spent hours selecting the brightest clothes in her closet. In the end, she chose a dress made of pink taffeta, which she paired with pink shoes and a pink rose from the shared garden of her parents' flat.[38] The dress seemed a little extravagant, but then, despite all the privations of war, silk taffeta had been rendered comparatively common by the requisition of linen and wool for airplanes and uniforms.

At the reception, with her pale skin highlighted by the tight curls of her red hair and set off by the pink of her dress, Elizabeth stood out among the young women, who far outnumbered the men. Looking around, she saw that most of the young men were foreigners, students from the far corners of the empire. One of them caught her eye. He held himself tall and erect, as though gazing down over everyone in the room. His features, she noticed, suggested refinement. An aquiline nose led with angular perfection toward a chin that was pointed. His skin seemed fair against the black luster of his hair and mustache, which was curled up at each end. There was a touch of the dandy about him—a rare sight in those gloomy years—and also, she thought with a smile to herself, the air of a swashbuckler.[39]

The female student to whom Elizabeth was talking noticed how her gaze kept turning across the hall. She finally marched over to the stranger (the war was changing women's ways, too) and brought him over. Ikbal bowed, as though to make up for the lack of courtesy. "*Sirdar* Ikbal Ali Shah," he said, enunciating every syllable with a flourish. Noticing Elizabeth's hands were empty, he marched off to fetch her cake and tea.[40] His eye landed on the single chocolate sponge among the plainer offerings on the buffet table. Thanking him, Elizabeth remarked that he had taken nothing for himself. He was pleased she had noticed, telling her that in the mountains of his homeland, his people drank only *green* tea. As Elizabeth looked at him, slightly startled, he warmed to his theme: "We are men of the sword and do not care for sugar buns."[41]

Elizabeth said little for the rest of the evening, but Ikbal did more than enough talking for the two of them. After months of solitude in his lodgings, the words seemed to flood out of him. He told her tales of his ancestors in the Afghan highlands, stories of gallant forebears during the Indian Mutiny, romances of his family palace at Sardhana. He could have gone on all night, but interrupting him suddenly, Elizabeth spluttered out: "Ten-thirty!" When Ikbal looked confused, then crestfallen, she explained her predicament, her promise to her parents, the scolding they would give her. As though living up to his ancestors' valor, he announced that he had his motorcar parked outside and would immediately drive her home. As they parted beneath the steps leading up to her family flat, Ikbal bowed again, even lower this time, and kissed her hand. Then he was gone, roaring away up the road.

Ikbal was far from the only Indian student attending dances and dating young British women, though such interracial relationships caused consternation in various corners, including Britain's nascent Muslim community. One such critic was Muhammad Marmaduke Pickthall, a prominent convert who would subsequently make a celebrated translation of the Quran under the patronage of the Nizam of Hyderabad. Writing in the *Islamic Review and Muslim India* (which had featured Ikbal's first publication), Pickthall warned Muslim students of the moral and reputational dangers they faced at British universities. "The temptations which assail newcomers from the East at every turn are inconceivable to Europeans," he wrote. "But the harm done to Islam by the misconduct of a Muslim here in England is inestimable. It gives English people an utterly false idea of Islamic notions of morality."[42]

The morning after the Flag Day tea party was a Saturday, and Elizabeth woke late. A letter was already awaiting her at the breakfast table. Though polite and proper, its brevity hinted at an intimacy already shared, asking her to tea that afternoon at Mackie's.[43] Later that day, telling her mother she was taking tea with a girlfriend, Elizabeth set out to walk to Prince's Street in Edinburgh's Georgian-era New Town. Mackie's famous tea rooms had an elevated view over both the neighboring neoclassical storefronts and the brooding Gothic turrets of the medieval castle. When she arrived—half an hour early in her anxiety to appear proper—Ikbal was already there. He'd reserved the best table, set apart from the others in its own bay window. His stories that afternoon offered a glimpse of a world she could scarcely imagine.

Merely to be in New Town's most elegant tea rooms would have filled her with excitement. After all, she lived in a flat on Argyle Park Terrace, which her father Charles, an estate manager for a Scottish aristocrat, rented for his family.[44] The building belonged to the Edinburgh Railway Company, which had divided it into seven such flats leased to lower-middle-class tenants. For the Mackenzie family it combined respectability with affordability, overlooking a park rather than the railway.[45] Both literally and figuratively, Ikbal was from the other side of town. At the time he began courting Elizabeth, he was living several miles away on Thirlestane Road in the more expensive district of Marchmont, his elegant Victorian villa surrounded by houses in the Scottish baronial style that resonated with his reading of Sir Walter Scott.[46] Marchmont was popular with wealthier students, being close enough to the university for them to walk to lectures.

In the weeks after they first took tea, Elizabeth and Ikbal were meeting every day. Then in the evenings, he sat writing. One evening in that autumn of 1916, he tried to piece together his confused thoughts in an essay about the war, about science, about religion. With labored prose and internal contradictions, he drew on the Darwinian education he received at the medical school to explain war as the "survival of the fittest," which was something all eras and all peoples accepted.[47] As in the hospital at Brighton, his thoughts then turned to the contrasting peace of Islam that was all the more appealing amid the clamor of distant gunfire, urging his readers to "turn with disgust from all that is superficial" and to instead "seek solace in the spiritual zone."[48]

He decided to send the essay (if such it was, at little more than a page) to the Indian Muslim editors of *The Islamic Review*, which had previously published the lecture he gave at the Edinburgh Indian Association. After all, the magazine was based at the mosque in Woking where the Muslim war dead received their last rites. Though the mosque was mainly attended by Indians, three years earlier its leaders had founded *The Islamic Review* as one of many new journals in which Muslims from across the empire were turning English into a new language of Islam. They did not necessarily see the British Empire, which provided the religious freedoms and practical mechanisms through which different versions of the faith could be practiced, as the enemy of their religion. Indeed, as far as Khwaja Kamal-ud-Din, the gentle Punjabi editor of *The Islamic Review*, was concerned, Muslims should be loyal citizens of the empire. "The British Raj [is] a blessing to India," he had written in the first issue of the journal. "We do believe that our community is better off under the present regime."[49]

Since the first years of the journal coincided with the war, many of its articles dealt with the violence and destruction of Europe, stressing by comparison the harmonious fraternity of Islam. Accepted for publication in the January 1917 issue, Ikbal's short contribution, "Peace of the Soul," fitted neatly this editorial line. The same issue contained an article on "The War and its Effect on Religious Ideas" by the Scots-Irish convert Yehya-en-Nasr Parkinson, author of *Muslim Chivalry*, a book on the gallant Arab warriors of yore. For Parkinson, Western civilization meant ceaseless conflict, so Ikbal's heartfelt little essay bolstered the contrast with the abiding peace of Islam.

Shortly afterward Ikbal sent a third article to *The Islamic Review*, to which he gave the theological title "Influence of the Soul on the Body."[50] It was a confused and confusing piece, caught between the scientific materialism he absorbed from his studies and the religious requirement for an irreducible soul. As a medical student addressing a readership of Muslims, he grappled for a compromise between the positions of faith and science in contorted prose that mirrored his internal conflict.

It was not clear which elements of Western civilization would survive the destruction of war, but Ikbal's trust in science would not. Though he remained enrolled at the medical school—he had to convince his father the nawwab he wasn't wasting the large sums of money being invested in his education—Ikbal was now attending fewer and fewer classes. Instead, whenever Elizabeth could join him, he drove her out to the Braid Hills golf course, southwest of the city, on the opposite side from the shipyards of Leith in the pure air of the Highlands. The club was almost twenty years old now, one of the last Victorian strides in the ascendance of golf as a gentlemanly pastime. (By the time Ikbal first picked up a putter, golf had even spread to Kabul, after the Scottish engineer James Miller taught the game to the Afghan King Habibullah, who promptly redeployed him to create three fairways instead of the hydroelectric dam he was meant to be building.)[51] Looking down from the Braid Hills fairway, Ikbal and Elizabeth could see every landmark in Edinburgh, then gaze down the coast to East Lothian and across to the waters to Fife. And after playing a bracing round together, they could escape the cold in the hotel, taking tea and cakes amid stained-glass and Gothic turrets. Public enough to be respectable, remote enough to be romantic, the Braid Hills Hotel was the perfect place for a secret Edwardian courtship.

There were also practical reasons for meeting outside the city. Aside from local prejudices about mixed-race couples, Elizabeth's father, Charles, had firm ideas about a daughter's place in the family. Not long into Ikbal and Elizabeth's relationship, Charles announced his plans for her marriage.[52] The son of his oldest and closest friend was coming home from France, he told her, injured but not irreparably so. Since Elizabeth had known the boy since childhood and had seemed fond of him, Charles and his friend viewed marriage as the natural next step of amity between their families. But Elizabeth objected. After her father pressed her for her reasons, she told him the truth. Charles Mackenzie was adamant in his response to being disobeyed. He had warned her about the fast types sitting out the war in lecture halls. And the background of this "Eastern student" was also troublingly uncertain. He even threatened to write to the university authorities and cause trouble for the intrusive Indian. But finally Charles accepted a compromise. His daughter agreed to sign a letter that he dictated, in which she declared an end to her friendship with Ikbal on the grounds that she was soon to be married.

Over the following weeks, she met Roy, her father's friend's son, as he lay recovering in an Edinburgh hospital. Her work at the flag depot filled her with conflict between duty and desire. Compared to the exotic world described in Ikbal's stories, the wounded soldier's longing for a life of Scottish domesticity settled over her like the winter clouds outside his bedside window. She slowly resolved to retract the statement in her forced letter and, returning home, wrote to Ikbal to tell him what had happened. He replied at once, with the extravagant urgency of a note delivered by a special post office messenger. Ikbal would wait for her that same evening, the note explained, outside the train station on Prince's Street. If the station lacked the respectability of their earlier haunts at Mackie's tea rooms and the Braid Hills Hotel, it at least had the assurance of anonymity. As soon as she arrived, he pulled up in his motor-car, and they were soon back in the Highlands, where the talk was inevitably of marriage. Ikbal asked Elizabeth to marry him, and she accepted.

Fortunately for Ikbal, his rival Roy's convalescence was over, and he was about to be sent back to France. The next day Elizabeth also broached Ikbal's introduction to her family, telling her mother she had invited a student friend for tea. Just as he had charmed her daughter, Ikbal lavished Margaret Mackenzie with compliments and tales of the vast vague hemisphere he called "the East." When tea was over and he departed, Margaret had to confess that she liked him. But Charles had not been won over. At twenty-one, Ikbal was actually a year younger than Elizabeth, but he had the polished manners of a more worldly man than he was. He was plainly too old for his daughter, declared Charles. Then there were all those stories he told of his eastern adventures. Ikbal was not to be deterred. He knew many Indian students at the university had secret Scottish girlfriends. What he was trying to do in seeking marriage was more honest, more noble. Of late, several Indian princes had taken British wives: it was the amatory fulfillment of the promise of empire. But when he sent a brief telegram to the Nawwab of Sardhana requesting his permission to marry, his father's reply was even shorter. It bore only two words: "Positively not."[53]

Chapter Two

JOURNALIST

thrown indeed into a temporary frenzy, by the epic
poetry of Sir Walter Scott

—Edmund Gosse, *Father and Son*

UNDETERRED, IKBAL AND ELIZABETH PRESSED AHEAD
with their plan to marry. When one of her friends warned her that
Ikbal surely already had a wife (or several wives) back in India, adding a cheap jibe about "Orientals," she became all the more determined.[1] Other friends said even worse things. For his part, Ikbal had
to listen to the advice of fellow students at the Edinburgh Indian
Association, who warned him that once British wives went out to
India, they flirted with other people's husbands, drank shamelessly
in public, and danced exclusively with their "own kind."[2] Pressures
mounted on the young couple from all sides, not least financial pressures, now that they were opposed by both sets of parents. Since
there was no question of a large wedding celebration, they decided
on a small and private ceremony, which took place on November 30,
1916, at 85 Hanover Street in Edinburgh's New Town.[3] It was an
odd place to marry, being the offices of David Gardiner & Company,
stationers and typewriter agents (presumably where Ikbal bought
his writing supplies).[4] But non-church marriages were common in
Scotland, and the room above the shop had the dual advantages of
being both discreet and affordable.

Before the civil ceremony, Elizabeth quietly uttered the brief Arabic confession of faith through which she converted to Islam, taking for her Muslim name the English-sounding Saira (though she would remain Elizabeth on official documents). Since her parents weren't present at the wedding—both her marriage and conversion were acts of rebellion—the legal witnesses were two older local women, a middle-aged commercial clerk, Isabella Williams, and Margaret Sinclair.[5] Far from the lavish ceremonies of a sirdar's marriage in India, their nuptials all but took place in secrecy. Elizabeth's father would never speak to her again.[6]

Yet she was not the first Scotswoman to marry a Muslim. There had already been several such marriages in the ports of Dundee and Glasgow, as well as farther south in English and Welsh ports like South Shields, Liverpool, and Cardiff.[7] The vast majority of those marriages had been with working-class sailors, often from Somaliland and Yemen, who had settled in Britain with jobs in the busy dockyards, then fallen in love with local girls who worked in the cheap lodging houses where they lived. So if marrying a Muslim wasn't unknown for women of Elizabeth's approximate class, being the wife of a sirdar was an altogether rarer—if still not quite acceptable—affair.

Despite defying their families, the couple were happy in the following months. One afternoon they took a drive out to Dryburgh Abbey, burial place of Sir Walter Scott. Set deep in the countryside some forty miles southeast of Edinburgh, it made a nice day trip of a little over an hour's drive in Ikbal's car. Although he now found it hard to celebrate war, he tried to hold on to his belief in valor, especially through the stories of his forefathers that he recounted to his bride. Sir Walter helped him, reminding him of chivalrous values from an age before the machines of death. It was a fine summer day, and in its tranquil setting the ruined monastery rendered the car ride not merely an afternoon out but, as he put it, a "pilgrimage to . . . where lies buried a masterful mind."[8]

When they returned to his lodgings that evening, he wrote

what he described as "the reflections which entered the mind of a foreigner" in Dryburgh Abbey. He began by comparing Scott's poetry to that of various "Oriental" poets so as to prove the former's "greater genius." Scott spoke to Ikbal's romanticism, a sentiment much in the air, as that same year back in India the Urdu novelist Abdul Halim Sharar adapted the Scottish author's tales of old Edinburgh to reimagine the history of the Muslim city of Lucknow. Ikbal was similarly enamored, declaring that in Sir Walter's martial ballads he used words "like a warrior, loving them not for their beauty, but as weapons of courage and national defence." It was a sentiment that fitted nicely with the jingoistic illusions of aging British editors. In the autumn of 1917, as thousands of young men perished in the "Battle of Mud" at Passchendaele, the elderly Scottish historian William Sanderson accepted Ikbal's essay for *The Border Magazine*.[9] On the cover of the issue in which it appeared, mounted Britannic warriors of yore rode bearing swords into battle.

Proud of his first few publications, Ikbal showed them to an older man whom he befriended through the Edinburgh Indian Association. Donald Mackenzie, a journalist, was interested in Indian folklore.[10] While he was no direct relative of Elizabeth, Ikbal perhaps felt he could trust this fellow member of the Mackenzie clan. It may also have helped that Donald liked to tell people he was a descendant of the Gaelic bard Rob Donn. In prosaic fact, Donald owed his prominence to simple hard work: he had raised himself up from the fishing port obscurity of Cromarty through journalistic stepping stones at provincial newspapers from Dingwall to Dundee and finally Edinburgh. As a folklorist, hack, and amateur Orientalist, his conversations offered Ikbal his first taste of the life of a professional writer. Although Donald's day job was as Edinburgh correspondent of Glasgow's *Bulletin*, he already had a dozen books under his belt. Admittedly the more recent ones had been war propaganda (he was clear-eyed enough to know that), with titles like *Great Deeds of the Great War*, but in his mid-forties, being too old to fight, he was merely doing his duty to maintain the nation's morale.

His other books, however, were studies of mythology and folklore, ranging from Scottish ballads to Egyptian and Indian legends. Like Sharar using Scott to reimagine Lucknow, Donald Mackenzie was a man for whom the empire provided new ways of thinking about his heritage. A few years later he even developed a theory that the British Isles had first been peopled by Buddhists who had sailed from India to plant the seeds of Celtic culture.

After reading Ikbal's few prose-poems, Donald encouraged him to produce more. So far none of his writings had been longer than a few pages—even his article on the grave of Sir Walter barely covered two columns on a printed page. But soon Ikbal was at work on his longest piece yet, a ten-page mystical war parable called "Visions of a Recluse."[11] Donald had just published two books on Indian myths, and as far as he was concerned, Ikbal was an Indian. The Scotsman was worldly enough to know the difference between "Hindoos" and "Mohamedans" and to know which of the two Ikbal was. Even so, most of the Association's members Donald had encountered were Hindus, and so far there had been no Islamic, still less Afghan, allusions in any of Ikbal's prose-poems. Moreover, the Hindu myths might still be considered Ikbal's heritage as an Indian Muslim, in the same manner that the pagan myths of Greece were considered the heritage of European Christians.

So under Donald's tutelage, Ikbal set about penning an even longer piece in the same Hindu vein as his first prose-poems. A few years earlier the Bengali Hindu poet Rabindranath Tagore had won the Nobel Prize for Literature for the English version of his "Song Offerings," *Gitanjali*, for which W. B. Yeats had written an introduction. Ikbal had already been echoing the translated Tagore in his imagery of rivers, floods, and temples, and now he responded to Donald's encouragement with another new piece that was twice the length of "Visions of a Recluse" and more ambitious than anything he had previously attempted. He titled it "The Hermitage of Sankara," in honor of the great Hindu sage of the eighth century, peopling its pages with a pantheon of Hindu devas and gandharvas, great gods like Indra and Brahma, and a seductive little nymph named Pramotoncha.[12] So beautiful was Pramotoncha that, seeing her walk past his hermitage one day, Sankara surrenders his hard-won control of his senses, then swaps a lifetime of abstinence for a single day of pleasure.[13]

Donald not only encouraged Ikbal to sit down and write, he also helped him to publish his work. Under his guidance, Ikbal collected the prose-poems he had written over the previous few years with the aim of assembling them into an anthology. It seemed a good proposition for both men, a collaboration to parallel that of Yeats and Tagore. Donald wrote a foreword, which proved a fillip in finding a publisher, and with his many connections in Edinburgh's tight literary circle, he helped set up Ikbal's book with the little publishing house of John Orr. In his foreword, he introduced Ikbal in vague terms as a man "of Eastern birth and descent" who possessed "strong artistic and literary leanings."[14] He erroneously explained that Ikbal's chosen medium of the prose-poem was a classical genre of Persian literature, and with vast exaggeration (Ikbal was fluent in Urdu and had some command over Persian), described the young author as a linguistic prodigy who could "speak and read almost all the Oriental languages."[15] Amid the awakening of national identity all around them—the "Scottish Renaissance" was entering full swing, with Hugh MacDiarmid collecting poems for the momentous *Northern Numbers* anthology to which Donald himself had contributed—Donald decided to paint Ikbal in similarly nationalist colors, as "an Eastern poet [who] dreams of his Motherland and voices in English the visions of his people."[16] All told, he claimed the anthology was "one of the most unique and remarkable collections of poems that has ever been composed or published in Scotland."[17]

Released in 1918, Ikbal's slender anthology brought together his prose-poems under the title *Eastern Moonbeams*. Inspired in equal parts by Scott, Tagore, and Yeats, it drew on the entwined nationalisms of the Indian and Celtic revivals, though his publisher (perhaps with Ikbal's input) chose a cover design with a turbaned dervish standing before a doorway bearing an Arabic inscription *Huwa al-khaliq al-baqi*, "He is the Creator, the Everlasting," which echoed the Quran. But never mind that the cover was at odds with the Hindu themes of the contents: vaguely "Oriental," it all perhaps seemed of a piece to its few British readers. Following Donald's cue, a few weeks later a review in *The Scotsman* praised Ikbal as "an Oriental linguist" who penned "dreamy and impassioned fantasias."[18] It was his first public persona.

It must have been a proud moment when Ikbal presented his first book to Elizabeth—even if it was dedicated not to her but to his "august and honorable father" (with "the profoundest sense of respect and of obedience").[19] Having been cut off by the nawwab since marrying against his command, Ikbal had written the dedication with an eye to the future, in hope of a family (and financial) reconciliation. But none was forthcoming. In stepped Donald, who took an interest in Ikbal's further professional development, or at least in his prospects of earning a living. With his fast car and fine clothes, Ikbal had proven himself good at spending money but had as yet shown no propensity for earning any. Although Donald wasn't directly related to Elizabeth, he apparently felt the responsibility of a paternalist patriot. So, with Ikbal's medical degree becoming less attainable by the week, Donald decided to guide him on the route to becoming a professional writer: not a writer of mythopoeic prose-poems but an expert author of political journalism. Donald had raised a family on a journalist's salary, and he knew well how to do it.

When Elizabeth announced she was expecting their first child before the end of the year, the young couple's financial needs became more urgent. Not only were their parents still opposed to their union;

as a mixed-race couple, it was also hard to find somewhere to live other than Ikbal's former bachelor quarters. Elizabeth's pregnancy amplified these problems. And so, still unqualified to practice medicine, Ikbal opted for the alternative modeled by Donald: he would write for a living. It was unclear, though, what he would, or indeed could, write about. Embellished prose about Indian anchorites was never going to make anyone a regular income. And the few articles he had so far published in *The Islamic Review* made little show of expertise, still less of authority. His inability to complete his B.Sc., let alone his M.D., further reduced the scope of what he might credibly write about. There was one qualification he did have, though, and that was who he was.

He turned first to his former experience teaching Hindustani at the Edinburgh Indian Association. In an attempt to elevate his credentials as a learned Orientalist, he now applied to join the Royal Asiatic Society.[20] Although he was admitted only as a Member rather than as a Fellow, this afforded him the right to place the letters *MRAS* after his name. Lacking a degree or other formal qualifications, it was the best professional endorsement he could manage, based as it was on his native language skills.

Next, he contacted Leopold Hill, a London publisher who specialized in language guides, including his *Briton Abroad* series of phrase books. So far the series had focused entirely on Europe, not least with *The Briton in France* and *The Briton in Germany*. What with the thousands of soldiers being shipped out to France, they had sold well during the war, with the France book entering its eighth edition by the time Ikbal proposed his own volume for the series, *The Briton in India*, with the subtitle: *A Pocket Interpreter.*

Leopold Hill accepted the proposal, so during the last months of Elizabeth's pregnancy, Ikbal put together around seventy pages of basic Hindustani.[21] In line with the other *Briton Abroad* books, they were the kinds of phrases a traveler might need, with sections on the train station, the hotel, the post office. Mindful of the likelihood that many of the troops diverted to the battlefields of France would soon be redeployed to India (particularly to the restless North-West Frontier with Afghanistan), Hill expected plenty of military phrases too. All told, the book had a most imperial, indeed imperious, air: almost every other phrase was a command in the imperative, including the infamous catchphrase of the British to their servants *Jul-dee Karo!* ("Make haste!")[22] But on the financial home front, the book advance didn't last long, and further royalties were slow in coming. It was also far from easy for an Indian to find work in Scotland outside the dockyards of the Clyde, where many an Indian sailor could be found, albeit not of Ikbal's class. Nonetheless, through his writings he was learning to make his "Indianness" an asset. Moreover, another option of identity was also available to him: although he had never set foot in Afghanistan, his ancestors had originated there.

By virtue of being an Afghan rather than a more commonplace Indian, he could offer the British unique insight on that turbulent but poorly understood country that bordered British India. In 1918, no one else in Britain could claim to offer such insider expertise, for as yet there existed no Afghan embassy, no Afghan community, and no Afghan students (compared with hundreds of Indians) at British universities. To Ikbal and his mentor, the uniqueness of his position became clear. The high stakes of the ongoing war, on which Donald had been reporting for years, were an opportunity for Ikbal to put his latent Afghan identity to use.

During the last weeks of Elizabeth's pregnancy, with data gleaned from the university library, Ikbal penned a series of articles that promised special insight into Afghanistan's place in the politics of the First World War. "Afghanistan and the War" was published in the *Near East*; "Afghanistan and the German Threat" was published closer to home, in the prestigious *Edinburgh Review*. "The Indian Frontier and the War" appeared in the *Asiatic Review*, and (perhaps with Donald's help) he even managed to place "Afghanistan and the Great War" in the distant *Los Angeles Times*.[23] In the wake of the recent Bolshevik takeover of the Russian Empire, concern had been voiced in the press that Red Russians would finally march into Afghanistan, then India. Responding to such concerns, Ikbal made his first moves in the great game of empire that Britain and Russia had been playing over Afghanistan for nearly a century.

Such was the level of public interest that his articles were further publicized in the *Scotsman* newspaper, which made much of the presence in Edinburgh of this authentic Afghan expert.[24] Ikbal might have hammered out more articles on his typewriter, but he fell victim to the influenza pandemic that would kill a quarter of million people in Britain alone. He was still in a nursing home when, on the last day of October, he received news that Elizabeth had given birth to a daughter at their rented rooms.[25] Later that night Elizabeth sat up in alarm as an insistent knock sounded on the flat's front door. It was Ikbal, standing freezing in pajamas that were soaked with his sweat. Delirious with sickness and joy, he had walked four miles from the nursing home.

As midnight struck along the nearby high street, she dragged him indoors. Elizabeth was as fortunate as her husband was reckless, for he didn't transmit the flu virus either to his baby daughter or to her weakened mother. But then it was a truly auspicious moment for a child to be born to a formerly Presbyterian mother and a Muslim father, because the day before the birth, the Ottoman and British empires had signed an armistice. Twelve days later, in a railway carriage in the forest of Compiègne, the Germans followed suit. The war was over. Ikbal suggested a name for their daughter, and Elizabeth agreed. She would be called Amina, a name derived from Arabic that carries two meanings: "safe" and "loyal."

Although on Amina's birth certificate, Ikbal listed his profession as "medical student," it was now clear that he would never finish his degree. As he recovered from influenza, he spent more and more time in the sections of the university library dedicated to Central Asia and Afghanistan. Because although the war had finally ended, the peace brought problems of its own, particularly across the Islamic world, what with the uncertain fate of the Ottoman Empire and the czar's Muslim colonies in Central Asia, now that the Russian Empire had been seized by the Bolsheviks. The few remaining independent Muslim states also faced uncertain futures, especially Afghanistan, so political journalists had more than ever to write about. From his library notes, Ikbal responded with an article on the Muslims of Central Asia. Whistling to the hawks of the imperial great game, he recommended that the British intervene to liberate Muslims from the yoke of Russian, and worse still, Bolshevik oppression.[26] His timing was perfect, seeing the article accepted by the highbrow *Contemporary Review*. Even so, he offered a strange kind of political commentary. Spiking realpolitik with romance, he quoted an exotic verse ("Chiefs of the Uzbek race / Waving their heron crests with haughty grace"), lifting it unattributed from a biography of the Afghan ruler Abd al-Rahman Khan by an old India hand, Stephen Wheeler.[27]

Meanwhile, Ikbal's relationship with Donald Mackenzie was nurturing another new interest: folklore, a subject on which Donald was a published authority. During those last months of 1918, Donald was correcting the proofs for his five-hundred-page *Indian Myth and Legend*. For Donald, collecting the myths of the Hindus, Jains, and Buddhists provoked the question of the absence of a Muslim mythology. After all, Muslims comprised around a quarter of India's population, so it seemed odd that they should have no legends of their own, particularly when their ancient Middle Eastern forebears (on whom he had already written another tome) possessed in Gilgamesh the greatest myth outside Greece. As winter wore on, Donald encouraged his protégé to develop a corresponding interest in the folklore of his own people.

His own people. That was easy for a Scotsman to say. A name like Donald Alexander Mackenzie left little ambiguity as to who *his* people might be, and where their national spirit might be found. For Ikbal, it was far less clear. Was it in India, with its many millions of Muslims? If so, which Muslims? They lived in so many places, followed so many sects, and spoke so many languages. Moreover, would any of their legends live up to the boisterous old ballads of Scotland? Maybe, maybe not. But the legends of the Afghans surely could compete, for after all, the Afghans were not so different from the feuding clans of the Highlands. To find out, Ikbal's only resource was the university library, from which he could borrow volumes on Afghan ballads by the French Orientalist James Darmesteter and the British soldier-scholar Captain Henry Raverty, as well as works by the colonial official William Crooke on the folklore of the North-West Frontier.

Through Donald, Ikbal was also introduced to the Scottish nationalist folklorist Lewis Spence.[28] Though raised in remote Monifieth, Spence's interests were broad and comparative, and he had written books on legends that stretched east to Babylonia and west to the Americas. Donald and Lewis were convinced that Ikbal's investigations into the legends of his Afghan ancestors could break new ground in the study of the grand mythic cycles that predated the diluted religions of Abraham, so they encouraged him to apply for membership of the Folklore Society in London. Aided by his affiliation with the Royal Asiatic Society, and giving his address as the Edinburgh Indian Association, he was accepted.[29]

The Edwardian intelligentsia took folklore very seriously. Between 1906 and 1915, Sir James Frazer, the Scottish grand magus of mythology, had published the third edition of his *Golden Bough*, in twelve recondite volumes. In an article for *Vanity Fair*, the rising poet T. S. Eliot had caustically praised Frazer's "stupendous compendium of human superstition and folly," but now the war had ended, *The Golden Bough* was rapidly going through several reprints as ancient myths seemed to sooth the wounds of modernity. While Frazer had been completing his sprawling magnum opus, another Scot, the pioneer anthropologist Andrew Lang, had become the leading figure of London's Folklore Society, over which he presided till his death a few years before Ikbal's introduction to the topic. As it had for so many writers from Scotland over the previous decades, folklore now offered Ikbal an entry to the cultural life of the metropole. On the basis of his membership of the Folklore Society, he was soon invited to London to present a paper on "The Folk Life of Afghanistan."[30]

When Ikbal addressed the society in its oak-paneled lecture hall, the meeting's chairman was Cambridge anthropologist Alfred Cort Haddon, best known for his studies of the Torres Strait Islands between Australia and New Guinea. Having heard of Dr. Haddon's zoological background, Ikbal drew on his abandoned medical studies to show his understanding of folklore as a branch of science. "Some would have us believe that the intellectual life of primitive peoples has evolved by a process governed by natural laws," he noted, before drawing on the Darwinian teachings of Sir William Turner to demonstrate the development of legends via comparisons with the biological laws of evolution.[31]

Even so, Ikbal knew full well he was a novice, and devoted the bulk of his paper to the content rather than the theory of folklore (though he did add that in arranging marriages "the Afghan gives some consideration to eugenics").[32] He then turned to customs surrounding marriage and childbirth, explaining that when a girl is born, as few as five shots are fired, whereas fourteen or more gunshots herald the birth of a boy.[33] Delivered, as the listeners were led to believe, by a speaker from Afghanistan, the lecture was a success. A spirited discussion followed between Dr. Haddon, Dr. Gaster, Mrs. Lake, and Mr. Abdul Qayum Malik, a fellow old boy of the Muhammadan Anglo-Oriental College who occasionally preached at the Woking Mosque. The minutes recorded that "the meeting terminated with hearty votes of thanks to Mr. Ikbal Ali Shah."[34]

However, back in Edinburgh with a three-month-old daughter, Ikbal faced a financial hole that no amount of folklore could fill. With no funds being sent by his father, he needed to find—and if necessary, forge—his way toward an alternative future. With the desperation of fading youth and its knowledge of lost chances, he opted for a bold move. On February 3, 1919, sitting for one of the last times in his secretarial office at the Indian Association, he wrote a four-page letter to David Lloyd George, whom he properly addressed as

"Prime Minister of the British Empire." Ikbal introduced himself not as an Indian, though, and thereby as an imperial subject, but as an Afghan, albeit from a family of "staunch supporters of the British Cause in the East." He was, he went on, an Afghan who belonged to the "family of the Laird of Pughman"—a turn of phrase that Sir Walter Scott would have enjoyed.[35]

After repeatedly pledging his loyalty (his family had "ever been first and foremost in defence of the British interest"), Ikbal worked his way toward the main purpose of his letter. Based on "my knowledge of my native country—Afghanistan," he offered Britain's prime minister his "humble services in connection with propaganda work." He had already, he explained, written several articles revealing Germany's secret designs in Central Asia, but now that the war was over, it was the Russians (nay, the Bolsheviks) who should be Downing Street's greatest concern. With his ability to read, write, and speak four major Asian languages, he continued, he could help the British Empire defeat the Bolshevik threat to its Eastern interests.[36] If only Lloyd George would let him.

The bait was soon taken, albeit for reasons Ikbal could not have foreseen when he wrote the letter: two weeks after he sent it, King Habibullah Khan of Afghanistan was assassinated while out on a hunting trip. (Some might have quipped he should have stuck with golf.) When the news reached London two days later, the mysterious letter from the Afghan in Edinburgh seemed like a gift from the great game's presiding gods. It was passed with alacrity to Sir John Shuckburgh, head of the political department of the India Office, which governed India from London. Meanwhile, the British government's main informant inside Afghanistan—an Indian Muslim called Hafiz Saifullah Khan—had just been expelled from Kabul, leaving an informational void at the very moment he was most needed.[37]

With skeptical yet keen interest, Sir John summed up the implications of Ikbal's letter in a short memo to his colleagues: Ikbal Ali Shah "claims to be the only Afghan in this country who is competent to speak with knowledge about the present political situation in C.

Asia."[38] It was an apt moment to play the part of an inside informant, moving between the worlds of the frontier and metropole: the week before Ikbal posted his letter, high-society artist Augustus John painted his iconic portrait of T. E. Lawrence dressed in Bedouin robes. With a curving dagger peeping out from beneath a nomad mantle, John sealed the sartorial image of "Lawrence of Arabia"—and of the politics of masquerade.

Events now began to move fast for Ikbal. The turmoil that followed King Habibullah's assassination caught the India Office off guard, allowing his fiercely anti-British younger son, Amanullah, to seize control of Afghanistan. Amanullah took decisively swift advantage of the fact that Indian troops were still stationed in Europe by launching a surprise attack on British India that would soon become known as the Third Anglo-Afghan War. The great game was back in play—and Ikbal's letter quickly qualified him as a politically important player. In London, his offer of inside information seemed suddenly invaluable.

In eager response, the prime minister's advisers requested that Ikbal be called for an interview with an eye to possible employment by the secretary of state for India.[39] It helped that Ikbal was evidently an aristocrat and gentleman: his title of sirdar was quite familiar to imperial officialdom, not least because the British commander-in-chief in Egypt (at the time Sir Lee Fitzmaurice Stack) also carried the honorary title of sirdar. And so Ikbal was invited to meet Sir John Shuckburgh.

Seizing the moment, before departing for London, Ikbal dashed off a note to William Crooke, folklorist and retired official of the Indian Civil Service with whom he had previously corresponded regarding his election to the Folklore Society. "Would you privilege me," he asked Crooke, by writing letters to friends, and providing their names and addresses, so Ikbal could call on them.[40] It was Ikbal's big chance to make contacts in the capital. "Time is very short," he urged. Crooke complied, also writing to the India Office to boost Ikbal's credentials.[41]

Ikbal further ensured that his arrival in London was preceded by a letter of reference from Sir Alfred Ewing, the principal of Edinburgh University, who assured the India Office that Ikbal was "well-intentioned" and "well-informed."[42] During his years as a student, Sir Alfred went on, Ikbal had gained "considerable influence with the Indian students," while his "constant effort has been to promote friendly relations with Britain." At a time when some Indian students were becoming increasingly vocal in the call for independence, his words were an assurance of Ikbal's loyalty as a British Indian subject. Little did Sir Alfred know that Ikbal was presenting himself to high officialdom as being from Afghanistan, not from India.

As these letters of recommendation were delivered to the palatial buildings of the India Office on Whitehall, Ikbal boarded his train to London. Short of funds as he was, on arriving he checked into the Shaftesbury Hotel in the working-class Seven Dials district.[43] Despite its dignified name, the Shaftesbury was a facility for "men of slender resources," where barrow boys from neighboring Covent Garden's fruit and vegetable market took lodgings. By contrast, the man Ikbal was going to meet was an old Etonian who had risen rapidly through the India Office to become secretary (effectively head) of its political department by his early forties.

At his first meeting with Sir John Shuckburgh, Ikbal presented himself as "a loyal Afghan" who was "convinced that the best interests of his country lie in the maintenance of close and friendly relations with the British Government."[44] Having spent the war years accepting or refusing many such offers of inside information, Sir John was shrewd to the point of suspicion, and when he questioned Ikbal further, the young man conceded that he had not been in Afghanistan for five years. But Ikbal managed to conceal the larger fact that he had never set foot in that country, and that it was India, not Afghanistan, that he had left five years earlier.

Since there was no Afghan embassy to which Sir John could turn for guarantees, he asked the mysterious young man for whatever insights he could offer. In response, Ikbal keenly recommended that the British should build railways in Afghanistan. It was certainly a novel proposal, given that the Afghan government had always firmly resisted the expansion of the British rail network from India. And sensibly so, since that very month trains were transporting Indian troops to fight on the Afghan frontier. When Sir John tactfully voiced doubt as to whether railways in Afghanistan were a realistic prospect, Ikbal turned the conversation to the spread of Bolshevism. A flash of alarm betrayed Sir John's bluff demeanor, and Ikbal seized his chance. There were Bolshevik agents all over Afghanistan, he declared, many in disguise as Pan-Islamists: they presented a most grave danger to British interests.[45]

Throughout the short Third Anglo-Afghan War (it lasted only three months), Ikbal met with Sir John in Whitehall several times for further "political conversations."[46] However, it was all on a gentlemanly basis; that is, without any consultation fee. This presented a dilemma to the increasingly penurious Ikbal, who felt forced to fiddle his expense claims: train fares costing £8 were said to have cost £12.[47] Although the discrepancies were noticed, they were overlooked. The insights of the only educated Afghan in Britain were too valuable to turn away for so inexpensive an indiscretion. And so, throughout the summer of fighting on the distant borders of India, Sir John listened to Ikbal expatiate about the importance of a British "grand strategy" for Central Asia. Lurking behind the Afghan decision to launch the war, Ikbal explained, were the real aggressors, the Bolsheviks. Against all obvious evidence, he even assured Sir John that "the Afghan nation has *no* inclination, of the least degree, to fight the British Government."[48]

Even though the new nationalist ruler Amanullah took pride in waging war on the British Empire—he was soon showing off his new title of *ghazi* or "holy warrior"—as far as Ikbal was concerned, Amanullah was actually seeking an alliance with the British. What was needed from the British side, then, was a vivid gesture of "strong friendship."[49] Given the circumstances, such a policy seemed either eccentric pacifism or wishful thinking. Instead, Sir John opted to bomb Afghan villages along the border. Ikbal's advice was bluntly ignored, then. But a door had been opened: he had succeeded in making himself known in the hushed corridors of imperial intelligence.

Although the war lasted only till August 1919, the urgent attention paid to Afghanistan during those few summer months saw Ikbal elected as a member of the Royal Central Asian Society.[50] Of the thirty newly elected members that year, only three weren't British; and of them, Ikbal was the only Muslim and, more importantly, the only "Afghan." Making use of his membership, he attended its twice-monthly meetings whenever he could afford to travel to London. Held in the society's headquarters at 14 Belgrave Square, the epicenter of the establishment, the meetings afforded him entry to the circles of brigadiers, explorers, and "old India hands" who advised the government on its policies toward Central Asia.

After the Afghan war ended with an armistice and no clear winner, interest still remained high in what the new ruler Amanullah would do next. As a result, Ikbal was invited to lecture at the society where, standing at the podium, he spoke with unexpected approval of the ruler who had just declared victory over the British Empire.[51] Still, Ikbal's account of recent battles, and of the bearded tribesmen of the frontier, held his audience captive. The lecture drew him again to the attention of the India Office, where memos circulated as to who this new expert informant really was. As H.R.C. Dobbs, foreign secretary to the government of India, phrased the matter, "doubt has been expressed . . . as to the genuineness of his Afghan nationality."[52]

Still, the Third Anglo-Afghan War had enabled Ikbal to make his name as an Afghan—at least outside the skeptical secret correspondence of the India Office. In the following months, he received more and more invitations to give paid lectures on Afghanistan across the length of the country, from the London headquarters of the National Indian Association to the Liverpool Geographical Society, the Yorkshire Philosophical Society, and the Royal Geographical Society of Scotland. His lecture in York was delivered to what one reporter described as "an exceptionally large audience." Airing to good reception his views in favor of British free trade policies, Ikbal declared that the Afghans must "open their doors to trade and allow foreigners, and above all the British, to come and assist them."[53] At this and several other points, several voices from the audience shouted, "Hear, Hear!"

Everything was progressing very nicely till, in October, somebody called Ikbal's bluff. He had given another lecture, this time to the Northbrooke Society in London. Named after a former viceroy of India, and based in the cultured surroundings of South Kensington, the Northbrooke Society was an offshoot of the National Indian Association, a gathering place for elite Indian expatriates. One such listener in the audience was Aziz-ud-din, a senior colonial official and commander of the Royal Victorian Order who, immediately after the lecture ended, wrote to inform the India Office's political department about a "fraud who calls himself Ikbal Ali Shah."[54] Aziz-ud-din declared himself not in the least fooled by the man who "was introduced as a genuine Afghan whose home was in Afghanistan," because as far as he was concerned, Ikbal instead "appears to be a Punjabee."

Worse still, the man to whom Aziz-ud-din wrote was Ikbal's key contact, Sir John Shuckburgh. But how could Sir John be sure? Reliable intelligence on Afghanistan was so hard to come by. Rather than cut Ikbal loose, Sir John decided he might still be useful. Perhaps there was something in the young man's excited ramblings about renewed Russian designs over India. He met Ikbal again and suggested he write reports on what he knew about Bolshevik activity in Central Asia. Although Ikbal knew nothing more about the matter than what he could garner between the library and his imagination, he agreed.[55]

Aziz-ud-din's letter had certainly been a close call, but because Ikbal knew nothing of it, his new career seemed to be taking shape nicely. His connection with Sir John was beginning to yield tangible results by way of much-needed employment. And recognition. Weeks later he was elected secretary of the Edinburgh Oriental

Society.[56] But financial concerns remained almost as pressing as before. So in the months that followed, he set himself the task of writing more political articles on topics he judged most relevant to the strategists surveying the emerging new order of the postwar world. For the leading Scottish newspaper, *The Scotsman*, he wrote an article on the Soviet threat to Afghanistan that made public the claims he had made privately to Sir John.[57] Given that the nascent Soviet Union was still fighting a vicious civil war to control its territories, Ikbal's alarmism was more than a little exaggerated. But he was learning that exaggeration, and if necessary imagination, was what made people take interest. He followed the piece in *The Scotsman* with a further "report" for Glasgow's *Herald* on the Bolshevik advance through Central Asia, then a longer ten-page exposé for the respected *Edinburgh Review*.[58]

While expanding his reach into the Scottish newspapers for which Donald Mackenzie had encouraged him to write, Ikbal also became a more regular presence at the Royal Central Asian Society in London. On one occasion, he gave a lecture to senior military officials about the Afghan government's relations with the Central Asian states that were rapidly being Sovietized, speaking as though he had an insider's knowledge.[59] Colonel A. C. Yate, who had traveled with the boundary commission that established the borders of Afghanistan back in the 1880s, listened keenly. A wary old player of the great game—Yate had made his name thirty years earlier with his *England and Russia Face to Face in Asia*—he could be an influential patron. In fact, Ikbal had already caught the colonel's eye. Following a lecture by Captain E. W. Sheppard on "Some Military Aspects of the Mesopotamia Problem" at a previous meeting of the Central Asian Society, Yate had stated that a fine solution to Britain's difficulties in Iraq had already been proposed by "Sirdar Ikbal Ali Shah, a well-known member of this Society and an Afghan of great ability."[60]

Indeed, Yate had declared, so brilliant were the sirdar's proposals that "they seemed worthy of the attention of our Foreign Office."[61] Ikbal was keen to reciprocate the compliment and cultivate the colonel's patronage. Accordingly, in the next meeting of the Royal Central Asian Society, he declared his allegiance to Yate's cause of maintaining Britain's influence in Central Asia. He explained that he looked forward to the day when a "complete and sincere friendship will be cemented" between the British Empire and Afghanistan, before adding that he hoped he could play his part in "the furtherance of that noble task." He ended his speech with the dramatic pledge that he was about to set off "to the East with this intention."[62]

First, though, he would have to make a shorter journey: to move his young family to Bristol, in the southwest of England. There, far from the many people in Edinburgh who knew him as an Indian, he could be free to reinvent himself as a citizen of Afghanistan. Even so, whether Indian or Afghan, living with a Scotswoman was no easier in Bristol than in Edinburgh, so Ikbal and Elizabeth looked for a house in Clifton, one of the most respectable parts of the city, where they might face less overt hostility. Eventually they found a landlord willing to rent them a flat on Cornwallis Crescent, part of a somewhat down-at-heels terrace of Georgian townhouses. Though the front rooms faced a high wall that left half of the house in permanent shadow, at the back there was an ample garden where Elizabeth could play with little Amina in a semblance of middle-class comfort. On paper at least, Clifton was known as a genteel neighborhood, home to many a retired colonial official. Ikbal had headed notepaper printed up for the letters he planned to write to editors, learned associations, and other men of influence.

Now that he was at the other end of the British Isles, and meeting people with no contact with Edinburgh, he began presenting himself as having been a "Lecturer and Examiner in Oriental Culture" at Edinburgh University.[63] He needed credentials and was willing to embellish and, if necessary, invent them. Spurred on by the needs of his wife and daughter, as 1919 rolled into 1920, he found himself forced to write for nearly any magazine that would pay him. With Afghanistan slipping from the front pages, he wrote on almost any topic imaginable. In "Aerial Warfare in Ancient India," he claimed to have found evidence for flying machines in the ancient Sanskrit *Mahabharata*. Published in the popular science magazine *Discovery*, it brought him his first bad review, which mocked his "merry-go-round-flights of fancy."[64] But with rent to pay in Bristol, Ikbal had to keep on writing, even if it was sometimes for *The Badminton Magazine of Sport*.

Partly under the influence of his folklorist acquaintance Lewis Spence, who at the time was compiling his grand *Encyclopaedia of Occultism*, Ikbal also turned to the supernatural subjects that were then much in vogue, as the aftermath of the First World War turned many people away from scientific modernity. Even Sir Arthur Conan Doyle, that doyen of rational deduction and alumnus of Edinburgh Medical School, became a prominent supporter of the Society for Psychical Research. With such high-profile promoters, the occult was not only in fashion, it was also in profit. Its most visible periodical, the monthly *Occult Review*, founded in 1905, sold in large numbers for a shilling an issue. Every prominent occultist wrote for it, from the genteel white magician Arthur Edward Waite to his depraved sinister shadow Aleister Crowley. Ikbal now joined them with an account of Afghan magical techniques in which he explained how the mullahs of Afghanistan used charms called "wazeefas" to summon genies, then control their vast powers.[65] *The Occult Review*'s editor was thrilled, and Ikbal soon followed up with an essay on the Afghan adherence to Sufism, the mystical form of Islam that had flowered over the course of a millennium.[66] He derived his information from the writings of British Orientalists like Reynold Nicholson of Cambridge, one of a new generation of late imperial scholars who wrote with profound sympathy for Islam, particularly for the poetic and philosophical teachings of the Sufis. Despite Ikbal's use of such secondhand sources, his assumed identity as an Afghan lent him an air of authority as he described the prestige and influence of Sufism in the little-known land of Afghanistan.

In the wake of the Indian Inayat Khan's founding of his Sufi Order in the West a few years earlier, in London then New York and San Francisco, interest in Islam's mystical tradition was growing beyond the academic circles of the Orientalists, particularly after Inayat Khan invented what he called "Universal Sufism," which detached Sufism from its Muslim foundations in a way that appealed to a broad church of liberal Christians, Theosophists, and occultists alike. When Ikbal presented Sufism to the readers of *The Occult Review*, he was responding to this interest but not necessarily agreeing with it, writing that a Sufi must behave as a "faithful follower of Islam" with full "obedience to its laws."[67] Though he conceded that different Sufi masters disagreed as to whether advanced practitioners had to continue obeying the Sharia after progressing on the path to divine union, he was unwilling to allow the enthusiasms of Western occultists to make him claim that Sufism was not part of Islam.

Commentators in the American *Theosophical Review* began treating Ikbal as an expert on the Afghan Sufis, whom he had actually never encountered. He promptly published another article on the subject for *The Hibbert Journal*, a prominent liberal theological magazine read on both sides of the Atlantic.[68] Much as he was enjoying this expanding readership, he hoped to influence the men who controlled the visible powers of the world of affairs rather than reclusive bohemians who spent their days summoning spirits behind the closed curtains of Kensington villas. But he had come to realize that his credibility had limits, something made painfully clear in conversations at the Royal Central Asian Society with men like Colonel Yate, who had marched across hundreds of miles of Afghan territory. Even a bespectacled don like Dr. Haddon, who presided over the meetings of the Folklore Society, had spent years exploring the Torres Strait Islands in the South Pacific. At a time when anthropologists were making "fieldwork" the acme of their authority, and journalists were roving ever farther across the planet's retreating borders, Ikbal needed the proven credibility of having "been there." So far he had pretended it. Now he needed to actually go to Afghanistan and take photographs to prove it.

Chapter Three

INFORMANT

So little did I understand what was allowable in the
way of literary invention.

—Edmund Gosse, *Father and Son*

In November 1920, after seven years in Britain,
Ikbal announced to his new circle at the Royal Central Asian Society that he was setting off to Afghanistan.[1] He had already written to Sir John Shuckburgh to request a preferential certificate to expedite his journey, declaring that he had been called home to attend to matters of state importance.[2] Keen to maintain the momentum of recent publications, he was soon sending back reports on his journey, describing strolls around Kabul in the airy language of travel articles that filled the popular magazines of the period. Kabul was a place of "continual *va-et-vient*," he wrote, and offered splendid opportunities for the philosophical flaneur. Then he turned, in his next article, to the Panjshir Valley, north of the capital, where the villagers were "true sons of old Asia."[3] Responding to British depictions of the Afghans as fearsome tribal warriors, he painted an altogether gentler picture, of farmers and craftsmen at work, citing a bucolic line from the poet Shelley.[4] Still, there was plenty of mileage to be had in stereotypes, and for *The Quiver*, he penned a piece in which he played happily on images of the tribal warriors and gun workshops of that "far and wild frontier."[5]

Yet soon Ikbal found he needed something more than recycled

clichés to entice editors to commission further articles. He needed a scoop, and soon found one. His next reports described treks into the mountainous far north of Afghanistan, where he witnessed Russian Bolsheviks busily building roads. He explained to his readers how he sneaked across the border into Soviet Central Asia to see just how far these roads went. Somehow, despite the ongoing Basmachi rebellion and the Bolshevik paranoia about spies that was fueling surveillance of each and every newcomer, Ikbal managed to wander for several months around the newly Sovietized cities of Bukhara and Samarqand, interviewing people and taking notes. What he reported back to British editors was extraordinary. Military garrisons had been assembled for the purpose of building highways designed to export Communism by armed force not only into Afghanistan but also from there into India.

This dastardly plot became all the more apparent when he followed up his investigations in the communizing khanates of Central Asia, whence he undertook an expedition across the Hindu Kush into the Indian border region of Chitral. There, on some of the highest mountain passes on the planet, he described Bolsheviks building more roads that would lay the entire subcontinent open before them. There was even mention of work on a secret railway. Given that Chitral was home to forty mountains over twenty thousand feet, the roads were testimony to the Bolsheviks' terrifying ambition, leading up inclines that no vehicle could yet climb. It was evidence of truly fanatical resolve. Was this not exactly what he had tried to warn Prime Minister Lloyd George about in his letter the previous year? Was this not what he had told Sir John Shuckburgh during their meetings at the Indian Office? Should they not have listened to him more carefully, taken him more seriously?

A series of articles on the Bolshevik advance now flowed from Ikbal's typewriter. Two strategic papers for _The Contemporary Review_ and _The Edinburgh Review_ warned of the "Bolshevist menace" and advised that Britain could best thwart the Communist advance by developing closer relations with Kabul.[6] The newspapers also took note, with Donald Mackenzie's Glasgow *Herald* quoting Ikbal as an expert who was "himself an Afghan."[7] Seizing on the recognition, Ikbal offered the *Herald* an equally alarmist piece on the spread of Bolshevism from Central Asia to within a rebel-rousing stone's throw of British India.[8] Here, as well as in two pieces he wrote for *The Graphic* and *The Field*, which he illustrated with photographs, he elaborated in detail on the Bolshevik roads.[9] All told, the articles described the British Empire's oldest nightmare—a Russian invasion of India via Afghanistan—finally on the verge of becoming a reality.[10]

Having paid for the photographic evidence, the editor of *The Field*, Sir Theodore Cook, was keen to make the most of his scoop. But he also felt patriotically bound to inform the secretary of state for India about the rather dapper young man who had called on him in London "with extraordinarily interesting information from Afghanistan."[11] Not that Ikbal was the only Indian to claim he had inside information on Afghan affairs that year: Abdul Ghani, the retired personal doctor of the Afghan king and erstwhile member of his legislative council, had just published his detailed *Review of the Political Situation in Central Asia*.[12] But nothing in Ghani's report matched Ikbal's incendiary talk of road-building up to the very borders of British India. Immediately, the authorities took note. Between London, Delhi, and Peshawar on the Afghan border, telegrams hummed along underwater and overland cables demanding to know whether what Ikbal reported was true. If the Bolsheviks had somehow managed to assemble enough men to build a military road inside British-administered territory in Chitral, then why, damn it, had none of the frontier agents spotted them?[13]

From the outset, Denys Bray, a long-standing frontier officer and now foreign secretary to the government of India, declared his suspicion. "Is this the so-called Afghan who lectured before the Central Asian Society?" he demanded in a telegram from Delhi. "If so, I fancy he didn't cross the frontier."[14] After all, the border with Afghanistan was the most scrutinized in the whole empire: no one passed it without official approval, let alone without being noticed. In response to Bray's inquiries, the British representative in Kabul dispatched a telegram to officials in Delhi confirming that Ikbal "has never been to Afghanistan."[15] In any case, he added, his account of roads, let alone whole armored divisions, crossing the mountainous roof of the world "sounds sheer nonsense."[16] Another high official telegraphed London declaring on no less an authority than the office of the viceroy that Ikbal had never been to Afghanistan and, far from having been born and raised there, came from Sardhana, a mere fifty miles from Delhi.[17] More damning still, he stated that in March of that year, Ikbal had been to see him and "tried to get me to take him to Kabul" but had been refused.[18]

As the investigation took shape, officials soon found gaping holes in Ikbal's tale of high-altitude espionage. The findings were summarized in a report that scoffed at the geographical lunacy of his claims. "His railways cross mountain tops and 12,000 foot passes with supreme disregard of such trivial obstacles," wrote Major A. F. Rawson Lumby of the India Office's military department.[19] So impossible was a motor road, let alone a railway, across the high passes of Chitral, he continued, that "it is obvious that Ikbal Ali Shah has never visited the country he so graphically depicts."[20] Still, "the limit to his effrontery" lay in the photographs in which he "palmed off" familiar places in British India as secret sites in the Afghan Hindu Kush and Russian Central Asia.[21] Major Lumby's internal report concluded that, far from trekking across fifty mountain passes to Bukhara, Ikbal's travels had merely involved spending time at his father's palace in Sardhana—if he had even traveled that far.[22] Responding to the report, Denys Bray voiced almost admiring astonishment: "He's an amazingly audacious fellow."[23]

Thus far the unmasking was a private one, conducted in secret telegrams that left both Ikbal and his public none the wiser of his exposure. So he continued to write to Sir John Shuckburgh as though nothing had happened; indeed, as if Sir John and his whole political department at the India Office still believed in his Central Asian adventures. Including his articles as proof of his findings, in November 1921 he wrote to Sir John requesting another meeting in London, this time with an eye to permanent employment. Explaining that he was giving up his medical studies, he gave the reason that his travels in Afghanistan and Turkestan had made him "unsettled."[24] So, he continued, he hoped Sir John would support him in pursuing a career with either the British government or the colonial government of India.[25]

A few days later Ikbal also wrote to Sir Theodore Cook of *The Field* asking for career advice. The letter had a plaintive tone: he presented himself as "a young man who is lost in a wilderness."[26] But next he took the kind of bold step he had made when he wrote to the prime minister almost two years earlier, this time by writing to the Right Honourable Edwin Montagu, secretary of state for India, to formally apply for a post in the Colonial Service.[27] Not for any position, though. He gave Montagu a list of the kind of jobs he would be willing to consider, at the top of which was a position in the Indian Civil Service, a class of officialdom so elite that even other British officials called them "the heaven-born." Moreover, Ikbal proposed that he would not sit an exam like every other applicant but should instead be given a position "without examination, as an exceptional case."[28] Should no place in the Indian Civil Service be available, then he might perhaps consider being head of a Political Agency, running a frontier district such as Chitral. After all, he had explored its high mountains. Or else he could be the British agent (effectively the ambassador) to one of India's chief princely states. At the bottom of his list was a much humbler role for which he was far better qualified: as "counter-propagandist" against the Bolshevik outreach to India.

Officials at the India Office were already on to him, though, and a week after he sent his application letter, knowledge of his inventions also reached the public. The source was an unexpected one: the perspicacious readers of *The Field*. Ikbal might reasonably have expected his ruse to pass without question among the riding and shooting readership of that self-described "Country Gentleman's

Newspaper," but he couldn't have been more mistaken. The polo-playing enthusiasms of army officers all over India saw *The Field* circulate in far-off places he had never anticipated. And from them, the editor, Sir Theodore, received numerous credible refutations of Ikbal's claims. He decided he had to act on them. Accordingly, in the December 1921 issue, Sir Theodore published no fewer than nine letters, most of them sent by officers stationed on the very frontiers Ikbal claimed to have witnessed being broached. One frontier officer wrote to identify a photograph that Ikbal had labeled as showing a Bolshevik-built road in northern Afghanistan as an "extremely well-known" section of the road on the Indian side of the Khyber Pass near Peshawar. Far from being built by Bolsheviks, it was designed by British engineers.[29]

That wasn't the worst of it. "Imagine my complete consterna-tion," the letter-writer continued, "when I saw in the lower pic-ture the camp which this unit [the 62nd Punjabis] occupied for ten months this year described as '*The White Tents of a Bolshevist Out-post.*'"[30] The photograph was not only misinforming; it was insult-ing, identifying loyal Indian soldiers as Communist invaders. Finally, the source of Ikbal's photographic evidence was revealed. Far from having taken them himself on his travels, they were stock photos supplied by Holmes Studio, a shop in Peshawar owned by the Brit-ish photographer Randolph Bezzant Holmes, who carried on a brisk trade with tourists seeking souvenirs of the "wild Afghan frontier."[31]

In fact, while Ikbal was supposedly undertaking his adventurous journey, he had been spotted several times in London.[32] To make matters worse, the company he seemed to be keeping cast doubt on the loyalty he had so keenly expressed in his letter to Lloyd George: in August he had been observed "hanging about the Ritz Hotel" try-ing to meet the senior Afghan official, Muhammad Wali Khan.[33] The latter was known to have led an embassy to Moscow two years earlier in which he had signed a treaty of friendship with the Soviets and persuaded Lenin to provide thirteen military aircraft to help the Afghans stand up to the capitalist imperialists of the British Empire.[34]

At the end of the investigation into Ikbal's Bolshevik reports, the foreign and political department in Delhi reported back to London. "Despite his romancing propensities," they concluded, "we are inclined to regard him as well meaning and potentially useful."[35] There were still high officials in London willing to overlook Ikbal's dalliance with hostile Afghan generals at the Ritz. Even so, "romancing propensities" were hardly the kind of expert qualifications Ikbal had hoped his reports would be taken for. He would be given no cushy career in the Indian Civil Service, and a few days before Christmas, he received a letter from the India Office declining his services.[36]

Even without the exposé, his financial needs and personal idiosyncrasies were combusting in a manner hardly conducive to building his reputation as a political analyst. At the same time as he had been writing reports about Bolsheviks, he had published articles that placed him on the wacky fringes of the culture of empire. Renewing his association with The Occult Review, he had written about "The Occult Lore of Burma," recounting anecdotes of ghostly women, jungle-dwelling werewolves, and a fearful class of necromancers called weza.[37] (A few years earlier his mentor, Donald Mackenzie, had published a book on Burma's folklore.) But if Ikbal hoped no one outside The Occult Review's secretive readership would take notice, he was disappointed, because the article was so sensational that mainstream newspapers picked up on it. Repeatedly citing Ikbal as the source, London's Evening News—read by hundreds of thousands of commuters every day—reprinted the juiciest parts under the startling headline "Woman Changed into Tigress."[38] But still Ikbal kept writing. Next, in a similarly fantastical report for Conquest: The British Magazine of Popular Science, he claimed to have discovered "A Hidden Race Roaming in Unknown Afghanistan," straining his credibility among even the great game's most hawkish players.[39]

In the meantime, the demands of family life in rented lodgings on Bristol's Cornwallis Crescent became ever more pressing, because Elizabeth was pregnant again. Ikbal did his best to resume lecture engagements and was offered a talk for the general public at the People's Palace on nearby Baldwin Street. Though the setting wasn't nearly as august as his former venues at London's Royal Central Asian Society or Royal Asiatic Society, the People's Palace was at least one of Bristol's largest music halls. Such speaker's fees helped pay the mounting bills—and there were more of them than ever when Elizabeth gave birth to a boy in the spring of 1922.[40] They decided to call him Omar. It was better known in Britain than most Muslim names. Moreover, for Ikbal and Elizabeth, the poems of Omar Khayyam, whose *Rubaiyyat* had been rendered into immortal English verse by the Victorian Edward FitzGerald, marked the point where their two worlds met in harmony.

Now that Ikbal had been so publicly unmasked in England, he decided to turn to the American press instead and wrote two articles for New York's prestigious *Asia* magazine.[41] Across the Atlantic there was far less chance of anyone learning of his true background, and so the contributors' section presented him to American readers as "an Afghan noble who, as his title [sirdar] indicates, is a member of the durbar [court] of the Amir of Afghanistan."[42] His contribution to *Asia* was based on what the editors took to be a genuine journey of secret espionage through Bolshevik Central Asia. As an advertisement for another of these articles explained, Ikbal was "an Afghan noble living in England" who had "succeeded in penetrating in the disguise of a mullah, or priest, into this inaccessible country."[43] He certainly knew how to give readers what they wanted, for the Muslim lands through which he claimed to have traveled in impoverished disguise were places where severed heads were shown off as war trophies by feuding tribes.[44] "Such absolute savagery," he declared, "I had never beheld anywhere."[45]

Back in London, though, these further tales of adventure were recognized as no less invented than his earlier reports. "He has concocted the whole story and has not traversed a yard of the journey which he attempts to describe," declared a secret India Office report on his American articles.[46] His claim to have walked from Chitral to the

Bashgul Valley in a single day, which would involve crossing a snow-bound pass of over fifteen thousand feet in midwinter, was declared to be "a physical impossibility."[47] He had also invented tribal uprisings that never happened, given the wrong locations for railways that did exist and fanciful locations for motor roads that didn't. All in all, the report concluded, "there is nothing in these articles which he could not have written sitting in London with the aid of a fairly good map."[48] Actually, he had written them in Bristol, but the point still held.

By now, officials were talking of Ikbal as "a fraud of the Rougemont type," comparing him to the nineteenth-century Swiss fabulist Henri Louis Grin, who under the assumed name of Louis de Rougemont had invented tales of extraordinary adventure in then-little-known Australia.[49] Sensing that this round in the game was over, Ikbal decided he had no alternative but to flee England—albeit for India rather than Afghanistan. Once he was there, he could try to find employment in the vast bureaucracy of the imperial Raj. And if that failed, he could always beg his father to resume the allowance that helped him live in such style during his student days.

As soon as Elizabeth, Amina, and Omar were ready to travel, on June 30, 1922, the family set sail from London for Bombay aboard the SS *Mantola*.[50] Though Ikbal hadn't been enrolled at university for over two years now, the passenger manifest listed his profession as "medical student." It was the most respectable claim he could make. They traveled second class.

Bombay came as a shock to Elizabeth and Ikbal alike. As they disembarked into the vast crowd of humanity surrounding the gangway, hooting cars jostled with loaded camels that towered over cyclists who weaved around bullock carts whose drivers pushed their way past wiry porters who were weighed down with impossible loads on their backs or, as often, their heads. Setting aside his departure via Bombay nine years earlier, the city was as new to Ikbal as it was to Elizabeth. His own India had been one of small towns—Sardhana, Aligarh, Meerut—whose prominent Muslim populations lent them a quite different flavor from this cosmopolitan port. The dockyards were filled with voices calling in a dozen languages he couldn't understand. The family was immediately accosted by local "guides" offering taxis, hotels, shopping, train tickets. The hawkers could spot greenhorns before they even stepped off the gangway. "India-returned" students who had forgotten the ways of their homeland were considered a particularly profitable subgroup.

From the vast Gothic monument to steam power that was Bombay's Victoria Terminus, they took a train over the high ghats that loomed precipitously over the coast, then chuffed through the baking plains of central India toward Delhi. With meals served by turbaned liverymen, the train seemed something more like the milieu of Ikbal's upbringing as described so many times to Elizabeth. Excited as he must have been at the thought of finally showing her his homeland, the reality likely proved far more complicated than he had imagined, for the Indian servants and English passengers would have been shocked at the sight of Ikbal sharing a sleeper compartment with the red-haired and lily-white Elizabeth.

Ikbal's search for a job with the colonial government meant that the family would have to stay for a while in the capital, New Delhi. Architect Edwin Lutyens was still completing its grand boulevards and palaces of government, but Elizabeth was more fascinated by the city's old Mughal monuments. She spent day after day wandering through the Red Fort, with its endless corridors and eerily empty halls of audience.[51] The fort had been the seat of the last Mughal emperor till just over sixty years ago, when her grandfather was a young man. Nearby was the jewelbox Moti Masjid, the "pearl mosque" built by the emperor Aurangzeb for himself and his wives. Here in India, Elizabeth's conversion to Islam finally began to find meaning. Before, it had been a merely expedient part of getting married to Ikbal, or perhaps a snub to her parents. But amid the marble mosques and domed Sufi shrines built during six hundred years of Muslim rule over Delhi, her abstract ideas about Islam began to take color and form. She stepped into the Moti Masjid, removed her shoes, and prayed.

From Delhi the family traveled the fifty-odd miles to Sardhana, where finally Elizabeth would meet Ikbal's father, the nawwab, and his sister Mahmooda.[52] By now, Nawwab Amjad Ali Shah had come to accept his only son's marriage to a Scottish woman. After all, she had borne him two children, including a boy. Along the train route to Sardhana, Ikbal, Elizabeth, and the children traveled via the old military cantonment at nearby Meerut, the site of the great rebellion—the "Indian Mutiny"—of 1857, which Ikbal's ancestor Jan Fishan had helped to suppress. As for the nawwab's residence, it was, in the words of the *Imperial Gazetteer*, "a fine house with a magnificent flight of steps at the entrance and extensive grounds," surrounding which were the twenty-eight square miles of sugar beet plantations that comprised the family estate.[53]

Despite the pomp that the nawwab tried to maintain in his palace, its rambling rooms were in poor repair. Although the East India Company had bestowed a rich pension of 1,000 rupees per month on his ancestor, Jan Fishan, along with lands once valued at 10,000 rupees per annum, his son, Ikbal's grandfather Nawwab Ahmad Shah had depleted the family's wealth through "speculations in indigo and personal extravagance," as *The Imperial Gazetteer* tactfully phrased it.[54] Ikbal was perhaps too proud to ever mention the matter, but back in 1895 the estate had been taken under the Court of Wards, and six years later his father Nawwab Amjad Ali Shah's debts had been paid off by a loan from the colonial government. By this point, the family's debts had reached the truly aristocratic sum of a million rupees.[55] Most of the income from the nawwab's estate subsequently went to paying off the loan. Of what remained, a great deal had gone to funding Ikbal's studies, and seven years at the most prestigious medical school in the empire had been far from cheap.

Ikbal and Elizabeth stayed with the nawwab for several weeks. Although to Elizabeth, the town of Sardhana may have looked tawdrier than Ikbal had described, it had its wistful charms, for as she soon would have learned, Sardhana had a most curious history. In the middle of the eighteenth century, when the Mughal Empire was being torn apart by freebooters from Europe, Persia, Afghanistan, and India alike, Emperor Shah Alam II had granted Sardhana to a Catholic mercenary from Luxembourg, Walter Reinhardt Sombre. Sombre's young Indian wife—known as Begum Samru through the Indian pronunciation of his name—subsequently inherited the estate and, having converted to Catholicism, constructed a splendid baroque basilica designed by an Italian architect from Vicenza. When Elizabeth came to Sardhana, Our Lady of Grace was still North India's largest Catholic church. Nor did the strange history of Sardhana end with Begum Samru. When she died in 1836, she left her lands to her Anglo-Indian step-great-grandson, David Ochterlony Dyce Sombre, but the East India Company refused to recognize him and seized control of the estate.[56] After Ikbal's ancestor Jan Fishan Khan aided the British in Afghanistan five years later, it was with the Begum's—and Dyce Sombre's—land that he was rewarded. There in 1864 Jan Fishan was buried in a dainty mausoleum that echoed in miniature those of the vanquished Mughal emperors.

Somewhat more of a modernizer, the next nawwab had ensured the palace was supplied with safe drinking water by having one of Cheavins's patented cast-iron water filters shipped out from England. With Britain's royal coat of arms on its barrel-like exterior, he had it proudly positioned in the courtyard, in front of the elegant veranda with its scalloped archways and baluster columns. But by the 1920s the palace's best days were clearly gone. Like so many members of the old aristocracy, the nawwab was living on borrowed time.

As Sir Sayyid Ahmad Khan, the founder of Ikbal's school, had realized half a century earlier, India's Muslim gentry would be better off finding places in the British imperial bureaucracy than leading hunting parties around their depleted estates. Ikbal now heeded that advice by again seeking a position in the Colonial Service. As far as he was concerned, his unmasking had taken place on the other side of the planet, so he appended copies of his publications to the letters he sent to Delhi in search of employment. He sent one such package to E. B. Howell, head of the foreign and political department, requesting a post in the consular service.[57] Presenting himself as an expert on Afghanistan, he expressed particular interest and aptitude for a posting to Kabul.

Unfortunately for Ikbal, as a result of the investigation into his claims of Bolshevik encroachments, Howell knew perfectly well who he was. He had no intention of taking the risk of placing Ikbal in the consular service, particularly in as sensitive a posting as Kabul. On that matter, Howell was adamant. Undeterred, Ikbal next offered his services for a planned expedition to the fierce frontier tribes of Waziristan.[58] Once again he was turned down.

This was altogether inconvenient, since living arrangements at the nawwab's palace were by now proving difficult. While Ikbal had been away, his sister Mahmooda had married Mirza Shakir Hussein Barlas, the scion of an old Mughal family, who had studied at Oxford then gone on to build a successful career as a barrister in Delhi.[59] Jobless and degreeless, Ikbal may have paled in his father's eyes by comparison. Perhaps tired of his father's recriminations for wasting vast sums on an education that had come to nothing, by September, though effectively homeless, Ikbal moved Elizabeth and the children out of the palace to stay with another Indian barrister he knew who lived in Meerut, the nearest large town to Sardhana.[60] This lawyer friend, Shakir Ali, had also been schooled at the Muhammadan Anglo-Oriental College, whence he too had traveled to Britain to complete his education, spending three years at the Lincoln's Inn law offices in London. Now he lived in the comfort of Meerut's cantonment which, with the more British ambience of its pretty cottages and flower gardens, may have suited Elizabeth (and, after nearly ten years away, also Ikbal) better than the crumbling palace.

Sending letter after desperate letter, Ikbal's peculiar talents eventually brought him to the attention of Laurence Rushbrook Williams, former professor of modern history at Allahabad University, where his contacts with the young generation of Indian intellectuals had helped him shape the gradualist wing of the nationalist movement.[61] Consequently, the mild-mannered historian had carved out a role for

himself as middleman between the colonial government and leading nationalists like Gandhi and Jinnah, though by the time Ikbal
came to his attention, Rushbrook Williams was being employed to
quietly prevent the spread of Communism among disaffected Indians. On the basis of Ikbal's journalism about the Bolshevik threat,
Rushbrook Williams sensed his potential as a helper—albeit an
unacknowledged one—in his own anti-Bolshevik ventures. He sent
Ikbal a letter offering what he euphemistically termed "experimental work."[62] A few months later Rushbrook Williams was appointed
director of the newly established Central Bureau of Public Information, a governmental public relations department founded in
response to the flow of propaganda from the Soviet Union. He spotted an opportunity to redirect Ikbal's earlier accomplishments in
supplying the British with false intelligence, by having him produce
counterpropaganda against the Bolsheviks instead.

Although it was far from the lofty position of assistant political
officer for which Ikbal had initially applied, he accepted the offer
nonetheless. Perhaps it might lead to greater things. In only a matter of weeks, he was proposing to his new manager what he enig-
matically referred to as a "Somewhat Larger Scheme."[63] What he
meant by this mysterious moniker was a grand plan for the colonial government to establish a School for Propaganda, over which he
himself would naturally preside as headmaster. As Ikbal explained
in the long master plan he typed as a lodger at Shakir Ali's table,
the graduates of the school would be trained in everything from fluent lecture delivery to mountain survival skills. Outdoing the secret
schools of the Soviets, Ikbal would create a new generation of Indian
loyalists who would lecture and publish in praise of British benevo-
lence. But the school was only one element of his "Somewhat Larger
Scheme"—it also involved recruiting a huge workforce of Muslim
propagandists, their credibility assured by selecting them from the
religious classes of Afghanistan and Central Asia. The best recruits
would be hajjis, with the prestige of having made the pilgrimage
to Mecca; traditional *hakim* physicians whom the common people

trusted; theology students from madrassas; and fakirs who roamed the land (Ikbal claimed) collecting rare botanical specimens for their alchemical experiments.[64]

In response, the General Staff Branch drew up a detailed critique, outlining the many reasons why the proposals wouldn't work.[65] Howell and Rushbrook Williams concurred, and Ikbal's school for spies got no further. Instead, under firm instructions to "keep a close eye on what he does," Rushbrook Williams employed him on a series of smaller tasks, like compiling information on the strategies of nationalists and Pan-Islamists as voiced in Indian newspapers.[66] Still, Ikbal kept on plotting his "Larger Schemes" and was soon writing to Rushbrook Williams with a new plan, this time to deploy the "spiritual influences" of a Sufi he supposedly knew among the Waziri tribes of the Afghan frontier.[67] After Rushbrook Williams passed the proposal up the chain of command, Howell replied tersely, telling him to make sure Ikbal was "choked off this idea."[68]

Within just a few months of taking Ikbal on, imperial officialdom was rapidly tiring of his schemes. Yet their position remained that, so long as Rushbrook Williams could control him, he was still "potentially useful." So Ikbal stayed on the shadowy staff of the Central Bureau of Public Information into 1923. But he became increasingly frustrated by the anonymous work of compiling reports on other people's journalism. Two years earlier it had been his own name appearing in prestigious magazines at the heart of the empire. Now he was stuck in provincial Meerut, near where his life had begun, except that rather than residing in his ancestral palace, he was lodging in a more successful schoolfriend's bungalow. After working for Rushbrook Williams for just over a year, he decided to return publicly to the journalistic fold. He joined Elizabeth, Amina, and Omar on a train bound for Simla, where he had found a job on a recently established newspaper, The Bulletin.[69] The journey, by pony and cart for several hours of the last steep section, was trying, not least because Elizabeth was heavily pregnant with her third child.

Still, as the summer capital of the Raj, Simla was the grandest "hill station" of them all. Its centerpiece, the Viceregal Lodge, was a rambling Scottish baronial edifice of a kind quite familiar to the young couple. Then there were the neo-Gothic Gorton Castle, the mock-Tudor library, and the Church of Scotland's St. Andrew's. But though the weather was cooler here than on the baking plains below, the social atmosphere was stifling. Nowhere in the whole empire was more snobbishly exclusive, and the British society wives of Simla prided themselves on maintaining a hierarchy stricter than the most Brahmanical caste codes.

Word would have gotten around quickly that Ikbal wasn't one of the rising Indian stars of the Indian Civil Service but was rather a low-level employee at an unknown newspaper. The best he and Elizabeth could manage was to remind people that he was a sirdar, the son of a nawwab. But in Simla, where the richest families of India's more than five hundred princely states were still regarded as socially inferior to "the gods" of the Indian Civil Service, Ikbal's association with the comparatively paltry estate at Sardhana would have counted for little. Worse still, many Simla wives had read Alice Perrin's *The Anglo-Indians* and Ethel Savi's *The Daughter-in-Law*, two hugely popular novels that depicted the "terrible fate" of British women who had broken racial taboos by marrying Indians.

In a rented bungalow surrounded by deodar trees and chattering monkeys, Elizabeth sat out the last months of her pregnancy. There, in the middle of June 1924, she gave birth to her second son, for whom Ikbal chose the name Idries. The name of one of the prophets mentioned in the Quran (often identified with the Old Testament's Enoch), it was not uncommon among Indian Muslims. But for Ikbal the name held a special resonance, for in Islamic esoteric tradition, Idries was identified with the mysterious Greek figure Hermes Trismegistus, the founder of alchemy and the other occult sciences.

The first months of the little boy's life were spent just a few yards in physical distance from the tea parties and bridge tournaments of the British elite, but miles away in social distance. In September, as the Simla season drew to a close, Lady Reading hosted a party for

350 guests at Viceregal Lodge, to which Ikbal and Elizabeth weren't invited. The party's oriental theme had nothing to do with India, still less with Afghanistan, for it was a Chinese Feast of Lanterns. The viceroy's staff wore black satin jackets and fake mandarin pigtails, with their eyes made up to look slanted; the guests dressed in Chinese costumes, some of them months in the planning. That night hundreds of paper lanterns wound their way through Simla, carried by Englishmen in Chinese costumes past the lane where, in a rented bedroom, baby Idries lay dreaming.

Ikbal's job at *The Bulletin* didn't last for much longer than a year, since Simla was already served by a glut of newspapers. By 1925 *The Bulletin* folded. But rather than learn the lessons of oversupply, Ikbal responded by trying to establish a newspaper of his own. The plan soon foundered when he was unable to afford a printing press.[70] With what money he had left, he took his growing family back to Delhi in the hope of finding journalistic work in the capital. There he managed to parlay his Edinburgh education into being given one of the positions reserved for the "England-returned" and was appointed editor of the English-language *Spectator*.[71] Yet still he harbored desires to move in the circles of high officialdom, and not merely as a newshound. With a new plan in mind, he rented a house next to the residence of the Afghan consul-general.[72]

Six years earlier in 1919, when Afghanistan had negotiated the right to establish consulates and embassies after the Third Anglo-Afghan War, the country had entirely lacked diplomatic personnel or even civil servants skilled in European languages. So by 1925, when Ikbal settled on his latest plan, his native-standard English appeared a better asset to Afghan officialdom than to its British counterpart. Two years after the doors to the Indian Political Service had been closed to him, Ikbal now introduced himself to the Afghan consul as a patriotic (albeit Indian-born) fellow Afghan, who spoke perfect English and had firsthand experience of the British in their homeland. He thus talked his way into the post of secretary to the Afghan consulate-general, which effectively meant overseeing correspondence in English. Concerned about what they called his "defection," British officials compiled another report on him, though fortunately it didn't take the charge of "defection" far. It concluded that his motives were material not political—that Ikbal would "stick to the party which pays him."[73]

Meanwhile Afghanistan, under the modernizing but anti-British King Amanullah, was again attracting a good deal of international attention. In 1925 former American war correspondent and budding filmmaker Lowell Thomas wrote a travel book on what he called "Forbidden Afghanistan." (Proudly signing his letters, "Lowell Thomas, Propagandist," he had the previous year published *With Lawrence in Arabia* to accompany his film that made T. E. Lawrence famous.) Reviewers acclaimed his *Beyond Khyber Pass* as a revelation of a land that time forgot, "unchanged in the last thousand years," with "shrouded girls, swashbuckling youths, peasants, princes."[74] Clearly fame and fortune were to be had in writing about Afghanistan, but now Ikbal was sequestered in consular filing rooms, his literary ambitions thwarted by a life of low-level officialdom.

Then early the next year, he heard that the recent conqueror of Arabia, Ibn Saud, was calling delegates to Mecca for a Congress of the Islamic World that would gather that summer. The international spotlight had been on Arabia since the Bedouin chief-turned-king Ibn Saud had defeated the former British protégé, Sharif Hussein, before finally subjugating Mecca in October 1924. In theory, the Meccan congress that Ibn Saud devised was meant to decide the holy city's future. The whole world would be watching, waiting for news of the outcome. But only Muslims would be permitted entry: no foreign journalists—not even Lowell Thomas—would be allowed anywhere near Mecca. For Ikbal, it was the opportunity he had been waiting for, releasing him from a future of tedious paperwork. When Elizabeth received a letter bringing news that her mother was dangerously ill in Edinburgh, he seized his chance.[75] She would return to Britain with the three children, while Ikbal would make a detour to Arabia.

Through his former role as editor of Delhi's *Spectator*, he managed to arrange an invitation to the congress. He took the cheapest route from Bombay, aboard the *Gurgestan*, one of many old steamers laid on for the pilgrimage.[76] The first days aboard ship were a shock. Down in steerage class, the ship's unscrupulous owners had packed in nine hundred pious passengers. There were fights from the moment they embarked: fights over space to lay down a sheet to sleep on; fights over space to stretch out and pray (especially difficult when everyone was meant to pray at the same time); fights over drinking water, claims of theft, infringements of honor. The modesty of wives and daughters was hard to protect in such crowded conditions, and the best way to defend one's honor was to proclaim it loudly. To make matters worse, it was the height of summer. Up on deck, the sun burned the skin within minutes; down (deep down) in steerage, it baked the flesh instead.

Ikbal was not in steerage class himself—that would have been unthinkable. (He was still a sirdar, albeit in a second-class cabin.) But he did go down for a look. It was so horrid and squalid, he tried to distract himself by perusing the other passengers. Perhaps there were men of influence aboard. A few days into the passage, he was attracted by the crowd that attended an elderly Indian gentleman. He learned he was Maulvi Abdul Wahid, a white-bearded Punjabi who led the Ahl-i Hadith, an Indian Muslim sect that sought to return to the fundamentals of the faith. It declared that if a belief or custom could not be found in the sayings of the Prophet, then it could not be considered Islamic and instead must be condemned. And the Ahl-i Hadith did a lot of condemning.

After listening to one of the Maulvi's morning sermons, Ikbal tried to give him a wide berth. But that was impossible aboard the cramped *Gurgestan*, so the Maulvi's followers took to following and haranguing him, since his linen suit and turned-up mustache certainly did not accord with the custom of the Prophet. Ikbal in turn took a dislike to the Maulvi's son, Ismail, whose vocal opposition to British rule had already seen him serve several jail terms in India, as Ikbal knew. Though Ismail's bushy beard was black with virile youth, he wore his hair clipped short, which, as the Ahl-i Hadith saw things, was the accepted style of the Prophet. To Ikbal, he seemed to possess a ferocious jaw, which jutted out as though to contradict and start a fight. Trying to avoid him, Ikbal nonetheless labeled Ismail with his worst insult: he looked like a "wild Bolshevist."[77]

After pausing to take on more coal (and passengers) at Aden, the *Gurgestan* sailed into the Red Sea. Though the swell eased, hedged in between the shores of Arabia to the east and Eritrea to the west, the heat grew worse. A small island came into sight through the blinding sunlight: it was Kamaran. The name must have circled around the ship in whispers, for in the wake of the cholera epidemics that had sailed out with previous pilgrims to kill millions worldwide, the island had been turned into a dreaded quarantine station. Everyone had to take off their clothes, hand them over to be disinfected, take an antiseptic bath, then spend twenty-four hours in an isolation camp.

On finally reaching Jeddah, whose white minarets announced the *Gurgestan*'s approach to the holy land, Ikbal disembarked ahead of the paupers belowdecks. He was looking forward to his reception, for he had two hosts, one official, one secret. The former was the Saudi governor of Jeddah, the official host to observing journalists at the conference. The latter was Stanley Jordan, the British vice-consul, for whom Ikbal had agreed to write secret reports.[78]

Along with some of the other Indian delegates, Ikbal was installed in a five-story building that had previously belonged to the Sharif of Mecca, the ruler before Ibn Saud's recent conquests. Built in tradi-tional Arabian style, its anchor stones at ground level gave way to mud brick and plaster, which led up to a breeze-catching top floor called a *mafraj*. Keen as Ikbal was to enter an ambiance of Eastern romance, his fantasies were dashed as soon as he walked in and saw cheap prints of British country houses tacked to the mud walls by dozens of rusty nails.[79] That first evening, the governor of Jeddah hosted a banquet of huge chunks of mutton, freshly baked loaves of round bread, and fresh apricots from the king's orchards at Taif. Then later that night Ikbal sat down to pen a report for Mr. Jordan.

Ibn Saud was eager to impress the delegates at his conference. After all, its aim was to legitimize his recent conquest of Mecca. Since he had to be seen to be making improvements, for special guests he laid on some of the first cars to ever enter the surrounding Hijaz region: five Ford trucks with seven spacious seats apiece. Painted with the insignia of the Red Cross–like ambulances, they were leftovers from the Great War, as were many of the first motor vehicles in the Middle East. An official guide sat with the delegates in each truck, tasked with ensuring that the passengers obeyed the strict Wahhabi code that Ibn Saud now promoted.

The first test came when Ikbal's truck stopped at the site of the tomb of Eve, mother of humankind, which for over a thousand years had been a traditional halt on the pilgrim road to Mecca. Since such traditions—or rather, "innovations" as the Wahhabis termed them— were precisely what Ibn Saud's followers opposed, this and many similar shrines had been destroyed. Ikbal had read news reports based on rumors that had trickled out of Arabia in the tumultuous last few years and wanted to see the destruction for himself. But his Wahhabi guide followed his every step, steering him away from the damaged areas while declaring it was his duty to prevent pilgrims from idolatrously praying at Eve's tomb.

It was still only seven in the morning when Ikbal climbed back into the Ford, but the sun was already high. Long after his lips dried out in the harsh air that blew through the open windows, the truck stopped at an oasis used by ordinary pilgrims riding camels or walking. Ikbal ran down a track littered with tin cans, dog carcasses, and the putrid corpse of a camel. Reaching the water's edge, he stared down at a shallow pool of discolored liquid.[80] As he looked on, appalled, his driver waded in, filled his tin, slurped from it, then tipped the rest back. For all his thirst, Ikbal couldn't bring himself to drink. On they drove till finally they reached the outskirts of Mecca. Ibn Saud's motorized concession to modernity stopped here, and Ikbal jumped out from the Ford, straddled a donkey, and rode toward the Kaaba—and a cup of clean water.

During the following days, he performed the rituals of the hajj with Muslims from every corner of Asia, as well as smaller numbers from Africa and a few from Britain, though in a subsequent article he carped that the "ceremonies were endless," such that there was "very little time left for sight-seeing."[81] Worse still, the mandatory Wahhabi guide who followed him everywhere was not only "grasping and unscrupulous" but also tasked with preventing pilgrims from using godless innovations like cameras.[82] So Ikbal sneaked around hiding his Kodak under his simple *ihram* robe, taking surreptitious pictures when no one was watching.[83] Then, on the appointed day, he was collected from his lodgings by a luxurious French automobile and taken to the royal palace, a grand white edifice near the center of the holy city, where he was met by Hafiz Wahba, a thirty-seven-year-old Egyptian journalist turned governor of Mecca and chief adviser to Ibn Saud. Hafiz Wahba conducted Ikbal through a series of reception rooms that led to an audience chamber some fifty feet long, its entire length covered with a Turkish carpet. At the far end stood Ibn Saud— all six foot four of him—on a platform. Ikbal greeted him as he would a king: "As-salam alaykum, ya sultan!"[84] Pleased to hear his title legitimized by a British subject, Ibn Saud stepped down from his dais and clasped Ikbal in his arms, kissing him on both cheeks in welcome. In return, Ikbal kissed his hand as though in fealty.

After an interruption for more prayers, Ikbal began the interview that he hoped to sell to a newspaper (and which Hafiz Wahba hoped would provide good publicity for the new regime). Tactfully posing his questions as ones that millions of concerned Muslims worldwide were pondering, Ikbal asked Ibn Saud whether his troops had really massacred thousands of men, women, and children in the assault on Taif; whether the king had really received a third portion of the booty on the grounds that the defeated were not true Muslims according to his own Wahhabi creed; and whether the Wahhabi forces had really destroyed the many Sufi and Shiite shrines that had graced Mecca for centuries.[85]

Though Ikbal asked courageous questions, Ibn Saud was as cool a politician as he was a soldier, and saw immediately that his answers provided an opportunity to justify his policies. He began by denouncing King Ali bin Hussein, whom he had just overthrown, for having sold Arabia to the colonial "enemies of Islam." Ibn Saud's conquests, by contrast, were motivated by higher principles, chiefly to secure "religious liberty" and put a stop to the immorality that the Ottoman former rulers had allowed to flourish in Mecca. What his Wahhabi followers were doing, he explained, was saving the Muslims from themselves, leading them (admittedly by force) from their immoral ways to the one true version of Islam. So yes, they had stopped all Sufi practices. But as for reports about massacres of the innocent, these were sheer propaganda. The dead were not innocent, he declared, for they had been rightfully killed.[86]

The interview over, next on Ikbal's agenda was the congress itself, though Ibn Saud's idea of a conference center was the intimidating setting of a secluded Turkish fortress that overlooked the holy city. Steeped in the romance of Sir Walter Scott, Ikbal reported that it reminded him of the castle of a medieval Arabian knight.[87]

When the idea of the First All-World Muslim Congress was initially mooted, delegates had imagined that its aim would be to negotiate for the future government of Mecca, which Ibn Saud would then hand over. As the delegates sat around two horseshoe-shaped tables, with the small group of Muslim reporters positioned on chairs behind them, it became clear that Ibn Saud was no man for negotiating.[88] He had already scaled back the remit of the congress to discussions of improving the administration of the hajj and the safety of those who performed it, helping his true purpose of legitimizing Saudi rule over Mecca by portraying the Wahhabis as protectors of the pilgrimage. Recognizing this purpose ahead of time, the independent Muslim states of Iran, Iraq, Turkey, and Yemen had refused to send delegates. But others had come: there were three delegates from Syria, three from Palestine, five from Java, seven from the Soviet Union, and twelve from India, along with several from corners of Arabia that Ibn Saud hadn't conquered. Comprising an awkward blend of Muslim colonial officials and anticolonial activists, the Indians at the congress had conflicting agendas. As for Ikbal, he took a special interest in anti-colonialists such as the Ali brothers, who a few years earlier had been the leading figures of the Khilafat Movement that tried to save the Ottoman Caliphate from being divided up by Britain and France.

Ikbal's other assigned task for the British consulate was to report on the degree of Bolshevik influence in Mecca, particularly via the delegation of Muslims sent by the newly formed Soviet Union.[89] Ikbal was determined to outwit them. Outside the congress meetings, he abandoned his habitual English suit, dressed as an Afghan tribesman, and pretended to be sincerely seeking the truth about Communist teachings.[90] Reprising his earlier warnings about Bolsheviks in Afghanistan, he warned Vice-Consul Jordan about their outreach to Mecca, declaring the leader of the Soviet Muslim delegation to be an "expert propagandist from Turkestan."[91]

Although Ikbal, in his reports to Stanley Jordan, stressed the dangers of the Communist menace, in reality the Bolshevists had little chance of succeeding at the congress. The Wahhabis knew exactly what they were doing in orchestrating the congress under the guise of Muslim unity. At precisely two o'clock (Ikbal was discreetly observing his watch, unsure if such Western innovations were permitted), the delegates were startled from the slumber of the afternoon heat by an explosion so loud, it shook the conference chamber in the isolated castle. To everyone's relief, it was merely a cannon salute to announce the king's arrival. The doors were flung open, and a dozen African guards entered, in red tunics, white breeches, and black boots up to their knees, with drawn swords, marching ahead of the king. When Ibn Saud was seated, the delegates were allowed to sit,

as his impresario Hafiz Wahba read his address to them, which justified his conquests and claimed his government was "being run on
the lines of the Quran."[92]

Five minutes after Ibn Saud left, the delegates fell into squab-
bling over the issue of who should be president and vice-president
of the congress. This was followed by a row over how such elections
should take place, since a simple ballot would give more votes to the
largest group (the Indians). Then they took up the question of the
official language of the congress, which being Arabic gave a natural advantage to native speakers from Arabia and Syria. Despite
the endless disagreements, over the next month the congress did
finally make a few decisions. First, the delegates agreed that there
should be future congresses. Second, they agreed that land should
be purchased to provide themselves with a permanent base. And
third, they agreed that a railway should be opened between Jeddah
and Mecca for ease of travel. As it turned out, none of these recom-
mendations bore fruit. By the simple act of hosting the congress,
Ibn Saud had gained the legitimacy he desired from the delegates.
Having seen what free discussion looked like, he decided against
hosting them again.

Meanwhile, Ikbal was compiling his secret reports for Vice-
Consul Jordan, as a result of which the British consulate in Jeddah
reported back to London that Bolshevik propagandists had made
considerable inroads to Mecca, not least in pushing the ideology of
the "Unity of Islam" as a front for their activities.[93] Yet despite journalistic concerns with what was then being called Pan-Islamism, the
disagreements at the congress belied the idea of Muslim unity. Reading Jordan's report back in London, a senior Foreign Office official
jotted down a comment on the cover sheet: the congress "shows how
hopelessly disunited Islam is."[94] While fully realizing that, as another
official put it, "Ibn Saud and his supporters stage-managed the conference cleverly," the British government still felt pleased with the
outcome.[95] The Foreign Office felt they could work with Ibn Saud,

who would shortly rename the lands he had conquered the "Kingdom of Saudi Arabia." His Wahhabi theology was of no concern to Whitehall: the main issue was that "attempts to fan the flame of anti-British prejudice fell flat" at the congress.[96] Whatever else they were, the Wahhabis at least didn't seem to be anti-British. The great game of empire was still in play, and Ikbal's reports had given useful tactical input.

Chapter Four

EXPERT

Their whole financial career had to be carried on with
the adroitness of a campaign through a hostile country.

—Edmund Gosse, *Father and Son*

IKBAL WAS PLEASED WITH HOW MATTERS NOW PROGRESSED.
He had his scoop! With the congress over, he made his way by steamship through the Suez Canal to London, where Elizabeth and his children awaited him. They rented a flat on Oxford Terrace, in a London
neighborhood that matched the standing he hoped to achieve.[1] A few
months earlier a secret report compiled in Delhi about his political
commitments had concluded that he was "not a man of settled con-
victions." Neither an Indian nationalist nor a defector to Afghanistan, his "sensational writings" were simply intended "to acquire a
reputation as an expert in a quarter of the world so little known and
still less penetrated by foreigners."[2] The trip to Mecca had provided
Ikbal precisely with that opportunity: to be considered an expert on
the region that was just beginning to be called the Middle East. No
sooner had he moved into his new flat than he began typing up articles from his travel notes.

Flicking through the London telephone directory, he looked for
a literary agent through whom he could sell his story about Mecca.
He found Harold James Shepstone, a journalist and editor of *Wide
World Magazine* who worked from his large home overlooking
Clapham Common.[3] A fellow of the Royal Geographical Society,

Shepstone had traveled extensively in Palestine, Egypt, and else-where in the region, where he had worked as the agent for several photographic firms.[4] One of the first of a new generation of roaming journalists, he had taken advantage of the rise of photography to sell images to the burgeoning market of popular magazines. As well as the *Penny Pictorial*, Shepstone sold many of his articles to U.S. magazines such as *Scientific American*, which had begun publishing him back in 1908, but by the 1920s he was using his many contacts in the publishing and photographic worlds to represent other authors.

Given his ties to the photography business (he also dealt in film supplies), Shepstone was particularly influential on the "magic lantern" circuit, delivering lectures illustrated with colored photographs that were hugely popular before Hollywood began making "talking pictures" toward the end of the decade. All told, Ikbal's adventure perfectly fitted the profile of Shepstone's agency, and the publicist congratulated him for secretly taking so many pictures.

There was as much public interest in the Mecca congress as Ikbal and Shepstone hoped. Even as famous a commentator on world affairs as Arnold Toynbee was writing about it. Yet Ikbal's instincts had been correct: being a Muslim lent him an advantage over other writers who were forced to write about the congress secondhand from a distance. Consequently, the July 1926 issue of *The Contemporary Review* featured Ikbal's seven-page account.[5] Its tone was surprisingly lighthearted, blending picturesque description more suited to a tourist brochure with derring-do inspired by the appearance that summer of T. E. Lawrence's *Seven Pillars of Wisdom*. He described how the donkeys of Mecca were gaily painted with bright-colored stripes, that shopping for souvenirs required a great deal of patience to bargain down prices.[6] While he could muster no tales of heroic camel treks to compete with Lawrence, he did claim to have dramatically seized control of the Ford on the long drive to Mecca, when his driver lost concentration.

In print, then, Ikbal was a man of action of sorts but also a man of ideas, for the article opened with a scene of him lying in the cabin of his pilgrim ship pondering the weighty question of whether "decayed and slumbrous Islam" was being awakened by Ibn Saud's "magical wand."[7] While he did mention some of the lighter evidence against Ibn Saud, overall he painted an attractive portrait, giving doctrinal reasons for why his actions were justifiable so as to purify the faith.[8] Although his previous articles and lectures for London's Folklore Society had celebrated the kinds of folk customs that Ibn Saud's followers were busy wiping out, Ikbal was not one to dwell on his own inconsistencies. Instead, following the Wahhabis' own propaganda, he tried to persuade his readers that Ibn Saud deserved credit for having "cleansed" Mecca and suppressed the immorality that had flourished there.[9] On closer inspection, the new ruler was a "Cromwell among Arabs" whose vision was to spread the spirit of unity among the fissiparous factions of Islam.[10]

It was a position Ikbal shared with other boosters of Ibn Saud, including the British former intelligence officer and Muslim convert Harry St. John Philby, who would help Ibn Saud establish his kingdom and was now busy writing his own account of the Wahhabis.[11] Part of the same imperial world as Ikbal, Philby had served in the elite Indian Civil Service which Ikbal had tried to join: when his son was born in the Indian town of Ambala, Philby had given him the nickname "Kim," after the eponymous Rudyard Kipling novel set there. But soon after Philby senior finished his book on Arabia, Kim rejected his father's faith by embracing Communism at Cambridge, where he was quietly recruited as a Soviet spy. For the game had many twists and betrayals, even between fathers and sons.

Meanwhile Ikbal was enjoying the bright light of publicity. Lured by the romance of Arabia and the hype around the congress, his agent Shepstone was convincing various magazine editors to publish Ikbal. After *The Contemporary Review*, he appeared in *The Spectator*, playing off the current reverence for T. E. Lawrence by presenting Ibn Saud as a similarly "stalwart desert warrior" and "man of vision."[12] Ikbal made a purpler pledge to readers of

The Saturday Review, for whom, remembering Sir Walter Scott's novels, he painted the Arabian ruler as a modern-day Sir Galahad.[13]

Later in July, *The Times* agreed to publish a long three-part article in which Ikbal wove together an account of his interview with Ibn Saud with lowbrow commentary on Meccan sightseeing.[14] Here, in the empire's chief establishment newspaper, he gave the Wahhabi message its greatest publicity to date via a purported verbatim record of Ibn Saud's rousing speeches.[15] Picking up on his piece in the London *Times*, in mid-August *The New York Times* published another of his articles, illustrated by his smuggled Kodak snaps, in which Ikbal quoted ten straight paragraphs of Ibn Saud's "gracious" words.[16] But even this was not good enough for Ibn Saud's keenest British supporter, Harry Philby, who after reading the article in *The Times*, wrote a letter to the editor to correct what he claimed were "several misstatements of fact." Philby declared the shrine of Eve had not been destroyed (it had); the delegates of Turkey and Yemen had not boycotted the congress (they had); and most importantly, Ibn Saud had helpfully forbidden delegates from discussing matters of state policy by colonial governments, such as Britain, who ruled over Muslim populations.[17]

Another respondent to Ikbal's *Times* articles was Arthur Field, a prominent socialist, anti-colonialist, and founding secretary of the Anglo-Ottoman Society, who after decrying Ikbal's "slanderous criticism" of several anti-British and pro-Soviet attendees at the congress concluded that "after sampling the effusions of the 'Sirdar,' one wouldn't hang a dog on such evidence."[18] Although the Western press was remarkably soft on Ibn Saud—the British government had after all supplied him with weapons—there were nonetheless millions of Muslims worldwide who were deeply opposed to his Wahhabi version of Islam. A few of them even found an outlet in the English media. Writing a letter in response to one of Ikbal's articles that ran in *The Times of India*, a representative of an Indian pilgrimage committee, Mahomed Yusuf Asfahani, took Ikbal severely to task for "saying pleasant things about Ibn

Saud."[19] He particularly objected to Ikbal's portrayal of the Wahhabis as "Puritans." They should be called what they plainly were, he proclaimed: "fanatics."

Still, despite a few such voices of objection, Ikbal did well out of his Arabian travels. The publicity was tremendous. Moreover, *The Times* paid him £50 for his articles; *The New York Times* only a little less; and the widely circulated *London Magazine* another £25.[20] These were then serious sums for a journalist. His new agent Harold Shepstone also managed to persuade the commissioning chiefs of the recently formed British Broadcasting Company to give Ikbal some of their precious airtime, otherwise dominated by scions of prep schools and Oxbridge. When the BBC's commissioning editor offered a standard fee of four guineas, Shepstone rejected it as far too little for his client, who "cannot see his way to accept."[21]

As Shepstone pointed out to the editor, "the number of Englishmen who had succeeded in penetrating into Mecca can be counted on the fingers of your hand," whereas Ikbal had been able to enter the city only "because he is a Mohameddan [i.e., Muslim], but no Mohameddan will give a Christian any particulars of the sacred city."[22] Ikbal, though, was willing to speak publicly because, having attended university in Scotland, he was "a little more broadminded." Even so, Shepstone hinted, the price had to be right.

Negotiations ensued, and eventually a fee, and a script, were agreed upon so that after the evening weather broadcast at 9:40 p.m. on an August evening in 1926, Ikbal read out on radio his account of "A Pilgrimage to Mecca."[23] He dwelled mainly on the adventurous aspects of his journey: how he was shot at for taking a photograph and chased by a mob when he lit a cigarette.[24] There were no cinemas or theaters in Mecca, he complained, and the hotels and sanitation were terrible. Positioned as it was in the prime Friday-evening slot, the program was an enormous coup. No one at the BBC seems to have noticed the socialist Arthur Field's warning from a month earlier to "accept all that this Afghan gentleman says with caution."[25]

Later that summer, Shepstone tried to keep up the momentum of Ikbal's broadcast by offering the BBC a series of programs on his other travels in the Muslim world. (He didn't mention that these were largely invented.) He would give a talk on the charm of Afghan life; another on Bukhara, the cradle of Sufism; another set in a Persian rose garden; one talk apiece on Arab and Afghan tribesmen; and a concluding lecture attesting to the similarity of the Middle East and Europe when viewed through their literature.[26] Ikbal was even willing to lower his earlier fee and accept only £15 for the entire series (a gesture that didn't seem so magnanimous to the commissioning editor, since it merely equated to accepting the standard rate that Ikbal had rejected earlier).[27] Though the BBC declined the offer, Ikbal was not to be deterred. Hearing mention of the poet Omar Khayyam on his radio one day in the autumn, he immediately dashed off a note to the commissioning editor, offering a talk on the poet's tomb in Nishapur.[28] Again, the editor wrote back to politely decline, saying the schedule was already full.[29] As soon as the BBC opened its doors, it had tightly closed them again.

Ikbal decided to try his luck once more at the India Office. Five years having passed since the showdown over his "Bolshevik Roads" reports, he wrote to his old contact Sir John Shuckburgh with a new offer of intelligence. This time he promised to reveal information about the Saudi takeover of Mecca.[30] Formerly a senior figure in the India Office, then in the Colonial Office, Sir John was now one of the government's key advisers on the Middle East. But he had learned his lesson from his earlier dealings with Ikbal and rebuffed him.

For now at least, the portals to high officialdom remained closed, and Ikbal had to turn back to publishing and the media. By November he moved his family again, this time to Westbourne Terrace on the cheaper edges of London respectability.[31] A short walk from Paddington Station, it could still help him in what he hoped would be his lecture-giving perambulations around the country. With their fixed scripts, color slides, and background music, "magic lantern" lectures were at the height of their popularity. Shepstone promoted Ikbal's talks on "the East" in an echo of the popular demand for magic lantern shows on the exotic or phantasmagoric. He also offered Ikbal a loan of projection equipment that saved him from having to buy it from expensive suppliers.

The evolving postwar order potentially offered many other openings for a man with the expertise Ikbal was claiming. He was still presenting himself in print as an "Afghan nobleman," making no mention of his Indian birth and upbringing.[32] During his four-year absence from Britain, he had let his memberships of the Royal Asiatic Society and the Folklore Society lapse. He let that be: money was still tight, and the fees for the Mecca articles were already spent on rent.

The Royal Central Asian Society was another matter, being a magnet for politicians, generals, and strategists. Despite its name, the society's remit comprised most of what is today called the Middle East. By January 1927, Ikbal was back there at the lectern, speaking on "Ferments in the World of Islam" by way of recent developments in the religious revival he saw taking place from Morocco to the Dutch East Indies (now Indonesia), and particularly in Afghanistan and Saudi Arabia.[33] Chairing the meeting was Sir Michael O'Dwyer, who in his opening statement introduced Ikbal as "eminently qualified" to speak on his topic "because he comes from an old Kabul family."[34] Turning to glance at his speaker—Ikbal was already known for a certain prolixity—Sir Michael announced his gratitude that Ikbal had "kindly consented . . . to limit his address to thirty-five minutes."[35] As it turned out, the lecture was an accomplished one. Talking about Ibn Saud and his fellow Muslim revivalists from the comfortable distance of London, Ikbal's hyperbole about their noble ambitions roused a good deal of sympathy. He finished his speech to loud applause.

Even so, several commentators that evening—some of whom had extensive direct experience of the Middle East—challenged Ikbal's assertions about the unifying spirit seizing hold of Muslims. Though he prickled at the critique, he conceded to the criticism offered by Sir Arnold Wilson, whose experience governing Iraqi Mesopotamia had earned him the nickname "the Despot of Mess-Pot."[36] For in challenging Ikbal's firsthand awareness of "recent developments," Sir Arnold undermined his basic claim to expertise: of having observed conditions in the many places he discussed. Ikbal had only one way to respond: he would have to make another journey. And this time he would have to take in not only Mecca but the entire region that the First World War and the breakup of the Ottoman Empire had placed under French and British control.

To make such an expedition possible, though, he would first need to raise money. The interest garnered by his Mecca reports led him to ponder the natural next step for an aspiring author: a book deal. Judging from the newspaper review columns he read in his cramped flat on Westbourne Terrace, every other British author seemed to be writing a travelogue in the 1920s. He too could write a book that would tell the dramatic story of his journey to Mecca. Or perhaps not his actual journey: it had been hard enough to wrangle a few paragraphs of copy for *The Times* from his half-day drive from Jeddah to Mecca. Perhaps instead he could write a more marketable version of the journey he had made. Or might have made.

During the months after his lecture at the Royal Central Asian Society, Ikbal worked hard at writing up his experiences in Mecca in book form. When it was finished, Harold Shepstone sold it to the London publishing house of H.F. & G. Witherby. Although Harry Forbes Witherby was personally more interested in books about birds, he did have on his list several travelogues by former colonial officials. He had just signed up the pseudonymous Ben Assher's *Nomad in the South Sudan: The Travels of a Political Officer Among the Gaweir Nuers*, part of Assher's successful series of *Nomad* memoirs (if memoirs they truly were—Witherby cared little about the veracity of his authors). Given the publicity already gained by Ikbal's recent pilgrimage, a book deal with this mysterious Afghan struck Witherby as a potentially sound investment. He bought advertising space in the *Times Literary Supplement* to announce Ikbal's "journey of adventure."[37]

Under the counterintuitive title *Westward to Mecca*, the book Ikbal wrote for Witherby recounted one of the oddest pilgrimages in Muslim history. The route he claimed to have taken on his quixotic peregrinations saw him begin in an unnamed princely state in central India, then move north to Lahore; thence northward (and upward) via a purposeless diversion through the Karakorum Mountains that separated India from China; thence a southerly retreat to the lowlands, before arcing northwest to the Afghan border. Then came a further backtrack down to the Indian city of Peshawar, which afforded an easy car journey up to Kabul. From there, it was a trek north for a month's rest in a village in the Panjshir Valley, followed by a northwesterly dash across scarcely passable mountain ranges into the newly founded Kirghiz Autonomous Socialist Soviet Republic, whence he moved westward—top secretly—through the Soviet cities of Samarkand, Bukhara, and Astarabad. After this highly effective infiltration of the Soviet Union, he escaped south into Iran via the Shiite holy city of Mashhad, made a pause for a literary pilgrimage to the tomb of Omar Khayyam, rapidly crossed the whole of Iran to Baghdad, and thence proceeded to Basra, where he boarded a boat for Bombay (where he had more or less begun), only to finally take a pilgrim ship to the Arabian port of Jeddah. From there, he admitted, he was driven to Mecca in a Ford.

Along the way, Ikbal described the most extraordinary adventures. In a high mountain cavern in the Karakorums, he met an alchemist who transformed base metal into gold before his very eyes (despite Ikbal having first declared him a dog of a Hindu).[38] In Bukhara, he sneaked into a Soviet conference, where an apparatchik offered him a high-ranking job as a language expert.[39] In the first-class dining carriage of a train from Peshawar, he felt annoyance as his gourmet supper was interrupted by a blood feud. (Gunfire ensued.) In Afghanistan's Panjshir Valley, he shared a cottage with a Norwegian named Rask, where they sat happily writing a book together till their "magic house" was enveloped in cold flames and other occult manifestations. On the steppes of Central Asia, he demonstrated such horsemanship (using techniques learned from English jockeys) that he beat a saddle-born Kirghiz chieftain in a point-to-point race. Time and again on his travels, Ikbal had to reach for his revolver, ready to dispatch tribesmen or bandits who stood in his way.

At the time, he was far from the only author writing invented or exaggerated tales of his travels. One such contemporary was Paul Brunton, whose account of supposed meetings with miracle-working holy men in *A Search in Secret India* became a bestseller. But what made Ikbal distinctive was that he wasn't writing about Hindu India or Buddhist Tibet. He was expanding the frontiers of the "mystical East" to Afghanistan. Yet it was a strange literary style he was developing, for he placed his anecdotes about alchemists and dervishes between dry strategic summaries of the development of Afghanistan's education system and the state of the Iraqi oil industry, aimed presumably at the solemn politicos of the Royal Central Asian Society. Then he turned to literary criticism in a chapter-long comparative study of the "philosophies" of Omar Khayyam and Shakespeare that demonstrated the intrinsic harmony of East and West.

Even so, manic deviations constantly flew from the topic at hand. Just when his pilgrimage to Mecca seemed to be finally on course with his arrival in Bombay, he decided to visit a cobra farm and devoted the best part of a chapter to describing techniques of venom extraction. Yet amid its manifold diversions and condescension to every kind of foreigner, one thing held the book together: the self-mythologizing of its narrator. If not in the resonance of his prose, then at least in the pose of his outsize persona, Ikbal had written an equal to T. E. Lawrence's *Seven Pillars of Wisdom*.

Not that everyone in Britain was in thrall to the new legend of Lawrence of Arabia. A few months after Ikbal's book was launched, it was reported that "Colonel T. E. Lawrence was burnt in effigy on Tower-Hill today by a crowd of British Communists after speakers had denounced the 'activities of British imperialism in Afghanistan.' "[40] Ikbal was no critic of empire, though, whether in Afghanistan or elsewhere, and he was hardly a friend of "Bolshe-viks," yet somehow he managed to avoid the denunciations of the leftists whose influence was growing in the literary sphere of the late 1920s.

It was just as well that *Westward to Mecca* was so weirdly unique because it wasn't the only work to appear just then about a jour-ney to Mecca. The same year saw the publication of Harry Philby's account of his own hard travels in *Arabia of the Wahhabis* as well as Eldon Rutter's *The Holy Cities of Arabia*, which admiringly detailed the pious new nation being built by Ibn Saud.[41] After wandering the world as a lost soul in the wake of the war, Rutter had found work in colonial Malaya and there converted to Islam.[42] Having spent longer in the Middle East than Ikbal—Rutter had served there during the war—Rutter's two-volume work had far more nuance than *West-ward to Mecca*. But despite their differences of style, Philby, Rut-ter, and Ikbal agreed that Saudi rule represented a modernizing leap forward for Arabia, whence a new spirit of progress would pulsate through the wider Muslim world.

Ikbal next found a publisher for a book about his Afghan "home-land." Based on Long Acre in London's theaterland, the Diamond Press had few authors on its list in 1927 and had just published a bodice-ripper called *Dawn of Desire* by the obscure theatrical agent turned spiritualist Nellie Tom-Gallon. After Ikbal's success with his newspaper articles, the Diamond Press was hardly the prestige pub-lisher he hoped to attract. But he was desperate to raise funds for his next journey.

If London's grand old publishing houses wouldn't open their doors to him, then there were many newer outlets for his ambi-tions, not least the literary journals that were flourishing during that decade. On the first day of spring 1927, he received a polite note from T. S. Eliot, to whom he had previously sent his compli-ments.[43] They had never met, but the two men had arrived in Britain as students within a year of each other, whereafter Eliot had found it far easier to integrate into Anglo-Saxon literary London. Ikbal

replied by sending Eliot an essay that he had entered for a student contest back in his Edinburgh days. Entitled "The Meeting
of the East and West," he hoped it might be published in Eliot's
journal, *The New Criterion*. The flagship of the modernist movement, its first issue had included Eliot's epoch-defining *The Waste
Land*, and in the five years since, every major modernist from Vir-
ginia Woolf and Ezra Pound to Marcel Proust had appeared in its
pages. Still, its avowed internationalism didn't seem to include the
colonies—at least not the Asian and African ones—though Eliot
did employ the aspiring Indian writer Mulk Raj Anand in a minor
editorial position. So to be published there would be a major coup
for Ikbal, if not in financial terms (its print run averaged only
seven hundred copies and Eliot was famously parsimonious with
fees), then at least in terms of prestige. As George Orwell later
wrote of the *Criterion*, "For pure snootiness it beats anything I
have ever seen."[44]

Eliot took his editorial role seriously and suggested major cuts of
Ikbal's essay, which as it stood was far too long, he explained by letter.[45] But if the cuts were carried out, he continued, the piece might
just be acceptable. Eventually he accepted Ikbal's much-shortened
essay, which as its opening line quoted Rudyard Kipling's famous
adage that "East is East and West is West and never the twain shall
meet."[46] Over the course of sixteen pages, Ikbal quoted a medley of
poets and philosophers from "East" and "West." There were Rumi
and Shelley, Hafiz and Wordsworth, the *Upanishads* and Sweden-
borg, the Sufis and Sir Walter Scott. (Scotland made a good showing
overall.) His general point was that all these sages were essentially
saying the same thing, and that that same thing had originally
been discovered in the East. What the philosophers of the Scottish
Enlightenment had debated, Ikbal explained, was the kind of topic
discussed on a daily basis in the highlands of Afghanistan.[47] Indeed,
most things the West claimed for itself had originally been discovered by the seers of the East, even so-called "Western" science.[48]
Still, in deference to Eliot's preference for the Hindu over the Mus-

lim scriptures—he had ended *The Waste Land* with three words in Sanskrit—Ikbal kept mention of Islam to a minimum. So while Sufis and Hindus made several appearances in the essay, Muslims per se received no mention at all.

A month after the essay came out in *The New Criterion*, a reader sent Eliot a letter with a stern critique of Ikbal's approach to the harmonious communion of East and West. "There is no method in it," declared D.C.J. McSweeney of the Colonial Office. "It is disoriented, it does no more than cite information (very vulnerable when you begin to infer from it)."[49] Though the letter-writer was scarcely qualified as a literary arbiter, Eliot took his criticism seriously. "It is too serious a matter to be overlooked," he noted in reply.[50]

Despite appearing in the *Criterion*, Ikbal still had many hurdles ahead of him, whether from colonial officials in Whitehall or from the book world's gatekeepers in Bloomsbury. Those hurdles were not merely methodological, in the way McSweeney implied. They were also racial and imperial. It was one thing for the high-minded Bloomsbury circle to have the son of a coppersmith like the lowly Mulk Raj Anand running errands after them. It was quite another to have a bumptious sirdar claiming social equality. Ikbal's brief breakthrough on paper notwithstanding, Bloomsbury didn't open its salons to him. Henceforth he would waste no more time with persnickety aesthetes and would return instead to the worldly arena of politics—while embracing the middlebrow book market that Eliot's modernists despised.

During the months he spent negotiating entry to the *Criterion*, Ikbal had made the difficult decision to move his family yet again. Even the margins of West London were proving too expensive. Like the aspiring poet Gordon Comstock in Orwell's *Keep the Aspidistra Flying*, forced to migrate south of the Thames from the West London edges of respectability, Ikbal likewise moved south, to the suburb of Mitcham. Seven miles from central London, Mitcham had the benefits of being just about affordable, just about respectable (if only by the standards of the lower middle class), and just a

fifteen-minute train ride from Charing Cross Station. Less appealingly, it was also heavily industrialized, home to many noxious factories making paint, varnish, linoleum, and fireworks, but at least
there was the green open space of Mitcham Common where Elizabeth could take the children: Amina, Omar, and Idries, by now aged
ten, six, and four. Ikbal rented a house for them on Wandle Road, a
street of small houses built for employees of local industries. Undeterred, on his embossed notepaper, he called his new home "Nashdom," the name of a country mansion near London recently built
for an exiled Russian prince by Sir Edwin Lutyens, the celebrated
designer of New Delhi.

Though Ikbal was fair-skinned and always wore a well-cut suit,
life in the suburbs was surely not straightforward. As Elizabeth
walked the children to Mitcham Common, the silent windows of
semidetached houses watched over their every step. It was hard
to tell, perhaps, if it was a neighbor twitching the net curtains, or
merely an aspidistra on the windowsill fluttering in the draft. With
their foreign-sounding names, the Shah children certainly stood out
in suburbia. Unable to blend in with other children, being similar in
age they grew up as a close-knit coterie, bonded by tales their father
told about their ancestors in the fabulous land of Afghanistan.

By day, Ikbal worked relentlessly at his desk, reviving his political journalism with a series of articles about Muslim rebels and
scheming Bolsheviks for *The New Statesman* and *The Contemporary Review*. Things slowly began to look up as he became something of a regular contributor, supplementing the income with more
magic lantern lectures.[51] It was a limited salary on which to base the
grand tour of the Middle East he was still planning, so later in that
spring of 1927 he decided to contact Mr. Garrett, a press officer at
the India Office. Ikbal announced to the surprised official his aim of
asking Ibn Saud to appoint him as the official representative of Britain's Muslim community at the next Meccan congress.[52] It was an
awkward meeting, made even more so when Ikbal finally asked for
governmental "approval and assistance" in the matter. In exchange

for funding for his journey around the Middle East, he offered to supply the India Office with a "report."[53] But Garrett, dubious, was unwilling to provide a subvention and turned the offer down.

Ikbal remained resolute. That October, with what money he had managed to save from his writings, he set out on a six-month journey through Turkey, Syria, Palestine, Transjordan, Iraq, Iran, and thence India. Such a circuit was far less daunting than it would have been just a decade earlier, because with the exception of Iran and Turkey, these countries were all now under British or French control. This wasn't the only outcome of the war. The campaign against the Ottomans, and the corresponding need to improve communications with Europe, had led to the rapid expansion of roads, making cars, buses, and taxis a common sight across the Middle East. So when Ikbal's steamship reached Istanbul, taxi drivers were waiting on the quayside of the Golden Horn. Still, to his delight as he disembarked, a group of Turkish sailors mistook him for a Cossack. In the months that followed, such experiences were repeated over and again as he reveled in the ambiguity of who he might be.[54] "Hanged if I can place you!" declared one bewildered Turk.[55]

Ikbal had been spurred into making his journey by Sir Arnold Wilson's sneer, at the Royal Central Asian Society, that he knew little of the modern Middle East. But when Ikbal encountered the region firsthand, he found the reality wasn't sufficiently exotic for his taste. Though in theory his sympathies lay with the Muslim modernists who had founded his school in India, like many a European traveler, part of him was nostalgic for an "East" that had perhaps never existed. He had read more works of romantic Orientalism than most Europeans, and bemoaned the loss of the picturesque Orient that European and increasingly American tourists similarly sought and enjoyed reading about. Strolling through Istanbul's Galata neighborhood, he carped at the lack of local color. Searching vainly for a glimpse of a fez, he mourned the loss of the "old Stamboul" made famous by the French novelist Pierre Loti.[56] Hoping to at least purchase what locals no longer wore, he went shopping for a fez in a souvenir market.[57]

Driving onward to Syria, he found French officials and their "bullet-headed African troups" now running the show. One night he found himself chased by Senegalese soldiers when they raided a *maison* he was visiting. His local guide shouted at him to run for his life, and as Ikbal recounted the event, he leaped through an upstairs window, whence after turning a neat somersault he fell headlong into the street.[58] A throwing knife was hurled after him, and as it whizzed past his ear, he turned to see African soldiers in hot pursuit. His spirit was roused: they had raised his "Afghan fighting blood," so he turned to taunt them. "Come on, you black sons of Shaitan!" he yelled. Summoning the commanding officer, who was also from Senegal, he denounced them as "howling savages," then ran for his life.[59]

His Afghan fighting spirit was also roused in rural Turkey, where the sound of a gunshot caused him to draw his revolver and ask with a shout whether this was a private fight or anyone could join in.[60] (Here were echoes of the American pulp cowboy novels he had come to enjoy with titles like *Shoot Out at Silver Mine*.)[61] Then in Kuwait, he fell into the clutches of an amorous Arab woman called Khawala, aged forty-five "if she was a day," with only three teeth and a smile like a tiger's. She dragged him to watch an Italian romance in the city's only cinema.[62] After she reached for his hand and laid her head on his shoulder, he turned to ask if she wanted coffee, then used the excuse to make a break for the docks, where he catapulted from a high quay onto a passing felucca.[63]

Ikbal's picaresque travels continued through Iraq (offering a patriotic opportunity: he found it far better governed than French-mandated Syria), then by car to Iran (another patriotic opportunity, where he bewailed that not enough was being done for British exports).[64] From there it was back to India, where in Bombay, depressed by the latest riot between Hindus and Muslims, he set off for the respite promised by a tour of Mahatma Gandhi's ashram. There he found not peace but delusion. The ashram lent him the opportunity to berate the leader of India's call for independence, declaring that Gandhi distrusted democracy in whatever shape it came. Far from leading his countrymen into the future, Gandhi wanted them to return to the ancient scriptural age of the Vedas, when gods were believed to have traveled in flying carriages.[65]

Ikbal concluded his demolition of the Indian National Congress Party by telling his readers that whatever national feeling Indians possessed was due to the British, since even the originator of the Congress Party was an Englishman.[66] (He made the same points in an article for London's *Saturday Review*.)[67] His prose then beat a political retreat as he headed for the Indian countryside in search of fakirs and magic.[68] But by now he had seen enough—enough to hold his own with the denizens of the Royal Central Asian Society, and certainly enough to write another book. Setting sail from Calcutta aboard the SS *City of London*, on April 23, 1928, he arrived back in England.[69]

Ikbal returned to find himself, if not a celebrity, then at least the author of *Westward to Mecca* and *Afghanistan of the Afghans*, both of which had been published during his absence. He quickly penned a follow-up on his latest journey, setting its opening chapters in Istanbul and giving it the title *The Golden East*. The year after it came out, Graham Greene made his name with the thriller *Stamboul Train*, while Agatha Christie was busy writing *Murder on the Orient Express*. Yet Ikbal lacked the dexterity or patience for an artfully constructed plot, so with such fierce competition in the market for travel books, he opted for lowbrow adventure of the kind written by Talbot Mundy. After blazing a trail of debts, aliases, and misdemeanors across British India, Mundy had started a new life in America as an author of theosophically tinged adventure tales, writing his first novel about Afghanistan before churning out Middle Eastern thrillers like *The Lion of Petra*, which featured James Schuyler Grim, or "Jimgrim," a multilingual spy who, apparently like Ikbal, could pass for a local from Delhi to Istanbul. Mirroring Mundy's popular works, Ikbal's new travel book developed his own ambiguous persona as the "Easterner" who could fit in anywhere. Yet for all its romance, nostalgia, and occasional racism, Ikbal's

Golden East was shot through with optimism about the future of the Middle East. Though he had little good to say about French rule in Syria, the wider region, under modernizing nationalists in Iran and Turkey, and the benevolent hand of the British in Iraq, Transjordan, and Palestine, seemed set on a steadily progressive course.

The reviews of Ikbal's three books were mixed. His most sympathetic reviewer was H.A.R. Gibb, a celebrated Orientalist (and Edinburgh alumnus) based at London's School of Oriental Studies, who evaluated *Westward to Mecca* for the *Journal of the Royal Institute of International Affairs*. Gibb decided the book must have been written ironically, calling it "a well-spiced Eastern revue, featuring Afghan raiders, alchemists, enchanted walls, watery blue-eyed Bolshevists, singing dervishes and mysterious caves." Correspondingly tongue in cheek, he rhetorically asked, "Is it all true?" before answering in conclusion, "How like the materially-minded West to ask such questions!"[70] Elsewhere Gibb reviewed *Afghanistan of the Afghans*, which "seeks to create a sympathetic understanding of the Afghans" and hence, he judged gently, "deserves in return a sympathetic hearing."[71] Even so, he had to admit the book suffered "from having been too hastily written and rushed through the Press, and is full of more or less serious slips."[72]

Like other jobbing authors, Ikbal did his best to capitalize on his new books by sending presentation copies to influential men of affairs. Announcing his triumphal return from "an adventurous journey" of fifteen thousand miles, just five days after his homecoming he wrote a letter to Downing Street on his embossed "Nashdom" notepaper, requesting a meeting with his old contact, Sir John Shuckburgh, by now the guiding figure behind British Middle Eastern policy.[73] In his letter, Ikbal explained that since he had now been able to make a close study of Middle Eastern affairs, his advice would surely interest the British government, adding with a characteristic flourish that he had met with "Kings, Divines, brigands & beggars." Hinting at the intelligence possibilities, he also mentioned having gone to a great deal of trouble to take photographs. Knowing well the social instincts of the imperial ruling class (Sir John was an old Etonian), Ikbal signed off by highlighting in parentheses his title of sirdar.

When a week later Sir John had not replied, Ikbal wrote again, and this time he raised the bait. In the six days since he penned the first letter, the scale of his journey increased from 15,000 to 25,000 miles.[74] If this exploratory feat didn't provide credentials enough, then there was also his recent book, *Afghanistan of the Afghans*, of which he politely asked Sir John to accept a copy. Lest the policy makers in Downing Street had forgotten Ikbal's earlier assurances that he was born and raised in Afghanistan, the photograph on the book's frontispiece would remind them. Unlike his father and fellow graduates of the Anglo-Oriental College, and even the Afghan aristocracy in Kabul, who all preferred European suits, Ikbal posed in a flamboyant rendering of traditional Afghan attire.

In May, he received a short note from Downing Street that summoned him to a meeting with Sir John Shuckburgh, who thanked him for his offer of gifting the book.[75] Unsure of Ikbal's aims, Sir John dashed off a separate note to L. D. Wakely, secretary of the India Office's political and secret department, asking if there were any issues on which he should be "specially reticent" during the upcoming meeting.[76] Wakely's reply confirmed Sir John's suspicions about Ikbal, and the two officials agreed on a strategy of "letting him talk and saying as little as possible in reply." Alluding to Ikbal's reputation, Wakely reminded his colleague that "you know of the tendency to 'romance' that he displayed some years ago."[77] Writing also to the diplomat Sir Lancelot Oliphant, Sir John described his visitor as "a young Afghan (or Punjabi: I believe there is some doubt as to his origin)."[78]

At the appointed time, Sir John conversed with Ikbal for over an hour at his Downing Street office. To the Englishman's surprise, the mysterious Afghan (or was it Punjabi?) wanted to discuss a plan for what he called "a Grand Muslim Conference for the Regeneration of Islam," which he hoped to oversee himself. The conference would

not focus on the political revival of Islam; indeed, discussion of politics would be banned altogether. Instead it would focus on cultural
matters. Ikbal's travels had convinced him, he explained, of the need
for a reunification of Islam, not in a political, but in a cultural and
educational sense by means of "a reversion to the true spirit of the
Quran." It was a phrase on the lips of every Muslim reformist of the
day, even as they differed enormously over what that "true spirit"
was. But if this revival could be brought about, Ikbal went on, then
religious fanaticism and political extremism would both disappear.
Moreover, once Islam was properly revived, all true Muslims would
realize that "their best hope for the future lies in close cooperation
with Great Britain."[79]

Listening to Ikbal outline his plans, Sir John tried to follow his
colleague's advice by saying as little as possible. So he could only
hold up his hands in quiet dismay when Ikbal suggested holding his
Grand Muslim Conference in Jerusalem. What with increasing ten-
sion between local Arabs and immigrant Zionists, the politics of Palestine were already complicated enough without Ikbal's intruding
on them. Sensing the room freeze, Ikbal backtracked and suggested
Cairo instead or (thinking on his feet now) perhaps even Albania.
Writing to his colleagues after the meeting, Sir John confided that
"the whole plan seems quite wild," and so he had, he assured them,
been "quite non-committal" in his replies.[80]

One can only guess what Sir John made of the book *Afghanistan
of the Afghans*, which Ikbal had presented him. It certainly opened
soberly enough, with two academic chapters on geography and history, followed, in a plausible progression toward ethnography, by
a chapter on family life, weddings, and dowries (a reworking of
two articles from his folklore days under the influence of Donald
Mackenzie). Then both tone and topic took a peculiar turn by way
of three chapters on witchcraft, necromancy, and the supernatural,
with instruction on hexes to subdue mothers-in-law and methods
to summon genies.[81] After fakirs and fairyland, next came the lore
of warriors via legends of Afghan heroes. Then after a debunking

excursus into Sufism (another reworking of an earlier article), with which he had apparently fallen out of sympathy, the book turned abruptly to the engineering of the Khyber Railway. There was no conclusion, indeed no ending as such, only an ambiguous formula at the foot of the final page: "(Usual ending.)"[82]

Returning to the lecture circuit, Ikbal was determined to weigh in on Palestinian affairs too. At the Royal Central Asian Society, he gave a lecture about British policy in Palestine based on what he had observed on his drive across the mandated territory during his recent journey of 15,000 (or 25,000) miles.[83] Chairing the debate that followed his lecture was Field Marshal Edmund Allenby, who back in 1917 had seized Jerusalem from the Ottomans. Officialdom was taking no risks with Ikbal's idiosyncratic suggestions, and the old soldier was there to firmly marshal the game of ideas. As it happened, Ikbal played his cards carefully, declaring Palestine under British control to be a land of progress where all sections of society were free to observe their own faiths.[84] He was no anti-Zionist. Afterward the British-edited *Palestine Bulletin* reprinted his speech with approval.[85]

Meanwhile, hoping Sir John Shuckburgh would see the wisdom of supporting (and funding) his "Grand Conference" in Jerusalem, Ikbal sent invitation letters to prominent leaders from around the Muslim world, including Amin al-Husseini, the outspoken Grand Mufti of Jerusalem. Given Sir John's support of Jewish immigration to Palestine, had he agreed to fund the conference it was unlikely that the anti-Zionist grand mufti would have attended, especially since Ikbal planned to ban all discussion of politics. But Ikbal's invitation letter was writ through with optimism, declaring that the old enmity between Shias and Sunnis would soon be gone forever, since different sects were now united in their desire to return Islam to its original purity.[86] It was Western scientific materialism that stood in the way, he continued.[87] For like so many in the decade after the First World War, the former medical student had turned on his science teachers to promote the revival of religion instead.

Rather than provide his correspondents with his address in the factory-filled suburb of Mitcham, Ikbal gave his address as Monomark House in Central London. Though it sounded official, it was one of Britain's first P.O. boxes, for Ikbal was trying to create his own grand version of the Meccan congress without even so much as an office. Worse still, there was far less consensus among the world's Muslims than he claimed, so his invitations met with little enthusiasm. Meanwhile Sir John also wrote back to give him the brush-off. (Hoping to preempt further letters, he added his doubt that further conversation would "serve any useful purpose.")[88]

As ever, Ikbal faced the more immediate need to make a living. No sooner had the British government declined to fund his conference than he was beseeching Sir Muhammad Rafique, a distinguished Indian judge and sometime member of the Viceroy's Council, for a paid position as secretary to the Woking Mosque, south of London.[89] Sir Muhammad refused, passing on the letter to the India Office, where it was remarked that Ikbal was now simply "out for money as much as notoriety."[90] Despite the occasional piece for *The Times* and *The Spectator*, Ikbal was unable to break into British broadsheet journalism, so had to satisfy himself with stringer positions on the London staff of two Indian newspapers, *The Civil and Military Gazette* (erstwhile employer of Rudyard Kipling) and *The Pioneer* (ironically, despised by Afghan nationalists). Based on his articles, the India Office's press officer now described him as "a bit of a liar in the sense that, like many freelance journalists (not all of them brown in color), he draws a long bow at times, to see whether the arrow will fall behind the bank counter."[91]

In his desperation, Ikbal was certainly drawing his journalistic bow longer than ever, for next he claimed to be a celebrated Afghan alchemist who devoted himself to "experiments that he hopes will one day make him richer than a thousand El Doradoes."[92] He told a reporter from *The Advocate* that, when his uncle was dying in Afghanistan, he had beckoned the young Ikbal to his bedside, pulled out a "well-worn manuscript" from under his pillow, and tried to speak but faltered and died. Ikbal had kept the manuscript, he told *The Advocate*, and someday would master its alchemical secrets to turn base metal into gold. "So far," the reporter noted wryly, "he has met with no success."

Undeterred, Ikbal publicly took up Couéism, a self-help method invented by the French psychologist Émile Coué de la Châtaigneraie and known for its repeated chant of "Every day, in every way, I'm getting better and better." (The later Beatles song aside, its most famous practitioner was the fictional Fleur Mont in John Galsworthy's 1924 novel *The White Monkey*.) For a brief time Ikbal served as vice-president of London's Coué Institute, giving lectures at Queen's Hall on Langham Place, the city's premier concert venue, which had an audience capacity of twenty-five hundred.[93] His promoters, in their eagerness to fill so many seats, billed him on posters as "Prince Ikbal Ali Shah, the Renowned Oriental Scholar and Mystic," whose skills now included the ability to cure "domestic discord, unhappiness, depressed spirits and general ill-health."[94] Taking note of this latest career change, an intelligence officer at the India Office filed the advert under a tab headed "Our Versatile Friend."[95]

There was more to come. Ikbal now began experimenting with a new kind of journalism in which he appeared as an Eastern counterpart to T. E. Lawrence, a man of action and adventure. His anecdotes became more and more fabulous—a favorite motif was being kidnapped in the desert.[96] In these "news" stories, he seemed as unfortunate as he was brave, repeatedly seized by "brigands" and "bandits," whether in Syria, Iraq, or Afghanistan. But there was also romance and intrigue, and in another newspaper article he claimed to reveal the mysteriously salacious truth about an occult dancer who had caused the collapse of the Ottoman Empire.[97] Recognizing the importance of women readers, he even penned magazine pieces on "Afghan beauty secrets" that revealed the martial makeup techniques of his homeland's fighting females.[98] Such articles sold well, placed by his agent Harold Shepstone in magazines and newspapers across the imperial Anglosphere, from Derby to Delhi, Bombay to Singapore, then all the way back to Aberdeen.

Since the India Office and Downing Street had turned their back on him, Ikbal next decided to write to Sir Eric Drummond, the Scottish secretary-general of the League of Nations. Having heard there was a vacant position as information officer for India, Ikbal included three pages of "particulars," detailing his war service, travels, diplomatic skills, and vast experience as a publicist.[99] He also assured Sir Eric that he was a fellow British subject. His application prompted an internal memo that recorded the league's perplexity. "It is extremely difficult to form any certain opinion about an applicant who puts his qualifications so high," noted an official from the league's information section, adding that while Ikbal's statement of being perhaps the world's most famous journalist was "patently absurd" (the press officer had never heard of him), he still possessed skills the organization might find useful.[100] Nonetheless, after much paper-shuffling, the application by this mysterious British Afghan who wanted to represent Indian affairs was passed over in favor of a more unambiguously Indian applicant.

Meanwhile Ikbal tried his chances again with the BBC. Explaining that he was an Afghan nobleman educated at Edinburgh University, he proposed a series of four radio talks with innocuous titles such as "Persians at Play" and "The Charms of Afghan Life."[101] The commissioning editor replied to decline the offer, but Ikbal was not so easily defeated.[102] On Christmas Day 1928, at his desk as usual, he wrote back to offer a "quite unpolitical" talk on life in Afghanistan, then followed up a few days later to suggest a broadcast that would secure friendly relations between Britain and Afghanistan (the latter being his own country, he emphasized).[103] This time the commissioner acquiesced.

Not long afterward Ikbal sent a congratulatory letter to Britain's new prime minister, Ramsay MacDonald, requesting a meeting.[104] Ikbal hardly shared the politics of the head of the Labour Party, but times were clearly changing, and Ikbal was nothing if not adaptable. The PM's office turned him down: Labour had been in office for less than a week before Ikbal's letter arrived, and they were rather busy, they explained. Still, Ikbal was alert to the shift in the political atmosphere marked by the triumph of MacDonald, an illegitimate farmworker's son, over the Old Etonians who were the usual masters of the game. Events in Afghanistan seemed to offer an Eastern mirror to these developments, when King Amanullah was overthrown by a rural Tajik rebel who, on account of his humble origins, was disparagingly dubbed Bacha-i Saqao, or "Son of the Water-Seller." The modernizing Amanullah, during his tour of Britain the previous year, had roused huge public interest with his fashionable unveiled wife, so his overthrow had captured the headlines. Bearded tribesmen had seized £750,000 from the royal palace, closed Kabul's only girls' school, destroyed Buddhist statues in the country's only museum, and made the burqa compulsory. Seizing the moment as he had a decade earlier, Ikbal lectured on the Afghan "revolution" wherever there was a fee to be earned, at venues as varied as Uppingham School and the Hull Royal Institution.[105] Even the Bouverie Society, a social club for London pawnbrokers, eagerly paid for an after-dinner talk now that Afghanistan was back in the news.[106]

This was just as well, because in a Croydon hospital Elizabeth had just given birth to a fourth child.[107] In a nod to the founder of the Ottoman Empire that had so recently been dissolved, the boy was called Osman (though in honor of Elizabeth's heritage he was given the Scottish middle name Ian). Shortly after the birth, the family moved out of the chemical air of Mitcham. On the proceeds of his recent lectures and journalism, they moved to the greener setting of Belmont, on the farthest outskirts of suburban London, renting a house near the railway station that allowed Ikbal easy access to the city. A simulacrum of rural life built after the coming of the railway, for its first decade the village had been called California Station—it only became the medieval Norman-sounding Belmont under pressure from housing developers. Likewise, Ikbal's ordinary commuter house bore the name Northdene, which he soon had emblazoned on his notepaper. There, beside Banstead Downs Golf Club, his children Amina, Omar,

Idries, and now Osman would all grow up, adopting their father's upper-class English accent. Ikbal had worked hard—exhaustively hard—to give them a foot up in life in their English homeland.

Despite digging deeper roots in the suburbs, Ikbal still harbored hopes of finding a place at the political gaming table of London's imperial establishment. So in 1930, settled in Northdene, he took the tried and tested route of joining a gentlemen's club by applying for membership in the National Liberal Club. Despite the fact that it was now a full decade since he had last been registered at Edinburgh University, in the application he stated his profession as "medical student," though he also added "author."[108] Two proposers followed up with recommendation letters. The first was Saeed Mohamedi, a Muslim doctor from India who declared Ikbal was a "liberal in politics & in every way eligible as a member of the club."[109] The second proposer was another Indian Muslim named Hamza Ali, who repeated exactly the same words.[110]

Founded fifty years earlier, the club's membership comprised a veritable pantheon of imperial politicos, including Winston Churchill, Gopal Krishna Gokhale, David Lloyd George, Dadabhai Naoroji, Sir Ramsay Macdonald, Sir C. P. Ramaswami Iyer, and Muhammad Ali Jinnah. All mingled on the equal terms of fellow club members, not least since Naoroji was the first Indian elected to the British Parliament, Iyer a senior Indian loyalist politician, Gokhale a prominent member of the independence-seeking Congress Party, and Jinnah the leader of the opposing Muslim League. Besides Jinnah, the club had other Muslim members, such as Abdullah Yusuf Ali, the Indian translator of the Quran into English, who stayed regularly in its grand neo-Gothic chambers beside the Thames near Parliament.[111] The club also attracted novelists and playwrights, including Bram Stoker, George Bernard Shaw, and Sir Anthony Hope, whose *Prisoner of Zenda* had been one of Britain's best-selling-ever novels. It was perhaps fitting company, for shortly before Ikbal joined the club, one of his short stories appeared in print beside the work of such distinguished authors as Somerset Maugham, Sir Walter

Scott, and Joseph Conrad—even if the anthology was called *Fifty Enthralling Stories of the Mysterious East*.[112]

By the time he was accepted as a member, Ikbal was proofreading his latest book, which he hoped would be accepted as a serious political study of contemporary Iran. As a follow up to *Westward to Mecca*, he gave it the title *Eastward to Persia*. In its introduction, Ikbal voiced clearly his long-standing belief that being a Muslim and being loyal to the British Empire were entirely compatible.[113] Setting himself apart from pro-independence members of the National Liberal Club like Gokhale and Jinnah, as well as anti-colonial firebrands like the Grand Mufti of Jerusalem, he pronounced his intention to refute "un-Islamic ideas that every white man is planning to usurp the freedom of this or that Asiatic country."[114]

In a considerable publicity coup born partly of an invitation to his thwarted Grand Conference in Jerusalem, Ikbal managed to persuade His Highness Sir Agha Sultan Mohamed Shah (better known as the Agha Khan) to write a foreword to the book. As the interwar era's most famous Indian Muslim luminary, the Eton- and Cambridge-educated religious leader was visiting London to defend the rights of Muslims against Hindus as part of the first Round Table Conference on India's constitutional reform. In his foreword to *Eastward to Persia*, the Agha Khan gave a ringing endorsement that the book ought to be "read by those in the West who want to see the East through Oriental eyes," a cue taken up by the reviewer for *Foreign Affairs*.[115]

More careful readers might have noticed that the contents and structure of *Eastward to Persia* almost exactly mirrored those of *Afghanistan of the Afghans*, published two years earlier. It began with Iran's geography and history, then moved on to folklore, magic, mysticism, and literature, turned abruptly to economic affairs by way of Iran's new railway, and finished with a survey of its flourishing petroleum industry. Along the way, accounts of flesh-colored ladies' stockings competed for coverage with tales of the goat-god Baphomet, who was purportedly still being worshipped from Shiraz,

Iran, to Charleston, South Carolina. In a kind of metaphysical free-for-all, Muslim mystical ideas were associated with everything from the Egyptian god Osiris to the Mexican Day of the Dead. Ikbal's ideological hobbyhorses could also be glimpsed prancing through each chapter, as he claimed the material civilization of the West was being resisted by a spiritual and political renaissance sweeping through the Eastern lands of Islam. Here were echoes of the recently published *Reconstruction of Religious Thought in Islam* by the illustrious Indian poet and philosopher Sir Muhammad Iqbal.

Yet if one theme pervaded *Eastward to Persia*, and so much of Ikbal's output, it was the admirable desire, paradoxically born from the tensions of empire, to help "the East" and "the West" understand each other. "Do Easterners look at the world so differently," he asked, "that it is not possible for them to find a common meeting ground?"[116]

Chapter Five

AUTHOR

On . . . books and lectures, therefore,

the whole weight now rested.

—Edmund Gosse, *Father and Son*

IT WAS SURELY WITH IMMENSE DELIGHT THAT IKBAL OPENED the embossed envelope containing an invitation to meet the King-Emperor George V.[1] After attending the reception at Buckingham Palace, he wrote it up for *The Saturday Review*. (How else was the world to know?) And he played the role of the Afghan for all it was worth, depicting himself as a wild tribesman more at home in a shower of bullets than at a sedate garden party.[2] He was driven to the palace together with retired colonial colonels, but no sooner had their car reached the gates than the clouds opened and rain began to fall heavily. While the long line of waiting guests was getting wet, Ikbal, in his long Uzbek robe and Astrakhan hat, remained cheerfully dry. After waiting his turn, his calling card was passed through six servile pairs of hands till it reached the footman before the throne. As Ikbal's title and name were announced, the king-emperor reached forward to shake his hand. But it was all over in an instant, and Ikbal was ushered into the gardens, where the rain now stopped and June sunshine broke through the clouds. There was light music and chatter all around, the decorous hum cracked only by a loud debutante gasp as a small party moved slowly through the crowds: it was the sovereign making the rounds of his guests. Ikbal's brightly striped robe caught his eye, and soon they were conversing about battles in Afghanistan, about Buddhist relics uncovered at Bamiyan, about the meandering route of the Helmand River. Ikbal was capti-vated, he wrote in his article later that week, by what the sagacious emperor knew about his distant homeland. All told, the day had a "magical effect" on him.[3]

Unfortunately, at the time he was breezily writing about being invited to Buckingham Palace, he was also fending off the milkman and baker. To make matters worse, he fell ill with a bout of the pneu-monia that he had first contracted in the postwar flu pandemic. But he struggled on. Writing from his sickbed, he initiated a new series of letters to high officialdom, this time to persuade the imperial gov-ernment to force his father to provide him with enough money to pay off his debts. Any pretense of having grown up in Afghanistan was now dropped as his letters made clear that his father was the Nawwab of Sardhana, where the family had been settled for several generations. Ikbal's debts were so serious, he explained, that bailiffs had already taken possession of his house, and he was facing five county court summonses through his inability to pay other bills. If the India Office didn't force the nawwab to cough up at least £200, then he would be carted off to a charity hospital, while Elizabeth and the children would be left to beg the Surrey Parish Council for their daily bread.[4] And if officials couldn't persuade the nawwab to send money voluntarily, then they should withhold the political pension he was paid for his loyalty and pass that on as a lump sum to Ikbal.[5]

His letter to the India Office in London triggered a flurry of tele-grams to Delhi, then Sardhana, where Nawwab Amjad Ali Shah was enraged. Indignantly replying in Urdu, he complained that he was already in debt to the sum of 22,000 rupees as a result of pay-ing for his son's extravagances.[6] Years earlier, the nawwab went on, he had expected Ikbal to become a doctor, then quietly serve the empire, but instead he had become a journalist whose writings were so obsequiously pro-British that now every Indian leader and newspaper abused him, which in turn affected his family in India.[7] So no: he would not send another rupee to his son. Instead, the nawwab declared, the imperial government should provide Ikbal with a steady job.[8] But there was of course no question of that. And so if Ikbal's father, the India Office, and the government at large wouldn't listen to him, then Ikbal still had the general public, whom he would now pursue relentlessly.

Published at the height of his financial troubles, *The Golden East* was well matched to the middlebrow section of the book market. Demand was high for gung-ho accounts of Eastern adventure written by the likes of Major Francis Yeats-Brown, who had recently followed up his hugely successful *Lives of a Bengal Lancer* with a book about Istanbul subtitled *A Decade of Plot and Counter-Plot by the Golden Horn.*[9] With its tales of mysterious dervishes and political intrigue, *A Decade of Plot* had much in common with Ikbal's own new potboiler, not least because its author, like Ikbal, was often in disguise. But the manly persona of *The Golden East* would never have dressed as "Madame Josephine," as Major Yeats-Brown did when going undercover.

The reviews were far better than for Ikbal's previous books. In the widely read *Bookman*, O. M. Green, editor of the *North China Daily News*, said *The Golden East* possessed "all the ingredients of an attractive book of travels, breezy style, skillful selection and illuminating comment."[10] But what set it apart from the countless other travel books of the 1930s was that "as an Asiatic, the Sirdar could go everywhere, see with Asiatic eyes and, with his comprehension of the West, interpret for Western comprehension." In *The Saturday Review*, to which Ikbal had been contributing a lot of late, he was similarly praised for these innate qualifications—expert insights borne from his identity as a Muslim and "Afghan gentleman . . . give him opportunities of contact denied a European."[11] It was as though the reviewer had followed Ikbal's script (or at least the book's preface). Following the glowing appraisal of Ikbal's book was a review of *Poems (1926–1930)* by Robert Graves, another aspiring author who had earlier tried his hand at tales of the East with his book *Lawrence of Arabia*, but the assessment paled by comparison.[12]

Soon Ikbal was under contract to also write a book on Arabia for A. & C. Black's *Peeps at Many Lands*.[13] In recent years this popular series had been diverted by the likes of *Peeps at the World's Dolls*, so Ikbal was commissioned to put it back on the masculine track established by boys' schoolmaster John Finnemore, who had written the stirring early works in the series. Although Arabia was now under Saudi rule, Ikbal charmed British schoolchildren with tales of romantic Bedouin traditions that the Wahhabis were busily stamping out as deviations from true Islam. Next, he updated the "Peep" at Turkey written by Julius van Millingen, who had been raised in Istanbul and spent his career at the Imperial Ottoman Bank.[14] Having only made a few stops during his drive across Turkey, Ikbal had no such long experience to draw on, but he did have his name, and readers would take that as qualification enough.

Drawn to Ikbal by the authority on Islamic affairs that came from his being a Muslim, other publishing houses opened their doors to him, and he now signed one book contract after another. First came a biography of the Prophet Muhammad, which the *Times Literary Supplement* judged "attractive and sympathetic."[15] Next he compiled a volume of selections from the Quran, during which he spent time with England's first resident Muslim religious leaders.[16] The most important figure he met was Moulana Abdul Majid, the Indian imam of the Shah Jahan Mosque at Woking, some twenty miles west of Ikbal's latest home in Belmont.[17] He also sought advice from Molvi Mohamed Ali, head of the mosque's missionary wing, who had written a proselytizing English biography of the Prophet and may have advised Ikbal to write a book similar to his own.[18]

Ikbal's biography was not the first such work in English. The earliest positive English biography of the Prophet Muhammad to emerge from British India had been written by the founder of Ikbal's high school, Sir Sayyid Ahmad Khan, back in 1870. Since then a growing number of authors had written sympathetic English accounts of Islam. They included the Indian barrister Syed Ameer Ali, who had helped found the Edinburgh Indian Association, and the British convert Muhammad Marmaduke Pickthall, whose appealing novels like *Saïd the Fisherman* featured many a Muslim hero (he also translated the Quran into sturdily Biblical English). The publication of Ikbal's new religious works coincided with the appearance of another English translation of the Quran by Abdullah Yusuf Ali, his fellow member of the National Liberal Club. In an effort to promote the best elements of Islam and bring them into harmony with liberal values, Yusuf Ali had published many previous books, such as *Muslim Educational Ideals*, though other believers were making less harmonious interventions in the literary sphere. In 1938, a decade after British Communists burned a statue of T. E. Lawrence, members of London's recently formed Anjuman-i Islam, or Muslim Society, adopted their incendiary mode of demonstration by burning H. G. Wells's *Short History of the World*, whose depiction of their Prophet they found offensive.[19]

Yet as Europe's empires showed signs of running out of steam, Islam held out the promise of both spiritual and political regeneration. Promoting Islam to a generation of postwar Britons who had lost faith in their own civilization, in the final chapter of *Mohamed*, Ikbal turned to the Prophet's lessons for the present, telling readers that only Islam offered a true brotherhood of man.[20] Amid the ideological crisis of the mid-1930s, the route to universal equality was Islam, not Communism. Still, Ikbal dedicated the biography to the Afghan dictator, Nadir Shah, whose reign he declared "nobly upheld the teachings of the Prophet"—at least till he was assassinated by a student activist the year after Ikbal's book appeared.[21]

Next came a monograph on Islam's main mystical tradition, Sufism.[22] It was written as a response to suggestions by an earlier generation of Orientalists that Sufism had originated in Buddhist, Hindu, or Christian practices. By contrast, Ikbal made the case that Sufism originated entirely within Islam, hence his book's title, *Islamic Sufism*. For over a quarter-century Cambridge's Reynold

Nicholson had also been arguing that Sufism had developed within Islam, but in 1931 his former student Margaret Smith had published *Studies in Early Mysticism in the Near and Middle East*, which revived the case for the origins of Sufism lying in Eastern Christianity.[23] Completed two years later, and siding with Nicholson, Ikbal's book pushed back against Smith and the earlier authors who gave the Sufis a non-Muslim pedigree.

Still, Ikbal could scarcely have written his book without recourse to the writings of more sympathetic Orientalists who in recent decades had presented Sufi doctrines in English. The longest translation in Ikbal's book comprised six Persian poems by Hafiz, which he took word for word and without acknowledgment from the translation by the redoubtable female explorer Gertrude Bell.[24] (Although Bell's book was still under copyright, she was unable to personally object, having died seven years earlier in Baghdad.) Nevertheless, in his preface, Ikbal did acknowledge the help he had received from leading Orientalists of the day, including Reynold Nicholson and Sir Thomas Walker Arnold who, unlike more disparaging scholars of a previous generation, had a deep fellow feeling for Islam.

This time Ikbal's publisher was Rider & Co., which had been established back in 1908 as the originator of the iconic Rider-Waite tarot cards. Since then it had promoted many oddball authors, but when Ikbal came knocking at its Great Portland Street door, it was surfing the crest of the postwar occult wave. At the same time as Rider signed up Ikbal, it also took on the first book by the British theosophist Raphael Hurst, who ran the Atlantis, an occult bookshop in Bloomsbury. Under his pen name Paul Brunton, Hurst too wrote of travels among India's fakirs and mystics. No longer a mere colony with nothing to offer Britain but raw materials for its industries, India was increasingly being seen as a treasury of ancient wisdom. However, Hurst's fascination was more with Hindu yogis than Muslim Sufis, and here lay Ikbal's market niche.

Islamic Sufism displayed none of the spiritual eclecticism of Ikbal's earlier works on magic, which had presented Muslim mysticism equally alongside manifestations of the occult from every part of the world. Now he insisted on the uniquely Muslim profile of Sufism, stipulating that there is "no form of Sufism other than Islamic."[25] Indeed, for the Sufi, the Quran is his "Textbook," and the Prophet Mohammed "the greatest Sufi of all times."[26] Most Sufis over previous centuries would have wholeheartedly concurred. But Ibn Saud and his Wahhabis, now in control of Mecca, fervently disagreed.

Having covered the spiritual dimensions of Islam, Ikbal's next book, *The Oriental Caravan*—published within months of *Islamic Sufism*—saw him turn to the religious heritage of "the East" as a whole; its subtitle promised nothing less than *A Revelation of the Soul and Mind of Asia*.[27] Next came *Lights of Asia*, in which he claimed all religions as the heritage of the East and not of the materialist West—an idea he shared with many British and American seekers of the time.[28] That didn't prevent him from conducting his research in the West, and the book's Jewish sections drew on meetings with the head of London's Liberal Jewish Synagogue, while for the Buddhist sections he received help from London's Buddhist Lodge, run by a Cambridge-educated convert with the distinctly un-Buddhist name Christmas Humphreys.[29]

Ikbal exhausted the world's religions within eighteen months, and so returned to his favorite topic of Afghanistan with a panegyric study of the exiled modernizer King Amanullah. By now Amanullah was living in Rome after being overthrown by the rebel Bacha-i Saqao, the lowly "son of the water-seller" who within months had himself been ousted by Amanullah's distant relative (and former army chief) Nadir Shah, to whom Ikbal had recently dedicated his biography of the Prophet.[30]

Having thus expanded his range to political biography, Ikbal next signed contracts for studies of the Turkish nationalist modernizer Kemal Atatürk and the liberal Indian Muslim leader the Agha Khan, whom he owed a favor for the generous foreword to *Eastward to Persia*.[31] The book market was still booming for travelogues, though, and regardless of having run out of journeys to document, Ikbal responded with *Alone in Arabian Nights*, an eager return from his recent pious orthodoxy to his old enthusiasms for the occult and magic.[32] There were even criticisms of Mecca as a city of extraordinary and unnecessary discomfort.[33] As for Port Said, it was a city of "sham romance" where tawdry shops sold "Arab" jewelry made in Birmingham, "Turkish" daggers from Sheffield, and fake "Egyptian" shawls from the factories of Turin. Worse still were the seedy dancers' booths where faded Parisiennes wriggled in supposedly Eastern dance moves.[34] He even admitted that the tomes on magic shown to him in a Levantine library turned out to be cheap French paperbacks one could buy for a few francs in Paris.[35] The harder he searched for the authentic spirituality of the East, the farther it seemed to slip away. So he turned instead to short stories, tales of Eastern romance compiled into a little book called *The Golden Pilgrimage*.[36] It was a period of extraordinary industry: his cigarettes must have burned constantly, with Elizabeth serving pot after pot of strong tea. Between 1932 and 1934, Ikbal published twelve different books.

He also tried to keep up with his journalism, not least concerning the high politics of empire. India was on many minds in London as the Round Table Conferences convened there to discuss Indian constitutional reforms, including the move to semi-independent "dominion" status. Although the leaders of the Indian National Congress stayed away, eighty-nine Indian delegates did come to London, including representatives of the Muslim League and of such Muslim princely states as Hyderabad. Writing for the British press, Ikbal seized the opportunity to berate Gandhi, the Congress, and the whole idea that India could be fairly governed by democracy (and thereby by its Hindu majority). The only way to rule India, he explained to readers of the *Daily Mirror*, was through benevolent autocracy.[37] The following weekend he wrote another article for *The Saturday Review* that celebrated the Muslim delegates from princely India as the conference's heroes, especially the ruler of Bhopal, "India's Bonnie Prince Charlie," who had attended Ikbal's old high school.[38] Much as Ikbal might have wished to be one of the delegates, having so often declared himself an Afghan and been investigated by the India Office, he had disqualified himself from being invited to discuss India's future. He would simply have to find other ways of shaping her destiny.

So in July 1931 he wrote to Alec Houghton Joyce, an experienced information officer at the India Office who had been appointed joint publicity officer to the Round Table Conferences. Having recently been introduced to him as one of the many journalists covering the conferences, Ikbal seized the opportunity to follow up with a plan to establish a journal on Indian affairs. It would cultivate friendship between England and India, particularly through the publication of "sympathetic articles," appearing twice monthly with plentiful illustrations.[39] As for the print run, that should be three or, better, five thousand copies per issue, priced at six pence.[40] Ikbal had thought about everything, not least his own position as editor in chief, bypassing the British old boys' networks of Fleet Street and providing a more regular income than freelance journalism. If Mr. Joyce were willing to help (that is, to pay), then the first issue could be put together within a couple of weeks, he explained. The sum of fifty pounds per issue would cover it, at least to begin with.[41]

Since it was Alec Joyce's job to oversee press coverage of India, he had already heard of Ikbal's tendencies. It had been to Joyce that a fellow press officer had earlier passed on his opinion that Ikbal was "a bit of a liar," albeit one who "eats out of our hand when occasion requires."[42] Wary of such a reputation, Joyce passed on the proposal to a senior colleague, whose plain advice to Ikbal spelled bad news: "I strongly advise you to let this project drop."[43] Anyway, other officials calculated that the journal would lose at least £150 per issue, and the India Office could not waste money investing in it.

As well as consorting with officials, imams, and Orientalists, Ikbal also renewed his acquaintance with the former Allahabad history professor Laurence Rushbrook Williams, who had employed him in India to write anti-Bolshevik propaganda (and to whom he had dedicated *The Golden East* in gratitude). Moving on from running the Central Bureau of Public Information in India, Rushbrook Williams had recently returned to London and been appointed director of Eastern Services for the BBC, effectively overseeing its growing broadcasts to the empire. Since Ikbal's last radio appearance in 1929, he had kept up a barrage of letters proposing talks for the BBC, to whose audiences he now offered to explain the political changes sweeping across the Islamic world.[44] He also proposed a series of travel talks that would summon happily exotic vistas in listeners' minds. His words would whisk housewives in Chipping Sodbury away to the Persian garden of Omar Khayyam or to the mysterious Kaaba in Mecca.[45] Given his earlier employment, Ikbal assured Rushbrook Williams there would be no "propaganda" in the talks.[46] Even so, the BBC declined the offers.

While Britain's state-dominated radio was difficult to access, the private sphere of magic lantern lectures continued to lend Ikbal an alternative platform. With Hollywood films just beginning to be recorded with sound and still being filmed in black and white, lantern slide lectures remained enormously popular. Not only were the pictures in color; the lectures featured atmospheric soundtracks via gramophone records that allowed Ikbal to intone a dramatic voice-over to images of distant places. He had been giving such lectures off and on for years, but now he expanded to seaside resorts such as Portsmouth's South Parade Pier.[47] After his agent Harold Shepstone arranged the bookings and placed adverts in local papers, Ikbal stayed on for weeks at a time, giving twice-daily performances of his "Oriental Films" for adults and children alike.[48] Here he was back in his guise as an explorer: one of his regular shows was called "Adventures in the Desert."[49]

The reviews of Ikbal's dozen recent books reinforced this impression.[50] For the highbrow *New Statesman*, he was nothing less than "an Afghan Odysseus."[51] Other reviewers praised his ability to explain Islam as an authoritative insider, reviewing him alongside works by such famous Orientalists as Edward Granville Browne.[52] Inevitably, there were some poor reviews too, including one by the influential soldier-scholar Lieutenant-Colonel Sir Wolseley Haig, who criticized the characteristically hasty preparation.[53] Another reviewer found the language of his travelogue *The Golden East* "reminiscent of a Chicago gunman."[54]

On the whole, though, Ikbal was riding the crest of a critical wave. Moving as he increasingly was in the circles of the university Orientalists, he now asserted himself as their scholarly equal by writing reviews of their books in return. He started at the top with the latest sympathetic study of Sufism by Cambridge's Reynold Nicholson, on whose work he had drawn for his own recent book on the Sufis.[55] But when Oxford's senior Arabist, David Samuel Margoliouth, dared to diverge from orthodox Muslim opinion, Ikbal wrote to *The Bookman* to correct the celebrated linguist on the grounds that, as "a son of Islam," he knew better.[56]

Yet despite Ikbal's prodigious efforts, the weight of his financial responsibilities could not rest on freelance writing and lecturing alone. With a wife and four children to support, not to mention the costs of maintaining an aristocratic image, he was forced to seek out a steadier source of income. Having long presented himself as an Afghan informant to the British, he now became a different sort of go-between by approaching the Afghan embassy in London, housed in a splendid Georgian palazzo across from the Royal Albert Hall. He was in luck. Having been established only in 1922, shortly after Afghanistan began to form its diplomatic cadre, the embassy needed someone with Ikbal's mastery of English, not to mention his many contacts. He was offered a position that reflected his earlier role at the consulate in Delhi: as official secretary. It not only gave him a regular salary; it allowed him to expand his address book, not least with several members of the Afghan royal family who served as ambassadors in the 1930s. His social ease among the British elite saw him act as chaperone for visiting Afghans, such as when he accompanied the Afghan Olympic hockey team to a dinner held in

their honor at the Grosvenor House Hotel.[57] The job afforded Ikbal
new travel opportunities too as a member of the Afghan delegation
to the League of Nations' World Disarmament Conference held in
Geneva between February 1932 and November 1934, as well as to
later meetings of the league's general assembly. On a few occasions,
he appeared in the assembly chamber alongside formally accredited
ambassadors from the United States, China, and the Soviet Union.[58]

Despite his modest official position as secretary to the Afghan delegation, Ikbal used these opportunities to blend his familiar skills
as a publicist with a new role as freelance diplomat. Hence in May
1934, he sent a long letter on the headed notepaper of Geneva's Hotel
Balmoral to Pablo de Azcárate, who oversaw the league's minorities
section.[59] In the letter (typed in impeccable French), Ikbal introduced
himself as an Afghan who had studied in Britain and was now working for the Afghan delegation to Geneva. The main substance of the
letter, though, was to offer his services in bringing the Muslim world
into the League of Nations' orbit. Specifically, this would involve
writing a book for a Muslim readership about the many admirable
activities of the league.[60] Persuaded by Ikbal's long list of qualifications, Azcárate promptly offered him a position as a *collaborateur
temporaire* with the league's *section d'information*. It came with
an ample salary of 800 Swiss francs per month, plus long-distance
train fares from London.[61] A few months later, wearing his latest
hat as an Afghan diplomat, Ikbal also approached Gerald Abraham,
head of the league's press office, for advice on how to help Afghanistan become a full formal member of the league. No stranger to
journalists and publicists, Abraham was intrigued by the "fascinating" Afghan who sauntered into his study, "with a face like a carved
image and speaking English as Matthew Arnold wrote it, with the
latest slang appropriately interspersed."[62]

Even amid the international society of Geneva, Ikbal cut quite
a figure. As the months rolled by, he tried his best to leverage his
minor positions as secretary and temporary employee into something rather grander. By the end of summer, he was proposing to the

league's new secretary-general a master plan to convince the whole Muslim world to cooperate with the league.[63] This was no longer a mere matter of writing a book; much to the dismay of the information section officials who were still paying him to write it, the book had fallen by the wayside. Rather, it was a far more ambitious proposal to bring together the leaders of Arab, Turkish, Iranian, Egyptian, Iraqi, and Indian Muslims, as well as the increasingly prominent Grand Mufti of Jerusalem. As for his own position, he suggested that he might be designated as the league's official "Liaison Officer to the Muslim World."[64]

Ikbal managed to get a written endorsement from the Aga Khan, the fabulously wealthy Cambridge-educated Indian Muslim leader who was by then a senior league official.[65] (A few years later he would be appointed president of the league's general assembly.) But officialdom in Geneva were unconvinced. Perhaps the information section had noticed that Ikbal had recently published a flattering biography of the Aga Khan.[66] At any rate, they were growing increasingly concerned about the lack of progress on the book he had been paid to write for a Muslim readership. By mid-October, Monsieur Pelt, the head of the information section, was writing to his colleagues with a dramatic report of Ikbal bursting into his office, brandishing a letter in Persian that he claimed (since Pelt couldn't read it) had been sent by the Afghan ambassador to London, and that demanded Ikbal's immediate return to England. The upshot, Pelt complained, was that Ikbal was trying to *forcer le main*—to force Pelt's hand into turning his temporary post into a permanent one.[67]

Although no such position was forthcoming, Ikbal returned from London to Geneva a few months later to attend the first organized conference of Muslims from across Europe.[68] Arranged by Shakib Arslan, an exiled Lebanese Pan-Islamist, and held in the genteel lakeside setting of the Hotel Victoria, the European Muslim Congress marked a milestone in the emergence of Muslim political consciousness in Europe. After Ikbal's foiled earlier plans of organizing an international Islamic conference of his own, he hoped this congress would promote a modern Islam capable of bringing about the harmonious union of East and West he discussed in his writings. But as it turned out, his influence on the proceedings was negligible, and as in Mecca a decade earlier, he had to be content with writing journalistic reports on its meetings. In one such article, he complained about the delegates' long-winded speeches and irreconcilable disagreements—at least until he himself intervened to restore the peace by reminding everyone that the interests of Muslims were best served by avoiding involvement in politics.[69]

As for his bid to be employed as the official League of Nations go-between with the Muslim world, it turned out he had again overplayed his hand—especially after he returned to London and informed Monsieur Pelt of the information section that he wouldn't be able to complete his promotional book on the league. Or at least not unless he was provided with a large comfortable apartment in Geneva in which to write it, he added, casually requesting that his outstanding bill at the Hotel Balmoral be paid as well.[70] With courteous sangfroid, Pelt wrote back to Ikbal (care of the National Liberal Club) to register his disappointment about the book, which he saw as being of potentially "great importance" in presenting the league's endeavors in a positive light to Muslims. But no apartment overlooking Lake Geneva was offered. Nor was an extension of his temporary appointment.

Although Ikbal continued to ask the league for employment for another four years—whether by proposing his book to different officials or applying to the secretariat as variously an Afghan, a British citizen, or an Indian national—his reputation in Geneva was tarnished.[71] Matters weren't helped when the league's head of personnel received a desperate letter from a Mademoiselle Houriet, complaining that she had never been paid for the translations into French of numerous letters she had made for Ikbal during his interactions with the league.[72] Whenever she had asked him to pay, he would put her off, she claimed, replying, "I know I owe you quite a good deal of money. I can't pay it just now, but will do so very soon."[73] But then Ikbal had permanently left for London, and though she sent him numerous polite reminders (even writing to the Afghan ambassador), she remained unpaid for her work. Since she looked after two elderly parents, she went on, who were entirely dependent on her, she couldn't afford to forgo the money she was owed, so in desperation she finally asked the league's personnel bureau to cover Ikbal's debts.

As if that weren't bad enough, a personnel file was compiled in Geneva containing claims that were extraordinary even by Ikbal's standards.[74] His fellow Muslims, far from considering him an ideal intermediary with the Islamic world, saw him as utterly untrustworthy, even as an employee of the British intelligence services. So much so that back in 1925, it was rumored, he had been forced to flee Mecca after attending the congress there. Similarly, at the recent European Muslim Congress in Geneva, the influential leaders he claimed as his allies had refused to begin their sessions in his presence for fear of being "under the eyes of London." Even books that bore his name, the file declared, had been written by his English wife.

Fortunately, the blue personnel folder was marked "not to be circulated," so its allegations were restricted to League of Nations bureaucrats. That was just as well, since Ikbal still harbored ambitions to influence British imperial policy. Rumors notwithstanding, by the mid-1930s his own writings were hardly helping his cause. Responding to an internal query as to the reliability of his publications, an official at the India Office noted his "tendency to make inaccurate or baseless claims as to his travels."[75] But that was not to stop him from writing books under another name, under another persona, for whom different and perhaps more credible claims might be made. So he now decided to write under a pseudonym. Or two. Or three.

The use of literary pseudonyms was common enough in the 1930s on highbrow no less than lowbrow bookshelves. There was the sardonically Japanese-sounding "Saki"; the Fu Manchu–inventing "Sax Rohmer"; and the class-defying everyman "George Orwell." There was even "Achmed Abdullah," the pen name of Alexander Nicholayevitch Romanoff, an American author of Orientalist pulp fiction who claimed to be the son of a Russian prince and an Afghan princess, and whose vast output included *Fighting Through: The Story of a Pathan Chieftain*, which reveled in adventures on the Afghan frontier, and *Mysteries of Asia*, which promised readers a vicarious peep at the veiled life of the East.[76]

Under the pseudonymous guise of the similarly named Syed Abdullah, Ikbal reinvented himself from twirl-mustached sirdar-about-town to bearded tribal warrior. This new persona also acted as a domestic literary catalyst, encouraging his wife, Elizabeth, to step away from her housework and write a book in which she in turn reinvented herself as a tribesman's consort. Now that their four children were all in school, Elizabeth had time to join the fictive literary game. Through her suburban typewriter, she remarried herself to Ikbal's new alter ego and became Morag Murray Abdullah, the hyper-Scottish wife of the Afghan frontiersman Syed Abdullah.[77]

Now in her forties, with her daughter Amina turning seventeen, the Surrey housewife perhaps looked back on her youth with nostalgia. Despite the many quotidian trials of life with a jobbing writer, her romanticized memoir voiced no regret. Opening with a tender verse from Omar Khayyam, the book was a testament to her love for Ikbal, her conversion to Islam, her discovery of dazzling Indian landscapes far from the dour skies of Edinburgh. Under her husband's tutelage, Elizabeth learned to reframe her identity, then sell it. And so in her pseudonymous autobiography, *My Khyber Marriage: Experiences of a Scotswoman as the Wife of a Pathan Chieftain's Son*, she was not the daughter of an estate manager but a high-society debutante who married the dashing scion of a tribal dynasty who lived in the Afghan highlands. Her book was a more adventurous competitor to memsahibs' memoirs, such as Maud Diver's *An Englishwoman in India*, that formed the "chick-lit" of empire.

For his part, Ikbal next donned the literary guise of a bluff English explorer modeled on the old army officers he had met at the Royal Central Asian Society. He became plain John Grant, as straight-talking as his name. As the audacious Englishman who dared penetrate the far reaches of Muslim Asia, he wrote *Through the Garden of Allah*.[78] Along with the familiar itinerary and the contradictory excursuses on modernism and magic, the book had several new twists. One was that Ikbal brought in another of his alter egos, Sheikh Ahmad, to share Grant's adventures in a kind of schizophrenia of pseudonyms.[79] Another was to task the fearless Grant with infiltrating a gang of Greek and Egyptian morphine smugglers, who were shipping their "satanic traffic" to London.[80] Disguised as Grant, Ikbal showed a startling familiarity with the drug world, vividly describing the sensation of smoking hashish and louche scenes in Eastern café bars where pretty girls injected morphine and sniffed crystals of white snow, slang for heroin.[81] All told, the *Garden of Allah* seemed a most unholy place, if a beguiling one nonetheless. It was snapped up by the Travel Book Club.

For his next book, he was back to an Afghan nom de plume, this time the name of a real person who had recently died a conveniently early death. Hence Ikbal became Habibullah Kalakani (better known as Bacha-i Saqao, "the Son of the Water-Seller"): the rebel who had overthrown the modernizing King Amanullah back in 1929. His rebellion and brief reign had been quickly reversed, and Bacha-i Saqao was soon hanged from a street post in Kabul. But though his uprising had made headlines around the world, no Western reporter had ever interviewed the infamous Bacha. Here Ikbal saw an opening and, testing the waters, published an article in *The Graphic* in which he claimed not only to be a relative of King Amanullah but also to have received a long letter that contained the full autobiographical confessions of the illiterate rebel he dubbed the Brigand King.[82] When Ikbal subsequently offered a complete book of the rebel's confessions to Sampson, Low & Co., the London publishing house was happy to believe he was merely the translator who penned an anonymous foreword. Ikbal's own name appeared nowhere. Ghostwritten amid the class struggle that found voice in Britain's 1935 general election, when the Labour Party gained a record 38 percent of the vote, the pseudo-autobiography was aptly titled *My Life: From Brigand to King*.[83]

Twenty years earlier China experts had fallen for Sir Edmund Backhouse's fraudulent *Annals and Memoirs of the Court of Peking*, based on an invented diary supposedly written by a court official called Ching-shan.[84] So Ikbal was hardly the first author to try such a ruse, though Backhouse had at least spent the previous decade in Beijing learning to read Chinese. By contrast, Ikbal's book deployed dramatic quoted speech that was entirely out of line with Afghan writings of the period, and its novelistic narrative was nothing like Afghan Persian prose. It also lacked the points of reference and (quite a slip for the punctilious Ikbal) the proper personal titles used in Persian works, even Khadim-i Rasul Allah, "The Servant of God's Prophet," which the rebel had bestowed on himself. (Only his enemies disparaged him as the Water-Seller's Son.)

A few well-informed readers spotted the ruse, though apparently not many. Having returned from military service in Afghanistan the year the book came out, Captain Felix Howland bought a copy out of curiosity, and after reading it wrote on the title page: "A purely fictitious work collecting many of the legends concerning Bacha-i Saqao. Obviously written by one unfamiliar with Afghanistan and one who is an Indian. Sirdar Ikbal Ali Shah?"[85] But Howland's was a private note on his own copy; the newspapers and their public took the autobiography at face value, echoing as it did the mood of social revolution. Still, behind the scenes, a few colonial officials did harbor suspicions. After the *Daily Mail* journalist Roland Wild published his own book on Bacha-i Saqao's uprising (Wild had been in Kabul during the preceding months), several British officials exchanged letters asking whether Wild really existed or whether he too was another of Ikbal's inventions.[86] It was becoming increasingly difficult for even expert readers to tell factual from forged information.

By the time *My Life: From Brigand to King* was published, Ikbal had invented two more pseudonyms: Bahloal Dana and Ibn Amjed. Meaning "son of Amjad" in Arabic, the latter contained a reference to his father, Nawwab Amjad Ali Shah. With this new nom de plume, Ikbal wrote a short story, "The Food of Paradise."[87] Trying his hand at fiction proper, he also set himself up as a reviewer of novels—and an opinionated one at that. "You cannot write human stories in a boiled shirt," he told readers of The Bookman. "English fiction is suffering from the boiled-shirt type of author."[88] But in the aftermath of Evelyn Waugh's widely imitated Vile Bodies, he certainly had a point when he observed that an "Oxford drawl confronts you in six out of seven English novels."[89]

Ikbal was convinced he could do better. He was no boiled-shirt type. He was Syed Abdullah, the son of the frontier. He was John Grant, intrepid explorer. He was Bacha-i Saqao, the Brigand King. And as he became a short story writer for the Evening Standard, he was now a teller of manly tales to bored London commuters. Soon one of his yarns was republished in The Standard's Book of Best Short Stories, alongside some of the era's most eminent stylists.[90] Peter Fleming, the then-better-known brother of Ian, offered a modernist story of drinks and revenge at the Stupor Mundi Studios in New York. Agatha Christie's rival Dorothy L. Sayers contributed a cunning capture-by-hair-dye ending to a dastardly criminal plot. The politically conscious Francis Brett Young was represented by a pitiful tale of refugees in Tunis. And Sirdar Ikbal Ali Shah supplied "The Sheik, the Sun and the Sack," in which kidnapping met high-jinks on camelback across Syria.[91] Reviving the persona of his travel writings, Ikbal was back in his Lawrence of Arabia get-up, riding dromedaries and commanding Bedouin. The narrator—an Afghan who partway through the story decided he is actually an Iranian Kurd—mocked and cursed the locals incessantly, calling them "desert Arabs" and "duffers" and denigrating one of them with the N-word.[92] With vile insults, lofty prose, and archaic dialogue, the tale was all yells and exclamation marks.[93]

Next Ikbal took up film reviewing, scrutinizing Otis Skinner's performance in Kismet for Film Weekly. Although the American actor had played the role for twenty years on Broadway, Ikbal concluded that he still couldn't do a proper Arab: he was merely as convincing an "Oriental" as could ever be feigned by a Westerner.[94] Not that

other actors weren't trying, since several other Eastern-themed stories had lately been made into films. The American pseudo-Afghan
Achmed Abdullah had written the screenplay for a film version of his
novel *The Thief of Baghdad*, which was a hit for Douglas Fairbanks
playing the light-fingered hero, Ahmed. Meanwhile the British novelist James Hilton was earning a fortune from his *Lost Horizon*, the
movie version of which made a household name of the fantasy mountain utopia of Shangri-La that Hilton invented. Although he left the
exact location of Shangri-La unclear, Hilton set the opening scenes
of his novel in the Afghan borderlands of British India, playing on
the region's mysterious reputation, in an echo of Rudyard Kipling's
The Man Who Would Be King.[95] In 1933 Frank Capra directed the
film version of *Lost Horizon*, to huge box office success.

Ikbal eyed a new opportunity here. While a younger generation
of artistically ambitious Indian Muslims were turning their student
years in Britain into modernist Urdu novels, such as Sajjad Zaheer's
Landan ki Ek Raat (One Night in London), Ikbal set to work on
a made-for-the-movies potboiler called *Afridi Gold*.[96] Published in
1934, it was the kind of novel that George Orwell called a "good
bad book." Like Orwell's own preferred good bad books—Austin
Freeman's *Eye of Osiris* and Guy Boothby's Tibetan thriller *Dr.
Nikola*—Ikbal's *Afridi Gold* satisfied Orwell's criteria of "an unin-
tentionally ludicrous book, full of preposterous melodramatic epi-
sodes" by which the reader might nonetheless be "amused or excited
or even moved."[97]

It was the story of Colonel Challenger of the India Medical Service, and of his adventurous daughter, who escapes her boarding
school to follow him to Afghanistan on his quest for the hidden gold
of the Afridi tribe. Ikbal had learned from watching films the importance of a strong female character, a potential leading lady. The
daughter, for all her pluck and spirit, soon finds herself kidnapped
by wild tribesmen, a hallmark of Ikbal's fiction. But they can't cage
her for long—she outwits them, blows up their village with dynamite, and escapes. And of course, she falls in love. Ikbal must have

been delighted when a reviewer described the novel as being "full of snap and sentiment" and "in the best film fashion."[98] Unfortunately, the movie moguls in Los Angeles didn't agree.

The great game of imperial politics soon called Ikbal back. In 1934 war broke out between the young state of Saudi Arabia and neighboring Yemen. Ikbal promptly wrote to the BBC's talks director on the notepaper of the National Liberal Club, offering to clarify for listeners not only what the war was about but also the beliefs of the Wahhabis.[99] Since the Royal Navy had been drawn into the war after rescuing Indian merchants from the besieged port of Hodeida, he also offered to elucidate the implications for "British Moslems."[100] It was apparently the first time he had used this phrase, its mention marking the emergence of a new political constituency. For by the mid-1930s, as the center and periphery of the empire increasingly converged, there were more Muslims in Britain to whom the state media needed to respond.

In March 1935, Ikbal and Elizabeth were among some two hundred such Muslims who gathered to celebrate the festival of Eid al-Fitr at the Woking Mosque with high-ranking British converts, Indian Muslims, and representatives of several other countries. In those imperial decades before mass labor migration, Islam was an elite religion in Britain, at least outside the dockyard districts that housed Muslim sailors. Among those present at the festive gathering were Lady Abdul Qadir, Lord Rowland Headley El Farooq, Sir Omar Stewart Rankin, Lady Rankin, the Egyptian chargé d'affaires, and a representative from London's Saudi Arabian legation. Addressed as "the Sardarina Shah," Elizabeth had come a long way since she was plain Miss Mackenzie, and blended right in.

That summer Ikbal also attended a reception at a new mosque in Southwest London, where over a hundred guests and worshippers squeezed in.[101] They included Sir Andrew Ryan, British consul to Jeddah, and Sir Telford Waugh, former consul to Istanbul (about whose book *Turkey: Yesterday, Today and Tomorrow* someone once quipped "Sounds like Boxing Day!"). They were gathered to celebrate the guest of honor, the Crown Prince of Saudi Arabia. Then in June the following year, Ikbal attended the celebration of the Prophet's birthday at the Portman Rooms on London's Baker Street, where the hundreds of gathered faithful included Indians, Iranians, Egyptians, Turks, Arabs, and Britons.[102]

By now, the Foreign Office estimated that there were also around eleven thousand converts in England, though the true number was probably considerably less than half that.[103] Even so, converts made up a sizable proportion of Britain's Muslim population, lending a British cultural—and certainly social—flavor to such occasions as converts adapted the basic requirements of the faith to their own familiar customs. Part of the appeal of Islam was that, through Indian imperial loyalists and aristocratic converts, it could be seen as entirely consistent with patriotic Britishness. Thus the Baker Street fête was hosted by the Muslim Society in Great Britain, whose president was Lady Khalida Buchanan-Hamilton, wife of the kilted Scottish convert Sir Abdullah Archibald Hamilton and a relative of Lord Curzon, the former viceroy of India.

Amid this growing Muslim presence in Britain, the BBC perceived there was an audience for a radio talk by Ikbal on "The Feast of Ramadan."[104] It was aired twice, at teatime. But when Ikbal offered another talk, this time for the recently inaugurated Empire Service, on the political scene in Saudi Arabia, the BBC sought advice from the Colonial Office. There Ikbal's letter triggered a flurry of communications with both the India Office (the script should be "carefully examined by an expert") and the Foreign Office (which did "not much like the idea").[105] Eventually J.C.S. Macgregor, the director of the BBC's Empire Service, turned down Ikbal's offer.[106] As it turned out, Ikbal was soon back on the airwaves with a talk for the Empire Service about the prime minister of Afghanistan, Mohammad Hashim Khan, who was visiting London on his way home from Berlin, where he had been cultivating contacts with Germany's new Nazi government.[107] As a result, hundreds of German advisers would soon arrive in Kabul.[108] Since Ikbal was known to support the regime

in Afghanistan via his writings in praise of the late king Nadir Shah
(who was Mohammad Hashim Khan's elder brother), he persuaded
the BBC to allow him to broadcast anonymously as "a fellow countryman" of the visiting Afghan premier.[109]

Besides the Empire Service, other new cultural initiatives were
responding to the unraveling international order of the mid-1930s.
Officials from the Foreign Office had recently established the British
Committee for Relations with Other Countries as a tool of cultural
diplomacy, aimed at countering the spread of fascism in regions on
the fringe of British influence. In September 1936, its cumbersome
giveaway name was abbreviated to the British Council. Within weeks,
Ikbal was calling its offices to introduce himself, and six months
later was writing to ask its director to support the foundation of
an Anglo-Islamic Society, explaining that he was the Afghan author
of twenty-eight books on "Oriental Lore."[110] Describing his long
career dedicated to bringing about an "atmosphere of friendliness"
between the Islamic world and the British Empire, he expressed hope
that such an Anglo-Islamic Society might bind Muslims to British
values. It was an agenda perfectly matched to the aims of the British
Council, which would soon dispatch dozens of young graduates to
Turkey, then to Cairo, ostensibly to teach English but primarily to
counter the growing influence of Nazi propaganda.[111]

The council's secretary-general, Lieutenant-Colonel Charles
Bridge, wrote to the India Office to ask advice about Ikbal. In reply
he was told that he "has written a good deal about Afghanistan, and
represents himself to be a subject of that country, where, I believe, he
has never been."[112] Still, the official replied, it might be worth meeting Ikbal to "ascertain in more detail what his scheme is." But the
Foreign Office urged more caution, on the grounds that Ikbal's "only
visible activity lately has been the publication of laudatory and inaccurate articles about the present Afghan régime."[113] Bridge heeded
the advice and turned Ikbal down.

Ikbal nonetheless kept himself busy, to say the least. In the following two years, leading up to the outbreak of World War II, he pub-

lished half a dozen new books. He ventured into new (and unknown) pastures in *Nepal: Home of the Gods*.[114] He then returned to familiar territory in *Modern Afghanistan*, which drew on his work for the Afghan embassy in London to provide a pro-regime account of recent history, emphasizing Afghanistan's inexorable path toward progress under the regal iron fist of its current rulers.[115] (He dedicated the book to Field Marshal Sirdar Shah Wali, the power behind the throne and brother of the assassinated king Nadir Shah, who had also been born in India and whom Ikbal likely met when Wali was ambassador in London.)[116] Next came a biographical compendium about Atatürk, Gandhi, and Ibn Saud whom, in a favorite phrase, he dubbed *The Controlling Minds of Asia*.[117] There were two more spiritual anthologies, including *The Spirit of the East*, a statement of his dualist vision of a materialist West and spiritual East, published by the same American press that that year reissued Lawrence's *Seven Pillars of Wisdom*.[118] Then, a few months before the outbreak of war, one of Ikbal's works finally reached the bookstores of the Middle East when his flattering biography of King Fu'ad of Egypt appeared in an Arabic translation issued by Cairo's government press.[119]

Back in Ikbal's household, that fearful season of 1939 wasn't all spent praising princes and pondering metaphysics. As Messerschmitts hovered on the horizon, his twenty-year-old daughter Amina wrote *Tiger of the Frontier*, reimagining the bedtime stories her father had told her by promising readers the "hair-raising adventures" of an Afghan chief called Shair Khan.[120]

Meanwhile Ikbal made another attempt to work for the British Council, or rather its more shadowy sibling, the Vansittart Committee for the Co-ordination of British Publicity Abroad. Newly established in a belated response to German and Italian shortwave radio propaganda, its mission was to project British soft power overseas through radio and other media. With around a dozen broadcasts already under his belt, Ikbal proposed that the committee employ him as an unofficial advisor on the "Oriental mentality."[121] When asked how this might work, he explained the offense caused by such films

as the recent *Lives of a Bengal Lancer,* which featured a scene where
an Afghan Muslim was splashed with polluting pig's blood for putting out the eyes of an English spy. (Ironically, the Oscar-nominated
screenplay, which had an Oxford-educated Afghan prince for the
villain, was co-written by the pseudo-Afghan American author
Achmed Abdullah.) By contrast, Ikbal suggested how cinema could
be deployed differently, not least in a way that would "avoid offending opinion" among Muslims.[122] Burnishing his credentials, he also
mentioned that he was an intimate of the Grand Mufti of Jerusalem,
Hajj Amin al-Husseini, who had become the most prominent Arab
critic of British policies in Palestine.[123] Whether Ikbal knew it or not,
the grand mufti had already established contact with Britain's enemies in Nazi Germany.

   As the propaganda war began to take shape in 1939, an internal memo at the India Office suggested that Ikbal "might be worth
considering" to produce "material and articles for publication in
Arab countries."[124] But between different departments, the creaking
bureaucracy of empire was slow in responding, and the British were
by no means the only players of this latest dangerous game. By the
time spring arrived, Ikbal, displeased by what he took as another
rejection and despite his patriotic overtures to the Vansittart Committee, accepted an unexpected invitation to give lectures in Mussolini's Italy. He was already known there through his writings,
albeit not always positively: sitting in his Italian prison cell earlier in
the decade, the Marxist theorist Antonio Gramsci had jotted sarcas-
tic comments in his notebook about Ikbal's ideas on Islam's potential to modernize.[125] But the opinions of Communists like Gramsci
hardly mattered now, for Ikbal had been invited to Rome by the Istituto per l'Oriente, the country's leading Middle Eastern research
center, which had succumbed to the patronage of ruling fascists. On
the apt date of April 1 he lectured via a translator to the *istituto*'s
assembled members, addressing the topic of "Cultural Movements
in the World of Islam Today" and basking in the appreciation of
his strategically rejuvenated importance.[126] Over the following days,

he met with representatives of Mussolini's government, who took a lively interest in what he told them about India's Muslims, their culture, conditions, and politics, as well as about the rebellious tribes of the Afghan frontier.

Just as it had been twenty years earlier during the Third Anglo-Afghan War, when Ikbal had written to Prime Minister Lloyd George, and just as it had been a hundred years earlier, when his ancestor Jan Fishan Khan had chosen to side with the British, the Afghan frontier remained one of the most vulnerable corners of the entire British Empire. By June, the Italian ambassador to Kabul, Pietro Quaroni, was plotting to rouse the frontier tribes to rebellion, to use Italian and German agents to depose Afghanistan's young pro-British king Zahir Shah, and to replace him with the pro-Axis former ruler Amanullah, who was conveniently exiled in Rome.[127] As Quaroni secretly laid his plans in Kabul, Ikbal sat in the Italian sunshine sending letters to officials in London that hinted that the Germans were also now courting him. But the stakes of the game were escalating rapidly. By the time he returned to London a few weeks later, Nazi sympathizers were being arrested there under the emergency laws of the new Defence Regulations.

Chapter Six

PROPAGANDIST

This patriotism was the more remarkable, in that
he had schooled himself, as he believed, to put his
"heavenly citizenship" above all earthly duties.

—Edmund Gosse, *Father and Son*

NO SOONER HAD IKBAL ARRIVED BACK IN LONDON THAN
he was summoned to the palatial headquarters of the India Office,
a short walk from Downing Street. His recent travels were having
the not entirely unintended consequence of making officialdom take
more notice of him, since in Rome he had been watched closely by
British spies. Yet Ikbal kept his aristocratic cool as Alec Joyce, the
India Office press officer, put him through a gentle grilling about his
activities in Italy. Joyce was adept at handling these subtle interro-
gations, particularly with intellectuals and writers. It had not been
long since he vetted the avowedly anti-imperialist George Orwell
about his motivations for applying for a position at the influential
Indian newspaper *The Pioneer*, for which Ikbal previously worked
as a freelancer.[1] But Ikbal was a tactician too, and throughout the
interview, he remained exasperatingly vague about his movements
in Rome, declining to name the people and organizations he had met
with.[2] In his report, Joyce described him as "noticeably less frank"
than in earlier meetings, suspecting he might have been "commissioned by Italian sources" and even might be accepting money to
write articles that put over the fascist position.[3] Indeed, Joyce added,
"quite casually on leaving, he happened to mention that he had the

right of free travel on German and Italian railways for assisting in travel propaganda."[4]

When they met again the following month, Ikbal announced that he was indeed writing Urdu articles for Indian newspapers based in Punjab and Calcutta, one of which bore the disconcerting title *Inqilab*, or "Revolution."[5] This was, he added nonchalantly, a result of his trip to Italy, whose officials had taken a gratifyingly "considerable interest" in what he could tell them about Indian affairs, particularly about Muslim opinion in India.[6] He also mentioned that he had listened with keen interest to Italy's overseas radio broadcasts, which in a "convincing manner" and "perfect Urdu" had criticized British policies toward the Muslims of both India and the Middle East.[7]

In those last months before the war, the Italians' Radio Bari broadcasts (which went out in seven languages including Arabic and Urdu) had become particularly worrisome to British officials. Italian agents had already distributed vast numbers of free or cheap radio sets among the Arabs, many with tuning dials fixed to the Radio Bari frequency, on which day after day the stirring sounds of Verdi alternated with invented or exaggerated reports of British crimes against Muslims. In response, the BBC had hastily initiated Arabic radio programming of its own, which in 1938 became its first foreign-language service, including lectures on Arab history, Quran recitations, and even a performance of Sufi chants by Yemeni sailors in the Welsh capital of Cardiff. As Ikbal coolly informed Joyce about the high quality of the Radio Bari broadcasts, it seemed as though he was taunting the man from the India Office that had so often turned down his requests for employment. The British government's fears about him seemed to be confirmed, at the worst possible moment. A week after Ikbal's meeting with Joyce, Italy signed the Pact of Steel with Germany.

When Ikbal met Alec Joyce again, he voiced his keen disappointment that neither the India Office, nor the Foreign Office, nor the British Council had taken up his earlier offers to help with "propaganda work" in the Middle East.[8] Before going to Rome, he had wanted to help the British, he opined, but as a struggling writer, he faced financial circumstances that forced him to accept offers of lecture and journalism work "on behalf of certain foreign organizations." As a result of accepting such "foreign" offers, he concluded, he was regrettably now unable to write "from a pro-British angle."[9] Alarmed, Joyce realized this was checkmate. It was May 1939: the stakes were too high to leave Ikbal roaming Europe as a propaganda pen-for-hire. Joyce recommended that he be found work, and fast.

As a result, Ikbal was promptly put in contact with Stewart Perowne, who had spent most of the preceding decade in Jerusalem, first as head of education in the Palestine Government Education Service, then as assistant district commissioner for Galilee. In the process, he had learned fluent Arabic and was appointed to the BBC's new Arabic Service. On their first meeting, Ikbal proposed to Perowne a series of programs about the condition of Muslims in Britain, which he suggested was an ideal topic to counter Italian propaganda about British persecution of Muslims.[10] Hinting that he had other irons in the fire, he told Perowne that arrangements had better be made soon.

The strategy of keeping up the pressure worked. Perowne contacted the BBC's Middle East program organizer, Evelyn Paxton, an Oxford graduate who had worked as a university professor in Egypt, where his keen interest in Arabic literature had led him to translate the autobiography of Egyptian modernist Taha Hussein.[11] Such proximity to the new Arab intelligentsia made Paxton the perfect figure to counter the Axis outreach to those same figures of influence. Having been appointed to the BBC only a few months earlier, Paxton in turn appointed Ikbal as one of his first scriptwriters. The arrangement was that Ikbal would write the scripts in English and submit them to Paxton, who would pass them on to advisers to check both their factual accuracy and their political slant. Only if a script passed muster would it be translated into Arabic and broadcast under Ikbal's name. That final part—the legitimacy lent by a Muslim name—was the most important element of all.

Over the two months leading up to Britain's declaration of war in September 1939, Ikbal wrote seven talks about the conditions of the different Muslim communities who lived in the British Isles. The literary quality of his scripts wasn't a matter of concern. Only a few years earlier, the BBC's founding director-general, Lord Reith, had sardonically assured listeners that "the programmes will neither be very interesting nor very good." Instead, the problem with Ikbal's scripts, Paxton found, was that his aristocratic prejudices slipped into them in ways that were counterproductive to the BBC's strategy for Middle Eastern outreach. They painted a "very disagreeable picture" of Britain's working-class Arabs (mainly families of Yemeni sailors who had settled around South Shields and Cardiff), whom Ikbal declared were notorious for their criminality.[12] Paxton contacted local police to check on this and learned it was untrue. Nor, as Ikbal also claimed, were these British Yemenis lapsed Muslims who were unable to recite the Quran (though Paxton's investigators did concede that they recited it with "a pronounced English accent").[13] As a result, Paxton had to inform Ikbal it was "impossible" to broadcast so scornful a talk to Arab audiences abroad. It was hardly a good start, and problems were soon found with his other talks too. Ikbal agreed to "re-condition" them, then work on others about Turkey, Iran, and India—and of course, Afghanistan.[14]

As soon as Prime Minister Neville Chamberlain announced that Britain was at war, Ikbal, despite his brief dalliance with Italian fascists, wrote to the secretary of state for India to pledge his loyalty to the empire.[15] There was no room now for the casual displays of ambivalence of a few months earlier. The empire was "so dear to my heart," he declared, that being unable to serve it made his life mentally "intolerable."[16] For he could be of great service "moulding Moslem public opinion" into a direction that favored Britain's empire.[17] Twenty years on, it was an echo of his letter to Lloyd George, a reprisal of his opening move in the great game.

Radio grew in importance during the war as Britain's nascent television programming closed down. The outbreak of war also had implications for Ikbal's domestic life. Realizing the danger of living in Belmont, close to the chemical factories of Mitcham, he moved the family a few miles north to Vineyard Hill Road in Wimbledon Park, on the outer edge of London.[18] He also had to think of other risks for his three sons—Omar, Idries, and Osman—who were now seventeen, fifteen, and thirteen. Having seen the fate of the Indian soldiers at the Brighton military hospital twenty years earlier, Ikbal hoped that keeping them in school might help them stay out of the war. But keeping the boys out of the war work also meant they could be of no financial help to the family. During the last summer of peacetime, he had arranged for a small local company, the Mitcham Printing Works, to reprint the publicity materials for his magic lantern lectures.[19] Branding him "The World-Famous Oriental Lecturer," the leaflets advertised his illustrated talks on "Persia Today," "Turkey Old and New," and "Mecca: The Cradle of Islam."

With Britain suddenly at war, though, romantic tales of exotic places were the last thing on people's minds, and families were all too aware that their husbands and sons might soon be fighting in such faraway lands. That the governments of Persia, Turkey, and Afghanistan were known to be close to Nazi Germany hardly helped the appeal of Ikbal's lectures, while the threat of air raids raised fears about gathering in lecture halls. For a while such gatherings were even banned. Once again Ikbal was struggling. While the BBC work would help, so far Paxton had committed to only seven talks, several of which he was unhappy with. Looking elsewhere, Ikbal wrote repeatedly to Miss Wade at the BBC's Empire Service proposing talks on the happiness of His Britannic Majesty's Muslim subjects.[20] Soon tiring of his repeated entreaties, she reminded him that she had his details on file, so he should save himself "the trouble of constant communication with us." Please, she entreated, "leave it to us to make the first approach."[21]

Just as he reached this latest financial low point, Ikbal received a telegram from India. His father, Nawwab Amjad Ali Shah, had died, leaving Ikbal heir to the political pension that the colonial government had long paid for the family's loyalty. At the start of December, as the war was gathering pace across the empire, Ikbal wrote a long letter to the under secretary of state for India recounting his financial difficulties.[22] What he was requesting was more complex than the simple continuation of his father's pension. He wanted it commuted into a lump sum based on a calculation of twenty years of future payments.

Over the next four months, as the complications of war kept escalating, the India Office in London and the Government of India in Delhi exchanged letters, reports, and encrypted telegrams about Ikbal's financial affairs. Noting that such pensions were paid "on condition of loyal behavior and active service in times of trouble or disorder," but still responding to the frantic tone of Ikbal's letters, the government eventually concluded that his family "should continue to have a monthly income to ensure them against starvation."[23] But the government would not commute the pension into a lump sum.[24] Ikbal was disappointed; it wasn't enough; and in October 1940, as bombs rained down on London during the first onslaught of the Blitz, he wrote to Alec Joyce at the India Office asking him to intervene.[25] Joyce had more pressing business to attend to.

Meanwhile Evelyn Paxton, Ikbal's erstwhile patron at the BBC Arabic Service, had become more wary after being advised of factual inaccuracies in Ikbal's latest talks. Reluctantly, he agreed to commission one more talk, this time on how the Nizam of Hyderabad was a Muslim ally of the British. (Indeed, "Faithful Ally of the British Government" was one of the Nizam's formal titles.) But when Paxton received the script, he despaired. It was brimming with Ikbal's obsessions with the exotic and incredible. Mindful of his Middle Eastern audience, he sent the script back to Ikbal with an accompanying letter. "Perhaps you will also agree," he asked, "that even if the story of the [Nizam's female] Amazon Guards is true, it might not be well received in some quarters where this talk will presumably be heard."[26]

Sensing that his time with Paxton was up, Ikbal wrote two letters to Sir Malcolm Darling, the first congratulating him on his appointment as head of the BBC's Indian Service, and the second offering his assistance.[27] He also wrote again to Joyce at the India Office, whom only months earlier he had taunted about his offers of work from the Italians, and to Lawrence Rushbrook Williams, his former controller in India.[28] He included with his letters a translation of a Persian "letter of credence" stating that he was a correspondent for the Afghan government newspaper *Islah*, whose editor had asked him to write a weekly newsletter. Since *Islah* was Afghanistan's main paper, a London newsletter would be a good way of feeding appropriate stories to the people of Kabul—and to the German and Italian agents gathered there.

Remembering Ikbal from their counterpropaganda work together fifteen years earlier in India, Rushbrook Williams took him up on his offer. He had spent many years in the subcontinent, forming a school of Mughal history at the University of Allahabad and writing a book on Babur, the founder of the Mughal Empire. With his sympathy for the old Muslim aristocracy, in April 1940 Rushbrook Williams recruited Ikbal for the wartime Ministry of Information. He had recently been made director of its Near and Middle East Section, based at the University of London's newly built Senate House—a forbiddingly fascistic-looking tower that, a few years later, would inspire Graham Greene's novel *The Ministry of Fear*, then reappear as the Ministry of Truth in George Orwell's *Nineteen Eighty-Four*. Ikbal's task there was to write articles for newspapers in India and anywhere in the Muslim world where Britain needed friends. In return, he would be paid the substantial monthly salary of fifty pounds.[29]

By now the Battle of Britain was in full swing. One night in early July, Ikbal's rented house in Wimbledon Park was hit during an air raid. Fortunately, the family were safely in a bomb shelter and no one was hurt, but Ikbal lost his library and most of the family's possessions. It was devastating for the family, not least after a life of perpetually moving house. For Ikbal, nothing now remained of his former life but the stories he told—and so too for his eldest sons, Omar and Idries, whose sole inheritance would be those fantastical tales.

The family had no choice but to make a fresh start and leave suburban London for pastures new. Through his connections with Rushbrook Williams, a fellow of All Souls College, Ikbal moved his family to the center of Oxford, where he was provided with a flat at 4 Turl Street, a narrow lane running adjacent to Balliol—that most prestigious of Oxford colleges that, back in the 1880s, had been the first to open its doors to the brightest and best-connected students from India. Perhaps Ikbal remembered the lecture given at his school in India by Syed Mahdi Hussain Bilgrami, who had explained the arcane social customs of Oxford University to would-be Muslim attendees. Be that as it may, Ikbal belatedly arrived in the city of dreaming spires, if not quite at its university.

There were by then many Indian students at Oxford, as well as the celebrated Indian professor Sarvepalli Radhakrishnan, who held the prestigious Spalding Chair of Eastern Religion and Ethics. Though Ikbal had no position at the university as such, the flat he was given on Turl Street did belong to Lincoln College, which rented out the ground floor as shops and the upstairs as accommodation to students. By the time Ikbal moved to Oxford, the college rented rooms to people involved in war work.[30] Its proximity to the Bodleian Library would allow him to work on the constant flow of articles he now had to write for the Ministry of Information. And just around the corner, there was a good school for his two younger sons to attend, Idries, now sixteen, and young Osman: the City of Oxford High School.[31] Though it lacked the prestige of the private prep schools where most university dons sent their boys—the high school was generally considered more "town" than "gown"—it was a respectable institution nonetheless. Housed in a Victorian Gothic building opposite the medieval Bodleian Library, the school also happened to be the alma mater of T. E. Lawrence.[32] On the main stairway up which Ikbal's sons would now walk every day stood a bust of "Lawrence of Arabia," and the main assembly hall featured a bronze bas-relief that Churchill had unveiled back in 1936.

Wearing brown blazers, caps, and striped ties with red and blue piping, every morning Idries and Osman made the short walk to school. Their lessons with the sons of the city's shopkeepers were not altogether easy, as there were no other Indian, or biracial, boys at the school.[33] An Indian Muslim called Mohamad Masud was briefly a guest of the headmaster while they were there though.[34] A student at Oxford's St. John's College, Masud showed the schoolboys what Indians were capable of, for he was a member of the Indian Civil Service, the "heaven-born" rulers of the Raj, which Ikbal had once tried to join.[35] But judging by his school reports, Idries didn't look likely to follow in Masud's footsteps. His best position was twenty-sixth in a class of twenty-nine.[36] On one report card, his form master tersely remarked of the sirdar's son, "Has attended at intervals. Superior attitude?"

Idries had at least one good excuse for his absences though: during his time at the high school, he fell seriously ill and was rushed into hospital for surgery.[37] Anxious for their son's recovery, Elizabeth and Ikbal nervously waited for news. After the surgery, a doctor told them that their son had failed to come out of anesthesia and was now in a coma. Having studied medicine for a couple of years, Ikbal was convinced it was down to the physicians' incompetence. He marched across Oxford to fetch his revolver from the family flat. Returning to the hospital, he summoned all the doctors together, then waved his gun steadily in front of them as he announced that, until he heard news of his son's recovery, he would lie in hiding outside the hospital and shoot the lot of them dead if they dared to go home. Turning on his heel, he marched outside and settled himself surreptitiously in the bushes beside the entrance. It was as though the frontiersman Syed Abdullah had leaped off the page into life, and effectively so. Elizabeth, who remained by her son's bedside, watched in wonder as the hospital room suddenly filled with medics bearing oxygen cylinders, resuscitation apparatus, and syringes of adrenalin. Idries was brought back from the dead in no time. At least that was how he later liked to recount the episode.[38]

The domestic drama resolved, Ikbal was immediately back at his borrowed desk. Penning articles that aided the war effort, as often as not, his new war work required him to write for British readers as propaganda on the home front. His most prominent outlet was *The Contemporary Review,* for which he had often written on political matters in the past. It was no longer the cutting-edge periodical it had been in its Victorian heyday, when its essays by T. H. Huxley and Matthew Arnold reshaped the mind of the nation through their debates about science and culture, but it was still influential among the educated classes. The main thrust of Ikbal's articles was to justify the government's policies in the Middle East.[39] Other articles he wrote—"Italy Versus Islam," ". . . And They Scorn Nazism"— made the argument from the other side, by showing how Islam was inherently incompatible with fascism.[40] At the same time, he wrote for newspapers in India. It was strategically important work, not least as the Raj's halfhearted entry into the information war had previously seen it appoint the donnishly inept historian Percival Spear as director of counterpropaganda against Goebbels's formidable Nazi lie factory.[41]

Ikbal was also writing regularly for *The Straits Times* and the *Singapore Free Press and Mercantile Advertiser,* the most prominent newspapers in British-ruled Malaya, which had large and influential Muslim readerships. Writing about the support lent by their fellow Muslims in Egypt and depicting the British Empire as the protector of Muslim rights, he encouraged Malays to support the war effort too by evoking, in the words of one article's title, "The Happy Lot of the Average Muslim in Britain."[42] With an eye to the semi-independent sultanates of Southeast Asia, where Japan was now sending its own propagandists, he advised that the best interests of small Muslim nations lay in supporting Britain. In other newspapers, he brought Islam squarely into the war effort by depicting the British Empire's struggle as a spiritual mission entirely in line with the teachings of the Prophet, whose biography he had previously written.[43] But Ikbal also had more troubling qualifications. Though it was over a decade since he had met Grand Mufti Amin al-Husseini in Jerusalem, it was only four years since he had bragged to the India Office of being his "intimate." That was now a dubious, not to say ironic, association, given that the grand mufti was being employed in Berlin as Ikbal's dark counterpart, spreading Nazi propaganda in Arabic by radio. Such broadcasts were beginning to have their effect too. As the Nazis seized the early upper hand in the war, Afghanistan's economy minister also visited Berlin to support the idea of a Berlin-Baghdad-Kabul axis.[44] If the plan succeeded, it would place Germany on the borders of British India.

Meanwhile, back in Britain, mosques were becoming an important new part of the great geopolitical game. After decades of delays, in August 1940 the East London Mosque was finally finished: three terraced houses had been converted to provide space for a prayer hall and hostel for Bengali sailors based in the nearby dockyards. The mosque's chairman was Sir Hassan Suhrawardy, a prominent Bengali who had been Calcutta University's first Muslim vice-chancellor. Ikbal now wrote to him suggesting that the mosque's cultural center should present Islam as a positive "social force" in Britain.[45]

While in Washington, D.C., authors turned diplomatic attachés such as Roald Dahl and Ian Fleming tried to drum up American support for Britain, from Oxford Ikbal tried to persuade Britain's Muslims that the United States was their ally too, deploying his powers of persuasion as a speaker at the Oxford Majlis.[46] Established in 1896 after the Oxford Union had refused entry to Indians, the Majlis was the university's second-oldest student society and the gathering place of Britain's rising Indian intelligentsia. While most members were Indians, the Sunday evening debates also attracted Egyptians, Malays, and other Muslims studying at Oxford. Now the Majlis's help was needed to save the empire that had brought them there. Accordingly, one February evening at 8:15, members gathered to hear Ikbal argue for the incompatibility of Islam with fascism.[47] He delivered a similar lecture on why the empire was good for Muslims at the Woking Mosque, which he complemented with a lecture for the Royal Empire Society, chaired by Professor Rushbrook Williams himself, about the Muslim affinity with liberal democracy.[48]

Such work for Rushbrook Williams's Ministry of Information went well through the remainder of 1941, but by the following spring, signs began to appear that Ikbal's employers were less than happy. Throughout the time he was working for the Ministry of Information, he had been constantly writing to Alec Joyce at the India Office. But since their tense interview on his return from Rome, Joyce had never trusted him. He refused to follow Rushbrook Williams's lead with further offers of work. The more standoffish Joyce became, the more personable Ikbal was in return. In one message, Ikbal confided that he thought he had seen Joyce rushing to catch the 4:40 train from Paddington Station and had run after him along the platform.[49] But he couldn't be sure it was him, he went on, for the gentleman at Paddington had been dressed in a flat cap and rainproofs, whereas he knew the dapper Mr. Joyce always dressed with pristine elegance. In another letter, he recounted his pleasure at hearing Joyce's voice on the radio, praising his admirable style of delivery.[50] But when after a barrage of letters Joyce eventually agreed to a meeting, Ikbal changed his mind and sent a last-minute telegram to cancel.[51]

When Ikbal was informed that his employment (and £50 monthly salary) with the Ministry of Information would end in October 1942, he decided to bypass Joyce and write directly to Leopold Amery, the secretary of state for India and Burma, requesting work from the India Office instead.[52] Drawing on his new Oxford connections, he declared he was writing at the recommendation of the Beit Professor of Colonial History at All Souls College concerning affairs of the "utmost importance." The Beit bait piqued Amery's interest, for he too was an Oxford history don and a fellow of All Souls. Even though Amery was rather busy now that the Japanese had invaded British

Burma and captured its capital, Rangoon, he called on six of his senior staff at the India Office to investigate who this self-proclaimed Afghan was and what his mysterious letter might possibly entail.

"For some time," began the ensuing report, setting the tone for what followed, "Sirdar Ikbal Ali Shah has been pestering us to subsidize him to put over the Muslim point of view through the Press."[53] For the past two years, it went on, he had been paid well to write articles on behalf of the Ministry of Information, but since his contract had been terminated, of late Ikbal had "made himself more of a nuisance than usual." He had even hinted that, since he was no longer on the ministry's payroll, he "might be forced to 'go over to Congress' "—to join the champions of Indian independence, including once-trusted Cambridge graduates like Subhas Chandra Bose, who were now aiding the Japanese assault on Burma that Amery was desperately trying to rebuff.[54] Despite this "hint of political blackmail," the report concluded, the authority lent by his Muslim name at the head of his publications was simply too important to lose.[55] Ikbal had to be placated.

After the Rome episode, the India Office was greatly alarmed at the thought of cutting him loose, stating that "the thought of his drifting into further financial difficulties is disturbing."[56] Considering Ikbal "a potential source of trouble if his energies are not being otherwise occupied," officials recommended he be found further employment.[57] Soon even the secretary of state for India was warning of Ikbal's threats to start "stirring up trouble" among the Muslims of London's East End if he wasn't found work to replace his lost salary.[58] Leopold Amery sent a personal letter to placate Ikbal, who sent a masterfully laconic reply to the effect that, as busy as he was writing books, he would consider giving up his leisure hours for the war effort.[59] But there were conditions, he added: there were only certain roles he was interested in. He would be willing to edit a new journal, which should be called *New Asia* and have a monthly print run of a thousand copies. He would be willing to undertake an official, government-sponsored public relations tour of India or the

United States. He would be willing to accept the position advertised in *The Times* that week with the BBC's Monitoring Service at Caversham Park, an aristocratic mansion in the countryside south of Oxford that had recently been requisitioned for the war effort. Or he would be willing to act as the official Muslim adviser to the BBC.

Ikbal was already well known at the BBC, whose senior staff now resisted the India Office's request to make more use of him, on the grounds that he could "not speak Arabic at any rate sufficiently well to deliver his talks himself." They had to be translated and broadcast by colleagues, which was expensive, time-consuming, and inefficient.[60] Furthermore, continued Paxton of the Arabic Service, "his name carries little weight in India, where he is regarded as a charlatan," unsurprising given that "he looks like an Indian edition of George Arliss and acts like the Old Man of the Sea." (A comically upper-class actor, Arliss was the first Briton to win an Oscar, playing the Victorian prime minister Benjamin Disraeli.) The coup de grâce came with Paxton's attack on the credibility of Ikbal's all-important name: "Oh! And incidentally, he is neither a Sirdar nor a Shah to the best of my belief."[61] Though this was not strictly true—Ikbal was an aristocratic sirdar albeit not a shah in anything but name—it was blowback from decades of imposture.

After Ikbal's attempts to gain work with the BBC Turkish Service were likewise rejected, he turned his attention again to its Indian Service with a letter inviting himself to visit its director, Sir Malcolm Darling, at his home in Evesham.[62] This time his persuasion tactics worked, and soon he was writing scripts for Urdu broadcasts, though as with his earlier talks for the Arabic Service, he wrote the scripts in English, then sent them for translation by BBC staff.[63] One of his talk topics was on Central Asia, aimed at showing how Muslims were worse off under Soviet than under British rule.[64] Another depicted the happy conditions of the Muslims of Cardiff.[65] A talk on Ramadan in England contrasted the religious freedoms of Muslims in Britain with those in the Soviet Union.[66] He was soon writing scripts about every community of Muslims from the Bosnians of

Yugoslavia to the exiled Tatars of Japan, presenting himself as the spokesman of Muslims worldwide, all of whose best interests lay with the British Empire.

Credentialized by the media, his work with the BBC introduced him to leading imperial historians and Orientalists, including A. J. Arberry, the Cambridge author of many works on the Sufis; R. B. Serjeant, a fellow alumnus of Edinburgh University and specialist on Yemen; and Lawrence Elwell-Sutton, a graduate of London's School of Oriental Studies and a future professor of Persian at Edinburgh, who would shortly head out to Iran to combat Nazi propaganda there.[67] These connections helped Ikbal revive his quest for formal qualifications as, now in his forties, he registered at St. Catherine's College, Oxford, for a postgraduate degree-by-dissertation.[68] His academic adviser was the septuagenarian Sir Richard Burn, Knight Commander of the Star of India and retiree of the elite Indian Civil Service, who had edited the volume on the Mughal Empire for the *Cambridge History of India.*[69]

Still, as it had twenty years earlier, the need for paid work distracted Ikbal from his studies. As the war continued, he began to demand from the BBC a higher fee of ten guineas, even for short broadcasts.[70] (Preferred by gentlemen, the guinea was worth five percent more than the common pound.) Reluctantly, Sir Malcolm Darling agreed, explaining to disgruntled colleagues that the higher wages were "justified by the Sirdar's scarcity value."[71] After all, his seal of Muslim approval on British policies was all important. Even so, Ikbal's relentless flow of letters with proposals for more work continued to cause headaches. As one internal memo noted, "he is prepared to sell articles on any and every subject."[72] To make matters worse, he was said to have become "the most awful nuisance," and "staff had to be warned about him several times."[73]

Still he continued his epistolary assault. After Paxton ceased taking his news items for the Arabic Service, Ikbal wrote to offer a short story entitled "The Secret of the Shrine," revealing to Paxton that his Arab nom de plume was Sheikh Ahmad Abdullah.[74] The latter was a crafty combination of Syed Abdullah, the name Elizabeth had given him in her fictionalized memoir of their early married years, and Achmed Abdullah, the pseudonym of the successful American pulp author Alexander Romanoff who had actually written "The Secret of the Shrine"—a story about a Muslim pilgrimage place whose visitors were shown to be fools when the shrine was revealed as the grave of a donkey. Paxton saw immediately that the story wasn't even Ikbal's to begin with. (It had appeared in London's *Evening Standard* a decade earlier.)[75] The lack of originality aside, Paxton also knew he couldn't broadcast it.[76] Half of his Muslim audience would already know it as a popular folktale, and the other half would "think we were making fun of their religious beliefs."[77] That was hardly propaganda's purpose.

Just when Ikbal's options with the BBC were running dry, he received a letter from Eric Blair, a name that a less aristocratic author might have recognized. Although in their ensuing correspondence Ikbal betrayed no signs of acknowledging Blair as a fellow author, he was better known as George Orwell. He had joined the BBC as a talks assistant for the Empire Service back in August 1941, but by the time he wrote to Ikbal, he was working as a talks producer for the Indian Service, where his immediate superior was Zulfiqar Ali Bukhari, a pioneering Muslim broadcaster from Lahore with whom Ikbal had already cultivated a relationship. As Eastern Services director, Professor Rushbrook Williams, Ikbal's long-standing supporter, was in overall charge of Orwell (and had first employed Ikbal as an anti-Bolshevik propagandist in India). Orwell was fully aware of the irony of his own role, not least after writing disdainfully about propaganda in *Homage to Catalonia*, his memoir of the Spanish Civil War. "Here I am in the BBC, less than five years after writing [*Homage*]," he confessed in a letter to a friend, "I suppose sooner or later we all write our own epitaphs."[78] Yet Orwell tried his best not to betray his socialist and anti-imperialist principles at the BBC, as he was tasked with bringing fellow writers to the airwaves to present Indian listeners with a noncolonial vision of British culture. He invited the novelist E. M. Forster, who was admired by many Indian intellectuals for his *A Passage to India*—itself dedicated to Forster's dear Indian friend, Syed Ross Masood, who also happened to be a graduate of Ikbal's alma mater, the Muhammadan Anglo-Oriental College, and of Oxford, where Ikbal was finally following him.

If it all looked rather cliquey, then it was after all the Empire Service. So as a critic turned custodian of empire, Orwell tried to promote fellow leftists whenever possible. Among Indian writers, his most regular guest had till lately been Mulk Raj Anand, a Marxist Cambridge graduate whose novels *Untouchable* and *Coolie* championed India's lower classes; Anand now interviewed British workers to assure Indian listeners that the struggle against Nazism was supported by fellow proletarians.[79] Like Ikbal, Anand had previously written for *The New Criterion*, whose editor T. S. Eliot also became one of Orwell's regular guests. But the publication of Anand's vehemently antiwar novel *Across the Black Waters*, followed by the arrival of Luftwaffe bombers over the factory towns of Britain, caused Anand to fall from favor among leftists like Orwell.[80] Enter Ikbal to help fill in the gap left by Anand's departure.

Amid the international struggle for the airwaves, Orwell's broadcast interviews added a subtle element of pro-British propaganda. Just as the BBC's Arabic Service was competing with Italy's Radio Bari, by 1942 the BBC Indian Service was facing competition from Subhas Chandra Bose's Radio Azad Hind (Radio Free India), which broadcast from Germany (then Singapore and Rangoon after they fell to Japan). Bose had escaped house arrest in India to reach Berlin via Kabul, where the Italian ambassador Quaroni had equipped him with an Italian passport. That Bose had considerable success in rallying Muslims and Hindus against the British cause exposed the overstatements in Ikbal's reports on Muslim loyalty, since India's independence movement had already been in full swing before the outbreak of war. Across the fighting frequencies, Bose mocked the BBC as the "Bluff and Bluster Corporation."

Back in London, Orwell was all too aware of the outright lies being broadcast on Axis radio stations, confiding in his diary, after hearing an Italian news report about supposed food shortages in London, that "we are all drowning in filth."[81] But he was determined not to stoop so low. *Through Eastern Eyes*, his regular program for the Indian Service, would explore ideas and inspire people, even unite them. But it would not knowingly deceive them.

It was regarding a section of this show that Orwell wrote to ask Ikbal to speak about what democracy meant for him as a Muslim.[82] The following Monday the two of them met for the first time over lunch in London. Since the program's title, *Through Eastern Eyes*, was more or less Ikbal's literary motto, he persuaded Orwell to accept several additional talks as well. One would be about the opening of a new mosque in Cardiff to replace one recently hit by a German bomb. That would be followed by a series of Ikbal's reports from the House of Commons, showing how committed Muslims really were to the workings of democracy.[83] Part of the arrangement was that Ikbal would read on air himself: the identity of who spoke was at least as important as what was said. Apart from the official monthly message of Sir Muhammad Azizul Haque, India's high commissioner to London, Ikbal's was the only Muslim voice on the Indian Service. Little wonder he now took to describing himself as "Muslim advisor to the BBC."[84]

However, having addressed Ikbal in his letters as plain "Mr.," the great social leveler Orwell soon found himself facing a lesson on proper form. On his headed notepaper, Ikbal replied that, while he had overlooked the matter when they first met, in future he should only be addressed as "Sirdar."[85] After Orwell obliged, Ikbal accepted a flow of new commissions, including a talk about the opening of a Turkish cultural center in London via a ceremony arranged by the British Council.[86] The latter had already invested in London's recently established Islamic Cultural Centre, though it did query its funding when the sole annual event of the center's intercultural pro-

gram turned out to be a visit to a margarine factory.[87] Undeterred,
the work of cultural diplomacy marched bravely on.

When it came to dealing with Ikbal, though, the usual financial
issues returned. Orwell had to make special arrangements to ensure
that his "Muslim advisor" received payment checks in less than
a week, sending colleagues an urgent memo that Ikbal was "very
reluctant to do anything until he knows what he will be paid" and
that he must on all occasions be addressed by his title "Sirdar."[88] But
a weekly check wasn't good enough, and Ikbal next insisted on being
paid in cash at his local Barclays Bank.[89] Fortunately, Orwell sympathized with the economic privations that writers were facing during
the war. "One can't write books with this nightmare going on," he
had written recently to a friend, since so many authors were forced
to live "a rather hand-to-mouth existence."[90]

However, Ikbal's financial demands weren't the only issue troubling his new patron. A little more than a month after he began
working with Orwell, it was discovered that Ikbal had sold the same
script about Muslims in America both to the BBC's Indian Service
and to its Near East Service. Having perused the two scripts personally, Sir Malcolm Darling declared the only differences were "two or
three verbal changes of not the slightest importance," adding that the
content, in any case, seemed "purest sophistry."[91] Ikbal was undeterred and a few weeks later wrote to offer Sir Malcolm a talk on
the Prophet Muhammad's birthday celebrations, which would prove
Britain's "liberal treatment" of the empire's many Muslims.[92] Playing on the name of Orwell's radio show *Through Eastern Eyes*, Ikbal
also proposed a book with the title *War Time Britain as an Oriental Sees It*, but the publishing house he contacted decided against
it.[93] Perhaps it feared that Ikbal might reveal too much of his recent
experience of cultural diplomacy as propaganda. But then, the war
was producing other dubious works about the smoke and mirrors of
imperial intelligence, including a novel set in wartime Cairo with the
implausible name *Nile Green*.[94]

Despite the difficulties of dealing with Ikbal, Orwell still needed him and so called on him again in March 1943 for a new series called *Books That Changed the World*. Its first season had focused on European works, particularly those whose views needed to be countered. R. R. Desai, an Indian postgraduate student at Cambridge, performed the desired demolition of *Mein Kampf*, though Orwell quietly made sure that *Das Kapital* was discussed more sympathetically by the left-wing economist Krishnarao Shelvankar.[95] Now for the second season, Orwell decided the focus should turn to books from Asia, and the first on the list was the Quran. Feeling he needed a Muslim to discuss it, Orwell turned first to the diplomat Sir Muhammad Azizul Haque, but he was about to sail to Bombay.[96] Desperate for a Muslim voice, Orwell turned back to Ikbal, who had in any case just reoffered his services.[97] Mindful of his own materialist principles, and of Ikbal's penchant for mystification, Orwell insisted that the talk should focus on the Quran's "social and political influence."[98]

When Orwell's offer came in, Ikbal agreed with alacrity, since just before Christmas, he had contacted Brigadier-General C.R.P. Winser about his latest financial "difficulty in educating his children."[99] It would be a script of only thirteen and a half minutes, but it might open the door to further opportunities.[100] Excited by the BBC's increased interest in Islam, Ikbal also offered a "passion play," in which he would dramatize the birth of the Prophet Muhammad to coincide with the annual Mawlid festival, but the proposal was turned down.[101] It was so hard to tell if Muslim listeners would be appeased or offended. A play carried too much risk; better to stick with scripture.

Ikbal's lecture on how the Quran had changed the world would be his last contribution to the propaganda war of the airwaves. Judging by his absence from a list of hundreds of "best books" (including several on India) recommended by Orwell, the latter seems to have held a poor opinion of him as a writer.[102] Nonetheless, the war economy offered many other openings for men of ideas, and Ikbal was

never short of those. He contacted Rushbrook Williams with a plan
to adapt the BBC Armed Forces program *The Brains Trust* into the
story of a war cabinet of Indian geniuses who could think the empire
to victory.[103] When that idea fell by the wayside, he claimed to be
heading a new Islamic Society based at National Liberal Club.[104]

After the long-awaited East London Mosque finally opened, he
had tried to gain influence over its accompanying Islamic Cultural
Centre, but the wealthy and well-connected Indian Muslims who
ran the center kept him at a safe distance—in Oxford.[105] In response,
he now established his own Islamic Research Bureau, appointing
himself as director.[106] Far from the dingy Whitechapel district of the
Islamic Cultural Centre, Ikbal's bureau boasted a swankier mailing
address in Eccleston Square, within London's most exclusive post-
code, SW1. The aim of his bureau was to present an anti-Congress
view of India; or it would be, he suggested to the India Office, if only
they would support it.

It was far from clear to anyone that this Islamic Research Bureau
really existed. Even the all-seeing eye of the Ministry of Information was unsure. After all, many new Muslim organizations were
being founded, some with clearly political aims, and the India Office
was struggling to keep track of them. There was also Ikbal's Muslim Culture League, which on its embossed notepaper, declared its
mission to be "the Interpretation of Islamic Culture for the Friendship of Mankind," but the careful reader might have noticed that,
despite claiming a deposed Turkish prince on its board of directors,
it was headquartered at Ikbal's grace-and-favor flat above the shops
on Oxford's Turl Street.[107]

His Islamic Research Bureau was a similarly paper enterprise, but
it was one the Ministry of Information was forced to take seriously.
Insofar as Ikbal's bureau might offset the influence of Gandhi and
Nehru's Indian National Congress, the India Office felt it might be
useful. Realizing this full well, Ikbal quietly suggested to officials
that prior to publicly associating himself with "Muslim League propaganda," he would need from the Ministry of Information an injec-

tion of funds.[108] This latest plan also involved the India Office buying large numbers of copies of a pamphlet that championed dividing India and founding a new country called Pakistan; the colonial government would distribute the pamphlet and effectively act as Ikbal's publisher. But on reading it, the India Office realized that the purpose of his Islamic Research Bureau was to promote the agenda of the Muslim League. It regarded the pamphlet as "a strongly partisan view of a highly controversial subject." So, mindful of appearing biased in favor of the League versus the Congress, the India Office now tried to distance itself from Ikbal.[109] He in turn decided to publish it himself under a new pseudonym.[110]

Calls for India's independence stoked Ikbal's long-standing concerns that Hindus would dominate the subcontinent, fears he shared with other Indian Muslims of his class. Led by urbane, British-educated lawyers like Muhammad Ali Jinnah, the movement for the creation of Pakistan out of part of British India offered the opportunity to realize the ideals of the Islamic modernists with whom he had long sympathized. Less than ten years earlier, the name "Pakistan" hadn't even existed, having been invented only in 1932 by an Indian student at Cambridge, Choudhry Rahmat Ali. A decade later, as the war brought India's independence closer to reality, the idea of Pakistan seemed a recipe for a Muslim utopia that would be as liberal as it was democratic.

Even if it was not, a separate nation for India's Muslims would rescue them from the perils of Hindu majority rule in an independent India where they would forever be outnumbered. Ikbal's imaginary homeland was moving again, this time to a country whose birth would mark the start of the postcolonial age. He hoped that the creation of the "Land of the Pure" (the meaning of the name *Pak-istan*) would bring into political reality the revival of Eastern spirituality he had proposed, off and on, for decades. After writing an article for *The Contemporary Review*, he published a booklet, *Pakistan: A Plan for India*, that tried to persuade both British and Indian politicians that the dreamers meant business.[111] In India the booklet met with a highly critical response among supporters of Gandhi and Nehru's Indian National Congress Party, who vehemently opposed the plan to cut the subcontinent in two, but in London the *Times Literary Supplement* praised how "the Sirdar neatly counters the Hindu Press repudiation of the Muslim claim to be a separate nation."[112]

Putting his Afghan dreams behind him, by 1944 Ikbal increasingly associated himself with inventing this new country. He hoped to use his connections at the India Office to reprint his pro-Pakistan pamphlet as a statement of British governmental opinion in support of a country that neither existed nor had even a draft constitution. Yet alongside politicos like Jinnah, such famous poets as Sir Muhammad Iqbal, those unacknowledged legislators of the world, were also now joining the Pakistan movement. As Ikbal saw it, only one point was still missing from the necessary triangle of proficiencies: a publicist—such as himself. So in July he wrote to Sir Feroz Khan Noon, an Oxford-educated imperial diplomat who worked with Churchill's war council as an adviser on India's Muslims.[113] Having met Sir Feroz via the East London Mosque, Ikbal tried to persuade him—and through him Jinnah, the leader of the Pakistan movement—of the necessity of establishing a Muslim News Agency in London. Its purpose, he explained, would be to counter the propaganda of Gandhi and the Congress Party by presenting the pro-Pakistan point of view to the British and American press. The agency, he continued, should certainly be sited somewhere central and prominent—say, Fleet Street or the Strand—and he himself could serve as its director.[114] It would cost Jinnah's Muslim League a mere £1,500 per year.[115]

To make Pakistan a reality would require more than the cooperation of Indian Muslims, though. So Ikbal wrote to Alec Joyce at the India Office, explaining that the movement would need some influential Englishmen as "cooperators," and to that end, he was having long discussions with leading intellectuals at Oxford and Cambridge.[116] For the plan to build the "Land of the Pure" required help from sympathetic Britons to outmaneuver the attempts by the Congress Party to prevent the required division of India. By the autumn of 1944, he was warning Joyce that the Congress had set up secret societies all over Britain, with branches active from Glasgow to Newcastle, Manchester and Birmingham.[117] Ikbal was now apparently spying on these British-based activists working for the Congress.[118] By raising funds from Indian petty traders and shop-keepers, and devoting themselves to "disloyal preaching," Congress secret agents, he maintained, were undermining the war effort in a way that would soon "harm the British in their own country."[119] To win the war, he hinted to Joyce, the British had better back the bid to build Pakistan.

Despite such dramatic claims, the India Office remained uncon-vinced, concluding that Ikbal's talk of secret societies was "just fan-tastic."[120] In response, Ikbal decided to bypass imperial officialdom by dealing more directly with the Congress threat, writing to Jinnah with warnings about Congress propaganda in Britain.[121] He signed the letter as president of the London Islamic Society, one of the paper organizations for which he had failed to find any funding. The warn-ings finally did lead Jinnah to establish a direct outlet for the Paki-stan cause in London. But that outlet was neither the Muslim News Agency that Ikbal had proposed, nor his London Islamic Society. Jinnah already had enough power struggles on his hands without handing over London to this mysterious erstwhile Afghan. Instead, Jinnah established a formal London branch of his own political party, the Muslim League. As its head, he appointed Muhammad Abbas Ali, a Bengali activist and law student, who used his flat on Tavistock Square as the unofficial embassy of Pakistan—a country that as yet didn't exist.[122]

Although by now it was unclear whose cause Ikbal was support-ing, the Ministry of Information continued to pay him to write for them. But after Hitler committed suicide in April 1945, Ikbal was given a mere month's notice.[123] As the war ended with the old world torn in pieces, an uncertain new age dawned over the empire on which the sun supposedly never set. The following March, Reuters reported that "a red banner on a white background proclaimed 'Pakistan or Muslim Revolt' as 5,000 people gathered in [Trafalgar] Square" to celebrate the first Pakistan Day—though still the country didn't exist.[124] But in July the landslide election victory of Britain's Labour Party promised to hasten India's independence—and with it the founding of Pakistan.

The end of empire—the loss of India especially—meant that Muslim affairs would soon no longer be a British concern. Exhausted by six years of struggle, British society was turning in on itself: soon everything from theater to healthcare would focus on the national, not the imperial. Meanwhile, positions of high influence in their liberated homelands awaited educated overseas Indians and soon-to-be Pakistanis. London began to empty out of its well-connected Indians. Though shorn of his war work, and shunned by the leaders of the Pakistan movement, Ikbal remained behind, with nowhere to go.

His blurred identities had been far easier to maintain in the world of empire than they would be in the new postcolonial order. Almost overnight, he became irrelevant. Whether as propagandist, informant, or entertainer, there was no longer a great game for him to play. In a Britain that was sloughing off its Indian empire faster than was decently possible, no one was interested any longer in Ikbal's expertise. Nor, with soldiers returning from the jungles of Burma and the deserts of Libya, was there any public appetite for trivial tales of Eastern adventure. Empire's sons finally turned their backs on foreign lands for stories about their home firesides. No publisher now cared for Ikbal's words; no propagandist had a use for his name.

For a quarter-century, dozens of books and hundreds of articles had sprung from Ikbal's frantically tapping typewriter, but now it fell into silence. He would write no more books about Islam or Afghanistan, about the high stakes of imperial politics or the harmony of East and West. The readers he had written for since his student days had no further interest in him, and soon there would be no empire for him to write for. The London-educated lawyers Nehru and Jinnah were about to assume leadership of India and Pakistan. And so as the architects of Pakistan rejected him, Ikbal returned to the bosom of the dying empire. Before the world into which he was born disappeared forever, he perhaps just had time for one final adventure. He was turning fifty, the age when a man looks to his legacy, and his son Idries was turning twenty-one. They would travel together on his last imperial hurrah. It was time to pass on the torch.

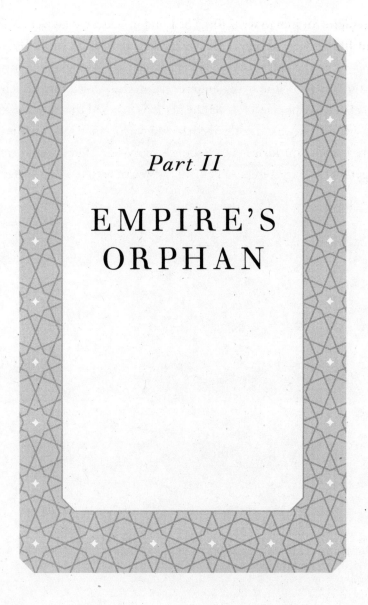

Part II

EMPIRE'S ORPHAN

Chapter Seven

APPRENTICE

... my Father's spiritual factotum ... a most efficient
coadjutor.

—Edmund Gosse, *Father and Son*

GROWING UP AS THE SON OF A SCOTTISH MOTHER AND AN
Afghan (or was that an Indian?) father had surely not been easy for
Idries Shah.[1] With his Mediterranean complexion, his difference
from the other boys at school was also inscribed in his name. Moreover, he was the son of a man with multiple names, each one claiming a different identity, and of a mother who had been Elizabeth
Mackenzie, Saira Elizabeth Shah, and Morag Murray Abdullah.
Even Idries's own name was sometimes in doubt. Back in November 1942, a few months after he left Oxford High School, his father
had made the first of many attempts to find work for him, offering his son's talents to the BBC's Overseas Service.[2] Idries's first job
almost evaporated before it began though, because Ikbal had given
the BBC a stage name for him, saying he was called Mansor. After
much back and forth, the booking manager prepared another contract, this time for "Edris Ali Shah," which as a result of the varied
English spellings of Muslim names would be Idries's legal and for a
while also his professional name.[3]

The contract was to perform in *Chief Scout*, a radio play being
produced for the African Service by an Oxford graduate who had
earlier co-created *The Brains Trust* and who had the implausibly

apt but real name, Douglas Cleverdon. He gave Idries his first job: to act, to impersonate, to play out the imperial fantasies of others. Considering that ordinary British soldiers at war were being paid about three shillings a day, at four pounds and four shillings for two days' work, the eighteen-year-old Idries was doing well. Especially as Ikbal managed to persuade the BBC to pay himself a chaperone fee of another two pounds and two shillings.[4]

While the war raged, Idries had spent his days, little acting roles aside, helping his father's propaganda work. From the Muslims of Bosnia to their co-religionists in China, the range of subjects on which Ikbal was writing articles kept his son busy compiling notes in Oxford's Bodleian Library. Although Idries didn't go to university—there were always financial struggles at home, and he in any case performed poorly at the City of Oxford High School—he learned enough about the adjacent university to pass for an undergraduate. The education he received under his father's tutelage involved no definable discipline, but it did introduce him to all manner of arcane texts that never crossed the desks of actual Oxford students. Reading about so many Muslim subjects would enable him to speak with vicarious familiarity about everywhere from Turkey to Java, to quote mystical poems translated by Orientalists, to recount anecdotes gleaned from a hundred travelogues—and to do it all in an Oxonian accent, the voice of credible authority.

In 1943, aged nineteen, Idries made his first foray into the literary world with a short article in the establishment magazine *The Spectator*.[5] Drawing on his abundant reading for his father, it sketched the economic and political motives behind calls for Pan-Arab unity coming from Egypt and Saudi Arabia. The following year he was writing about Turkey for *Chambers's Journal*, the Scottish outlet that had published one of his father's first articles a quarter-century earlier.[6] Championing the great secularizer Kemal Atatürk, just as Ikbal had in his biography of him, Idries recounted the progress of modernizing reforms and women's emancipation in a piece of politically informed if picturesque journalism (digressions on Angora cats notwithstanding). In September 1944 he reappeared in *The Spectator* with a letter to the editor about the deadlock between the Congress Party and the Muslim League over the division of India after independence.[7]

Just as, a century earlier, the high politics of empire had afforded an opening into the media for Ikbal, the international politics of decolonization now did the same for Idries. Within two months of the German surrender in 1945, he published an article in *War Illustrated* about fighting in the Levant as France tried to reassert control over its mandates in Syria and Lebanon.[8] The sober piece of analysis explained the recent founding of the Arab League in Cairo and the respective positions of the British and French governments as they struggled to come to terms with the new reality of Arab nationalism. With no academic degree to open a path into a profession, Idries was following in his father's footsteps. Mirroring Ikbal's war work by writing on the tangible forces of Muslim politics, he planned to make his name as an expert on the new great games of the postwar order. But the serious twenty-year-old would not indulge in his father's occult fantasies; nor would he descend into the shadowy realms of the propagandist.

Like other young men of his generation, both Indian and British, Idries took India's coming independence to be inevitable. But he was no nationalist. His father's son, in the summer of 1945 he declared his allegiance to the dying empire by becoming a fellow of the Royal Empire Society, to which his father had lectured during the war. When it was founded as the Colonial Society back in 1868, its aims had been to provide a meeting place for people interested in Indian affairs, but since then it had become a vehicle for imperial loyalism with a membership that stretched from Singapore to Canada. In the year Idries applied for membership, the society's magazine *United Empire* had its aims emblazoned on the cover of every issue: "To promote the preservation of a permanent union between the Mother Country and all other parts of the Empire: and to maintain the power and best traditions of the Empire."[9]

On September 12, 1945, Idries's membership was approved after being proposed by Sir Frank Brown, honorary secretary of the East India Association and a long-term supporter of educational projects, particularly for Muslims.[10] With a long career as a journalist for the *Bombay Gazette* and *The Indian*, of which he had been editor, Sir Frank knew Ikbal and sympathized with his son's journalistic ambitions. So Idries was elected as companion, first class, of the Royal Empire Society, while his younger brother Osman was approved as companion, third class.[11] Soon to be orphaned by the empire's unraveling, the family was not only continuing the loyalist politics of their ancestors but being cannily pragmatic too. Aside from his first two years of childhood in India, Idries had spent his life in a Britain which would soon shed responsibility for Indians. His brothers Osman and Omar were in the same boat. Ikbal could see that if his sons were to remain in Britain, it would be wise to distinguish them from the Indian and Pakistani nationalists who were now sailing home. For Ikbal's children, England was home.

Before Idries had the time to publish further articles that would anchor his career in London, he was drawn into his father's last imperial adventure. It would not take him to the Middle East he had recently written about, still less to the Afghanistan he had been told about since childhood. Instead, their destination would be Argentina and Uruguay. Having spent the war behind his desk, Ikbal was now finally asked to venture into the field, though not as a soldier or a spy, nor even as a roving propagandist. He was to sail to Buenos Aires as a meat inspector, accompanied by his son as secretary.

For now at least—the autumn of 1945—Britain still ruled over India, Malaya, and parts of the Middle East, and it did so through an army that included tens of thousands of Muslims, many still stationed overseas. Every army marches on its stomach, but in the case of the British Empire, what went into those stomachs was subject to varied ritual requirements. Different groups of Hindus needed food that didn't break caste taboos (and certainly not beef); for Muslims, meat (but not pork) had to be slaughtered according to halal rules.

During service in India, that had rarely been a problem, but the scale on which Muslim troops were deployed outside India during the war had made supplying halal meat very difficult. Muslim soldiers had often been given the same tinned ham rations as British soldiers. Ikbal was tasked with resolving this festering problem. Having put his typewriter to rest and been laid off by the Ministry of Information, he embarked on the path of action, with a commission from the Ministry of Food. His mission was to investigate a reliable supply from South America of canned halal beef.[12]

On December 19, 1945, Ikbal and Idries boarded the *Drina* from East London's bomb-battered dockyards.[13] Sailing with them were twenty-one other passengers, a mixed bunch of engineers, commercial agents, car mechanics, and the manager of a textile mill from Manchester.[14] Having listed himself on the passenger manifest as a "government official," Ikbal easily held his own in such company. The only passenger who was hard to handle was a retired diplomat, Sir Robert Michell, former ambassador to Chile, who discreetly dropped the "Sir" when he signed the manifest. But these other passengers were probably of little concern to Idries. After being raised on tales of his father's adventures, he was finally accompanying him on one of his missions. He had recently turned twenty-one; he was coming of age.

The place to which they were heading was terra incognita in more senses than one. It didn't matter to Ikbal that he knew nothing about South America, but it did matter that South America didn't know anything about him. No sooner had they disembarked than he contacted the *Buenos Aires Standard*, South America's most respected English newspaper, to announce their arrival. On January 8, the *Standard* repeated what Ikbal told its reporter:

> The Sirdar Ikbal Ali Shah, Oxford University research student and a noted authority on Oriental political history, arrived here yesterday on the Royal Mail liner "Drina." He was accompanied by his son, who is acting as his secretary. . . . He

expressed a keen desire to know this country, of which he had heard and read so much about. Spanish is one of the few modern languages he has never learned, but he hopes to speak it well before he returns to England.[15]

Over the next nine months, father and son made their way through Argentina then neighboring Uruguay. For Idries, the gray Atlantic had been no match for his father's tales of the resplendent East; nor would their journey involve the kinds of adventures Ikbal described in his travel books. There were no bandits lurking at each corner, and no dramatic escapes from kidnappers. Nor was Ikbal constantly reaching for his revolver (though he may have kept up his insults to locals). Instead, within a few days of arriving, he called at the offices of the British Council, introducing himself and his son to Sir Eugen Millington-Drake, the council's chief representative in South America.[16] An old Etonian and Oxford boating blue, Sir Eugen was captivated by the "tall, distinguished-looking man" who strolled into his office, and he took a special shine to Ikbal after he said he was "an exceptional cricketer" who, like Sir Eugen himself, had played for Oxford.[17]

But even though Sir Eugen was a senior diplomat—not least as a key player in the Battle of the River Plate, the first naval battle of the war that took place off the Uruguay coast—Ikbal refused to reveal the purpose of his journey. It was, he hinted mysteriously, "a mission directly under the India Office," which he was "not at liberty to reveal."[18] Since Ikbal had introduced himself with the title "professor," Sir Eugen tactfully changed the subject and proposed a lecture tour of the British Council's various institutes in the region. Gracefully but rather grandly, Ikbal turned down the offer. His secret duties were too important for such distractions.

Charmed though he was, Sir Eugen sensed something wasn't right, especially after he asked his guest when exactly he had played for Oxford. Stumbling for an answer, Ikbal had claimed the years 1933 to 1935, when he would clearly have already been approaching middle age.[19] When Ikbal and Idries left his office, Sir Eugen wrote to the British Council's London headquarters for corroboration about these mysterious visitors. His telegram triggered an epistolary explosion. After numerous notes were exchanged between the India Office, the Foreign Office, and the British Council, back in the southern hemisphere Sir Eugen was informed that the reason his visitors were being so "mysterious" was that their sole responsibility was "investigating the methods of killing employed in the South American slaughter houses."[20] Instead of admitting he was sent by the Ministry of Food—associated with the unglamorous tedium of food rationing—Ikbal had linked his "secret mission" with the more prestigious India Office. But by the time Sir Eugen found out, Ikbal and Idries had moved on to the destination of their hush-hush duties: the Anglo Meat Packing Plant in Fray Bentos.

A small Uruguayan town of twenty thousand inhabitants, Fray Bentos lay around two hundred miles upriver from Buenos Aires. A sprawling complex of nearly seven hundred acres, its British-owned meat factory included a vast slaughterhouse, where 1,600 cows and 6,400 lambs were butchered every day, before their meat was quickly canned and transferred to a warehouse on the banks of the Uruguay River. The killing and canning continued night and day. By the time Ikbal and Idries stepped off their steamboat, the war boom in canned corned beef had lured a workforce of more than five thousand to the town surrounded by jungle. But the stench of carcasses from the five-story slaughterhouse hung like an infernal miasma in the humid air. If Fray Bentos was hardly a diplomat-class destination, then, it was a strategically vital one, because during the war the Anglo Meat Packing Company had fed Britain's armies with over two hundred different meat products. For countless British soldiers, its nostalgically labeled "Hereford" corned beef had been the edible equivalent of the poems of *A Shropshire Lad*. Since not every imperial soldier was a Christian, Ikbal's mission was to assess whether the plant could ritually slaughter cows by hand. While his father discussed Arabic phrases with Argentine butchers, Idries stood by taking notes.

In March 1946—with the colonial Indian Army still needing feeding for another eighteen months before independence—Ikbal and Idries's month of meat-inspecting was over and they sailed downriver to Montevideo. With its fine Italianate buildings, Parisian boulevards, and statues of liberators on horseback, the little capital of Uruguay struck them as a place where they might spend some time. As the sun shone over its elegant avenues, the prospect of returning to a bombed-out Britain was far from enticing. Looking for opportunities, Ikbal led Idries to the royal embassy of the Netherlands and forced an introduction on the startled Dutch ambassador. Since the postwar Netherlands was facing problems in its own Asian colonies, Ikbal proposed a solution to their difficulties with the Muslims of Java. What was needed was a diplomatic intervention by "leading Indian co-religionists."[21] Actually, Ikbal suggested, he would be willing to go on such a mission himself. When the ambassador, Count Bentinck, mistook the name Sirdar Ikbal for "Sir Darikbal," Ikbal apparently saw no need to set him right. After all, it seemed an appropriate title for one of Britain's last imperial emissaries.

The costs of their hotels were mounting, though, and with their meat-slaughtering mission complete, London began inquiring about their return home. So on the basis of his links to Oxford's St. Catherine's College through the dissertation he was still meant to be writing, Ikbal decided to reach out to Uruguay's only university. Wandering around the late-nineteenth-century edifice, Ikbal and his son came to what looked like an important office. It belonged to Dr. Félipe Gil, secretary-general of the University of Montevideo. They knocked at the door. Fortunately, Dr. Gil could speak English, as a result of a recent stint in America, where he had spent time at Princeton.[22] Having admired the pseudo-Oxford quad in New Jersey, he was excited to meet two gentleman scholars from Oxford and eagerly introduced them to the university rector in his neighboring office. The timing seemed fortunate for all parties, since the rector, Don José Pedro Varela, was trying to raise the international standing of his university through affiliations with overseas dignitaries and scholars. That very summer Sir Eugen Millington-Drake of the British Council was to be awarded an honorary doctorate, and Don José was keen to organize public lectures by what he called *releventes personalidades.*[23] He must have listened keenly as Ikbal rattled off his résumé, including his self-bestowed title of professor.

For the past seventy years, Uruguay's intellectuals had been fighting a philosophical battle between positivist materialism and spiritualism.[24] Fortuitously, Rector Varela was less committed to materialism than were many of his colleagues, and he invited Ikbal to lecture on his suggested topic of the spiritual life of Islam. The following week Ikbal delivered his lecture in the large Salón de Actos Públicos. The university gazette described the event as an *"extraordinaria versación en temas de cultura y filosofía orientales."*[25] And extraordinary it was—the young Catholics of Montevideo had surely never heard of Dhu'l-Nun, or al-Ghazali, or Junayd of Baghdad, or any of the other great Sufis of distant times and places.[26] At his histrionic best, the former lantern slide lecturer revealed through his translator the secret doctrine of Hallaj, who had declared "I am the Truth! I am God!" ("YO SOY LA VERDAD! YO SOY DIOS!" boomed the translator's echo in turn.)[27] As hundreds of young people listened in wonder, Idries sat in the audience, learning.

Such was the success of the lecture that it convinced Rector Varela to appoint Professor Shah as the University of Montevideo's official representative to America, Europe, and Asia.[28] The appointment letter defined his assignment as being to encourage "effective cultural interchange."[29] The transatlantic telegraph cables were soon buzzing with diplomatic angst. At the Foreign Office in London, Sir Evelyn Shuckburgh (whose father, Sir John, had been the first official to entertain Ikbal's schemes back in 1919) heard of Ikbal's dealings with the university and half-admiringly pronounced that "the Sirdar 'pulled a fast one' at [the university's] expense."[30] However, when the India Office learned of Ikbal's politically fraught proposal to the Dutch ambassador, they were simply furious. "As he is accompanied only by his son, who acts as his secretary, he is hardly entitled to call himself the Head of a Mission," stated an official, adding in further clarification that "he is not in South America as a representative of the [India] Office and we are not pleased that he has been so describing himself."[31] There was more. "We certainly do not regard him as a representative of Moslem India," the India Office telegraphed categorically, adding for final good measure that "he would be a most unsuitable person to entrust with a mission to Java."[32] Ikbal's manager for his halal meat mission, Lieutenant-Colonel John Finlay of the Army Requirements Branch, was no less forthright: "This chap Iqbal [sic] Ali Shah is nothing if he is not enterprising. I want him back in this country as soon as possible."[33]

On October 17, 1946, father and son, their mission aborted, disembarked in London from the *Darro* of the Royal Mail Lines.[34] In the nine months they were away, much had changed in Britain. J. B. Priestley's novel *Three Men in New Suits* was voicing the optimism of the large majority who had voted the Labour Party to victory and established the welfare state. But for Ikbal and his son, it was a brave new world they faced on their return. Aside from Ikbal's roving commission from the University of Montevideo, they were both coming back unemployed amid a vast labor market of demobbed soldiers whom the new national politics pledged to prioritize.

They had not been home three days before Ikbal called Alec Joyce, his old contact at the India Office, saying he would like to "re-new our old association" over lunch at the National Liberal Club.[35] When Joyce showed no interest—the Labour government had pledged to be out of India in under a year, so the India Office was closing down— Ikbal phoned Professor Rushbrook Williams, hopeful of finding work.[36] Meanwhile Idries was planning his own career as an expert on all things Islamic, and soon after their return, he managed to place a two-page article on Persian carpets in *Chambers's Journal*.[37] While mostly factual, his aperçu of textile history emphasized what he called "Shah Carpets" and included a story "related in the East" about a prince and a weaver. It had the distinct ring of his father.

Tales of the East were all well and good, but after the endless sunshine of Montevideo, they had returned to England's coldest winter in three centuries. From early January, huge snowdrifts closed roads and railways, and domestic electricity was stripped back after coal deliveries couldn't reach power stations. As the snowfall continued, across Britain crops froze in the ground, stirring fears of famine. BBC radio broadcasts were restricted, with television suspended entirely, while magazines were ordered to cease publication and daily newspapers to reduce their size. The media that had fed Ikbal's family since his marriage to Elizabeth seemed suddenly on the verge of collapse. Britain, exhausted by war and sloughing off its empire with catastrophic haste, seemed to be finished.

At the end of January, Ikbal wrote to Sir Gordon Vereker, the British ambassador to Uruguay, with plans to return there with Idries.[38] Sir Gordon immediately cabled London in alarm, asking if "anything can be done to have this most unwelcome project nipped in the bud?"[39] Although the Foreign Office responded with alacrity, that didn't settle the ambassador's nerves.[40] In order to do so, the dwindling India Office agreed to place on official record that, if the British government should ever again "need expert advice by a Mohammadan on any 'hallaled' meat question in Uruguay," then the Foreign Office "would prefer that we did not re-employ Ali Shah."[41] Such was the diplomatic anxiety in Montevideo that the Foreign Office even looked into the dubious legality of blocking Ikbal's passport.[42] On contacting the Passport Office, they learned with consternation that Ikbal had grander plans than they realized: he had applied for a new passport that would be valid for travel not only to Uruguay but also to Saudi Arabia, Iraq, Turkey, Syria, the United States, and the whole of Europe.[43] The reason he supplied was his status as international representative of the University of Montevideo, which had appointed him Professor of Oriental Literature and Philosophy.[44] Learning of this, the British embassy in Montevideo launched its own investigation and contacted Dr. Félipe Gil.[45] Shocked to hear what Ikbal was planning (though no one was certain what that exactly was), Gil explained that Ikbal's vague letter of affiliation had been supplied only "at his own request."[46] Far from being a professor and overseas representative, "the Sirdar was, and is, in no way connected officially with the University."[47]

If the distant University of Montevideo was disowning him, back in Oxford, Ikbal had no intention of surrendering his self-bestowed professorship, which he now used to ask the BBC to broadcast his take on the impending birth of Pakistan from "an Indian Muslim point of view."[48] The head of the nationwide *Third Programme* replied that he was "interested to learn that you have now added a professorship to your other honours."[49] But two weeks later Charles Curran, future director-general of the BBC, tactfully wrote to decline Ikbal's offer due to the need for careful treatment of the situation in the subcontinent.[50] It was now just a week before India's, and Pakistan's, independence and the horrendous massacres of Partition were already underway: the new national frontiers would be baptized in the blood of millions. Moreover, in an article published that month, Ikbal was now making the case for carving two more nations from the ruins of British India, including another Muslim-ruled state based in Hyderabad.[51] But no one was listening, least of all the new rulers of independent India, who instead chose to invade Hyderabad with battle tanks inherited from the British.

As Ikbal was contemplating his retirement from literary and political affairs, another loyalist Afghan sirdar and erstwhile imperial subject was looking back on his life too. Under the title *Royals and Royal Mendicant*, the memoir that Sirdar Muhammad Abdul Kadir Effendi published that year described a life that closely echoed the main orchestrations of Ikbal's career.[52] The son of an Afghan ruler pensioned off by the British after the Second Anglo-Afghan War, Sirdar Muhammad had also opted for the literary life rather than the fighting ways of his forebears. But even though, back in 1922, he had been the first-ever Afghan to publish a novel, as Britain and India pulled away from each other, both of these loyal sirdars were about to be forgotten, and their literary lives along with them. Published by minor presses in Madras and Lahore, Effendi's novel and autobiography went unnoticed by readers in Britain.

Nor did the new postcolonial world that had just been born have any need for Ikbal's imperial expertise. It was time for the new generation. Fittingly, two weeks after Britain's handover of India, he tried to find a job for his son Idries with the Reuters news agency. Based on their vaguely commercial ventures in South America, Ikbal had already approached the British Board of Trade about a career for Idries, but they rejected the suggestion.[53] He next called on the Commonwealth Relations Office, asking them to intervene with either Reuters or one of the American news agencies in London, explaining that Idries had assisted him in preparing the many articles he had written for the Ministry of Information during the war, had done some freelance work of his own, and had published several letters in *The Spectator*.[54] Currently, he added, his son was conducting "historical research at Oxford" (the city serving as an ambiguous equivocation for the university).[55]

Reuters replied that they had "very much doubt" that they could find an "opening for the young man," though they agreed to peruse Idries's curriculum vitae.[56] Accustomed to employing Britain's brightest graduates, Reuters were apparently unconvinced by Idries's lack of qualifications, so Ikbal turned back to his old antagonist Alec Joyce, the press officer at the India Office, requesting a personal introduction for his son to the directors of other London news agencies.[57] Complaining that Ikbal had been "a nuisance to me for many years as a free-lance journalist," Joyce refused to have anything more to do with him: "I shall ignore his letters."[58]

Oxford's South Asian graduates were now heading off to take up high positions in India and Pakistan, but that was not an option for Idries. England was home, and he had anyway grown up considering himself Afghan, not Indian, still less a citizen of that new country called Pakistan. So, with no professional doors open to him in London, Karachi, or Delhi, Idries had to remain in the rented family flat on Turl Street, where he had little option but to continue helping his father.

With the end of the empire, Ikbal was turning away from the great game of politics to focus solely on occult and mystical matters. He continued to receive invitations for paid lectures, aided by his refusal to relinquish his title "professor" (whatever was being said in Montevideo). The title was useful in these changing times. The imperial hierarchy that had valued his title sirdar was gone, and independent India was stripping its inherited princes and aristocracy of their power (though their pensions would continue to be paid). Meanwhile social leveling, and the rise of the meritocracy, were creating a new hierarchy in which it was better to be a professor than a nobleman. By May 1948, Ikbal was lecturing on "Philosophy as a Key of Happiness" at Amsterdam's Indisch Instituut, whose public announcements identified him as a professor at the University of Montevideo.[59] He was becoming an early postwar purveyor of the fashion for Eastern wisdom, albeit as exported from Uruguay.

It was well timed. Those first years after the war were seeing a revival of the mystical themes that had fascinated the Western intelligentsia after the First World War, when T. S. Eliot had worked the Hindu *Upanishads* into *The Waste Land* back in 1922. Twenty years later, in *Four Quartets*, Eliot had turned to the *Bhagavad Gita*, the same work J. Robert Oppenheimer was to quote when he watched the first atomic fireball over the New Mexico desert: "Now I am become Death, the destroyer of worlds." As the war ended, Aldous Huxley had published *The Perennial Philosophy*, an anthology of Eastern and Western mystics compiled in an attempt to identify what he called the "highest common factor" in all the world's religions. In Islam, that factor was Sufism, he decided. Accordingly, Huxley's book was peppered with quotations from the medieval poems of Rumi, which he and other Western intellectuals were identifying as the quintessence of Islam.

The onset of the atomic age also led Huxley to write the novel

Ape and Essence, which began with the sentence: "It was the day of Gandhi's assassination."[60] Juxtaposing his embrace of Indian mysticism and pacifism with dystopian fears of the apocalypse, Huxley described a future after nuclear weapons had destroyed every trace of civilization. Meanwhile Orwell's *Nineteen Eighty-Four* described a different dystopian future, where the government controlled people's thoughts through a Ministry of Truth that was modeled on the wartime Ministry of Information where he and Ikbal had worked.

As political writers envisioned bleak destructive futures, Britain's mythologizers turned back toward magical pasts. In 1948, as Ikbal began his first lecture tour as a professor of Oriental philosophy, Robert Graves's *The White Goddess* gave birth to a new mythology for postwar Europeans whose forebears, he claimed, had worshipped a peaceful goddess before being enthralled by the male god of war. Then in 1949 the obscure former colonial servant Gerald Gardner published *High Magic's Aid*, in which he tried to recover Olde England's ancient religion by inventing a nativist past of stone circles and pentagrams.

Amid this magical revival, Ikbal turned away from Muslim topics to write a treatise on the occult, drawing on dozens of rare grimoires in the libraries of Oxford, London, and Paris, from which Idries, as his assistant, took notes. The resulting book—*Occultism: Its Theory and Practice*—focused mainly on Europe, especially Britain. For like Gardner's *High Magic's Aid*, it was a response to a nation turning in on itself, as well as to the huge public interest stirred by Graves's *The White Goddess*.

The topics of Ikbal's *Occultism* were many and marvelous: magical rings, witches' hexes, devilish apparitions in the guise of black dogs, infernal hierarchies, Witch-Finder General Matthew Hopkins, and the necromantic anecdotes of Benvenuto Cellini. As Ikbal wrote it all up, he used the voice of the objective describer: striking a sober tone was all the more important now that he was throwing in his lot with the lowbrow likes of novelist Dennis Wheatley, whose *The Haunting of Toby Jugg* was a recent bestseller.

By 1951 the postwar fascination with magic was given a legal boost in Britain when, amid much publicity, the Witchcraft Act of 1735 was replaced by the Fraudulent Mediums Act. So long as it was sincere, casting spells and worshipping horned gods was now entirely legal— and across the British Isles many people were keen to try their hand, or wand. Published the following year in response, Ikbal's book gave detailed instructions on how to perform dozens of different spells, whether for attracting the opposite sex or for gaining "advancement in social and economic fields" (much more like Ikbal).[61] Other chapters focused on demonology, the conjuring of spirits, and the alchemy he had briefly practiced in prewar suburbia. There were precise prescriptions of the mephitic paraphernalia that each spell required, with dozens of diagrams—magic squares and talismans, alchemical laboratories and inscriptions on wands—to guide the aspiring thaumaturge. Ikbal's old interests in "the East" had not disappeared entirely either. For there were sections on Arab and Hindu magic, and a few Indian books were cited, such as Swami Dayal's *Inder Jall*, whose Urdu Ikbal had learned back in his schooldays. In such subtle ways, the old culture of empire quietly seeped into the new national culture of the early 1950s.

All told, Ikbal's *Occultism: Its Theory and Practice* was a recipe book for the would-be magician that echoed Gerald Gardner's claim in *High Magic's Aid* that "the Magical Rituals are authentic" and derived "from Magical MSS in my possession."[62] By the time it was published, his son had learned much from helping him to prepare it, learning what it meant to be not only an author but also a self-publicist and self-declared authority. As Idries contemplated his own career, Britain's political concerns with Islam were fading into the imperial sunset. But the bright moon of magic was ascendant, and so as he reached his late twenties, while helping with his father's *Occultism,* Idries began researching his own first book.[63] It too would focus on magic, with many details in common with his father's tome. There would be sections on summoning spirits, on "devil-worshipping" Yazidis, on manuscripts preserved in Paris's Bibliothèque Nationale. Idries also borrowed his father's voice of objective description of the occult and his method of anthologizing material from many different sources. Yet he would have to outdo his father. His book had to be more ambitious, its scope more comprehensive than Ikbal's main focus on Europe. Instead, Idries determined that he would write the definitive study of the arcane traditions of Egypt, Babylon, China, Japan, India, Tibet, Arabia, Persia, and the Africa he designated "Ju-Ju Land."[64] He would spend five years researching it, supporting himself as best as he could.

When Ikbal began his writing career, he had been cut off by his father. But he treated his own son differently, opening whatever doors he could and taking him along on his travels, whether to Latin America or "the Orient," whose magic Idries was now researching. So in 1951, when *The Times*—which a quarter-century earlier had paid for Ikbal's scoop on the Mecca congress—agreed to a follow-up article on how the holy city had changed since 1926, Ikbal took twenty-seven-year-old Idries along with him.

Despite the tale of hard travel that Ikbal had told decades earlier in *Westward to Mecca*, he had been one of the first pilgrims to reach Mecca by car. By 1951 the pilgrimage had been made even easier by the advent of air travel, which now took father and son directly from London.[65] They arrived in July, two months ahead of the half-million Muslims who would come that year for the hajj.[66] Ikbal was pleased by what the Kingdom of Saudi Arabia had built with oil money since his last visit. Having complained decades earlier about the poor hygiene, hotels, and lack of cinemas, he was delighted with the comfortable accommodations and clean water.[67] In Riyadh, King Saud's officials arranged for father and son to stay in the royal guesthouse.[68] Though cinemas were still banned, the shops were piled high with American goods of the kind rarely glimpsed in still-rationed postwar Britain. Ikbal described not seeing a single old car during his visit, since only the newest models were in use.

In the days that followed, Idries attended his father's audience with King Ibn Saud and his senior Wahhabi clerics at the royal guesthouse.[69] Though Arabia's Sufi mystics had been suppressed by the Wahhabis—and magicians were subject to the death penalty—there was still much for Idries to learn during his weeks in the holy land of Islam. But it was also becoming time for him to grow out of his father's shadow. A year after their return from Mecca, he set out on his own Middle Eastern journey. He didn't share his father's former concerns with the great game of empire: in January 1952, just before his departure, the Egyptian nationalist Gamal Abdel Nasser had led a military coup that rang the death knell of British influence in the region. But the powers of the visible world were not Idries's concern. Already at work on his monumental study of magic, it was as an expert on the world's hidden forces that he planned to make his name. Yet becoming an authority on what he called "Oriental Magic" still required a degree of credentializing travel to that Orient, or at least some part of it. Consequently, just as Ikbal had journeyed through the Middle East to write his first book, *Westward to Mecca*, Idries set off on his own eastern *Wanderjahr*.

His itinerary began on the Thames Estuary aboard a sailing vessel that belonged to an English friend from his London gentleman's club,[70] perhaps the National Liberal Club, where Ikbal was still a member, and where Idries stayed with him when they were in London.[71] To fly to the Middle East would ruin the romance, and unlike his father, Idries had neither newspaper editors nor kings to sponsor him, so he and his friend sailed south to the movie-tinseled port of Tangier, where they parted company. Idries had hoped to travel onward to Libya but hadn't thought to arrange a visa in advance.[72] He was new to all this. Hence it was back on a boat to Europe, this time to Marseille, where he bought a ticket with Messageries Maritimes to Alexandria, from where it was an easy train ride down to Cairo.[73] Its exotic alleys appealed to him more than the bars and beaches of Alexandria. Besides, Lawrence Durrell had already captured the market for books on Alexandrian decadence, so instead Idries spent three months in Cairo learning to speak some Arabic.[74] He was following a path that was already well trodden by Europe-

ans. It was in Cairo forty years earlier that the French metaphysi-
cian René Guénon had similarly studied Arabic before becoming a
Sufi at the hands of the Swedish convert Ivan Aguéli. Then Guénon
in turn inducted into Sufism the British student of Arabic Martin
Lings, who in 1951 convinced his compatriot Charles le Gai Eaton
to embrace to Islam as a Sufi.

By the time Idries arrived, though, Cairo's little circle of European Sufis had been broken by the anti-British riots that accompanied Nasser's revolution. But as yet, Idries had shown little interest
in the Sufism that had been only one of the mystical topics his father
had written about. If anything, he was more interested in finding a
way to return to the anti-Sufi kingdom of Saudi Arabia. In Cairo,
he learned that the Saudi delegation was visiting the newly founded
nationalist Arab League, including Prince Faisal, whom his father
had met on his recent trip to Arabia. Idries rushed to the hotel where
the delegates were staying and, like a courteous member of a gentleman's club, had his visiting card sent up to the prince.[75]

Sitting nervously in the lobby, he was called up to the royal suite
to meet Prince Faisal, who as minister of foreign affairs was sitting
with the Saudi ambassador to Egypt. Seizing his chance after his
prior visa mishaps, Idries asked permission to make the pilgrimage
again to Mecca. The next morning he collected his visa from the
Saudi embassy, and a few days later took the train from Cairo east to
Suez, where he boarded one of the many ships to Jeddah.[76] He spent
the next few weeks in Mecca and Riyadh, lodging again at the royal
guesthouse and being granted an audience with Ibn Saud in a rerun
of his visit with his father the previous year.

He then boarded one of the kingdom's new American airplanes
to Port Sudan, on the African side of the Red Sea, from where he
took an air-conditioned train to the Sudanese capital, Khartoum,
still under British rule, spending a few days driving around before
flying to Beirut.[77] There he relaxed in the Western atmosphere of the
city's wealthier Christian sections, lounging in seafront cafés and at
the lovely clifftop campus of the American University, founded by

Protestant missionaries in the previous century.[78] But he soon moved on to Jordan, where he followed by taxi what was already the tourist route to the splendid ruins of Petra.[79] In the wake of the 1948 Arab-Israeli War, the Old City of Jerusalem was ruled by Jordan, so it was an easy day trip from the capital Amman to visit the Dome of the Rock.[80] He had so much ground to cover, so much to catch up with, after his suburban upbringing in Belmont; he needed to authenticate himself in "the East" of which his father had always talked.

Having dashed around the Middle East, it was over to Cyprus, still a British crown colony, where he headed for the mythical birthplace of Aphrodite at the archaeological site at Kouklia. It was the home of the White Goddess, whose cult the poet Robert Graves was famously resurrecting.[81] Finally, he popped over to Turkey, where he finally began to search for the Sufis suppressed by the secular edicts of Atatürk, of whom his father had written an admiring biography.[82]

On returning to England, Idries, following his father's example, briefly tried to straddle the roles of political journalist and travel writer. For the long-established Catholic journal *The Tablet*, he wrote a sober strategic assessment of Cyprus's place in nascent Cold War geopolitics.[83] Rather than wax lyrical about Aphrodite's birthplace, he analyzed the relative positions of Greek nationalists, Turkish secularists, and the small but active cadre of Communists. Full of facts and figures, it was based on the kind of research he had done for his father during the war. Next, Idries wrote up his journey to Mecca.[84] Unlike Ikbal's gilt-edged scoop a quarter-century earlier, his article made it into neither the New York nor the London *Times*, for now that Saudi Arabia was full of American technicians, Washington had no shortage of intelligence. Instead, he sold his story to *Wide World*, an American boys' magazine: his tourist piece summoning the "authentic atmosphere of the *Arabian Nights*" appeared behind a cover image of three Boy Scouts on a character-building hike.[85]

Another article concerned the policies of the recently formed National Health Service, focusing on Britain's postwar public health campaign against tuberculosis; this appeared in the *Illustrated*

Weekly of India via his father's old journalist contacts in Delhi.[86] Finding outlets for other articles was far from easy, though. He had no pals from prep schools to open the doors to Fleet Street, and the endless array of little magazines that had been his father's bread and butter had not survived the great literary cull of the war. So it was perhaps with mixed feelings that Idries accepted an offer to become a regular contributor to *The Countryman*.[87] Based at the rustic address of Sheep Street in the market town of Burford near Oxford, *The Countryman* was the humbler counterpart to aristocratic *Country Life*. Far from being read by the puppet masters of empire for whom Ikbal had written in such publications as *The Contemporary Review* and *The Times*, its proudly parochial pages were usually the preserve of Cotswold farmers and country vicars.

Idries published these articles under the name "Sayyid Edris Ali Shah." Since independent India had abolished the aristocracy that had been loyal for so long to the British, he was unable to inherit his father's sirdar title, still less the more exalted nawwab of his grandfather. But his family lineage did afford him one honorific: that of *sayyid*. Signifying descent from the clan of the Prophet, by the twentieth century the title was claimed by literally millions of Muslims across Asia and Africa. But among English readers who had little idea what it meant, it held a degree of cachet, and looked all the more exclusive when prefixed with the definite article. So in his early publications and on his headed notepaper, he was "The Sayed Edris Ali Shah" or simply "The Sayed Idris Shah."[88]

Finally gaining his financial independence, Idries rented a flat of his own, in a redbrick Victorian terrace in London's Swiss Cottage neighborhood where he could now devote himself to his writing.[89] There too he would take his first steps into the artistic milieu taking shape in Northwest London a decade after the war. When the lease expired midway through writing his book *Oriental Magic*, he moved to another inexpensive flat in a subdivided terrace shared with two other tenants, Peter and Alfred, though several Indians and Arabs, likewise leftovers of empire, lived along the same road.[90] With many large Victorian houses converted into flats, Swiss Cottage was popular with renters, and it was as close as Idries could afford to literary Hampstead, which had been the favored home of émigré artists since before the war, including the Bauhaus founders Walter Gropius and László Moholy-Nagy, as well as the British artists Ben Nicholson and Henry Moore. Many cultured Viennese Jews had also settled there after fleeing the Nazis. By the 1950s, Swiss Cottage had also developed an artistic subculture, mainly of German speakers who gathered in the coffeehouses below Finchley Road. From Idries's flat, it was less than a five-minute walk to the Cosmo restaurant, where German and Yiddish mixed with snatches of Russian, French, and the Spanish of the waiters. After the donnish atmosphere of Oxford, he could watch and learn much in this new milieu.

Despite his few articles and book reviews, his career as a freelance journalist was leading nowhere, and with rent to pay, like Ikbal before him, Idries needed regular paid work. He tried to patent an Afghan-style charcoal heater that he hoped would catch on in Britain's bleak postwar winters, but the project failed.[91] Fortunately, an alternative opportunity arose through his father, and Idries left the world of heating appliances forever to take up a position as London agent for Radio Kabul, Afghanistan's state broadcaster. Ikbal still kept contact with both the Afghan embassy in London and the radio world. (His colleague from BBC days, Zulfiqar Ali Bukhari, was by then the director of Radio Pakistan.)[92] Building on his meager journalistic credentials, Idries was tasked with overseeing news reports gathered in London and commissioning scripts for the station's occasional broadcasts in English. Even if the focus of his work was on British affairs, the job still afforded him contacts with the few Afghan citizens who were then resident in London.

Ikbal's connections also helped his elder son, Omar. Longing to see his ancestral homeland and unable to settle into a steady career in England, Omar had traveled to Kabul, which as the Cold War began to bite was rapidly modernizing under rival aid grants from the Americans and the Soviets. Unable to speak Persian, Omar similarly found work as an announcer for Radio Kabul's English broadcasts, which his brother was helping to script back in London.[93] Their careers seemed to be developing in tandem. But despite staying in Afghanistan for two years, Omar showed no intention of writing about his travels.

Instead, it was Idries who harbored hopes of inheriting their father's roles of author and explorer. In the summer of 1953, having learned from Ikbal the importance of having sponsors (though there was no longer an India Office to ask for support), Idries wrote to an influential member of New York's Explorers Club, Lowell Thomas, who was also America's most successful travel writer and broadcaster.[94] Thomas was the man who had manufactured the living myth of "Lawrence of Arabia" based on the dramatic footage of T. E. Lawrence and his Arab companions that he filmed during the First World War. Thomas had also written about Afghanistan in two heavily promoted books, *Beyond Khyber Pass* and *Adventures in Afghanistan for Boys*, published in the same year as Ikbal's *Afghanistan of the Afghans*. In his letter, Idries now informed Thomas about his plans to mount an expedition to follow Alexander the Great's route to India, exploring the unknown region of the Hindu Kush known as Nuristan, where blue-eyed descendants of Alexander's men were said to survive in remote snowbound valleys.[95]

A generation earlier there had been much interest in Britain about the fate of Alexander in Afghanistan, prompting the Anglo-Hungarian explorer Sir Aurel Stein to write *On Alexander's Track to the Indus*. But with the end of the British Empire, it was now America that was making vast investments in "area studies" by sending anthropologists and other social scientists to research Afghanistan. Hence Idries asked Thomas for help in finding funding from wealthy U.S. organizations. Specifically, he needed money for three Jeeps and plenty of filmmaking equipment, as well as a deal for distributing a movie, because—going one better over his father—he planned to write a book, present slide lectures, but also make a film about his adventures.[96] As he sat waiting for Thomas's response, Idries recognized the lingering allure in Britain of the old imperial legend of a lost Greek kingdom in the East. So he sent a letter for publication in *The Countryman*, announcing his plan to visit his "homeland" to investigate the links of Nuristan's blue-eyed inhabitants to Alexander's Macedonian soldiers.[97] Looking for support wherever he could, he also approached the Paris-based Institut International d'Anthropologie, where he had previously made contacts while researching his father's books on magic at the Bibliothèque Nationale.

In the mid-1950s, as the world recovered from war and travel became easier again, stories of remote adventures reemerged in both the old and new media. Lowell Thomas was about to start filming *High Adventure*, a TV travel series for CBS, while Eric Newby, a London fashion retailer who had served in the Indian Army and learned Urdu during the war, was planning the climbing expedition that would lead to his laconic travelogue, *A Short Walk in the Hindu Kush*. A few months earlier Denmark's Henning Haslund-Christensen Memorial Expedition had also set off to research and film in the Afghan province of Nuristan.

Unfortunately, as Thomas and the potential sponsors at CBS and the Explorers Club saw immediately, Idries lacked any of the qualifications or experience demanded by such risk-laden and logistically complex ventures, so his proposal was turned down. His Jeep tour had never been feasible anyway: there were not even dirt roads in Nuristan; Newby and the Danish expedition had to hike and ride on horseback. However much he dreamed, Idries was no rider of horses like his ancestor Jan Fishan Khan, though like his father before him, he had inadvertently invented roads across Afghanistan.

Chapter Eight

OCCULTIST

To adopt a scheme of religious pretension, with no
belief whatever in its being true.

—Edmund Gosse, *Father and Son*

IN THE MONTHS BEFORE IDRIES'S FIRST BOOK, ORIENTAL
Magic, appeared in 1956, Britain's literary scene was going through
its biggest revolution since the heyday of T. S. Eliot's modernists.
In May that year, John Osborne's *Look Back in Anger* premiered
at London's Royal Court Theatre, whose press officer coined the
phrase "angry young men" to describe the new movement. By looking to working-class themes, the disparate authors who gathered
under that banner triggered a seismic shift in the cultural landscape.
Not that all the Angry Young Men were truly working class. The
privately educated Osborne grew up in the Surrey village of Stone-
leigh, less than three miles from Belmont: his prep school, Belmont
College, even shared its name with Idries's childhood suburb. But
like Idries, Osborne didn't go to university, and both bore a sense
of exclusion from the dominant culture. While Osborne and the
other Angry Young Men articulated their exclusion in terms of class,
Idries, as the son of a sirdar and grandson of a nawwab, perhaps felt
excluded based not on class but on race.

Although the theater held no attraction for Idries, the new prose
works of the decade apparently did. The same year that produced
Oriental Magic and *Look Back in Anger* also saw the publication of

Colin Wilson's *The Outsider.* Written while its author slept rough on Hampstead Heath—effectively on the doorstep of literary London— *The Outsider* blended Sartre and Nietzsche into a watered-down existentialism in which history's greatest minds shared a single personality type. For Wilson, the man on the margins was not the downtrodden prole of the Parisian socialists. He was the spiritual revolutionary, the Nietzschean whole man, the only person awake in a city full of sleepwalkers. His book became a sensation. Unlike the other modish writers of the moment, Wilson had invented a category that Idries could inhabit, especially since *The Outsider* included a more cosmopolitan cast than the plainly Anglo-Saxon characters invented by the Angry Young Men in the nationalizing aftermath of empire. One of Wilson's heroes was an Eastern mystic called Gurd-jieff, a man of mysterious provenance whose cryptic utterances had entranced the salons of interwar Paris. Idries too was an outsider. And Wilson showed him that an outsider could still have influence, not only despite but because he was from elsewhere.

Still, for the moment that was all theoretical, and Idries faced the immediate problem of persuading a publisher to accept his next book. The mid-1950s were a time when small publishers still flourished in London, many of them founded by Jewish émigrés such as George Weidenfeld. After working for the BBC with Orwell during the war, Weidenfeld had founded his publishing house in 1948, showing what was possible for outsiders to achieve in British cultural no less than commercial life. The Viennese art publisher Phaidon was also rees-tablished in Hampstead exile. But Muslims made little progress in British publishing by comparison with the prominence achieved by Jewish editors like Weidenfeld. The only notable Muslim publisher was still the Woking Mosque, but it issued only religious works, leaving translations of Muslim literature in the hands of Orientalist publishers like Luzac and Zwemer, both of Dutch origin.

India's Hindus and Parsis had made slightly more progress. In 1946 the New India Publishing Company had been established in London to promote Indian authors with socialist and nationalist leanings (a requirement that placed both Ikbal and Idries beyond the pale). For a few years, it had flourished, issuing a pioneering anthology of Indian English poetry edited by the Parsi poet Fredoon Kabraji. The end of empire soon had its literary impact, as by 1950, the New India Publishing Company had closed after its editor, Mulk Raj Anand—erstwhile errand-runner for T. S. Eliot—sailed home to India. Fredoon Kabraji stayed on in Britain with his Welsh wife, but his supply of authors dried up as the 1950s saw an exodus of Indian intellectuals to the liberated subcontinent, including Krishna Menon, who had helped found London's spectacularly successful paperback line, Penguin Books, before departing to become India's defense minister.

In 1956, seeing the subsequent opportunities for a publisher on Asian and Islamic topics, Idries founded Octagon Press. Its first publication was by Afzal Iqbal, a Pakistani diplomat stationed in London, who had previously been a reporter for the imperial All-India Radio when Ikbal was working for the BBC's Empire Service.[1] Now Afzal Iqbal had written a book on the Persian Sufi poetry of Rumi. Since the book had already been published the previous year in Lahore, a British edition presented an easy first publishing venture for Idries, but it was important nonetheless. The Cambridge Orientalists Reynold Nicholson and A. J. Arberry had written earlier studies of Rumi, but this was the first book on Rumi by a Muslim author to be published in Britain. Given that the leading London publisher George Allen & Unwin had recently reissued Nicholson's study, signing Iqbal seemed a shrewd response to what looked like rising interest. As it turned out, a review in the *Journal of the Royal Asiatic Society* of Iqbal's *The Life and Work of Jalal-Ud-Din Rumi* complained that it was "written entirely in superlatives" and "marred by exaggerations" and "prosaic translations."[2] The Orientalists guarded their gates.

If the reviews for Idries's first book as a publisher were disappointing, he held out hope for his first book as an author. The manuscript for *Oriental Magic* was now complete: all he needed was a foreword by a notable figure, of the kind Ikbal had garnered from the likes of Donald Mackenzie and the Agha Khan. He called on Louis Marin, deputy president of the Institut International d'Anthropologie, whom he had met during his research in Paris. Already eighty-six, Marin was long past his prime as a scholar, but his longevity had bequeathed on him a list of positions that appeared under his name on the flyleaf of *Oriental Magic*: member of the Institut de France and director of the École d'Anthropologie de Paris, as well as deputy president of the Institut International d'Anthropologie.

Marin's foreword presented *Oriental Magic* as a work of "scientific method," drawing on Lucien Lévy-Bruhl, a founder-member of his institute, whose 1931 *Le surnaturel et la nature dans la mentalité primitive* had pioneered the anthropological study of occult beliefs (though it was now much outdated).[3] Idries had relied on the even earlier Victorian likes of the Egyptologist Sir Ernest Wallis Budge (several of his father's books also featured in his bibliography), leaving him unprepared for the structuralist revolution that was about to overturn such old methods of colonial anthropology.[4] As an outsider to the university seminars where Cambridge's Edmund Leach was bringing Claude Lévi-Strauss's *anthropologie structurale* to Britain, Idries missed the changes that were gathering on the intellectual horizon.

Still, *Oriental Magic* was a scholarly book of sorts, opening with a general argument that magic had spread internationally through cultural diffusion and was thereby comparable across different cultures. Despite a few sensational titles, the chapters focused in anthropological mode on specific regions, whether India and Iran or China and Japan, and its academic tone generally remained impersonal, except when Idries slipped in the occasional family anecdote. At one point his father's story about a holy man in a Himalayan cave made a reappearance, and he cited another yarn about an Indian alchemist cited from his mother in her guise as Madame Morag Murray Abdullah.[5] But what most distinguished *Oriental Magic* from the anthropological studies to which Louis Marin compared it was its argument that magic wasn't merely the mode of symbolic thought described by the rationalizing anthropologists. It was potentially a means of harnessing "hitherto little understood forces . . . to individual and collective advantage."[6] For twenty-five shillings, Idries was telling his readers that magic was real. Appearing at a time when the occult novels of Dennis Wheatley were bestsellers—*The Ka of Gifford Hillary* came out the same year—it was what many readers wanted to hear.

In writing on the exotic and occult, Idries was occupying one of the few spaces on Britain's bookshelves that remained open to Indian writers. The demise of the empire meant that interest in the far-off political questions that had partly paved Ikbal's writerly way had faded with the last colonial bugle. The following year, when the later Nobel laureate V. S. Naipaul published his first novel *The Mystic Masseur*, he too used the old tropes of Eastern exoticism. But while the Oxford-educated Naipaul knew how to mix the social satire of Evelyn Waugh with the imperial settings of Somerset Maugham, Idries recited his research on alchemists and juju dolls straight-faced. He won no literary prizes to match Naipaul's early success, but the reviews of *Oriental Magic* were still good. Swami Akhilananda of Boston's Vedanta Center praised the "fascinating book" written by "Dr. Shah" (though the swami disliked the comparison of Hindu gurus with African witch doctors), and even America's prestigious *Journal of Asian Studies* judged it "well-written and interesting," albeit "likely to appeal to the reader without a strongly developed scientific interest."[7] India's *Time and Tide* praised the depth of research by this "Afghan ethnologist," while back in Britain the Folklore Society advertised it lavishly.[8] As it had for his father, the folkloric fringe of the chattering classes was opening Idries's first door to the cultural establishment.

Soon after the publication of *Oriental Magic*, Idries received an invitation to Cambridge from the archaeologist T. C. Lethbridge, and he eagerly replied to accept.[9] Lethbridge was curator of the university's Museum of Archaeology and Ethnology. After a respectable career as a pioneering excavator of Anglo-Saxon burial sites,

Lethbridge had lately become convinced he was unearthing the lost gods of Olde England, sounding an academic echo of Graves and Gardner's magical writings in his own book, *Merlin's Island*. Articles in the London *Times* and the *Standard* reported on his claim to have discovered three vast figures of a warrior, a goddess, and a sun god carved into the chalky earth of Cambridgeshire's Gog Magog Downs. Soon he turned to writing about ghost-hunting with dowsing rods. Within a year of contacting Idries, Lethbridge would be forced to resign from Cambridge. But thereafter his rapid reversal of fortune—from dishonored don to media magus—was most instructive. Academia might well mock the study of magic, but the wave of public interest in the occult was swelling. While Idries didn't get to lecture on his book at Cambridge, he continued to correspond with the increasingly famous Lethbridge.

Idries's sequel to *Oriental Magic* was published the following year in London and New York.[10] *The Secret Lore of Magic* was shrewdly based on extensive summaries of old works that were out of copyright.[11] Like Ikbal's *Occultism* only more so, it was a recipe book for the aspiring magician, covering ritual and white magic, spirit-summoning and talismans, along with the all-powerful grimoire of Honorius the Great. It offered spells galore: spells to make music, spells to test chastity, spells to become invisible, spells to kill enemies, spells to be warm in the cold, even spells to make camels fight. Evidently some spells were more useful in London than others, though the section on talismans described a ring that would render its wearer respected and learned.[12] In dense scholarly prose, Idries described manuscripts perused in the ancient libraries of Oxford and Cambridge and the astonishing prices that Parisian bookdealers demanded for such arcane bibliographical rarities.[13]

Navigating an unsteady course betwixt the occult and Islam, between *Oriental Magic* and *Secret Lore*, Idries published his travel book *Destination Mecca*.[14] With its breezy style and concern for comfortable hotels, it bore many similarities with his father's *West-*

ward to Mecca. Obsessive accounts of taking photographs and getting hold of camera film went on for pages, along with expatriate anxieties about the availability of American cigarettes and worldly tips on how to deal with Arab porters.[15] The book's opening scenes in a London gentleman's club and the flattering chapter on King Saud seemed very much a romp through Ikbal's world.

Yet in fundamental ways, it was very much not, for by the time Idries arrived in the Middle East, European power over the region was gone. Although Idries had been witness to these seismic shifts in geopolitics, he showed no desire to write about them. The Suez Crisis took place while he was writing his account of Egypt (and the city of Suez itself), yet he kept political commentary to a minimum.[16] His authorial persona was as a cultured denizen of London clubland. As the title of the opening chapter put it, he was a "gentleman at large," while casual references to Oxford tutorials hinted at a university education.[17] Writing as the Englishman abroad that he very much was, Idries echoed the laconic tone of such interwar travelogues as J. R. Ackerley's *Hindoo Holiday* and presaged the Indian Nirad Chaudhuri's *A Passage to England*, published two years later, with its sense of traveling through a diverging world of nation-states that till recently were connected by empire. Yet all told, Idries's *Destination Mecca* was a polished piece of writing: the natural dialogue was a far cry from Ikbal's blend of *Boy's Own* magazine and the gung-ho yells of G. A. Henty. Idries's descriptions of places were vivid and light on cliché.

The Middle East as depicted by Idries was no longer the land of bandits and camel trains long familiar to the Anglophone imagination. Nor was it the region described in *Arabian Sands* by his decade-older contemporary, Wilfred Thesiger, which recounted hard travels with the last traditional Bedouin across Arabia's desolate Empty Quarter. Though both authors were born in distant places—Thesiger in Addis Ababa, Idries in Simla—*Destination Mecca* was written in a contemporary voice that contrasted sharply with Thesiger's conservatism. Instead of Thesiger's antimodernist paean to the desert, Idries's Middle East was a region of bustling beach resorts and shining aerodromes, where American consumer goods could be found even in Mecca.

Idries's book appeared during a time of complicated currency controls when even a trip to Paris had become difficult. As a result, the nationalizing 1950s nurtured far fewer works of British literary travel than the interwar decades. The obstinate Wilfred Thesiger aside, what books were published were no longer about imperial escapades but about the glamour of the kind of sleek places summoned so effectively in the first James Bond novels. As postwar rationing gave way to consumerist adventures with caviar, Ian Fleming captured this new luxury ethos in his own travelogue, *Thrilling Cities*. But unlike Idries, not even James Bond could travel to Mecca, still less enjoy a dry martini there. Idries was finding his niche.

Destination Mecca also offers an early glimpse into a new post-colonial sensibility that was both British and Asian. Its class-ridden foibles are almost stereotypically English, as is the feeling of being a fish out of water in this unfamiliar Arabian version of "Abroad."[18] Yet as the pages turn, the clubby character of the opening chapters gives way to a new and as yet unclear persona. Out of line with the breezily skeptical tone of the rest of the book, the last two chapters read like appendices added after it was contracted to Rider & Co., publisher of Gerald Gardner's *Witchcraft Today* and several of Ikbal's books, including his *Occultism*. Set vaguely in Turkey, the penultimate chapter of *Destination Mecca* describes a supposed journey to a Sufi monastery, albeit with none of the previous chapters' credible sense of place.[19]

The final chapter turns to the mountain borderlands of Afghanistan, where Idries finds the Fakir of Ipi, the holy leader of a "strange guerrilla state" in Waziristan.[20] The fakir was a real enough figure who had led an uprising against the British in the 1930s. During World War II he had been funded by Italy and Germany to revive his rebellion. Then, after the subcontinent's independence, he launched

a guerrilla war against the fledgling nation of Pakistan.[21] Idries made
no mention of such awkward facts, though, and declared the dangers of political Islam to be the invention of Orientalists.[22] The Fakir
of Ipi was not to be feared, he explained. Despite his bodyguards,
with their explosive belts and hand grenades, he was "strangely gentle," and merely a "dreamer."[23]

At thirty-two, Idries had published two books on magic and a
travelogue. For the first time, he seemed to have prospects, and he
moved to a nicer flat in a neoclassical terrace.[24] Located in the corner of Northwest London called Little Venice (locals argued over
whether the name was given by Byron or Robert Browning), the
neighborhood had ongoing literary connections. John Masefield,
a sailor turned poet laureate, and J. R. Ackerley, author of *Hindoo Holiday*, both resided there, while the modernist poet Stephen
Spender previously lived next door to Idries's flat.[25] V. S. Naipaul,
the ambitious young Indian writer from Trinidad, was lodging
a mere mile away when Idries moved in, and his *Mystic Masseur*,
Suffrage of Elvira, and *Miguel Street* appeared at the same time as
Idries's first three books.[26] Although both had fathers who were
published authors, Idries had no exotic childhood to draw on in the
way Vidia Naipaul turned his late imperial life into the literary art
that beguiled London's cognoscenti—*The Mystic Masseur* won the
John Llewellyn Rhys Prize, following the fashion for Caribbean and
Indian settings sparked by the previous two winners, John Hearne
and Ruskin Bond. The time had not yet come though for tales of
immigrant life in London, of being raised between cultures in Britain; and Idries in any case had no desire to tell the world about his
suburban mixed-race childhood.

Idries's links to the suburbs had been severed now anyway. His
father had finally made peace with the Congress Party that had come
to rule over India, and he had accepted Indian citizenship.[27] Together
with Elizabeth, Ikbal had taken to spending most of his time on the
family estate in Sardhana, though they lodged with Idries whenever
they visited London.[28] Cast aside by the empire he served, Ikbal had

turned to the nationalists he had long scorned, talking his way into a post as Indian cultural representative to the Middle East, which would afford him continued opportunities to travel.[29] The focus of Ikbal's now few writings also took a new turn, as he promised the Indian government a book on Indian relations with Kashmir. Since India was struggling with Pakistan to legitimize its de facto control over the disputed region, Ikbal used the book—or at least the promise to write it—to help his case to cash in his pension.[30]

After independence back in 1947, all such "political pensions" had become the responsibility of the Indian government. Ikbal had decided to move back to India in the hope of consolidating it into a lump sum, as he had first tried to do back in 1940. Since many other former Indian allies of empire were trying to do the same, officials in Delhi were concerned that Muslims might cash in their pensions only to emigrate to Pakistan and take the funds with them, so Ikbal needed to be particularly careful in the legal declarations he made.[31] For though he had no interest in moving to Pakistan (especially as it entered its first military dictatorship), he did have plans to settle in Morocco.

Painting himself as an impoverished Indian patriot, Ikbal explained in his deposition that he was in dire financial straits through having incurred a large debt on his travels researching his book on Indo-Kashmir cultural relations.[32] He wrote the letter from the Wheeler Club of the recently departed colonials in Meerut, where he and Elizabeth had lodged with Ikbal's lawyer friend in the early years of their marriage. Officials in India's Ministry of Home Affairs took him at his word, and his pension was signed over as a lump sum. Not long afterward he moved to Tangier, where with his cashed-in pension, he bought a house on Rue de la Plage, at the isthmus of the Muslim world and Europe. Like his earlier book for the League of Nations, his book for the Congress government on Kashmir never appeared.

Despite occasional visits to London, Ikbal now lived far enough away that his shadow over Idries receded. Now a man of letters in his own right, Idries began holding court at the nearby Cosmopolitan restaurant.[33] Back in the 1930s, its émigré owners had tried to recreate the lost atmosphere of the Austro-Hungarian Empire, and Sigmund Freud often went there in the last exiled year of his life.[34] By the time Idries showed up, the name had been fashionably shortened to the Cosmo, but the old menu of *Weisswurst, Sauerbraten,* and even rarer lager beer ensured there were many loyal clients, including the actor James Mason and the young spy novelist Frederick Forsyth.

One Tuesday evening in 1959, a less familiar figure sauntered over to what had become Idries's regular table, beneath a portrait of Carl Jung.[35] Jack Bracelin introduced himself as having an active interest in magic and said he had read Idries's books. Joining the table for drinks, the two men began to talk. Jack dropped hints that magic wasn't only preserved in the old manuscripts that Idries described in his writings but was still alive and well. What was more, magic and witchcraft were being practiced right now in London.

Tall, thin, and pale, Jack Bracelin had served during the war in the Palestine police force and had then spent ten tedious years as a paint salesman. Reading a book had subsequently changed his life, and that book was Gerald Gardner's *Witchcraft Today.*[36] The 1951 abolition of the Witchcraft Act had made possible a neopagan revival in Britain, enabling Gerald to take his coven out of the semi-legal underground of Bloomsbury's Atlantis Bookshop basement. By 1956, Jack had contacted Gerald and was soon afterward initiated by Doreen Valiente, one of the first priestesses of the new religion that she and Gerald called Wicca, claiming this was the true name for what Christians had long denigrated as "witchcraft."

On the Hertfordshire outskirts of London, Gerald purchased a few acres of woodland for his followers to practice the pagan ceremonies he was busily inventing.[37] As though it were a suburban golf course, he called it the Fiveacres Country Club, an elegant solution to the problem of finding a discreet cover for naked moonlit gatherings in leafy groves. After predictable misunderstandings arose with his local caretaker, Gerald decided to bring in the recently initiated

Jack Bracelin from London and entrust him with managing the club. Not only was Jack Bracelin more broad-minded, his eagerness and humility were a useful combination. His days of selling paint now over, Jack took to his new responsibilities with gusto, increasing the membership of Fiveacres with adverts in *Health and Efficiency,* the magazine of the budding naturist movement. However, the sacked caretaker took revenge by writing to the Central Council of British Naturism with claims that the club was a cover for the ritual sexual abuse of children. Jack was quick to respond.[38] Paid for by Gerald's colonial pension, lawyers issued a writ for libel that saved both Gerald and his new religion. By the time Jack met Idries at the Cosmo, he was the witchmaster's right-hand man.

Not long after that first meeting, Jack agreed to introduce Idries to the Bricket Wood Coven, who convened full-moon sabbaths at the Fiveacres Country Club. The most eye-catching of the witches was Jack's elfin girlfriend who, though she now went by her neo-pagan name Dayonis, came from a family of Jewish immigrants from Armenia.[39] Among the other young people Idries now met was Austrian-born Frederic Lamond, a shy Cambridge economics graduate who commuted to London from his gypsy caravan at Fiveacres. Lamond's path to witchcraft had been paved by membership of the Progressive League, a social reform group, co-founded by H. G. Wells, whose lofty causes stretched from world government to rights for nudists.[40] Among the coven's older members was Edward Grove, a retired colonel in the Indian Army.[41]

Idries was most keen to meet the man who claimed to have rekindled Wicca from the pagan embers of yore. He already knew Gerald's historical novel, *A Goddess Arrives*—it had inspired a chapter in his *Destination Mecca*. There, in an incongruous turn from the holy places of Islam, Idries had headed to Cyprus in search of Aphrodite's temple at Kouklia, following the hero of Gerald's novel, a Londoner mystically transported to ancient Cyprus in the days when Aphrodite stepped naked from the waves.[42]

By the time Idries met him, Gerald was already famous. Ever

since the tabloid *Sunday Pictorial*'s witchcraft exposé three years earlier, Gerald had courted the press and television cameras—much to the dismay of his more respectable middle-class followers.[43] After opening a Museum of Witchcraft, he began styling himself "Dr." Gardner, saying he had been awarded doctorates in philosophy and literature by the universities of Toulouse and Singapore.[44] (There was no truth to the claims.) Yet the two men found they had much in common. Both Gerald's and Idries's turn to the witches of Olde England had begun in the East. At sixteen Gerald had sailed from his native Liverpool to Ceylon and spent ten years as a tea planter, then moved as a rubber planter to Malaya. There, after the price of rubber collapsed, he was employed by the public works department as principal officer of customs.[45]

After he retired and returned to England, he turned from amateur Orientalism (having written a short book on the *kris*, the traditional Malay dagger) to the Folklore Society, publishing an article on traditional English talismans in the same journal for which Ikbal had earlier written about the folk charms of Afghanistan.[46] Through his new folklore circle, Gerald learned of Margaret Murray, whose 1921 *The Witch-Cult in Western Europe* had pioneered the revisionist thesis that witches were neither devil's disciples nor puritans' delusions but survivors of pagan nature religions that flourished before Christianity. (Like Gerald and Idries, Murray also had colonial roots, being born in India and raised in Calcutta.) When Gerald retired to the English countryside, he met a group of Murray enthusiasts who met in a wooden village hall named Ashrama Hall, after the retreats of Indian yogis.

That rustic outpost of the imperial imaginary became a cauldron for the revitalizing ingredients of England's supposed old faith. There Gerald was inspired to write his Wiccan bible, *The Book of Shadows*, with Doreen Valiente. What Gerald said of *The Book of Shadows* could equally have been said of Idries's *Secret Lore of Magic*: it "is not a Bible or Quran. It is a personal cookbook of spells."[47]

The Wicca that Gerald was concocting was a new homegrown

creed, to coincide with the nationalization of everything from railways to religions. Underlying his claim to be transmitting the wisdom
of Olde England was an invented story that he had been initiated by
an elderly witch called Dorothy Clutterbuck.[48] Apparently, no one
among Gerald's growing audience knew he had plagiarized many
rituals for his *Book of Shadows* from sources ranging from Rudyard
Kipling's *Puck of Pook's Hill* to manuals by the Victorian magician
MacGregor Mathers.[49] Here Gerald's witchcraft overlapped with
Idries's magic, for in researching *The Secret Lore of Magic*, Idries
had studied many of the same texts on which Gerald too relied.

Despite the dubious authenticity of his sources, Gerald demonstrated to Idries how writing books could be used to gain not only
readers but followers—something Ikbal had never taught him.
For Gerald's part, Idries's reputation as an expert on magic awoke
a complementary interest. In Gerald's large London apartment in
Holland Park, amid Regency terraces and foreign embassies, they
took to meeting frequently, talking magic for hours on end. Eventually the publicity-hungry Gerald trusted Idries enough to ask him to
write his biography. Idries agreed on condition that he could publish
it through his own company, Octagon Press.

Idries needed to acquire a book that would sell well. After publishing the study of Rumi by the Pakistani diplomat Afzal Iqbal,
Octagon's second undertaking had been a new book by Ikbal, reprising his early role as anti-Communist political expert amid the conflict unfolding in Vietnam. Idries had done his editorial best to lend
the book the appearance of serious reportage.[50] But the reviews of
Ikbal's *Viet-Nam* were damning. In the *Journal of the Royal Institute of International Affairs*, the Southeast Asia specialist Patrick
Honey was merciless: "The general outlay to this book, its index, its
bibliography and the absence of illustrations, would suggest that it is
a serious academic work," he began, but "the numerous elementary
errors which occur throughout lead me to doubt whether the author
has ever visited the country about which he is writing."[51]

The familiar critique got worse as the reviewer took pot shots at Idries, noting that "the publisher has left uncorrected the mistakes in the English language committed by the author [which] make this book very difficult to read."[52] A professor at London University who had lived in Vietnam during the early years of the war, Patrick Honey was all too aware of the high stakes of misinformation and stated his final verdict in no uncertain terms: "This book is heavily biased, meretricious, frequently inaccurate, and badly written. It cannot be recommended."[53]

It was altogether a bad year for both Ikbal and Idries, because in August 1960, their beloved wife and mother Elizabeth had died unexpectedly, aged only sixty-four. Just the previous year she and Ikbal had gone back to India, retracing their first journey together.[54] Now Ikbal would remain alone in Tangier, the Moroccan port that till a few years earlier had been an international zone, neither one place nor another, where Paul Bowles and Jean Genet had talked literature with Mohammed Mrabet and Mohamed Choukri. It was a fitting place for the final years of a man whose career had tried to connect the East and West.

In London, meanwhile, Idries mourned the loss of the mother who was his last living tie to his British roots but he kept himself busy with his biography of Gerald Gardner.[55] His publishing company needed a book that would sell, though notoriety was a double-edged sword. By the time Idries finished writing *Gerald Gardner, Witch*, the tabloids were making links between Gerald's witches and church desecration, child abuse, and even ritual murder. The libelous headlines were as salacious as chapter titles from a Dennis Wheatley novel: "Black Magic Killer" and "Murder at Black Mass."[56]

Still, what sold newspapers for Fleet Street could also sell books for Octagon Press. Taking tea with the economist-by-day and witch-by-night Frederic Lamond, Idries admitted that when he interviewed Gerald, he sometimes wished he was a *News of the World* reporter, because what Gerald told him was "marvellous material for an exposé!"[57] But at the same time, Idries didn't want his own name dragged through the tabloid mud.[58] Even as Gerald reveled in the attention, inviting journalists to his flat, Idries seems to have become more nervous. He had never stalked Dayak pirates through the backwaters of Johore with a revolver in his belt like the indomitable customs officer Gerald. Moreover, with most of his career still ahead of him, he had much to lose. So he decided to publish Gerald's biography under a pseudonym. Gerald's sidekick, Jack Bracelin, agreed to give his name to the book, since he had already been named in the newspapers anyway.[59]

The biography Idries wrote under Jack's name described a life of adventures in Malaya involving smugglers' dens and opium eaters, magicians and mediums. But fundamentally, it was a book about secret power. In one anecdote, Idries described how, during the Battle of Britain in 1940, Gerald had summoned witches from across southern England to gather in the New Forest at midnight, where they performed a ritual that in centuries past had defeated both the Spanish Armada and Napoleon.[60] That same summer Winston Churchill had declared, "Never in the field of human conflict was so much owed by so many to so few," but little did he know that among those few were the seventeen witches who danced naked that night for Gerald Gardner's Operation Cone of Power.

Despite making such extraordinary claims, Idries wrote in the sober tone of a biography of a retired brigadier. There was no need for purple prose. Helped by its unique material, *Gerald Gardner, Witch* was a more compelling read than any of the three books Idries had published under his own name, its dialogue capturing the character of a man who was, if nothing else, a raconteur and showman. In becoming Jack Bracelin and channeling Gerald Gardner, Idries liberated himself as a writer.

His liberation wasn't only literary. By listening to Gerald recount every fantastic detail of his life, Idries learned how to break free from the life laid out by his upbringing. Gerald showed him that magic wasn't a matter of somber prose and solemn ceremonies. It was about perception, illusion, even delusion. Gerald's life showed that fiction and reality could be merged. On one of the many evenings they spent together, Gerald even confessed he had entirely invented Wicca.[61] By purloining sections of forgotten old texts to compile *The Book of Shadows*, he taught Idries how to make a new religion seem old. With his wizardish goatee, he showed him how to look the part too. And above all, in basing his authority on a claimed initiation by a mysterious witch called "Old Dorothy," Gerald reiterated Ikbal's lesson about the aura of authenticity. When the biography appeared in the spring of 1960, Gerald invited Idries to take over the management of his Museum of Witchcraft just as Jack was managing Fiveacres.[62] But Idries recognized that the British public were unlikely to believe that a man with the name Idries Shah was the heir to Olde England's witches. For Idries to claim the kind of authenticity Gerald had found through his tale of Old Dorothy, he would have to look to the land of his ancestors.

Chapter Nine

AMANUENSIS

I began to perceive, without animosity, the strange
narrowness of my father's system.

—Edmund Gosse, *Father and Son*

IN JANUARY 1961, IDRIES SET OFF WITH GERALD TO THE
Spanish island of Mallorca. Almost a decade after his journey to
Mecca, this was to be an altogether more pagan pilgrimage. The two
men were heading for the village of Deià to meet the high priest of
the Mother Goddess: the poet Robert Graves. Gerald was lonely (his
wife of thirty years had died the previous year), and for all his talk
of the winter solstice, the old colonial despised the English winter
and liked to spend the worst of it in the warm south. When Idries
had suggested they go to the Mediterranean together, Gerald had
agreed, announcing in a letter to a friend that he would be away "for
two or three months," adding that he was traveling with Idries, who
"always tries to do the flying carpet trick."[1] He would soon see the
truth of his words.

As soon as they reached the Mallorcan capital of Palma, Idries
posted a letter to Robert Graves from their hotel, the economical
Pension Pullman. He introduced himself as the author of several
tomes on magic who was now conducting research for a book on
ecstatic forms of religiosity, which involved experiments of witches
munching on hallucinogenic mushrooms.[2] In case this was not
intriguing enough, Idries added that he was accompanied by "Dr."

Gardner, the leader of England's witches and director of the Museum of Witchcraft.[3] For all his bohemian ways, Robert Graves was a man of letters—an Oxford classicist, a sometime literature professor, a prodigal but proudly reclaimed son of the establishment—so it seemed important to present a respectable appearance. Careful to pay homage too, Idries explained that he and Gerald would be honored to meet, and salute, the great bard. Adding a final dash of literature for good measure, Idries ended the letter by passing on greetings from the Indian poet Fredoon Kabraji, one of Robert's former protégés, whose daughter Idries had begun dating in London.

Robert had already been made aware of Idries's activities. The previous summer Jack Bracelin had written the poet several letters introducing himself as a "leading member of the St Albans coven of witches" and describing experiments on the effects of psychedelic fungi "under strict scientific conditions."[4] The letters had described Idries making tape recordings of whatever mystical revelations poured from Jack's mouth after he munched a handful of *Agaricus muscarius.*[5] Four weeks before Idries posted his own letter from the Pension Pullman, Jack (or perhaps Idries writing under his name) had written again, this time inviting Robert to attend a mushroom-eating symposium that would purportedly take place at the May and Baker Research Laboratories.[6]

There were good reasons for sending odd epistles about psychedelics and witchcraft to the celebrated poet. Robert was already rethinking his ideas about the Greek goddesses who haunted and taunted his imagination, especially his theories about the ecstatic cults that surrounded them in antiquity. Perhaps the frenzy of the bacchants had been something more than alcoholic stupor. Rather than being drunk on gallons of retsina, maybe ancient Greeks had eaten the mushroom *Amanita muscaria.* It was a question Robert had already taken up with several correspondents, including R. Gordon Wasson, a retired American merchant banker and pioneer "ethnomycologist" who in 1957 had published a much-discussed article in *Life* magazine called "Seeking the Magic Mushroom."[7] His catchy name for the psychedelic fungus soon caught on. Inspired by Wasson, Robert had gone public with his psychedelic revisionism a few months before Jack had written to him, declaring in his *Food for Centaurs* that the roots of European religion lay with mushrooms or other mind-altering substances.[8] After the technologically enhanced atrocities of World War II, artists and intellectuals had lost faith not only in Europe's scientific achievements but even in the rational foundations of Western civilization. In 1951 E. R. Dodds, Regius Professor of Greek at Oxford (and president of the Society for Psychical Research), had published *The Greeks and the Irrational*, nudging Socrates from his throne with an image of ancient Greece driven by dark passions and unconscious forces. A decade later Robert's *Food for Centaurs* took the battle against reason beyond academia. His radical claims attracted much publicity, prompting Jack, then Idries to write to him.

In the wake of the war, both Robert and Gerald Gardner had published paeans to a new paganism. Robert's *The White Goddess* had been issued by the preeminent literary press Faber, while a year later Gerald's *High Magic's Aid* was printed privately for an obscure occult bookseller. But both books provided the pillars for many a new temple to the old gods. Still, the two men were of quite different status in the wider realms of culture. While Gerald's academic credentials were invented, Robert was about to be elected Oxford Professor of Poetry; while Gerald's novel of ancient Cypriot magic was an overwrought hit of the underground, Robert's novels on ancient Rome were highbrow bestsellers. Moreover, Robert and Gerald were theological as well as temperamental rivals. Were it not for Idries, Gerald would never have agreed to set foot on Mallorca. With his ribald jokes, he was like Caliban on Prospero's elegant island.

The only Gardner in whom Robert had previously shown interest was the film star Ava Gardner, who was one of his many glamorous guests on Mallorca. (He learned that a living screen goddess could be more demanding than a dead Greek one.) Still, Robert had heard of Gerald, a few years earlier having drawn on his *Witchcraft*

Today as the basis for a short story Robert published in *Punch.*[9] So after receiving Idries's letter, he wrote back to arrange a meeting. At four p.m. on Tuesday, January 17, 1960, the three mages assembled in Granja Reus, the swankiest *cafetería* in Palma.[10] Over Spanish brandy and black *cafés solo*, the conversation soon leaped from sorcerers to Sufis, from Greece to Afghanistan. By Sunday, Idries and Gerald were guests at Canelluñ, Robert's seaside villa in Deià, the serene outpost for his writing.[11] When Idries and Gerald visited, there was still only one short street in the village, over which hovered the poet's imposing stone house. That Sunday Gerald was quickly edged out of the conversation.[12] Robert was fond of fanciful genealogies, preferring a Welsh bardic ancestry to his maternal German lineage, so Idries made the extraordinary suggestion that the poet was also a descendant of the Prophet Muhammad. After all, Idries claimed such a lineage himself as a *sayyid*, which would make him and Robert relatives.

Having come prepared to make this most curious claim, the next morning Idries wrote Robert another letter from his hotel, hailing the poet as a fellow member of the Prophet's clan and including a corroborating article on "The Family of Hashim" from *The Contemporary Review.*[13] (A few months later he would send the same article to the archaeologist-turned-occultist T. C. Lethbridge.)[14] In three action-packed pages, the author "William Foster"—likely Idries in bland disguise—explained how the Hashim clan had once been the true leaders of Islam but were now represented only by one pure branch, which hailed from Afghanistan. That branch was the holy lineage of Jan Fishan Khan, whose heirs would soon "form a leadership for the Moslem republic which many feel is the coming thing."[15] Lest Robert fail to join the genealogical dots (plenty of wine had flowed the previous day), at the end of the article Idries added with a pen the four generations that linked him to Jan Fishan via Ikbal and the Nawwabs of Sardhana. How astonishing it must have seemed that the urbane, Oxford-accented Afghan who had sat chain-smoking Rothmans while telling Robert about Sufi mystics and Persian wine poems should be on the cusp of founding what would surely be a most bohemian Muslim republic. As Robert read the article the next morning, utopia seemed within reach.

. During the weeks in Mallorca that followed, Idries and Robert formed an increasingly close bond. The Spanish that Idries had picked up in Uruguay gave him a cosmopolitan air that appealed to the multilingual poet, as did his talk of Eastern languages, of which Robert knew nothing. They shared connections with Oxford too, where Idries had taken to saying he had abandoned his studies in disdain. More importantly, they were kinsmen of a mystical hierarchy that would soon usher in a new world. Sidelined then abandoned, Gerald had to fly in one of his priestesses, Lois, to keep him company.[16] Not only had Idries found a more powerful wizard in Robert, he had also found a more glamorous Gardner in the actress Ava. From Palma, Robert, Idries, and Ava flew to Madrid to watch a *corrida* with a celebrated bullfighter.[17]

Meanwhile, Idries had demoted Gerald with a new nickname: *mali*.[18] As the Urdu word for "gardener," it seemed harmless enough, but in India, *malis* were low-caste servants of the kind Idries's grandfather had employed by the dozen. Letting the subtle insult pass over Gerald's head, he used what he had learned from writing Gerald's biography to spin a yarn that Gerald, via his descent from Colonel William Linnaeus Gardner of the Indian cavalry regiment Gardner's Horse, was entitled to the rank of an Indian prince.[19] Moreover, Idries explained, his elder brother Omar was in Delhi arranging for Gerald's investiture. The pride of the former colonial customs officer piqued, Gerald left Mallorca for London, where he made ready to sail to Bombay.

The witchmaster out of the way, Idries devoted himself fully to Robert. He was no longer his father's secretary, nor any more the sorcerer's apprentice. While there was much he could learn as the amanuensis of a world famous poet, he was seeking not another master but an influential disciple, or at least a supporter. Night after night he told the poet about magic and witches, ceremonies and

Sufis. In less than two weeks, the aging avant-gardist began experimenting with magic mushrooms.[20] By the auspicious date of the spring equinox, Idries was back in London, writing to tell Robert of plans to procure a stash of mescaline from someone who had started a mescaline cult in Hampstead. It would enable Idries to conduct a comparative study of the mystical experiences induced by hallucinogens and those induced by the traditional methods of the Sufis.[21] Having gone to Mallorca as the secretary of an English witch, Idries now began to reinvent himself as a Sufi.

As practicing Muslims committed to the moral guidance of Sharia, the vast majority of historical Sufis had abhorred intoxicants (and those that didn't favored hashish or opium, not mescaline or mushrooms). But by framing Sufism in terms of mystical experience rather than moral purification, Western writers of the 1950s and '60s had already begun to blur the boundaries between Sufism and psychedelia. In 1954 Aldous Huxley had published *The Doors of Perception*, a philosophical essay about his experiences on mescaline. Robert Zaehner—Oxford's Spalding Professor of Eastern Religions—was also soon experimenting with the drug, replacing his all-too-regular whiskey with a postprandial dose of mescaline. As a scholar of Sufism, Zaehner's short psychedelic season predated Idries's comparison of Muslim mystics with mescaline eaters. In his 1957 book *Mysticism Sacred and Profane*, he described listening in awe, in his tasteful rooms at All Souls, to Berlioz's *Te Deum*, while gazing in wonder at "a Feraghan [Afghan rug] of extraordinarily rich design with a basic coloring of deep, glowing russets."[22] Nonetheless, Zaehner ultimately decided that true mystical experiences couldn't be induced by drugs. Instead, it was Gordon Wasson, the retired vice-president of J.P. Morgan, who promoted magic mushrooms among a wider public through books that theorized the importance of mushrooms as the basis of early religions.[23] Through a kind of Protestant psychedelic theology, Wasson reasoned that because these were the earliest forms of religion, they were also the truest.

Robert was already familiar with Wasson's writings through his research for *Food for Centaurs*, but after another visit from Idries, he wrote excitedly to Wasson about a breakthrough in their shared search for the role of psychedelics in ancient history. Recounting his latest conversational marathon with Idries, Robert described how "at the end of 24 hours' talk about poetry and other things, he came to mushrooms." Idries had then said he had an Indian cousin whom he had sent undercover on Robert's behalf to investigate Hindu rituals by "impersonating a Brahmin."[24] At that point, Idries had revealed that Hindu Brahmins prepared a trippy elixir from the urine of fellow priests who had eaten sacred cowpats offered to their gods.[25] Even Ikbal played a cameo role in this plot to steal this Brahminical ambrosia. For as Robert explained to Wasson, Idries's father had informed Idries that "SUMA is the name of a tree-fungus in Afghanistan (where some of the Vedas were written)."[26]

In the spring of 1961, Robert invited Idries to return to Mallorca and spend part of the summer with him.[27] By now Idries was slowly settling into his new persona as a Sufi, describing himself as such in letters to acquaintances like T. C. Lethbridge.[28] Yet it was a strange kind of Sufism he was espousing, having little in common, apparently, with the teachings of twelve centuries of Muslim mystics. But then, he considered himself an adapter of Sufism, extracting what seemed most relevant to modern times, and sometimes that meant adopting modern jargon. Hence Idries's Sufism was about what he called "ecstatogenic processes," metaphysical phenomena that were entirely in accord with the laws of science—if only scientists would investigate them![29] After all, it was the decade of Dan Dare, Sputnik, and the H-bomb. Idries next informed Robert and Lethbridge that he had made scientific experiments that proved that static electrical forces underlay the psychic powers of the Sufis.[30] He told them he had spent the last twenty years practicing hypnosis too, which apparently also had something to do with Sufism.[31]

These skills were soon called on, for shortly before Idries returned to Deià, Robert wrote in desperation asking him, when he arrived, to cure the mental ailments of an unnamed member of his household. Idries agreed, requesting photographs of the patient to help him prepare a course of hypnosis.[32] In July, he was back in Mallorca, though a vacation *chez* Graves was never really relaxing—one of Robert's rejected goddesses or sidelined children was always shouting and screaming.[33]

Still, throughout that therapeutic summer, Idries echoed Robert's deriding of conventional psychiatry. The poet had already collaborated with William Sargant, who moved on the dark side of the psychotherapy moon with interests in brainwashing, indoctrination, and thought control.[34] For his part, Idries belittled mainstream psychiatry as the work of amateurs whose "claptrap" risked turning people into "zombies."[35] What mentally ill people needed was a healer who blended Eastern insight with a strobe light—a psychologizing Sufi for modern times.[36] Such ideas were much in fashion among artists and intellectuals: Alan Watts, the self-styled "philosophical entertainer" to the nascent counterculture, had just published *Psychotherapy East and West*, in which he blended Buddhist, Daoist, and Yogic teachings with doses of Freud and Jung.

Over the next two years, Idries visited Deià repeatedly, staying at La Posada, the guest house Robert had built for his friends. Their bond deepened as Idries further promoted the idea of their shared kinship and ancestry.[37] Through his visits to Mallorca, Idries learned a good deal from Robert about medieval European literature and came to speak very good Spanish. Robert learned from Idries in turn and began lecturing on the notion of *baraka*, an elusive Arabic term for "blessing" that Idries claimed had secretly inspired the medieval troubadours with whom Robert had long identified.[38] With his connections to Gerald's neopagans, Idries also told the poet that his *White Goddess* was being debased by the new witch cults, though in the case of the Scottish nationalist witch Major Boothby, he asked Robert not to reveal that it was he who had been spying on the major's militant coven.[39] Where there were cloaks, there were daggers.

By 1962, Idries's influence was such that Robert's older friends were warning him to be careful. He responded by telling them to follow Idries's teachings themselves.[40] For teachings of a sort there now were: hints about arcane knowledge, talk of meetings in Eastern hermitages, quiet allusions to secret societies, the oblique recounting of old fables recast as Sufi parables that listeners were too bashful to confess they didn't understand.

When Idries wasn't staying in Robert's rambling compound, which regularly hosted visitors from every branch of the arts, he was back in London working on a follow-up to his books on magic and witches. Having moved to Steele's Road in Hampstead, he completed a history of secret societies.[41] Some of its chapters served familiar fare: the Knights Templar, the Rosicrucians, the Assassins (all fascinating to Robert). But others dealt with darker sects, like the Balkan Skoptsi, whose name, he explained, meant "The Castrated"—a reference to their initiation by bloody hatchet.[42] He devoted a chapter to the Triads of Malaysia, about whose smuggling rackets the former customs official Gerald had told many a tale. Another turned to the cult of the Black Mother, a chapter that Robert, in his own idiosyncratic religiosity, used as the basis for an Oxford lecture on the Sufi origins of Sicily's black Madonnas.[43]

In his earlier works, Idries had paid scant attention to the Sufis, but he now devoted an entire chapter to them.[44] Set far from the distant East, it described a gathering of Sufis in a country house in Sussex, their beliefs seeming little different from those of the Templars and Mithraists of adjacent pages. The book's author made no suggestion that he was a Sufi himself; though, as far as readers were concerned, the author wasn't Idries Shah. After being Jack Bracelin (too rustic) and William Foster (too plain), he had now assumed a more mysterious moniker, a name from nowhere, albeit with echoes of conversations with the classicist Robert. Now Idries was Arkon Daraul, an *archon*, one of the "lords" of ancient Greece.

He kept up his new name for his next book, *Witches and Sorcerers*.[45] It was a follow-up to *The Secret Lore of Magic*, written for the same publisher, who the following year would publish the first *Doctor Who* annual. Despite sensationalist lapses, Idries tried to uphold the scholarly tone of his previous books. His years as an Oxford outsider still haunted his prose, which had more of the self-taught high seriousness of Colin Wilson than Vidia Naipaul's ironic Oxonian wit. The thirty-five chapters surveyed mostly familiar figures: the witches of Salem, Cornelius Agrippa, the Doctors Dee and Faustus, and Matthew Hopkins the Witch-Finder General.

What was new about *Secret Societies* and *Witches and Sorcerers* was the coverage the two books provided of contemporary practices that Idries had encountered at meetings of various cults around London. In the respectable suburb of Putney, he entered a basement where sixty young people gyrated in ecstasy before a statue of a Peacock Angel.[46] There was, he wrote, "no slit-eyed oriental or turbaned sheik" in sight; the dancers were all converts to a sect imported from Syria.[47] He spent an evening with James, a bank clerk from the north of England and graduate of a redbrick university who had turned his tiny apartment into a magician's laboratory.[48] It seemed to work: James had recently had a win on a football sweepstake. Whereas thirty years earlier Ikbal had hobnobbed with London's upper-class converts to Islam, his son was surveying the larger spiritual marketplace of the early 1960s in which Gerald's Wicca and the straitlaced Sunnism of Lady Khalida Buchanan-Hamilton were no longer the only alternatives to Christianity.

Idries's pseudonyms may have proved useful when he was out exploring, or "trawling," as he preferred to say. The problem was that the names he had so far adopted weren't entirely credible in person. While he might easily pass for an Italian, he looked rather less like a Jack Bracelin, and no one looked like they could really be called Arkon Daraul. Enter Omar Burke, a somehow honest alias that sounded as though its bearer might indeed be half Indian and half Scottish.[49] The year 1962, in which Omar Sharif starred in *Lawrence of Arabia*, was a good time to take the name Omar (even if it did already belong to his brother). Idries wrote to introduce Omar Burke to Robert, describing him in the third person as a casual but intriguing acquaintance, a dependably trustworthy chap, who also happened to be a Sufi and an admirer of Robert's poems.[50] Burke had mentioned, Idries continued, that he was interested in publishing in American magazines (he could apparently write extremely well), so perhaps Robert could put him in touch with some editors?[51] Idries would handle the paperwork, since Burke had agreed to submit all his writings through him. And Burke had much to write about, having recently explored Tunisia and Iran and even sneaked into Mecca to spend time with the Sufis there.

Robert suggested in reply that Burke try *The Atlantic*, to whose editor Idries sent a letter under Omar Burke's name, proposing an article and explaining that Robert Graves had suggested he write.[52] A few weeks later Idries wrote back to Robert, announcing that Burke had just telephoned with disappointing news that the editor's response had been lukewarm.[53] Since Burke was dashing off to India—hence the urgency of the phone call—Idries asked Robert to follow up with *The Atlantic* on his behalf. As it turned out, the editor still passed on the proposal. Idries had to publish Burke's first piece in the Edinburgh-based *Blackwood's Magazine*.[54] Far from cracking the rich American market that every British writer set their sights on, Burke appeared in the pages of a relic of empire that still published tales of adventure by old India hands who now held sway over little more than their typewriters.

In December 1961 and again the following month, *Blackwood's* published two articles by Omar Burke. The first, "Solo to Mecca," served to introduce Burke to readers: Idries patched together aspects of his own and his brother Omar's upbringing to present his alter ego as the son of Scottish parents whose mother had given him his unusual name through her love for the poems of Omar Khayyam.[55] Despite his name, Burke explained in this first article, he was not a Muslim. Nevertheless, drawing on the old imperial trope of the infidel explorer who sneaks into Mecca, he planned to inveigle his way to the Kaaba as Sir Richard Burton had done a century earlier. After a few desultorily touristic escapades, Burke eventually succeeded in making a whistlestop pilgrimage to Mecca via a day trip in a station wagon. He also journeyed to Pakistan, where he spent a month in a secret Sufi monastery in the remote Afghan borderlands. It was there, he confided to his readers, that he first heard the name of Idries Shah, whom the master of that distant hermitage described as a "mysterious figure" who roamed around the planet teaching people.[56] What was more, the Afghan dervish whispered to Burke, Idries Shah was the current "Grand Sheikh" of the Sufi path.[57]

Having successfully launched Idries as a Sufi master, Burke's second article gave an impression of Sufism that might appeal to Britain's freethinking avant-garde. It related a journey through Tunisia, a camel caravan crossing of the desert to a remote Sufi monastery in a far oasis described as the Clapham Junction of the Sahara.[58] Riding beside Burke was Hamid, a Sufi master who revealed the true nature of reality by telling simple stories. As they plodded through the sands, Hamid explained that Sufism was the original source of all religions and that all the world's great religious teachers had been Sufis.[59] Along the mirage-laden way, Burke wondered whether the Sufis' ecstatic experiences were similar to those derived from taking mescaline or mushrooms. When he finally reached the oasis and joined the Sufis in their dance, his experiences echoed those described by Gordon Wasson, the American expert on magic mushrooms.[60]

As though Robert's circle in Deià had slipped south into the Sahara, the oasis was Idries's Sufi-tinged fantasy of bohemia. His actual travels that year, though, had little to do with the discomfort of camel treks. A few months after the article appeared, he wrote to Robert from an Istanbul hotel, describing holidaying on the Black Sea's beautiful beaches and relaxing on the Princes' Islands, the favored resort of Turkey's secular elite.[61] Far from lodging with Sufi Bedouin, he was staying in the Park Hotel, whose spacious suites boasted modern bathrooms, in-room telephones (a luxury in the Turkey of the early 1960s), and views over Istanbul's most Westernized neighborhood.[62]

By contrast, in the stories Idries was telling as Omar Burke, imperial nostalgia met the nascent counterculture in accounts of psychedelic camel treks through the mysterious East, as though such tales eased the pain of decolonization's many disasters. Taking the cue from a section about the mountain lair of the Ismailis in Idries's *Secret Societies*, and reworking James Hilton's Shangri-La novel, *Lost Horizon*, in another article Burke described a journey to the hidden mountain of the Ismailis in remote northwestern Iran. One of the readers of the article was Reginald Hoare, a wartime intelligence officer turned follower of George Gurdjieff, a spiritual teacher of indeterminate ancestry from the Caucasian edges of the old Russian Empire.

Gurdjieff had found his first followers in Paris, where he seemed to appear from nowhere after the First World War with tales of "meetings with remarkable men" throughout the lands of the East.[63] Since his death in 1949, his followers had struggled to find a successor, and the reins eventually fell into the hands of Englishman Russell Page, who had previously been married to Gurdjieff's niece. But Russell Page turned out to be no leader.[64] And so when the Gurdjieffians of Paris looked to him for guidance, he in turn searched for a new master through his contacts with Reginald Hoare's circle of Gurdjieff followers in London.

That circle was being led by the retired businessman John Godolphin Bennett. A graduate of London's School of Oriental Studies, Bennett had met Gurdjieff in Istanbul in 1920 when he was working as a Middle East adviser to the British government. After a subsequent career in the solid fuel industry, Bennett had founded his Gurdjieff-inspired Institute for the Comparative Study of History,

Philosophy and the Sciences. Taking advantage of strapped state finances at the end of the war, he had then bought a country mansion in Surrey, called Coombe Springs, from the British Coal Utilisation Research Association. Reggie Hoare had become a regular visitor. But as time passed, Gurdjieff's disciples in Surrey had become disillusioned with Chairman Bennett's mundane management of their spiritual affairs. By 1962, they were looking for a new leader, preferably one who came from "the East" like Gurdjieff himself. One of those seekers was Reggie Hoare, the reader of Omar Burke's article.

A few weeks after the appearance of that article naming Idries as the "Grand Sheikh" of Sufism, Chairman Bennett was organizing a seminar on Gurdjieff's psychology. Opening the morning post at his orderly desk, he read a letter from Reggie Hoare, excitedly explaining that he had just read the most extraordinary article about secret Sufi monasteries whose teachings were unmistakably connected to Gurdjieff's.[65] Surely, Reggie went on, the author of the article (a mysterious chap called Omar Burke) had discovered the source of Gurdjieff's doctrines—perhaps even the sanctuary of the Sarmoung Brotherhood, where Gurdjieff claimed to have studied.

Reggie had already written to the editor of *Blackwood's* magazine asking to be put in direct contact with Burke. A few days later Reggie received a letter from Idries, who explained somewhat awkwardly that he was in fact Omar Burke. By the time Chairman Bennett in turn replied to Reggie, the latter had gone ahead and met with Idries. Moreover, he had taken with him four fellow institute members. Bennett was furious. Having previously been disappointed by several Eastern teachers, he was wary about falling for another one, not least now that he was leading a spiritual fellowship of his own. But Reggie Hoare was persuasive. He and his wife arranged to bring the mysterious author, whom he understood to be from Central Asia, for dinner at a prim London restaurant, where the chairman and Mrs. Bennett would join them.

After all the buildup about Sufi monasteries in the mountains of Iran and the Sahara, Idries perhaps appeared disappointingly metropolitan. Nor did the evening much improve after that first impression, for Idries seemed restless, smoking incessantly and seeming too intent on making a good impression.[66] When Mrs. Hoare, who was Russian, asked where he had learned such perfect English, Idries said he'd learned it by sitting on his own in a cave reading Shakespeare.[67] After the dinner, Bennett complained that Idries "spoke impeccable English and but for his beard and some of his gestures he might well have been taken for an English public school type."[68] As for Idries's allusions to the Sarmoung Brotherhood, Bennett thought he might have learned as much from a glimpse through Gurdjieff's writings, which also made cryptic allusions to Afghanistan.[69] Mrs. Bennett, who had long suffered from her husband's many mentors, was even less impressed, later telling friends that Idries had clambered bizarrely over the restaurant's furniture.[70]

All told, the dinner was a disaster, so for the rest of the summer, Idries seems to have busied himself with reading everything he could about George Gurdjieff, the mysterious man from the East who had so impressed Bennett's circle. He may have already taken an interest in Gurdjieff from Colin Wilson's *The Outsider*, but he had much more to learn. As well as describing the fantastical Sarmoung Brotherhood, Gurdjieff had also recounted amusing anecdotes about the fictional Mulla Nasrudin that he first heard as folktales during his childhood in Russian-ruled eastern Turkey.[71] The adult Gurdjieff, for his refined Parisian followers, had then recast the rustic wisdom of Mulla Nasrudin as "subtly philosophical questions."[72] Idries would also now have read the Sufi "teaching stories" that Gurdjieff recounted, and he would have learned about the exercises he set for his students, especially the "Stop" exercise, during which students had to freeze in whatever position they were in when the master shouted "Stop." It was meant to break established habits of behavior and so pave the way to freedom.

Meanwhile Chairman Bennett decided to put his peculiar dinner with the urbane, table-tottering Afghan behind him and go back to teaching seminars at his institute. But as the summer months rolled by, Idries continued to meet Reggie Hoare, who relayed to Bennett his claim to be Gurdjieff's successor. By fall, the chairman conceded. He trusted Reggie not only as a fellow Gurdjieffian of forty years standing but also as a former wartime intelligence operative. In the autumn of 1962, Bennett invited Idries to speak at his institute. A few years earlier Pak Subuh, the Indonesian Muslim founder of a new religion called Subud, had spent several weeks there, after which Bennett had written a book that briefly spread Subud worldwide.[73] Now Idries stepped onto the same platform. That day the English followers of George Gurdjieff gathered at Coombe Springs to meet a man announced as having recently arrived from Afghanistan; little did they know that he had been raised a mere seven miles away, in Belmont.

It is not surprising that Idries seemed at ease that day: he was in his native habitat. But Coombe Springs, the home of Bennett's institute, was different from the suburban house where he had grown up: it was a grand country mansion set in seven acres of landscaped gardens. The overall effect was enhanced by the Djamichunatra (or "Djami," as younger followers preferred), a ninety-foot-tall, nine-sided hall designed by the architect Robert Whiffen in the form of Gurdjieff's cosmic key, the enneagram, for performing ritual dances.[74] Close to London, Coombe Springs attracted hundreds of visitors every weekend, drawn more by the funky Djami than by Chairman Bennett's Sunday talks or the formal dinners with a high table from which he presided.[75]

Idries needed something special to face the large Sunday crowd. It was a new experience for him—he was more used to convincing people through intimate conversations and the solitary work of writing. But he came prepared. Rather than adopting Bennett's country gentleman look with tweeds, pipe, and halting professorial speech, Idries came dressed in a camouflage boilersuit.[76] With a matching cap pulled down over his eyes, he completed the look by dangling a cigarette from the corner of his mouth. An incongruously proletarian presence at Bennett's bourgeois assembly, he arrived early and spent the weekend conspicuously pushing a wheelbarrow around the gardens. When after Sunday lunch to everyone's surprise the tall guerrilla gardener stood up to speak, it looked like a revolution was going down: the servants were taking over the mansion. Instead of accepting the leather armchair provided for the chairman's guest speakers, Idries sat cross-legged on the floor among the young seekers in the hall, who were gripped as he began to speak.

Hinting at ties to the illuminated masters of Shangri-La and to Gurdjieff's mysterious Sarmoung Brotherhood, he announced that he had been sent from the East by "the Guardians of the Tradition." For that, he quietly confided, was the true name of the Sarmoung Brotherhood. With slowly cultivated suspense, he pulled a document from his boilersuit pocket and read it aloud. With its suitably portentous title of "The Declaration of the People of the Tradition," the text was long and convoluted, and full of vague imperatives.[77] No one could quite tell what it all meant, but the gist seemed to be that there was a secret doctrine that was the preserve of an invisible hierarchy, who had now decided the time was ripe to share it with humankind. Idries ended his pronouncement by declaring that the invisible hierarchy was currently seeking individuals with the capacity to digest their higher knowledge. Lest his audience miss the implication that he was the hierarchs' representative, he ended by plainly telling them so.[78]

Through his father's stories of the dazzling East, and his own travels under the Mediterranean sun, Idries had glimpsed a way of life more vital than the gray concrete that characterized Britain's cities in the early 1960s. With the frowning earnest seekers at Coombe Springs, he was trying to share that sense of being alive, of being awake to the possibilities of existence and imagination. If necessary, he would use the skills of invention that Ikbal had taught him—and the sense of the absurd that led him to deliver his "Declaration of the People of the Tradition" in the shabby overalls of an avant-gardener.

One regular visitor who was present that day was Ivan Tyrrell, a student at Croydon Art College. Despite his interest in Gurdjieff, he had always found Chairman Bennett's lectures too formal and stuffy.[79] Listening to Idries was an altogether different experience, "a breath of fresh air: modern, irreverent and serious all at once."[80] After Idries read his "Declaration" that Sunday, Ivan and other members of the institute gathered eagerly around him. Blending Wilson's *Outsider* with his reading of Gurdjieff, Idries talked of humanity being asleep, of people being unaware of life's purpose and possibilities, even though they had the potential to achieve higher consciousness: to stop being sleepwalkers (Wilson's pop existentialism), to be awake (the prime command of Gurdjieff). Courtesy of Chairman Bennett's years of groundwork, Idries was finding a new, and younger, audience.

Bennett himself was still not fully convinced, though, so every week through 1962 and into '63, the two men held private meetings that continued for hours as Idries tried to convince the chairman that he was who he said he was.[81] The research Idries had done for his books and all the tales he had heard from his father provided an endless resource for his weekly disclosures. Though Bennett was older by far, it was he who drove up from Surrey, traversing the whole of London to meet Idries in Hampstead.[82] Who went to whom notwithstanding, Idries had excellent manners and was usually able to put people at ease. But he made no secret of his goal, telling Bennett he sought to "validate himself," to prove that he was the messenger of the People of the Tradition (or "the Hidden Directorate" as the bureaucratic chairman preferred).[83]

John Bennett had spent his entire life (not to mention his fortune) on his spiritual search, so before he got into his car to drive to each meeting, he prayed for a sign. One day when he was halfway to London, an answer popped into his head: he must pray together with Idries. When he mentioned this, Idries agreed, though on his way home, Bennett realized his request had been ignored—they hadn't prayed after all. It wasn't Idries's thing. Though Idries now talked endlessly about Sufis, the early London mosques his father had attended were not for him; nor were the growing number of Muslim immigrants who now went to them. Many of those working-class worshippers, particularly those from India and Pakistan, had been devoted to Sufi masters back in their homelands, to traditional miracle workers able to look after their quotidian worries about health, jobs, and children. But Idries had no interest in the spiritual affairs of Muslim factory workers; nor for that matter did other middle-class Britons. Someone else would take care of them.

Instead, Idries's talk of self-discovery and psychology was aimed at the Anglo-Saxon seekers who flocked every Sunday to Coombe Springs, where he was becoming a regular speaker. Conveniently, Gurdjieff's *Meetings with Remarkable Men* had just been posthumously published, lending Idries access to its tales of Central Asian Sufis, to whom he laid claim as an Afghan from an ancient Sufi lineage. To seal Idries's connections with the source of Gurdjieff's teachings, the respectable-sounding Major Desmond Martin published an article purporting to report his discovery of the home of the Sarmoung Brotherhood during an intrepid hike through Afghanistan's Hindu Kush.[84] Still more conveniently, the major confirmed Idries's claim that Gurdjieff's teachers had been Sufis.

Meanwhile the London-based members of Bennett's institute, in turn, introduced Idries to Russell Page, who was still struggling to hold together Gurdjieff's followers in Paris. After a meeting that went on for hours, Russell too accepted Idries's claim to have been sent by the same Central Asian masters who had illuminated Gurdjieff. In a letter to Solita Solano, the lesbian poet and erstwhile secretary of Gurdjieff, Russell proclaimed, "This man is from the source which G found and where he learnt all that he knew and was. This man and his family and ancestors far way back belong to and have worked as a part of the source and in fact his grandfather helped G and then all things that G made in his [teaching] plan in Afghanistan."[85] And so, Russell continued, "the entire G activity lies here, for Mr. Shah lives in London."[86]

While this was good news for Londoners, it was less convenient for the rudderless Gurdjieffians by the Seine. So Idries came up with a solution: he would send his elder brother Omar to France.[87] After all, his possession of higher knowledge came through their ancestral Afghan lineage, and Omar had inherited a share too. Soon afterward, in 1963, Bristol-born Omar moved to Paris to reside there with his new followers, renting a space for them to live and setting everyone to raise funds.[88] First he told them to sell all their books (especially those by Gurdjieff). Then part of the building he rented in the Latin Quarter's picturesque Passage Saint-André-des-Arts was turned into a shop called Le Troubadour, which his followers replastered and decorated, transforming the upstairs rooms into a *tekkia*, or Sufi lodge.[89] Everyone was encouraged to spend as much time with Omar as possible. Even vacations—group camping trips to Spain, then Turkey—became part of their discipleship.[90] They were told to address their new leader as either "Agha," "Sir," or "Master," and to write private letters to Master Omar explaining their deepest desires.

Their next instructions were to cease Gurdjieff's spiritual exercises and to call Idries and Omar's teachings "The Tradition." But what replaced Gurdjieff's doctrines was a mélange of more recent provenance, for Thursday meetings in Paris now began with the chanting of a Buddhist mantra, followed by tape recordings of Idries reading what were said to be Sufi teaching tales.[91] In these lectures, speaking softly in his elegant voice, Idries blended what he had read of the occult with Orientalist translations of Persian poems and the Sufi stories recounted by Gurdjieff, who had perhaps invented them himself.

Henceforth Idries and Omar would carefully conceal their English childhoods and imperial pasts. The accent Idries had acquired in Oxford could stay—after all, the British were raised to obey it—but otherwise he would now present his identity as Afghan, editing from his family history the alliance of his ancestors with the British that had been points of pride for his father and forebears. Instead, he cultivated a new postcolonial persona of pristine authenticity. Idries had already turned away from his father's great game of imperial politics to focus on the world's invisible forces instead. Now he would play with the occult energies of identity. Before the crowds at Coombe Springs, he learned the art of speaking on behalf of somewhere else, of being the spokesman of the People of Tradition from faraway lands.

Idries approached his fortieth birthday as a man purged of his past. But his new identity still had to be made official—and where better than in the newspaper of record, *The Times*? There an article by an anonymous correspondent now appeared, titled "Elusive Guardians of Ancient Secrets." It purported to be a report from Afghanistan's Hindu Kush, in whose distant mountains the correspondent had gained entry to a secret circle of Sufis. Amid scenes redolent of Rudyard Kipling's tales of the Afghan frontier, *Times* readers learned that, at the climax of their ritual chants, the Sufis called out "Idd-rees Shaah!"[92]

Meanwhile back in suburbia, it was time for Idries to settle his domestic arrangements. In the autumn of 1963, he married his girlfriend, Cynthia Kabraji.[93] Much like Idries, Cynthia was born of an imperial union between an Indian man, who originally came to London as a student, and a woman from the Celtic fringe of empire. Her father, Fredoon Kabraji, the son of a colonial civil servant, was a Zoroastrian who in the early 1920s had sailed from Bombay to take up a place at University College London.[94] Failing to finish his degree, like Ikbal, Fredoon took up poetry and came to know the Indian writer Mulk Raj Anand, who worked with Eliot and Orwell. He then married his Welsh girlfriend Nellie Wilkinson, who gave birth to the triplets Christopher, Eleanor, and Cynthia, who received a cultured upbringing on Primrose Hill near Hampstead.[95]

As a Bombay Parsi, Fredoon belonged to India's most Anglicized community; in London he became the gently bohemian author of *A Minor Georgian's Swan Song*, an anthology of poems with a cover of a naked boy sketched in the style of Eric Gill.[96] A charcoal portrait in the frontispiece showed Fredoon himself, huge eyes blazing above cheekbones as delicate as a bird's. In the preface he declared his admiration for Yeats, Orwell, and especially Edmund Gosse, whose name reappeared in one of the poems.[97]

Remaining in Britain after India's independence, Fredoon helped found the New India Publishing Company and became a close friend of Robert Graves.[98] It was Fredoon who first cultivated in Robert an interest in Indian poetry in English, leading Robert to promote another Parsi poet called Keki Daruwalla. For her part, his daughter Cynthia had visited Robert in Mallorca before Idries ever set foot there.[99] Raised in a cosmopolitan corner of London that Idries didn't enter till he was thirty, Cynthia knew many of her father's literary friends. Still, Idries was some years older than her, and having traveled to the Middle East and South America, he had an international air that seemed debonair in the gray London of the early 1960s. As they grew closer, he revealed another side of himself, playful and humorous. When she introduced him to her father, Fredoon's first words were "I hear you are a very funny man."[100]

By the time they married in 1963, Cynthia had acquired a new name. "Cynthia" was one of the names of the Greek goddess Artemis, about whom Robert had written a chapter in his *Greek Myths*. But so European a name would hardly do for the consort of an Afghan Sufi, so Cynthia became Kashfi, a play on a Persian word that meant "She Who Discovers." It also had the Hollywood cachet of being the name of Marlon Brando's wife, Anna Kashfi—a Welsh woman who claimed to be Indian.

Three years had now passed since Idries first met Robert, but they kept up their conversations through regular visits and letters. The poet was keen that Idries should write a book on the Sufis, prompting Idries to ask him whether his American publishing contacts would be interested.[101] After Robert agreed to act as go-between, Idries sent him a book proposal called "The Sufi Way," hinting at how much it would help if Robert would endorse it.[102] He agreed, but suggested a snappier title: the book should simply be called "The Sufis."[103] Idries followed his advice, sending the proposal to Doubleday, a New York publisher with which Robert had profitably worked for over thirty years and that had published his psychedelic *Food for Centaurs*.[104] Robert ensured that his own literary agent carried out the negotiations, and when he also agreed to write a foreword, a contract was quick in coming.[105]

In between meetings with Bennett's Gurdjieffians, Idries wrote regularly to Robert for advice about royalties and taxes on overseas sales.[106] For writing his foreword, Robert would receive 10 percent of all royalties—not a bad share for penning twelve pages of a four-hundred-page book. But for Idries, the Doubleday contract marked a decisive shift in his career, projecting him from the occult byways of Grub Street to the top-tier publishers of Broadway. It also coincided with his marriage to Kashfi, allowing them to move to a detached Georgian residence in North London, with steps leading up to a graceful portico.[107] (Idries's sister, Amina, moved into the ground-floor rooms.)[108] Their street ran off Abbey Road where, a ten-minute walk away, the Beatles were recording *A Hard Day's Night*. There, amid London's creative ley lines, Idries sat down to write *The Sufis*.

He also continued his correspondence with Robert in which, business matters aside, the poems of Hafiz (in English) rubbed shoulders with Wasson's psychotropic experiments and the hidden meanings of *The Arabian Nights*.[109] But when Robert suggested that Idries consult the works of A. J. Arberry, professor of Arabic at Cambridge and author of numerous studies of Sufism, Idries poured scorn: Arberry and his fellow Orientalists had no understanding of Sufism whatsoever.[110] Idries would show them the true meaning of Sufi teachings.[111] Still, he admitted, he was happy to use the translations from Arabic and Persian made by Arberry and other Orientalists like Reynold Nicholson, H.A.R. Gibb, Louis Massignon, and Miguel Asín Palacios.[112] At once building on and rejecting the Orientalists' studies of Sufism, *The Sufis* would mark Idries's coming of age as a writer, as he exorcised the ghosts of Wilson, Gardner, and Gurdjieff by summoning the spirits of his own cultural heritage—albeit solely on the Afghan rather than the Scottish side.

Early in 1964, just before *The Sufis* was published, Gerald Gardner was sailing home, after wintering in Lebanon, aboard the cruise
liner *Scottish Prince*. He died en route and was buried in Tunis in
the Christian Cimetière du Belvédère.[113] It was an ironic end for
an English witch, but for Idries, the closure was timed perfectly:
interred with his former mentor were the British occult roots of the
Sufi master from Afghanistan.

Chapter Ten

MYSTIC

. . . he took a human being's privilege to fashion his
inner life for himself.

—Edmund Gosse, *Father and Son*

REFLECTING THE DAWN ON THE CULTURAL HORIZON, *THE
Sufis* mirrored the new spirit of the 1960s.[1] Like the collage technique of the Pop artists, it was a work of assemblage, mixing a mul-
titude of sources, from folktales and academicisms to digressions on
Freemasons and nuggets from *The Jewish Encyclopedia*, all placed
beside the cryptic utterances of the Sufis. With no formal structure,
it was a book to dip into, like the *I Ching* popularized by Carl Jung.
Suddenly, Sufism was the thing in hip London happenings. For bohemian readers, Robert's foreword presented Sufism as a form of "spiritual freemasonry" that belonged not to Muslims but to everyone,
via an eclecticism that linked the medieval mystic Ibn Arabi to the
Irish goddess Bridget, with court jesters and Druids thrown in for
good measure.[2]

Following Robert's cue, Idries downplayed the Islamic basis of
Sufism to present it as a freestanding system that could be neatly
detached from its Muslim foundations. Although, since their origins
in ninth-century Iraq, the Sufis had placed great emphasis on the
moral strictures of Sharia, Idries made no mention of the awkward
requirements of Islamic law, and wherever possible he overlooked
the doctrinal context in which Sufi ideas had developed. Though

the Quran was the foundation of Sufi thought, his most substantial reference to the scripture was a two-page appendix on its esoteric meaning.[3] While Sufism could, he admitted, be taught through
Islam, the latter was no better a vehicle than any other religion or,
indeed, no religion at all.[4]

The Middle Ages had seen plenty of Christian Sufis, he claimed,
and more recently, even Charles de Gaulle and Dag Hammarskjöld
were secretly Sufis.[5] (An ecumenical but deeply Christian Swede,
Hammarskjöld had once cited Rumi amid the cultural diplomacy of
being secretary-general of the United Nations.)[6] Idries also declared
Sufism to be the true source of Sikhism and of many Hindu mystical groups.[7] Though this statement had some historical credibility,
his assertion that Zen also derived from Sufism was factually untenable.[8] But in the religious markets of Britain and America, where
promoters of Zen and Yoga had been active for decades, to claim
Sufism as their origin was a canny way of co-opting the competition.

The ideas and style of The Sufis differed markedly from Ikbal's
Islamic Sufism, written four decades earlier. Following the Orientalist format, Ikbal had focused mainly on organization and doctrine,
making it clear that Sufism was part of Islam. Idries, by contrast, all
but eschewed questions of organization and doctrine and minimized
references to Islam. Although the book contained some leaden scho-
lasticisms, he dropped the scholarly mantle he had worn in his previous works. At over four hundred pages, The Sufis had the heft of a
learned tome, but unlike the expensive editions of the Orientalists, it
was an affordable mass-market work that would reach more readers,
and sell more copies, than any of the books by the learned professors. By shifting the tone from studying Sufism to teaching it, Idries
found a viable form of originality and readability.

While this elision of the Muslim religious profile of Sufism was a
historical travesty, it was based in Idries's conviction that Sufism was
in essence a learning system that could be adapted to any cultural
context. The trappings of Islam were not important, or at least not
essential. This approach meant that the message of The Sufis chimed

in harmony with some of the loudest philosophical and theological voices of the early 1960s. Echoing the vagabond existentialism of Colin Wilson's *The Outsider*, Idries's Sufism-without-religion dovetailed with the criticisms of organized religiosity made in the 1963 book *Honest to God* by the radical bishop of Woolwich, John Robinson. This unlikely bestseller drew on the existentialist theology of Paul Tillich to shatter the image of God as the heavenly overseer of humans; instead it recast the distant deity as the palpable "ground of our being."[9] In chapters with provocative titles like "An End to Theism?," Robinson called for "a break with traditional thinking" and a rejection of the need for "a particular code of morals" to allow people to embrace science and secularism.[10] *Honest to God* sold over 300,000 copies in the year running up to the 1964 publication of *The Sufis*.

As the latter's publisher knew, its place in the market was clear. A few years earlier the Tibetan lama Lobsang Rampa had written *The Third Eye*, revealing the esoteric teachings of Himalayan Buddhist masters. It was a huge hit, and by the time *The Sufis* appeared, Rampa had published five successful follow-ups, despite *The Daily Mail* revealing him to be a plumber from Devon called Cyril Hoskin.[11] If Lobsang Hoskin was dominating the Buddhist end of the market, the absence of a popular Sufi competitor offered plenty of commercial potential for Idries and his publishers. And with good reason: his book offered an exhilarating vision of mystics who had dug an infinitely deep well of wisdom. To a generation caught between the dreary Church of England and the godless Chairman Mao, a sip from its pages of parables felt liberating.

For if the spirit of Idries's book was very much of its British time and place, the cast of characters it quoted was drawn mainly from the medieval Middle East. *The Sufis* opened with an epigraph by Sana'i of Afghanistan, who told readers they were all asleep. This would become a keynote for Idries's concept of Sufism as a teaching tool for waking people up to their full human potential. The epigraph was followed by lively summaries and free translations from Rumi, Attar,

Ghazali, and other Sufi luminaries.[12] Even so, rather than to the Arabic and Persian manuscripts that Idries hinted he had consulted, the only proper citations were to Western studies of Sufism. For in order to reauthenticate himself as heir to an Afghan Sufi lineage, he immersed himself in Orientalism. Somewhat ironically, perhaps, he relied especially heavily on the Christian scholars Reverend W.H.T. Gairdner and Father Miguel Asín Palacios, whose ecumenical linking of Dante's *Divine Comedy* to the teachings of Ibn Arabi prefigured many of Idries's arguments.[13] Hence Sufism, Idries proposed, was the key influence behind every European spiritual impulse, from Catholic mysticism to Morris dancing.

While Idries's book cohered perfectly with culturally eclectic trends in the West, it could hardly have offered a greater contrast with influential books being written in the Middle East at the time, particularly those promoting anti-Sufi versions of Islam, whether Wahhabi or Salafi. By the 1960s, the combined forces of those sundry fundamentalisms were spreading from Arabia, Pakistan, and Egypt and robbing the Sufis of political influence almost everywhere in the Muslim world. In 1964, the same year *The Sufis* was published in New York and London, in Cairo the former literature teacher Sayyid Qutb wrote *Ma'alim fi al-Tariq* (Milestones). In it, he presented a plan of revolutionary violence through which "true Muslims" were called on to overthrow any government, Eastern or Western, that stood in the way of Sharia. Whereas Idries won readers by whittling away at religion to present a Sufism without Islam, Qutb espoused a politicized Islam that denounced the quiet mysticism of the Sufis as un-Islamic too. And so, for different reasons, in both the West and the East, Sufism was being detached from the religion for which it had served as the mystical life and soul for more than a millennium. While *Milestones* went through dozens of editions and translations, no one in literary London took notice. Carnaby Street was swinging; and the radicalized readers of Sayyid Qutb's dangerous book seemed far, far away.

Among the many reviews garnered by *The Sufis*, only one seri-

ously objected to Idries's approach. The MIT-trained Iranian scholar
Seyyed Hossein Nasr had just published an academic work entitled
Three Muslim Sages: Avicenna—Suhrawardi—Ibn Arabi. Nasr
declared Idries's book to be "an exposition of Sufism from which
Islam seems to have been subtly eliminated and Sufism presented as
an occultism and an esotericism 'floating in the air.' "[14] This denial of
the Islamic character of Sufism, he wrote, was a dangerous falsifica-
tion, for Muslims no less than for Westerners. In the *Journal of the
Royal Asiatic Society,* Cambridge's A. J. Arberry, whose reputation
Idries had derided to Robert, knowingly explained that "the author
of this book, eldest son of the Nawwab of Sardhana . . . is styled
in the publishers' advertisement as Grand Sheikh of the Sufis." Yet
Arberry couldn't help but enjoy the book's winning contrast to dry
academic treatments of the topic and concluded that *The Sufis* was
"a strange mixture of erudition and eccentricity."[15]

Such scholarly appraisals were small fry compared to the reviewer
for *The New York Times,* who was captivated by the playfully
serious teachings of this Afghan Sufi.[16] (The previous year James
Michener, in his best-selling novel *Caravans,* had paved the way by
portraying Afghanistan as a beguiling land of romance.) In London, meanwhile, reviews appeared by important literary figures of
the younger generation. Lured by Robert Graves's foreword, Ted
Hughes leaped onto the book with wide eyes, calling it nothing less
than "astonishing" and declared the Sufis the "biggest society of
sensible men there has ever been on the earth."[17] In *The Spectator,*
the disenchanted ex-Communist novelist Doris Lessing reviewed
the book. Lessing, after experimenting with Yoga and spending
afternoons in London's occult bookstore Watkins, had been turning
in her prose from the political to the psychological.[18] Hers wasn't a
review in the conventional sense, but a series of nonsequiturs about
inelasticity of thought and secret psychic languages. Freud was
mixed with the wisdom of the Bedouin; fashionable Tarot cards
were referenced, and everyone seemed to be covertly a Rosicrucian,
a Knight Templar, or a Sufi. They were all the same, if one only

understood—and Idries Shah clearly had. It was only artists, she concluded—people like herself and Robert Graves—who would "get" the book.

Doris Lessing first heard of Idries through the wife of Reggie Hoare, whom she met through her interest in Gurdjieff. A few months before she wrote her review, Idries had written her a letter introducing himself, and after reading *The Sufis*, Doris wrote back to ask him to take her on as his student.[19] Not only was she enchanted by what she read: as a novelist versed in the subtleties of "show not tell," the storytelling teaching mode of *The Sufis* spoke to her. The book also confirmed what she had read in Rafael Lefort's *The Teachers of Gurdjieff*, a text she had eagerly underlined—and that claimed that Idries spoke from the true source of Gurdjieff's teaching, to which Doris had previously been attracted.[20] By now, Idries was establishing his own teaching circles beyond Coombe Springs, which drew not only on Gurdjieff's use of "teaching stories" (albeit now solely of Sufi provenance) but also on Gurdjieff's dancelike exercises, which had more ties to the avant-garde Paris of the 1920s than to the traditional rituals of the Sufis, which prioritized formal prayer and reciting Allah's divine names as *dhikr*, or "remembrance."

Not long after Doris met Idries, the Chicago novelist Clancy Sigal, who had lived with her in London as her lover, went around telling people that she was having an affair with this mysterious man from Afghanistan.[21] She wasn't, though. Her budding relationship with the teacher she was told to address as "Shah" bore no physical intimacy, and for decades her letters to him would remain respectful and formal. But the inner void created by her rejection of Karl Marx had left Doris searching for a spirituality to replace her dreams of universal political brotherhood. With its Persian echoes of her childhood in Iran, Idries's cosmopolitan Sufism seemed to answer the deep needs of the novelist. For his part, Idries now had the approval not only of seventy-year-old Robert but also of one of the most influential young stars of the literary underground.

As *The Sufis* found its way into bookstore windows, Idries maintained his regular meetings with Chairman Bennett and his Coombe Springs Gurdjieffians. Bennett finally professed he was convinced.[22] The former Coal Board director now accepted that Idries was the Sufi master he said he was; that he was the spokesman of the People of the Tradition; that he had been sent by the Hidden Directorate; and that he was the one for whom Bennett had searched for decades. But now, Idries told him, words were not enough: the secret masters required tangible proof that their authority was accepted.[23] Bennett would have to surrender not only his followers but also his institute and the Coombe Spring estate, via a deed of gift, to the People of the Tradition.[24] Idries reportedly made plain the Hidden Directorate's demands: "the gift must be absolute, irrevocable, and completely voluntary."[25]

In the summer of 1965, Chairman Bennett held his final seminar at Coombe Springs and informed his long-standing followers of his plans. Shortly afterward Idries drove down from London to convey the urgency of the handover, since the Hidden Directorate said the time was nigh. Several of the institute's members revolted at the idea of signing over the estate, with its large Edwardian villa and seven acres of gardens, so, former corporate man that he was, Bennett turned to his institute's governing council. As the turmoil rolled on into autumn, he called an extraordinary general meeting of the members of the council of the Institute for the Comparative Study of History, Philosophy, and the Sciences. When the council convened, Bennett presented the proposal that Coombe Springs be gifted to the People of the Tradition, arguing long and hard in its favor. Eventually the motion passed. Coombe Springs, including its furniture and land, was signed over as a deed of gift to a new charitable foundation called the Society for Understanding the Foundation of Ideas.[26] Its initial letters cleverly spelled SUFI.

Bennett's secretary Helena Edwards was allowed to stay on, working in the same position for Idries, who needed an assistant to arrange the activities of SUFI.[27] But Bennett, together with Coombe Springs's long-term residents and his wife, moved into a semidetached house in neighboring Kingston-upon-Thames. Of the many members of the former institute, Idries allowed a select group to continue coming to Coombe Springs, "young people to work with and to become part of his entourage," as one witness later recalled.[28]

Unlike Bennett, with his businesslike indoor seminars, Idries made use of Coombe Springs's gardens, taking his new followers outside to sit for lessons on Mulla Nasrudin, the folkloric figure who cropped up in Gurdjieff's books and whom Idries now presented as the epitome of Sufi wisdom. Although Idries usually donned the tweed jackets and corduroys beloved by denizens of the 1950s book world, one afternoon, not long after founding SUFI, he appeared in a dark cloak, with a white scarf draped over his head and shoulders.[29] His brother Omar, visiting that day, donned a Bedouin robe and checked keffiyeh scarf of the kind Omar Sharif had recently worn in *Lawrence of Arabia*. Before they went into the gardens, Idries had his acolytes dress up in costume too, with Moroccan djellabahs for the men and caftans for the women. Once they were outdoors, with everyone sprawled around him on rugs, Idries sat cross-legged on a leopard skin, after the custom of Indian holy men, reading from a book on a wooden Quran stand in front of him. When someone took a photograph later that afternoon, the young men stood up to show off their swords while Omar brandished the musket that completed his tribal outfit. Idries often talked of his ancestor Jan Fishan, a man who, long ago in a land far away, had, he said, been both a Sufi and a warrior. That fine summer day in the English sunshine, posing with weapons and playing Afghan soldiers must have seemed like harmless fun.

As the months rolled by, Bennett rarely heard from Idries till he received an invitation to a celebration billed as Midsummer Revels.[30] When the day came, Coombe Springs's acres of grounds were filled with pavilion tents for acrobats, magicians, and belly dancers, in a free festival to launch SUFI on swinging London.[31] There were pop, folk, and jazz musicians too, along with a band playing what was said to be Afghan Sufi music. The nine-sided Djamichunatra was turned over to honky-tonk piano sessions by aspiring Swedish film-maker Leon Flamholc.[32] The famous father of "zany" comedy, Spike Milligan, was invited too.[33] Lasting two days and nights, the Mid-summer Revels was Idries's bid for the attention of the new gener-ation. Hundreds of young people turned up, many in Eastern robes and costumes. It was August 1966: the Beatles had just released *Revolver*, and as Buffalo Springfield sang that year, something was happening here. A new great game had begun.

Gurdjieff's days at Coombe Springs were over, just as surely as Chairman Bennett's were. And to make doubly sure, Idries had pub-lished a refutation of Gurdjieff's teachings under a new pseudonym, Rafael Lefort. *The Teachers of Gurdjieff* purported to be a study of his ideas, but reversing the flow of influence, it revealed that the true source of Gurdjieff's thought was the teachings of Idries Shah.[34] Though it had hardly taken "a real effort" to invent the anagram "Rafael Lefort," that didn't prevent Victor Gollancz, hero of liter-ary Hampstead and founder of the Left Book Club, from publish-ing the book.

When the summer ended, Coombe Springs was sold to a prop-erty developer.[35] Bennett reported that the estate went for £100,000, a colossal sum at a time when a starter home cost only £2,000.[36] The developers soon tore down the large house and the enneagram-shaped Djami that Frank Lloyd Wright had once visited, and twenty-eight luxury homes were built in the huge empty footprint.[37] Not long afterward Idries made arrangements for the purchase of Lang-ton House, a Regency mansion with eight bedrooms and a colonial-style veranda overlooking twelve acres of grounds.[38] It had been built in 1815 for the Powell family, whose Lord Baden-Powell founded the Boy Scouts and inspired the radio play that lent Idries his first public role. Located in a tranquil village near Tunbridge Wells, the house was adjacent to a Gothic Revival church by Sir Giles Gilbert-Scott and a village green overlooked by a country pub called The Hare.[39] Amid this most English of scenes, where cricket was played every

Sunday, Idries could raise the family he was starting with Kashfi, in a setting superior to that of his penny-pinching childhood.

Langton House was to be the base for various new ventures. Once he settled in, Idries founded the Society for Organising Unified Research in Cultural Education, or SOURCE. Though it sounded like a mystical equivalent to Ian Fleming's SPECTRE, featured in the previous summer's Bond film *Thunderball*, SOURCE was actually heir to Bennett's Institute for the Comparative Study of History, Philosophy and the Sciences. Idries presented its activities in terms of science and psychology as much as of Sufism.

An imposing octagonal structure with strikingly patterned doors was built in the garden at Langton House, but to distinguish it from Bennett's demolished Djamichunatra, it had one side fewer. Inside, its eight walls were covered with flashing lights and display gauges, for this was the Studio, designed by Dennis Fry, a professor of experimental phonetics at London University. Here, in what might be said to resemble one of Ken Adam's sets for the Bond movies, Idries would make recordings for his growing number of followers in London, New York, and Paris.[40] But the nerve center of SOURCE was an elegant book-lined study, where the reels of the tape recorders on Idries's desk turned for eight hours at a time, recording *pensées* for two secretaries to transcribe.[41]

Surrounding Langton House were gorgeously landscaped gardens, which the former Paris Gurdjieffian Russell Page was tasked with reviving.[42] On their walks around the acres of gardens, Idries revealed to Russell secrets about the medicinal herbs of the East, while the two men traded anecdotes about royal acquaintances: Idries about the House of Saud, Russell about the Duke and Duchess of Windsor, whose garden at Gif-sur-Yvette he had once transformed.[43] Since Russell had toured India and lived in Cairo (in swish Zamalek, naturally), they always had much to talk about.[44] And much work to do too. For Idries was recreating the palatial life of his forebears, on the opposite end of the disappeared empire.

◆

OMAR ALI-SHAH, two years older than Idries and residing in Paris with his own former-Gurdjieffian followers, took note of his sibling's success. He had inherited little of his father's work ethic, spending years drifting between jobs, traveling around Europe and farther afield, but he was still the sirdar's eldest son, whom the end of empire had robbed of his place in the imperial hierarchy. Having watched many doors open to his bookish younger brother and followed his blossoming relationship with Robert Graves, Omar made contact with the poet and presented himself as a Sufi master too. After all, Idries's claim to represent a family lineage of Sufis meant that Omar also had a claim to mystical mastery.

From Paris, Omar began corresponding with Robert, albeit taking a different tack—or rather two different tacks—from his brother. First, Omar made an appeal to Robert's artistic sensibilities by presenting himself as a fellow poet (albeit a Sufi one), indeed as an heir to the classical Persian poets. Since Robert liked to claim descent from ancient Welsh bards and had previously encouraged several Indian poets to write in English, he invited Omar into his circle in Deià as a bardic apprentice, as he had many before him. Then Omar made a second appeal, this time to Robert's military side: Graves was a former captain in the Royal Welch Fusiliers, a war memoirist in *Good-bye to All That*, and an early biographer of Lawrence of Arabia. So Omar told everyone at Deià that he was a retired general in the Afghan Army. Officer class, of course, like Robert, only far higher in rank than Captain Graves, nicely leveling their relationship. Strutting together, tall and erect, the two soldiers-turned-poets cut quite a figure in the villages of Mallorca.

Omar was quite unlike the other guests in Deià, scrawny beatniks and bespectacled literature graduates whose puny conversation was no match for his manly tales from the Afghan Army and wine-soaked couplets of Sufi verse. It didn't harm that the handsome Omar shared his name with the suave Egyptian actor in David Lean's film about Lawrence of Arabia that had recently been shown everywhere. Just as the Greek Christian Omar Sharif (born Michel Chalhoub) excelled in his role as an Arab warrior, so did the Scottish-Indian Omar as his Afghan Sufi counterpart.

Returning to Paris, Omar lodged with one of his followers at the quintessential Left Bank address of 167 Boulevard Saint-Germain, a two-minute walk from the existentialists' café, Les Deux Magots.[45] That winter of 1966 the two statues of Chinese mages that lent the café its name looked on serenely as Jean-Paul Sartre and Omar Ali-Shah imparted wisdom to the young acolytes who crowded around their tables.

Back in London, Idries's *The Sufis* was the literary talk of the town. Even in Paris, Omar heard reports of huge demand for the book, with long waiting lists for back orders.[46] The wonders that Robert had worked for his brother's career being plain to see, Omar began to lay plans for his own collaboration with Robert, to whom he now sent letter after letter. Having already presented himself as an expert on Sufi poetry, his letters became tutorials on the Persian classics, with excerpts from Rumi accompanied by exegetical commentaries to convince Robert of both his literary and mystical mastery.[47] From Rumi, Omar's letters turned to Sa'di, whose *Bustan*, or "Rose Garden," he was translating. He asked Robert for feedback.[48]

As for Idries, SUFI and SOURCE were not his only new ventures, and running short of neat acronyms, he also established the Association for the Study of Traditional Teachings. For Idries in some sense saw himself as a man of science, a Sufi psychologist. Despite occasionally donning Eastern outfits at Coombe Springs, he disdained the desultory dress of the Indian gurus who were then becoming popular, preferring tweed jackets and corduroys, with formal shirts, though not usually a tie. It was the look of the man of letters he was becoming. To connect his new organizations to more formal centers of learning, he contacted Sussex University which, designed in bold concrete, was the most progressive of the new universities founded in the 1960s. In February 1966 he delivered a guest lecture there, invited by trendy academics keen to "practise this other way of thinking."[49] As the fortunes of the Sufis fell toward their nadir in the Middle East, with the ascent of Salafis and Wahhabis, in Britain Idries had his Sussex lecture published by Octagon Press under the learned title *Special Problems in the Study of Sufi Ideas*.[50] Sales were not the point this time, for the aim was intellectual respectability, which Idries had craved ever since his youth as an Oxford outsider. And if a book's title sounded sufficiently tedious, then its contents must assuredly be scholarly.

Idries wasn't concerned with profiting from such self-published symposium proceedings, for he had just reached a publishing deal through Robert's literary agents, A. P. Watt.[51] Founded in 1875, it was the oldest literary agency in the world, its list of former clients reading like a roster of Britain's most financially successful authors, including H. Rider Haggard, H. G. Wells, Wilkie Collins, Arnold Bennett, Lewis Carroll, and Arthur Conan Doyle.[52] A couple of generations earlier, A. P. Watt had made a household name of Rudyard Kipling, that most gifted of empire's imaginers who made "the great game" a famous phrase.

Idries's representative at Watt was Hilary Rubinstein, who had previously launched the meteoric career of establishment outsider and Booker Prize winner Kingsley Amis. Through Rubinstein's negotiations, Idries now signed with Jonathan Cape, the highly respected publisher of Doris Lessing, who put in a good word with commissioning editor Tom Maschler.[53] Still in his early thirties, Maschler had made his reputation with an important anthology of new writers—Colin Wilson, John Osborne, Kenneth Tynan, and Doris herself—which in effect made him the impresario of the Angry Young Men (as well as Doris, the self-declared Angry Young Woman). In his introduction to the anthology, Maschler had claimed to be "uncovering a certain pattern taking shape in British thought and literature."[54] And so he was: his authors, whether the son of a Leicester factory worker like Wilson or the daughter of poor white

Rhodesian farmers like Lessing, came from outside the Oxbridge establishment that Ikbal had memorably derided as the "boiled-shirt school." A decade before Idries signed with Cape, Wilson's *The Outsider* had captivated readers with its homespun existentialism, its lambasting of the sleepwalking masses, its summaries of Gurdjieff, and its veneration of Lawrence of Arabia. With his similar teachings, now Idries was to join Wilson and the other ascendant outsiders on Tom Maschler's list.

Two years earlier Maschler had made Jonathan Cape a fortune by buying for £250 the British rights to *Catch-22*, a novel by then-unknown Joseph Heller. Maschler trusted his instincts, and when he read *The Sufis* (Doris had kept telling him about it) he was intrigued by an unnumbered chapter called "The Subtleties of the Mulla Nasrudin."[55] Idries probably first heard tales of Mulla Nasrudin from his father, before coming across the Mulla again in the writings of Gurdjieff, who had recast the old figure of folklore as a poser of "subtle philosophical questions."[56] But where Idries had got his ideas from was of no concern to Tom Maschler: as a publisher, he had a brilliant eye for the book market. He saw at once that the Mulla was in sync with the zeitgeist.

When Maschler had got past the fusty academic opening to Idries's chapter, he found the stories that followed were vivid and funny. They were about one of the great types of world literature: the idiot savant who always laughs last. The stories typically went like this: Once Mulla Nasrudin worked as a smuggler.[57] Every day he crossed the border with the panniers of his donkeys loaded with straw. And every day the border guards stopped and searched him. Tipped off about his smuggling, they knew the Mulla was up to something. But no matter how much they searched, they could never find anything hidden in his panniers. Finally, from frustration, they promised him immunity if he would tell them what he'd been smuggling all those years. He answered with one word: "Donkeys."

There were plenty more such tales. They were folklore, so they belonged to everyone, and there was no need to cite sources or worry about permissions. Moreover, Idries told them well, channeling his natural gifts as a raconteur and humorist. When he presented the Mulla Nasrudin tales to his growing number of students who gathered at Langton House on weekends, they became Sufi teaching stories. But to his publisher, that was neither here nor there. They were appealingly written, and at least potentially, they were literature that sold well. Zany tales were in vogue: Maschler had recently published two books of nonsense stories by John Lennon and sold 400,000 copies in Britain alone.

So Tom Maschler invited Idries for lunch at Soho's L'Escargot, the fashionable restaurant of choice for editors with expense accounts.[58] For all the high seriousness with which Idries talked that day about Mulla Nasrudin, he was made aware of the tales' financial potential too. Shortly after that meeting, Maschler began negotiations for him to write a whole book of Nasrudin stories. A few weeks later Idries responded with plans to found a limited company into which Cape should channel the anticipated royalties.[59] He also put a good deal of thought into publicity, asking the publisher to send three thousand postcards to the SUFI mailing list proclaiming "How Mulla Nasrudin Invented Truth."[60] When the book came out in November 1966, a copy was sent to the head of talks at the BBC.[61]

The Exploits of the Incomparable Mulla Nasrudin, the book Idries wrote with Maschler's encouragement, was both a commercial and a literary achievement.[62] Benefiting from Robert's feedback, his prose lost its old verbosity and found a sprightly verve.[63] His academic tendencies were shorn away into an introduction of just over a page that informed readers that while Sufis used the tales as spiritual parables, others could read them just for fun. The hundred stories that followed were often a mere paragraph in length. But the writing was exquisite, with beautifully pared sentences, such that the Mulla's wisdom slipped from page to mind without troubling the eyes on the way. The reviews were uniform in praise. *The Birmingham Post* called *The Exploits* "a humorous masterpiece," while to progressive readers of *The New Statesman*, Doris Lessing testified that it contained "the secret of life, no less!"[64]

All in all, it was writing, and editing, of a high order. What was more, it captured the carefree spirit of the time, for as 1966 rolled into 1967, wise fools were appearing everywhere. A few months after the book launch, the Who reached number three in the charts with "Happy Jack," the lyrical tale of a cheery simpleton who lived on a beach. Next the Beatles took up the theme with "The Fool on the Hill." Then in the summer of '67, Pink Floyd released *The Piper at the Gates of Dawn,* with its wistful echoes of *The Wind in the Willows* and the innocent world of childhood. For the flower children of the Summer of Love, Idries's harmless mullah seemed to be one of their kind, an Eastern companion of the *Piper* and *Alice in Wonderland.*

It wasn't only the stories that captured the imagination of a partly stoned readership. It was also the illustrations by Richard Williams, the Canadian-born artist whom people were calling "the English Walt Disney." Bringing Richard Williams on board had been quite a coup. The year before he took on Mulla Nasrudin, Williams had animated the credit sequence for the Peter Sellers and Woody Allen comedy *What's New Pussycat?* Then straight after finishing the Nasrudin book, he designed the title sequence for David Niven's spoof of the Bond films, *Casino Royale.*[65] To capture the Mulla's mix of frantic energy and airy lightness, he used simple line drawings that faced the stories like the visual record of an idyllic acid trip. To stare at them was to fall into an oriental fantasy where Andy Capp met Aubrey Beardsley. Soon *The Sunday Times* was discussing plans to feature the Mulla as a regular comic strip.[66] Cape knew they were on to a good thing and promptly commissioned a joint follow-up from cartoonist and storyteller to be called *The Pleasantries of the Incredible Mulla Nasrudin.*[67]

By this time, Idries was working on a range of potential spin-offs via a company he founded with the name Mulla Nasrudin Enterprises. In psychedelic spirit, its correspondence was sent on colorful paper headed with a warped *Rubber Soul* font. Its office was on Soho Square, the heart of London's media district, which as well as housing Mulla Nasrudin Enterprises also became the headquarters for the Society for Understanding the Foundation of Ideas.[68] Minutes from the neon lights advertising Soho's sex shows, a sign by the front door was emblazoned with the society's initials: SUFI.[69]

With its strip joints and jazz clubs, its advertising agencies and film companies, Soho was where art and commerce were inseparable. Idries and Richard Williams, well connected to the film world, soon thought of turning the Mulla Nasrudin stories into a feature-length cartoon.[70] It would not merely be lucrative, it would bring Idries's teachings to a far wider audience. Idries wrote to Tom Maschler, promising that a ninety-minute animated film could be ready in two years.[71] Rumors soon spread that the voice actors would include Vincent Price, Donald Pleasance, and Sean Connery, though it was the comic actor Kenneth Williams of the *Carry On* films who recorded the initial vocal track.[72] The project got as far as recording scratch tracks, temporary dialogue recordings to allow animators to pace out their sequences. Robert wrote from Mallorca to recommend that the score be written by his friend Ramón Farrán, a Catalan musician who had already written music for a version of the Nasrudin stories staged in Deià.[73] But a film was a complicated venture that would ultimately need support from one of the big American studios, and gradually the project petered out. The world would never hear the sound of the Mulla getting funky, though Idries did still plan to market a Mulla Nasrudin plush toy.[74]

That the Pink Panther (films on which Williams later worked) almost had a Sufi rival showed the resonance of the Mulla stories with the counterculture. Freed of the responsibilities of rule, the orphans of empire found Eastern ideas, clothes, and music all the more enchanting. At the same time that Idries established Mulla Nasrudin Enterprises on Soho Square, a two-minute walk away on Greek Street, the fashion designer Thea Porter opened her boutique that sold couture versions of Afghan coats and Moroccan caftans to the likes of Brian Jones and Cat Stevens.[75] Born in British-ruled Palestine and raised in French-ruled Syria, she was another of empire's orphans, nostalgic for the bright world of her childhood. At the height of Mulla Nasrudin's success, Pink Floyd wore her costumes on the cover of *The Piper at the Gates of Dawn*.[76]

Yet Idries moved at several degrees of separation from the hippies who were becoming some of his keenest readers. By now he was regularly trying to get rid of them when they turned up at Langton House, though still they would linger on the adjoining village green, waiting for the chance of an autograph or a word of wisdom.[77] Whereas Idries's soirées preferred guests like Doris Lessing and J. D. Salinger, his former associate Jack Bracelin was living at ground zero of hippie London.[78] Jack had renounced Wicca, but he hadn't lost the libertarian spirit that led him to the witchmaster Gerald Gardner in the first place. He had opened a nightclub in Soho, around the corner from Idries's office. It wasn't meant to be a snooty table-service haunt for aristos, like Annabel's on Berkeley Square. No, Jack's joint was a happening—Happening 44, in fact—where psychedelic missionaries like the Deviants, Soft Machine, and Pink Floyd performed. As the chords from their guitars stretched longer and longer, Jack became an early exponent of the light show.[79]

Idries viewed hippiedom with a strong dose of establishment mistrust. But in the summer of 1967, when Scott McKenzie's "San Francisco (Be Sure to Wear Flowers in Your Hair)" reached number one in the British charts, Idries became all too aware of the Californian source of the new cultural spirit spreading to London. In San Francisco, interest in Sufism was growing, fostered by Samuel Lewis, the Jewish son of a vice-president of the Levi-Strauss jeans company. Lewis had spent decades blending ideas from Sufism and Zen, but while recovering from a heart attack that summer, he had a dream in which God commanded him to serve as the spiritual leader of the hippies. As his reputation spread around the spiritual marketplace of the Bay Area, hipsters soon gave him the nickname "Sufi Sam."

By the fall of that year, Idries was in on the action, albeit through a weekend seminar in the respectable setting of San Francisco's Sheraton Hotel.[80] To arrange this and other events, a new organization was set up in Los Altos as the U.S. counterpart to SUFI and

SOURCE, albeit run independently. It too needed a clever acronym, so it was called the Institute for the Study of Human Knowledge, or ISHK, which sounded like *ishq*, the Persian word for the passionate love so often invoked in the poems of the Sufis, if not a major theme of Idries's writings.[81] He usually presented Sufism in terms of psychology, science, and the self, but on the West Coast they loved the touchy-feely stuff.

Back in London, Idries and his brother Omar tapped into the commercial potential of counterculture clothing fashions by opening a pair of shops on Portobello Road, where well-heeled hippies were kitting themselves out at vintage stores with empire-nostalgic names like I Was Lord Kitchener's Valet.[82] They began by selling antiques that Omar acquired from Parisian flea markets; then when the Beatles donned Afghan sheepskins for the cover of *Magical Mystery Tour*, they quickly changed to selling Afghan coats and colorful caftans.[83] Idries didn't work in the shops himself, though, any more than he attended Jack Bracelin's happenings. At work in his Soho offices and Langton House, with his recording studio and secretaries, his output began to approach his father's level of productivity.

In 1967 Cape issued his *Tales of the Dervishes*.[84] (The American publisher tried to tempt Robert into writing another foreword, but he declined—with Idries's rise to fame, their relationship wasn't quite the same.)[85] Billed as a collection of teaching stories, *Tales of the Dervishes* contained dozens of short stories purportedly collated from Sufi classics and obscure manuscripts, such as a tale about four magic treasures, three bejeweled rings, an ogre, and a dervish. There was nothing from the magnificent works of metaphysics into which so many Sufis had distilled their souls. But that was never Idries's interest. He was a storyteller, whose stories had an appealing simplicity that belied a certain profundity. Doris Lessing wrote a glowing review in *The Observer*.[86]

Still, his success wasn't based solely on literary merit. It also rested on the legitimate lineage claimed from his ancestor Jan Fishan Khan who, now that the empire had ended, was presented as a Sufi master rather than a horse-riding ally of the British. Not that the romance of empire had disappeared from the bookstores at large. *Tales of the Dervishes* reached the shops just before *Retreat from Kabul* by the Scottish author George Bruce, whose gung-ho depictions of the colonial past led one reviewer to describe him as "belonging to the drum and trumpet school of history."[87] Nods to the spirit of the 1960s notwithstanding, Bruce's detailed account of the disastrous British defeat at the end of the First Anglo-Afghan War was highly accurate but for one notable absence: Jan Fishan Khan, the valiant Afghan warrior who sided with the invaders.[88] As Idries cultivated his origin myth in which the collusions of empire played no part, the omission suited him well.

In addition to Spanish translations in the Latin American literary capital of Buenos Aires, the following year saw Idries publish several other new books.[89] *The Way of the Sufi* was an introductory primer that began with a long survey of Orientalist studies, then moved onto extracts from Sufi poets and a selection of "teaching stories." The publisher was unsure what kind of book they were dealing with. It seemed to be some sort of scholarly text, but when on this assumption they asked Idries to expand the bibliography, he accused them of behaving like pedantic academics.[90] Published simultaneously, *Caravan of Dreams* was a more hastily prepared hotchpotch of typed-up recordings and jotted-down notes. In contrast to *The Way of the Sufi*, in which Islam appeared nowhere, its opening contained several sayings of the Prophet Muhammad. But then it was back to Mulla Nasrudin's pithy wisdom and more "teaching stories," such as the tale of Mushkil Gusha (Problem Solver), which Idries seems to have taken from a collection of folktales collected in early-twentieth-century Iran by David Lorimer and his wife Emily.[91] A military intelligence officer turned linguist and folklorist, Lorimer had recorded the story in the Kermani dialect of Persian from some "poor and pious women," though Idries's *Caravan of Dreams* recast it as a supposedly Sufi parable.[92]

His next volume, *New Research on Current Philosophical Systems*, again struck a more academic note.[93] The introduction described it as an investigation into philosophical teachings and psychological techniques from "the East." Such talk was in vogue in the wake of the Buddhist guru Alan Watts's *Psychotherapy East and West*, though in Idries's invocations of science there were also traces of his father's medical education. But whereas Ikbal's generation had tried to reconcile science with Islam, in a more secularizing age his son jettisoned any mention of the Quran, or of organized religion in general. Idries's Sufism was psychologizing, with no need for the external buttress of creeds and morals. Instead, the purportedly scientific methods he described in *New Research* had names like "The Pointing-Finger Teaching System," which seemed to involve puzzling your students by pointing at things that weren't actually what you were referring to.[94] It was a Sufi counterpart to Watts's Zen, whose sane-crazy monks liked to point a finger at the moon as a lesson in looking at the moon not the finger.

As though it were a modish sociology dissertation, *New Research* included a questionnaire that had supposedly been sent to an international colloquy of distinguished metaphysicians. All had bizarre biographies. One had been raised in Bukhara but then fled to Albania (an odd place of refuge, with its Mao-inspired ban on religion, though one where few readers were likely to track him down).[95] Another contributor lived in the Gobi Desert of Mongolia (again safely out of reach, if also ruled by Communists).[96] The names of these mystical boffins ranged from the plausible (Edouard Chatelherault) through the unlikely (Gyn Aksu) to the outright invented (N. Awab Zada). As any reader with a modicum of Persian might have noticed, the latter was a pun on Nawabzada, "Born of the Nawwab." Wrapped in a riddle, the pseudonymous contributor was the son or grandson of the Nawwab of Sardhana. In another chapter, Ikbal's old alter ego Sheikh Ahmad Abdullah made a return, only now he was supposed to be an Arab expert on hypnosis rather than a boisterous Bedouin chief.[97] Similarly back in print was Ikbal's bluff British explorer John Grant, who in the decades since his last outing had become a gentleman scholar of Babylonian magic.[98] He had also gained a doctorate and aged remarkably well, since he had already been writing his memoirs when Ikbal invented him thirty years earlier. And making a posthumous literary appearance from beyond the grave was Elizabeth, or rather Morag Murray.[99] Even Arkon Daraul got a look-in with a citation of his *Secret Societies*.[100] He had a Ph.D. now as well. Yet even though the book was published by Idries's Octagon Press and bore his literary fingerprint throughout, the name Idries Shah appeared nowhere.[101]

While his more commercial books were coming out with Cape, Idries was keeping Octagon Press busy. It published studies of Sufism by the Victorian Orientalists Edward Henry Palmer and Edward Armstrong Johnson, who were not only long dead but long out of copyright.[102]

Then came the strangest of all Octagon titles: *The Book of the Book*.[103] In coffee table format, glossy and expensive in black and gold, it looked like it belonged in a fashionable art gallery, especially because only nine of its nearly two hundred pages had anything printed on them (and then only a dozen lines). For those patient enough to leaf through in search of them, those few sentences spun another teaching tale about some kind of Ur-book written by a dervish that had then been given to a king, then taken by a man named Mali (a nod to Gerald Gardner), who finally entrusted it to a Sufi from Bukhara. And that was it. It was a book about a book. Only there was no book. Postmodernism *avant la lettre*, it was either a gag, a scam, or a psychological teaching tool of the subtlest refinement.

◆

FOR IDRIES, THE FINAL YEAR of the 1960s was an annus mirabilis. The BBC program *The Critics* awarded Book of Year to *The Way of the Sufi* and *Reflections*, prompting journalist Nina Epton to praise him on the radio.[104] He became a member of London's exclusive Athenaeum Club. And his fan base in California was growing.

Ikbal must have been proud of his son as he sat out his retirement in Tangier. Since Elizabeth's death nine years earlier, he had writ-

ten no more books of his own. Nor had he joined the hash-smoking
authors who gathered down the road around American novelist Paul
Bowles. Unlike Bowles and company in their caftans, Ikbal kept to
his smart English suits and trilby, while his grandly faded villa recreated the aristocratic world of his childhood.[105] Property was cheap
in Tangier—prices had never recovered since 1956, when it lost its
status as an international zone and tax haven, and the wealthiest
expatriates left. His villa on Rue de la Plage was a five-minute walk
from the Grand Socco, the fabled market square where the imperial cosmopolitanism of prewar times lingered among the exiles
from American morals and Middle Eastern revolutions.[106] Ikbal's
elegant gateway was guarded by a local sentry (unskilled labor was
also cheap) dressed in what occasional European visitors took to be
the traditional garb of Afghan warriors.[107] Idries and Omar liked to
visit the villa that symbolized their father's triumphal return to their
ancestral glory.[108] Yet Ikbal could afford it only by cashing in the
political pension that had long been paid to his forebears.

With what little funds he had left, and the trickle of royalties and
library lending fees, he kept a loquaciously cheerful local housekeeper called Zohra, whose little daughter Fatima brought life to
the crumbling villa.[109] Each morning he would stroll along the neighboring Corniche, then sit in his favorite corner of the Café de France.
Or he might enter the gently decaying Hôtel Cecil, a former resort of
European royals with the decor of a colonial Indian club, where tea
was served on rosewood tables beneath walls decorated with mus-
kets and sabers.[110] From there, Ikbal penned letters to the likes of
Robert Graves, proffering insights into the poetry of Rumi.[111] In his
Tangerine exile, he often found his thoughts turning to old acquaintances too. Writing to Sir Evelyn Shuckburgh, he recalled his father
Sir John, on whom he had frequently called in Downing Street. He
cherished many fond recollections of their shared efforts to hold
together an empire ruled over by sirs and sirdars.[112] From time to
time, these quiet days of retirement were interrupted as Idries's
growing fame brought his father visits from young acolytes en route

to Marrakech. Though this new generation sent no calling cards ahead, he dealt graciously with their impromptu arrivals.

One afternoon in the spring of 1968, Ikbal received a more glamorous visitor than the usual hippies who traipsed to his villa. Beverly Kelly was the Hollywood wife of actor James Coburn, then filming the casbah caper *Duffy* in Tangier. Having dabbled with Eastern mysticism and the teachings of Gurdjieff, Coburn and his wife had heard on the counterculture grapevine about the Sufis, Idries Shah, and the omniscient Afghan father he quoted in his books. "Yes, madam, what can I do for you," said Ikbal, opening his front door and introducing himself: "I am a professor of oriental religion."[113] Beverly explained that she and her husband had recently read Idries Shah's *The Sufis*. Ikbal affirmed it was written by his son, then added, "You have come to the horse's mouth."[114] He invited her indoors and, happy to have a listener, regaled her with tales of the East that had enchanted Elizabeth half a century earlier. Over the following week, Beverly returned every afternoon to hear more stories, bringing along her daughter and, when filming wrapped, her husband, who picked up a caftan in the Tangier bazaar.[115] When James Coburn met the elderly professor, there were no formalities: the actor immediately embraced Ikbal and held him for three minutes straight.

With his acid-infused chic, Coburn didn't represent the Hollywood of Rudolph Valentino's *Sheikh* and Gary Cooper's *Bengal Lancer*, which Ikbal had enjoyed in former times. But as Coburn liked to tell it, from that first moment of meeting, it was like they were already old friends. Except that Professor Shah took the position of Coburn's Sufi master, or *murshid*, as, for the next year, the two men formed an unlikely partnership. When Coburn went to Spain to play a CIA assassin in the dismal thriller *Hard Contract*, Ikbal spent two months as his guest in the beach resort of Torremolinos, charming everyone on set with anecdotes recounted in his cut-glass accent and with the curry cooked by his housekeeper Zohra, who he insisted should join them.[116] Then there was the time they met up in London, where the actor picked up his *murshid* from the British Library in his bright red Ferrari to take afternoon tea at the Royal Overseas League, the genteel club for impoverished old empire hands of which Ikbal was now a member.[117]

Then back in Tangier, it all came to a sudden end. On November 4, 1969, Ikbal was involved in an accident near his villa on Rue de la Plage. The road there was steep, climbing up from the coast, and he was hit by a reversing Coca-Cola truck.[118] At seventy-five, Sirdar Ikbal Ali Shah, aka Sheikh Ahmad Abdullah, aka John Grant, aka the Brigand King Habibullah Kalakani, was dead. The man who had faced down Pathan bandits and escaped kidnapping by Bedouin, who had mastered alchemy in suburban Surrey and advised the British Empire, was no more. Back in London, *The Times* carried a short, dignified obituary that emphasized his noble lineage and scholarly credentials.[119] It made no mention of his ventures in misinformation, his many aliases, or his grand designs for the destiny of nations.

For their part, the Congress Party nationalists who had taken charge of India would make sure that Ikbal and his kind were written out of the story of empire. Ikbal had had no time for Gandhi and the Congress; nor would their followers now have any time for him. Henceforth the story of British India would have no place for the complex interactions, the cultural comprises, the friendships, and even the opportunities of empire. After Ikbal died in Tangier, the history of empire's loyal Indian sons would be buried, lest it raise questions about the way the past would be told. His remains were returned not to India, still less to Afghanistan, but to England, where he was laid to rest in the Brookwood Muslim Cemetery, near the Woking Mosque for whose journal he had written his first articles. A few months before his funeral, the remains of the Indian soldiers who had died at the Brighton Pavilion hospital were reinterred at Brookwood. In death, Ikbal was reunited with the empire's other Muslim sons—in their different ways, all wounded in service.

As Ikbal's generation faded away, his sons Idries and Omar

focused their attention on guiding their fellow orphans of empire. Omar, now directing the former Gurdjieffians of Paris, followed his brother's lead by telling his students to stop calling their belief system "The Work," as Gurdjieff had, and to call it "The Tradition" instead.[120] Even so, elements of Gurdjieff's teachings remained part of both Idries and Omar's repertoire, including the "Stop" exercise in which everyone had to freeze in their position when the master shouted the word.[121] Though it seemed like a children's game, it was meant to break habits of thought and behavior. There was other fun, too, when Omar took his followers on camping trips to Morocco, which the lure of mysticism, music, and marijuana had placed firmly on the hippie trail.[122] The former Beat poet Brion Gysin was promoting Morocco's Master Musicians of Jajouka as devotees of the Greek god Pan, playing down the Muslim dimensions of Sufism to present them as bacchanalian Sufi revelers. With the royal dictatorship of Morocco being celebrated as a hippie Utopia, Brian Jones of the Rolling Stones came to record Jajouka's musicians, while Robin Williamson of the Incredible String Band bought instruments in Jajouka village to play on *The Hangman's Beautiful Daughter*, and Led Zeppelin's Robert Plant went to Marrakech to meet other traditional musicians. As Omar and his followers headed south, Crosby, Stills & Nash were telling hipsters everywhere to take the "Marrakesh Express."

✦

OMAR HAD NO COUNTRY mansion to rival his brother's, yet he had now persuaded Robert Graves to collaborate on a venture that might outdo Idries's books. By sending Robert his poetry over the past few years, Omar had prepared the way for a proposal that they translate together the most famous of all Persian poets: Omar Khayyam.[123] Omar explained that his family owned an ancient manuscript of Khayyam's *Rubaiyyat*, which would serve as the basis of their translation.[124] When Robert expressed interest, Omar mailed from Paris what he told Robert was his own translation from this family manuscript that dated from 1233—which made it older (centuries older, he suggested) than any known *Rubaiyyat* manuscript in the world.[125]

Although Khayyam had been a religious skeptic, perhaps even an atheist, and was better known in the Muslim world as a mathematician, Omar persuaded Robert that he had actually been a mystic whose epicurean songs about women and wine were the essence of Sufi teachings. After several years of discussions with Idries (perhaps with bountiful quaffs of *vino*), Robert found this idea strangely plausible. But then, except for Saudi Arabia, at the time secular governments ruled the entire Middle East, and vineyards planted by French settlers still flourished from Morocco to Syria. After Robert responded keenly to the proposal to collaborate, Omar heightened his enthusiasm by letting months pass by before replying in detail. He had had to dash to Afghanistan, he explained, on a matter of national importance.[126] Back in the old country, he added, he should at least be able to consult the manuscript kept by his relatives in the hidden valleys of the Hindu Kush.[127]

Competition in the Khayyam market was stiff, though. From Robert, Omar learned with alarm that eight years earlier A. J. Arberry of Cambridge, the Orientalist who translated many volumes of Persian verse, had published his own revised *Rubaiyyat*.[128] The problem for Omar was that Arberry had worked from what he claimed was the world's oldest authenticated copy of the *Rubaiyyat*, reliably dated to 1259 and kept in the Chester Beatty Library in Dublin. Robert, having just finished his term as Oxford Professor of Poetry, was impressed by the credentials of his Cambridge colleague and voiced concerns about the implications. Omar was quick to respond, denouncing Arberry as a "cheap hack," with such a poor command of Persian that he misunderstood Khayyam's key terms.[129] Worse still, Arberry had made the grave error of declaring that Khayyam had never been a Sufi. As the heir to a Sufi lineage himself, Omar knew better, and told Robert as much. He also knew that Khayyam was actually an Afghan and not from Iran, as the Orientalists (and Iranians) liked to claim.[130] Robert need not worry about Arberry and his cronies, Omar assured him. Together they would prove the experts wrong.

Although Idries chimed in to reassure Robert about Khayyam's importance as a Sufi, Robert couldn't help but have concerns.[131] If the Shah family manuscript was only twenty-five years older than the one Arberry had already translated, it didn't seem much of a discovery. Omar soon found a solution, telling Robert he was negotiating for access to an even older manuscript, dating from 1207.[132] It was kept in Balkh, the Afghan "Mother of Cities" near which, he said, Khayyam's family had once lived. What was more, Arberry didn't even know it existed.[133] Robert was reassured. Between Omar's understanding of Persian Sufism, and Robert's poetic gifts in English, together they would produce a translation to stun the literary world. It would outdo not only Arberry's erroneous renderings but even the much-loved Victorian *Rubaiyyat* of Edward FitzGerald that had been through scores of editions over the past century.[134]

It was a good time to be translating lost texts of Eastern wisdom. Harvard psychologists Timothy Leary and Richard Alpert had recently published their adaptation of the *Tibetan Book of the Dead*, sending ripples through the counterculture. A couple of months before Omar and Robert began work on their *Rubaiyyat*, John Lennon came across Leary and Alpert's translation in London's Indica gallery and bookshop, then went home to use a line from it as the opening of "Tomorrow Never Knows." If Tibetan Buddhists could be recast as pioneers of psychedelia, then the poems of Khayyam could be presented as the libertine essence of Sufism.

Robert had translated Latin and Greek poets for decades, but in recent years he had been reaching beyond his competence to translate texts from Hebrew, albeit with the help of learned collaborators. One such work, *The Nazarene Gospel Restored*, paved the way for his *Rubaiyyat* by audaciously claiming to have "restored" the true message of Jesus which the Christians had corrupted.[135] More recently, he had followed up his hugely successful *Greek Myths* with

The Hebrew Myths, written with the Hungarian Hebraist Raphael Patai, whom he met in the New York apartment of the "mushroom man," Gordon Wasson.[136] During their stays in Deià, Omar and Idries had almost crossed paths with Raphael—and Omar was certainly an unusual successor to the erudite Zionist who, in addition to Hebrew, read German, Hungarian, Latin, Aramaic, and Arabic.[137] But Omar needed no degrees like Raphael Patai: his authority lay in who he was, or at least who he said he was.

From the opening paragraph of Robert and Omar's *The Original Rubaiyyat of Omar Khayyam*, they flaunted their discovery of the world's oldest manuscript of Khayyam's poetry.[138] Robert mocked Arberry for believing the Chester Beatty manuscript to be the oldest in existence, and despite his lack of Persian, felt confident enough to declare that all previous translations were "clumsy," "slipshod," and "faulty."[139] And though earlier translators denied it, Robert stated that he had it on the personal authority of Idries Shah that the *Rubaiyyat* was indeed a mystical Sufi text, having been taught as such by his great-great-grandfather, the Grand Sheikh of the Hindu Kush, whose teachings were followed throughout Afghanistan.[140] After Robert's introduction came Omar's "Historical Preface," though being unfamiliar with the work of Iranian scholars like Muhammad Ali Furughi and Ali Dashti, or even the writings of the Orientalists, Omar was unable to lend his preface the scholarly appearance of some of Idries's books.

Still, it was meant to be about the poems; and there, over the following pages, they finally were in print: for the first time in almost a millennium, the *Rubaiyyat*'s 111 authentic stanzas were revealed in their correct order. Robert was particularly insistent on this point.[141] For all his expertise, Omar had somehow neglected to tell his collaborator that the word *rubaiyyat* is simply the plural of the Persian word *ruba'i*, a "quatrain." It signified, not a single long work of many stanzas, but a collection of many individual four-lined ones. They had no correct sequence.

With Robert at the peak of his fame, the translation garnered tremendous attention, not least for its fashionable claim that Khayyam was a Sufi, and soon it was selling well. A positive early review in *The Sunday Times* augured even better sales, and Idries sent Robert a note of congratulation.[142] Next the novelist Anthony Burgess wrote a review for the prominent literary magazine *Encounter*, which had previously carried a long laudatory piece on Robert and Raphael's *Hebrew Myths*.[143] But Burgess was more widely read than the average Anglophone man of letters, and had studied Persian as part of his efforts to master Malay when he taught at the elite Malay College in Kuala Kangsar. While making no claim to linguistic mastery, Burgess explained, he knew enough Persian to see that the two sample verses provided in the original language from the "Shah family manuscript" were the same as those in Oxford's Ouseley manuscript, which a century earlier FitzGerald had used for his famous translation. Something was amiss. Meanwhile, *The Times* commissioned a review by Major John Bowen, a soldier-scholar of the old school who had previously published his own translations of Persian poetry, including of Khayyam.[144] Bowen too hinted that something wasn't right.

Although Doris Lessing leaped into the affray with a defensive piece for *The New Statesman*, it wasn't enough.[145] Laurence Elwell-Sutton—a prickly Irish professor of Persian who had briefly worked with Ikbal during the war (both had been assigned to the BBC's Middle East Service)—immediately guessed that Robert's collaborator was the son of the propagandist he remembered from the 1940s.[146] After the war ended, Elwell-Sutton had found employment in academia, compiling Persian language guides, translating folktales, then writing a biography of the Prophet and a survey of Iranian politics. But by 1970, he was at work on a book about Omar Khayyam, which drew him to the new translation.[147] He sent a letter to Major Bowen, whose *Times* review he had read and whom he had also known during the war, when they had both served in Iran. The two men quickly confirmed one another's suspicions. Together they pledged to solve the riddle of the mysterious manuscript.

Chapter Eleven

LUMINARY

After his literary misfortune, his conscience became
more troublesome than ever.

—Edmund Gosse, *Father and Son*

IN HIS STUDY AT EDINBURGH UNIVERSITY, A FEW DOORS
from the Indian Association on George Square that Ikbal had once
frequented, Laurence Elwell-Sutton pondered the opening lines of
his new article for the *Journal of the Royal Central Asian Society*:
"A recent publication has stimulated interest once again in the Persian poet Omar Khayyam," he began plainly.[1] But a puzzle lay at the
heart of this new publication.[2] He then spent two-thirds of his article building up to Omar and Robert's translation, working his way
through the sketchy data on Khayyam's life and the still more perplexing problem of what he actually wrote. Having lived in Tehran,
Laurence knew many Iranian scholars, and described their attempts
to determine which of the fifteen hundred quatrains attributed to
Khayyam he could genuinely have written. The collective critical
efforts of Sadeq Hedayat, Mohammad Ali Foroughi, and Ali Dashti,
he explained, had settled on only around fifty *rubaiyyat* as reliably
authentic.[3]

Underlying every serious discussion of Khayyam, he continued,
was the question of manuscripts. When critical study of the poet
had commenced in the early nineteenth century, the oldest had been
Oxford's Ouseley manuscript, dated to 1461, which was 330 years

after Khayyam's death. Edward FitzGerald had used this manuscript for his celebrated Victorian version. But in 1948 another
manuscript had been bought by Irish American mining magnate Sir
Alfred Chester Beatty. A bibliophile with bottomless pockets, the
"King of Copper" had been advised by A. J. Arberry of Cambridge,
who dated the manuscript to 1259, a full two centuries before the
Ouseley version.

All this background was mere buildup, for now Laurence turned
to the "mystifying" third manuscript used by Omar and Robert,
which, in being purportedly transcribed a mere thirty years after
Khayyam's death, kicked its rivals out of the codicological playing
field. Such a "sensational discovery," was, Laurence admitted, every
scholar's dream. The problem was that it was nothing more than a
dream, for there was "not the slightest doubt" that its "authenticity
must be rejected."[4]

Laurence dropped his bombshell discreetly. He didn't declare that
Omar and Robert were frauds, merely that their manuscript was.
Not that there was any evidence of its existence, he went on, since its
translators had revealed only that it had been discovered in Afghanistan by General Omar Ali-Shah (the military title appeared in the
publicity materials), whose family had secretly preserved it for eight
hundred years. One might ask how it had survived the Mongol inva-
sions to become one of the oldest Persian manuscripts in existence
anywhere, but far from addressing that question, Omar and Robert had provided no evidence whatsoever to prove it even existed:
no photograph, no facsimile, no colophon; no specific information,
papyrological or paleographical; not even its precise location.

This lack of detail seemed initially like a dead end, because if
there was no manuscript to examine, then its authenticity was
impossible to disprove. But Laurence wasn't willing to leave matters there. An experienced literary scholar, he knew that when the
material evidence of a manuscript was missing, scholars still had the
internal evidence of the text, so he turned to that for his article's final
thrust. There was something very strange, indeed altogether unique,

he wrote, about the Shah-Graves *Rubaiyyat*. For despite the translators' claim to have preserved the original sequence intended by Khayyam himself, neither their ordering nor their selection of verses appeared in any of the dozens of known manuscripts. But a certain printed version of the *Rubaiyyat* did contain exactly the same verses in exactly the same sequence—though it was not a Persian edition but an obscure English translation, published in 1899 by the eccentric violin-collector-turned-palm-reader Edward Heron-Allen.[5] So closely did the Shah-Graves *Rubaiyyat* resemble Heron-Allen's version that it even included Heron-Allen's mistakes.

A diffident man in person, on paper Elwell-Sutton paced these final blows with sadistic pleasure. He scrutinized the sample transcriptions that Omar had provided to lend the book a scholarly appearance, then compared them with the correct versions, demonstrating that Omar's Persian was quite literally "meaningless." None of this necessarily suggested a "deliberate forgery," for perhaps Omar and Robert were "genuinely mistaken."[6] All they had to do to clear the matter up, he concluded, was to allow scholars to examine their manuscript. The Orientalist had thrown down the gauntlet.

The article reached Omar and Robert separately via their publisher, together with Major Bowen's review from *The Times*. They quickly exchanged letters between Deià and Godalming, the village where, as the fruit of his various enterprises, Omar was now living in a country retreat that, if rather less grand than his brother's Langton House, was only a short drive from where they had both been raised. Over the following weeks, he wrote to Robert over and again, reassuring him that the manuscript was real, and that bringing it to Britain for experts to inspect would be merely a matter of time. Persuaded and reassured, Robert published an indignant riposte to Bowen and Elwell-Sutton.[7] "Omar Ali-Shah entrusted me," he began; for it was a matter of trust, he explained, and Omar was an honorable man, as was his brother, who was nothing less than the Grand Sheikh of the Sufi *Tariqa*.[8] As for the manuscript, it had been presented to their ancestor by a sultan. It was all beginning to sound like the bibliographical parable from Idries's *Book of the Book*.

Meanwhile Omar was sending Robert more assurances that far from his manuscript being a forgery, the Oxford manuscript on which earlier translators had relied had in fact been copied from his family's Jan Fishan manuscript, named after his warrior-turned-Sufi forebear.[9] Under pressure from Robert, Omar also wrote a long letter to *The Times*, trying to defend their translation but literally slipping into their critics' noose.[10] For in seeking to justify his rendering of the word *kamand* ("noose"), he came up with three definitions that couldn't be found in any Persian dictionary.[11] Finally he reiterated his assertion that the *Rubaiyyat* was a single poem and not a collection of quatrains—a truly amateur error.[12]

As the months rolled by, more criticisms and responses were exchanged in public, attracting attention on both sides of the Atlantic. Although in public Robert stuck by his man, in private he pressed Omar to reveal the family manuscript. Omar, now that even Robert was calling his bluff, adopted a stance of offended hauteur. The manuscript's custodians, he said, knew it to be authentic but did not value the opinions of Orientalists, so they refused to allow such so-called experts to inspect it.[13] When Robert replied by asking again, Omar said he was sorry for the public blows Robert was receiving, but Robert was an "old warrior" like himself who could stand up to his enemies.[14] Raising the stakes still further, Robert then did exactly that, writing to the *Sunday Times* to brand his critics "a lot of imbeciles."[15]

For his part, Laurence Elwell-Sutton responded to Robert's insults with a more detailed review in *Delos*.[16] Edited by Donald Carne-Ross, a distinguished translator of ancient Greek verse, the journal specialized in translation, boasting an editorial board headed by the poet W. H. Auden and the critic George Steiner. Though an article in *Delos* wasn't as public as a letter to *The Times*, it afforded Laurence the space to resume his dissection with torturous precision. He devoted long sections to semantic misreadings, issued scalpel-cold responses to Robert's condescension about "scholarly Persicologists" who "needed psychiatrists," and drew distinctions between formal qualifications and Omar's "claim that he 'read and spoke classical Persian' (whatever that may mean) as a child."[17] Then he took up a new issue: Omar and Robert's claim that Khayyam was a Sufi, which Omar (following Idries) had stated "all native-born experts in Persian language and literature" believed.[18] Laurence declared that he had "searched hard" for Iranian scholars who took this view but had not found a single one. But he had found many—he rattled off a list of eminent Iranian men of letters—who flatly rejected the idea that Khayyam was a Sufi. The assertion that he was, Laurence continued, was not merely a factual mistake; it was "cashing in on the current craze for 'pop orientalism' " and, as such, was an "indulgence in phony exoticism."[19] For good measure, the Irish professor also sued Robert for libel.[20]

Omar responded by sending Robert further notes of reassurance. Elwell-Sutton, Omar explained, far from being the scrupulous literary scholar he pretended to be, was part of a conspiracy cooked up by fanatically anti-Afghan Iranians who as Shiites were sworn enemies of the Sufis.[21] As for the striking similarity between their own translation and the Heron-Allen translation that the professor claimed to have detected, Omar explained, this was because the manuscripts used by Heron-Allen and by FitzGerald were both based on the more ancient Jan Fishan manuscript.[22] But by now it wasn't only Robert and Laurence who were asking to see the manuscript—directors at Cassell, Robert and Omar's publisher, were asking as well.[23] When their letters went unanswered, one of the directors telephoned Omar repeatedly about the "odium" being attached to the company's reputation.[24] Omar always had an explanation at the ready. Since the controversy couldn't conclude till the whereabouts of the mysterious manuscript was identified, someone would have to travel to the Hindu Kush and find the secret valley where Omar said it was hidden. Laurence Elwell-Sutton knew just the man who could do it. It was time to bring Major Bowen back from retirement.

Born and raised in India, John Bowen had spent the war years patrolling the Afghan-Iranian borderlands, and was happy to return there. Although it was a long overland journey from London, hippie camper vans were now leaving every week with copies of *The Sufis* stashed in their glove compartments. Not that the hippies were Major Bowen's kind of company, mind you. In fact, they seemed to him the living argument for bringing back national service. But he had faced far worse dangers than poisoning by patchouli oil. So though the empire was gone, he was glad to be offered one last mission and play one final round of the great game.

✦

NINETEEN-SEVENTY WAS the easiest time in history to be traveling to Afghanistan. During the late 1960s, many hotels had opened there, as plans were submitted to the World Bank to improve the country's tourist infrastructure.[25] Afghanistan hadn't been talked about so much since the Third Anglo-Afghan War, when Ikbal had written to Prime Minister David Lloyd George. But now the talk wasn't about defending the thin red line. It was about breaking down internal borders, the frontiers of the mind—and Kabul was reputedly the best place to do that. Not that it was without its dangers: the budding Californian folk singer Craig Smith had been beaten and raped in Kandahar. Several other hippies had ended up dead, a few buried in the Christian cemetery in Kabul's Sherpur Cantonment, originally intended for British soldiers who fell in the Second Anglo-Afghan War. But it was so cheap there, especially the dope, and all along the hippie trail from Istanbul's Pudding Shop, rumors abounded of heroic figures like Helmut the Hash King of Kabul, in a stoner's take on the medieval legend of the Old Man of the Mountain.[26] Months before Major Bowen's departure, the publication of the first *Flashman* novel about a louche British antihero in the First Anglo-Afghan War meant even the memory of empire was going to pot.

John Bowen was no devious Harry Flashman, though. He liked

to play with a straight bat. Even his poetry had to be served straight. He was so incensed by the adulterous old goat Robert Graves (to say nothing of the man he dubbed "Svengali Shah") that he was willing to roam the Hindu Kush to unmask them.[27] When he packed up his old kitbag and hit the increasingly busy road to Kabul, he had just two clues to guide him. First, he had learned from old British records that before Jan Fishan Khan had been (as he put it) "expelled" from Afghanistan and settled in India in 1842, his family had lived in the village of Paghman, not far from Kabul.[28] Second, Robert and Omar had asserted that the manuscript was guarded by Idries's and Omar's eighty-year-old relative, who had so far refused to reveal it because, as Robert put it, "to be challenged by a lot of imbeciles naturally upsets the old man."[29]

After reaching Afghanistan, Major Bowen spent several weeks riding through the mountains that Omar and Idries claimed as their homeland. It was like his war years, only then he had been hunting Nazi spies trying to sneak across the border and influence the Afghan government. Finding no one in the highlands who had ever heard of the Shah brothers, still less of Idries's leadership of all of Afghanistan's Sufis, he headed back to the capital, where he contacted two eminent scholars, the poet Khalilullah Khalili and the editor of the *Karvan* newspaper, Abdul Haq Waleh. Serious and principled men, they were both intrigued and appalled by what Bowen then told them.[30] As it happened, Abdul Haq had met Omar fifteen years earlier: as vice-president of Radio Kabul, he had hired Omar as an announcer for English broadcasts. At that time Omar "knew very little Persian," he recalled, and only "picked up a smattering" during his two-year stay.[31] Little wonder, Bowen concluded, that he had copied Heron-Allen's mistakes.

Now that Bowen had two well-connected Afghans to help him, the question of the manuscript's existence could finally be settled. Abdul Haq Waleh recounted what happened next for the readers of the *Kabul Times*:[32]

Major J.C.E. Bowen. . . . began his investigation by spending twenty-four days in the Hindu Kush trying to find the Afghan principality which, according to Graves, was ruled by the Shah family. Travelling on horseback he crossed and re-crossed the watershed at 13,500 feet without finding a single principality let alone the "Royal court of General Ali Shah's father." . . .

But Bowen's literary crusade took an optimistic turn when Professor Khalili told him that the "old man of eighty"—the man referred to by Graves—was alive and well at Paghman, sixteen miles from Kabul and incidentally nowhere near the Hindu Kush. Immediate arrangements were made for the old man to be brought to Kabul for an interview. It was a scenario somewhat reminiscent of the meeting between Stanley and Livingstone when Major Bowen shook hands with Mir Jamaluddin, aged eighty-five, head of the Shah family. But Major Bowen's expectations were not to be fulfilled. Yes, Jamaluddin said, he was related to Omar Ali Shah because they had a common forefather five generations back. They had never met, however. Jamaluddin had not heard of the priceless manuscript, nor of Robert Graves, nor indeed of Omar Khayyam![33]

The revelations didn't end there. For if the manuscript was a fraud, then was its inventor one too? With the help of Abdul Haq, who as a journalist could draw on many local informants, Bowen now investigated the claims that Omar and Idries had made about their family's lineage in Afghanistan. To start with, there was no record that Omar had been a general in the Afghan Army.[34] And when Bowen interviewed Jamaluddin, the head of the branch of the family that Jan Fishan had left behind in 1842, he was told that the closest his relations had ever come to royalty was when he was once put in charge of looking after the prime minister's car.[35] Instead, the family's aristocratic ascent had been the outcome of empire. As nawwabs and sirdars, Jan Fishan Khan's heirs were sons of the British Empire; and as mystics and Sufis, they were its postcolonial orphans.

When Bowen returned to England, he set about tying up the loose ends of his inquiry by looking into other claims that the publicity for *The Original Rubaiyyat* had made. The publicists' account of Omar's Oxford education and his earlier accomplishments as a translator had previously seemed credible enough, but the findings in Afghanistan now rendered everything suspect. Taking the train to Oxford, Bowen asked the university authorities to check for any record that Omar Ali-Shah had ever studied there.[36] He had not. Next, Bowen looked into Omar's claim to be a leading scholar. That was likewise false, he established, for the Bodleian Library, which held a copy of every book published in Britain and many thousands published in Iran and Afghanistan, didn't hold a single book under his name.

Triumphant, the old soldier finally sat down to write his own book on the affair.[37] As he saw it, Omar was a modern-day version of James MacPherson, the eighteenth-century Scotsman who invented the Gaelic bard Ossian; and Bowen was playing the role of Samuel Johnson, the great unmasker. But his labors would result in no *succès de scandale*, because lacking a literary agent, Bowen ended up giving his book to an obscure provincial publisher. Few people noticed it, just as no one in New York or London read the revelations in the *Kabul Times*. Meanwhile Omar's profits on the *Rubaiyyat* were being paid into his Swiss bank account.[38] He scoffed to Robert that Bowen had spent £800 on the trip to Kabul only to prove nothing.[39]

Increasingly irate in Edinburgh, Laurence Elwell-Sutton refused to give up. Hovering over a typewriter, his would be the hands of hubris. It was the summer of 1970; the 1960s were over, and it was now time for a reality check. Having taken on Omar, his scornful gaze turned toward Idries in a review of his two latest books. In a meandering essay for *The New York Review of Books*, Laurence traced the history of Sufism from its origins to the present day.[40] In the twentieth century, he explained, the Sufis, having been rejected by Muslim modernists, Wahhabis and Salafis alike, had reached the end of their history. Yet their lowest point was not in Saudi Arabia, he said, but in the West, where "self-styled Sufis" like Idries Shah had cashed in on the success of Yoga and Zen. (Lest anyone in America was unsure who Idries was, Laurence explained that he was the brother of the man who had recently duped Robert Graves.) As for Idries's new *Way of the Sufi*, it was a "schoolboy essay" based on "the gleanings of its author's sessions in the public libraries." Although its publisher had "comically inflated" Idries's other book under review—first presented as seminar papers at the trendy University of Sussex—Laurence condemned it as a "rag-bag" of tales and proverbs whose common features were "constant errors of fact," "slovenly and inaccurate translations," and "misspellings of Oriental names."

Idries had sat quietly on the sidelines during the *Rubaiyyat* affair, but now that the negative publicity began turning toward him, he reacted with alacrity to the spiteful review, though with discretion nonetheless. In a letter to Robert, he denounced Laurence Elwell-Sutton as the least distinguished scholar in his field (he was Britain's only professor of Persian), then sided with his brother, explaining there was no point in producing the family's Khayyam manuscript because so-called experts were unable to tell a genuine manuscript from a forgery.[41] But Idries didn't demean himself by writing to the letters pages of magazines and newspapers like Robert and Omar. Instead, Doris Lessing wrote to *The New York Review*, listing every one of Idries's achievements, both factual and fantastical.[42] At nearly a thousand words, her published letter read like a public relations statement, the gist of which was that Idries was simply a genius; everyone said as much; so why couldn't the misguided professor see it too?

The New York Review promptly printed Laurence's rejoinder. (There was nothing like a good spat for the "Letters" page.) The many endorsements that Lessing mentioned were meaningless, he wrote loftily, because none were from anyone with any knowledge whatsoever of Islamic literature, religion, or philosophy. Not that this would put off Idries's admirers, he conceded, because the "Hampstead intelligentsia will have swallowed this buffoonery with the same enthusiasm with which they have gulped down the rest."[43]

He had a point, because soon Idries had three new book contracts with leading publisher, Penguin, a deal due largely to Doris, who had written to Penguin proposing that they reissue his earlier books as mass market paperbacks, including with her letter one of his self-produced publicity brochures.[44]

As the innocence of Haight-Ashbury faded in the dawn of the new decade, Idries gave his next books serious-sounding subtitles, such as *Studies in Experientialism* and *Analogical and Action Philosophy of the Middle East and Central Asia*.[45] But he didn't give up his "teaching stories," publishing another volume of them called *The Dermis Probe*, based on Rumi's famous medieval fable about blind men feeling their way around an elephant that represented the universe, unable to see the whole for the separate parts they clumsily groped. A contemporary take on an old story, Idries's version was about a man who devoted his life to studying goldfish.[46]

By now, Doris could be relied on to champion almost anything he wrote. In *The Guardian*, she declared that *The Dermis Probe* offered "something new for the West."[47] Indeed, so important were its insights that California's RAND Corporation was allegedly using its teachings to develop special human brains capable of solving the world's biggest problems.[48] Doris's own books also increasingly drew on her discussions with Idries: she dedicated her *Four-Gated City* to him, and her subsequent novels featured Sufi themes and Persian terms that carried faint fond echoes of her childhood in Iran.

Having begun his career in the imperial radio drama *Chief Scout*, by 1970 Idries was back at the BBC, making an episode called *The Dreamwalkers* for the TV documentary series *One Pair of Eyes*.[49] It was broadcast over a year before *Ways of Seeing*, the celebrated series by art critic John Berger, preempting its critique of Western "ways of seeing." Six days before Christmas, with only three channels to choose from in Britain, millions tuned in to watch as in the

opening shot, Idries sat telling an animal story to a group of children; then the screen switched to a scene of London commuters,
walking like zombies while Idries intoned, "There is an old saying:
man is asleep: must he die before he wakes up?" The camera went
back to the children; then to a pinstripe-suited toff sprawled over a
sofa in a fancy drawing room; then to Cockney housewives nattering
on park benches; then to a wild-eyed hippie; a group of football fans;
followed by a troop of monkeys. Interludes of mind-bending music
alternated with orotund apothegms about dream-walking, and the
need for deconditioning.

For many viewers it must have been quite baffling, but Idries
proved himself to be an engaging presenter who in interviews with
ordinary people managed to put them at ease before the camera.
It was certainly experimental TV programming, and Idries made
no attempt to dilute his message about the importance of freeing
one's mind from the shackles of convention. Along the way, he tack-
led important questions, such as the trade-off between freethinking
individualism and maintaining the collective social glue. Human
evolution still had so many possibilities, he promised viewers, if
only we could break our psychological limitations. But what pre-
vented many people from doing so was the tragic Western prison
of pessimism.

Prodding the minds of the TV-watching masses was a worthy
endeavor, but in the background the Khayyam affair was still blazing. Several months before, a detailed exposé had appeared in *The
Sunday Times*.[50] Increasingly implicated, Idries wrote reassuringly
to his editor, Tom Maschler, declaring that his critics were pedantic nobodies.[51] When other articles questioned the ancestry claimed
in the blurbs to his books, he wrote again to assure Maschler that
he had documents proving not only his long spiritual lineage but
his possession of five royal titles too.[52] Like Robert, Idries seemed
to subscribe to the adage that an artist's first creation is himself.
In an overblown stratagem of damage limitation, he issued a silver
publicity dossier through his own publishing house that elaborated

his official biography. His family stretched back, it proclaimed, to the Sassanian emperors who ruled Iran almost two thousand years ago. The claim neatly coincided with the 2,500th anniversary of the founding of the Persian Empire, which in October 1971 saw a vast tent city set up at Persepolis, with meals by Maxim's of Paris served on Limoges dinnerware for guests of the shah of Iran.[53] No longer a loyal orphan of the British Empire, whose old titles like sirdar now counted for nothing, Idries was declaring his independence by claiming ties to the Middle East's last living empire.

Questions continued to be asked, though. Robert, after waiting so long for the Khayyam manuscript, turned exasperatedly to Idries to intervene, reminding him that when they first met, he had been no more than the "secretary of an old fraudulent witch-doctor."[54] In reply, Idries pledged that the Guardians of the Tradition would soon supply the elusive manuscript.[55] But since neither they nor the manuscript existed, by the end of 1972 Idries decided to cut the Gordian knot by effectively severing relations with his brother Omar, who had become too much of a liability.[56] Omar left England again for France. From there he would gradually reach beyond the English-speaking realm, where his reputation had been ruined, to Spain, then Brazil, Argentina, and Mexico.[57] Forced to differentiate his teachings from those of his brother, Omar gradually made his Sufism more Islamic, even including prayers in Arabic.[58]

That was not Idries's way. For him, the essence of Sufism was about personal liberation, about freeing one's mind to reach one's fullest potential. Accordingly, he presented his Western followers with a psychologized Sufism with as little Islamic baggage as possible. And he did so by dealing with his followers as individuals, addressing them one on one, in small teaching groups, or as readers of his books. Larger communities were neither his concern nor his métier. Although by the early 1970s many Muslims from across the former Indian empire, in what was now Pakistan and Bangladesh, were settling in Britain, they were not his congregation; nor, since he had been raised in England, were they truly his people. Other new

religious leaders would have to claim them instead. For in contrast
to his father's time, the new spokesmen for Islam in England were
no longer imperial elites with patrician titles, Oxford degrees, and
memberships of the National Liberal Club. They were now more
likely to be alumni of small-town madrassas in rural Kashmir and
Sylhet, where Britain's new Muslim immigrants originated. Far from
Langton's serene village green and the seminar rooms of fashionable Soho, their England was a country of Midland car factories and
northern textile mills.

Abandoned in their terraced slums, those other orphans of empire
were left to find their own answers to the great questions of life.
Some turned to proletarian mystics such as Sufi Sahib, a Pakistani
factory worker from Birmingham, but as time passed, more and
more were drawn to anti-Sufi preachers whose supporters' deep
pockets dripped with oil.[59] None of Hampstead's highbrows showed
any interest in such immigrant affairs, for all their fascination with
Sufism and fashionable taste for Moroccan decor. Meanwhile many
of Britain's mosques began to change, as the Sufi Islam that had
flourished in the Indian subcontinent for nearly a millennium withered in the cold winters of exile.

Distancing himself from Omar wasn't Idries's only strategy for
recovering from the *Rubaiyyat* scandal into which his brother had
drawn him. Idries would also confront his enemies—if not by the
sword, like the Jan Fishan Khan he regularly invoked, then by the
pen and publicity. Through his assistants, he sent his publicity dossier to newspapers, magazines, and educational institutions worldwide, stating the credentials of his royal Afghan, Iranian, and Sufi
lineage.[60] He successfully weathered the negative publicity. In a letter to Robert's wife Beryl, he recounted with delight that his American sales had shot up by 22,000 copies since Elwell-Sutton's attack
in *The New York Review*.[61] In the United States, his publishers
described how his writings were now "enormously popular," particularly in California, where Mulla Nasrudin's cartoon-accompanied
wisdom was proving particularly successful in Los Angeles.[62]

Meanwhile Doris Lessing renewed her campaign to promote Idries among East Coast highbrows. In the eight years since she first met him, her work had been profoundly shaped by the man she always addressed as "Shah" and whose Octagon Press published her groundbreaking 1974 novel *Memoirs of a Survivor*. Set after an unspecified disaster called simply "The Crisis," it marked her turn to science fiction, a then-niche literary taste she shared with Idries, who had long admired the spiritualized sci-fi of Clifford D. Simak.[63] After Idries encouraged her in embracing a genre the critics viewed with scorn—urging her to think for herself—she reportedly offered his press the first book of her *Canopus in Argos* series, which blended interstellar futurism with Sufi motifs from her mentor.[64] (Idries's writings also influenced some of the Sufi themes in Frank Herbert's *Dune* novels.) Though some of Doris's friends were wary of Idries's role in her life and art, he helped her not only to recognize the great theme of her writings—the disintegration of the self, society, and the world at large—but also to achieve the personal integration to stand outside this morass and depict it.[65]

In gratitude, she painted Idries in newspapers as the world's chief Sufi spokesman, whose followers included psychiatrists, doctors, philosophers, mathematicians, and (as though they confirmed his Eastern credentials) Egyptologists. As heir to the medieval mystic Mahmud Shabistari, Idries was the world's supreme guide to the inner space explored in her novels. In an article for *Vogue*, she explained that his stories showed "an ancient way to new freedom," since Sufism even offered a route to women's liberation.[66] Then, in a long review of Idries's latest book for *Encounter*, where Elwell-Sutton had denounced him, she responded to the professor's critique with ever greater praise for her teacher.[67]

Laurence Elwell-Sutton would not be silenced, though. "In this age of instant coffee and pre-packed fish-fingers," he sighed in a letter sent in response to Doris's review, "it is perhaps naïve to be exasperated by synthetic philosophy and reconstituted mysticism."[68] Far from being the heir to an ancient Sufi lineage, as Idries's publishers kept repeating, his ancestor Jan Fishan Khan hadn't been a religious teacher at all. He had been a man of action, an imperial hero, "the buccaneering leader of a troop of Afghan horse who sided with the British." Jan Fishan had been "an amiable ruffian perhaps," Laurence conceded, "but hardly a Sufi!"[69]

Once again, the critique failed to undermine Idries's appeal, especially when his next book, *The Magic Monastery*, channeled the romantic myths of empire through a title evoking the mountain hermitage in James Hilton's *Lost Horizon*. The lingering legend of Shangri-La was still inspiring many young Westerners to travel to Afghanistan and Nepal. (Tibet had been off-limits since the Chinese invasion.) Heading east across Turkey by train in 1973, the American author Paul Theroux met hippies whose Idries Shah books "had the chewed-over look Korans have" (an ironic remark, given the book's lack of references to Islam).[70] Whether on the hippie trail or in more lofty literary venues, Idries was coming through his brother's *Rubaiyyat* scandal more lauded than ever. His books were appearing in French, Italian, Dutch, Spanish, and German translation. The University of Geneva appointed him as guest professor of ecumenical studies. In America, it was claimed, his writings were being taught in three hundred accredited courses on sociology and psychology.[71] UNESCO bestowed awards on his work as part of its International Book Year, while in distant Buenos Aires, where he had once taken notes on meat-packing, the Argentinian subcommittee of UNESCO held an International Sufi Book Week that featured his books center stage.[72] Intellectuals everywhere seemed to be promoting Sufis; everywhere, that is, except in the Islamic world itself, where Sufis were increasingly followed only by the marginalized and poor.

With too many followers now to attend his seminars in person, Idries set up a recording company to distribute his teachings by the new technology of audiotape.[73] Just as his father had favored the modernizing Muslim reformers of the previous generation, Idries saw cassettes as a natural successor to books in bringing Sufism to a wider audience. He had also become an accomplished speaker, increasingly comfortable before the microphone in his home studio, so the recordings captured his casual warm tone and the sense of sincerity that girded it. Under the trading name Seminar Cassettes, the company promised "audio cassettes by leading thinkers," effectively Idries and a handful of followers, such as Doris.

Then came a bibliographical harvest to rival the best annual yields of his father. There was a new Mulla Nasrudin book; a compendium of "scriptures from the East" (a borrowing from Ikbal); and an invented travelogue by his alias Omar Burke, who had been silent for a decade.[74] Idries's diasporic Indian contemporary V. S. Naipaul also turned to travel writing with *An Area of Darkness* and *India: A Wounded Civilization*, but the romanticized Afghanistan in Burke's travelogue couldn't have been more different from Naipaul's stark critique of Indian society. For Naipaul, tradition meant caste and corruption, nepotism, and hocus-pocus. For Idries, as spokesman of the "People of the Tradition," it meant Eastern wisdom to heal the Western psyche. Moreover, according to Omar Burke, the lands of Islam were chockablock with Sufis, who seemed to pop up on every corner from Kabul to Cairo.

As a publisher as well as an author, Idries was promoting not only his own and his alter egos' books. His Octagon Press had come a long way since Ikbal's disastrous book on Vietnam (though it never again published Ikbal in his lifetime). While Idries's brother Omar was by now persona non grata, Octagon Press did publish his sister Amina's book of Afghan folktales, which charmingly recounted old legends about genies, princes, and flying horses with none of her brother's insistence on their psychological inner meanings.[75]

However, Idries also wanted to branch out as a publisher, and Octagon Press began to dabble with some of the darkest fears of the decade. *The New Threshold* was a manifesto on population control by the Club of Rome, a think tank that raised early warnings about the environmental consequences of continued economic growth but that conspiracy theorists saw as a right-wing plan to take over the planet.[76] Having been founded by the Italian industrialist

Aurelio Peccei and the British chemist Alexander King (who both featured on Idries's Seminar Cassettes), the Club of Rome counted Idries as a member for a while. *The New Threshold* was his attempt as a publisher to follow up on its multimillion-selling predecessor, *The Limits to Growth*.[77] But the club's political and economic concerns were not his true calling, especially as the Sufis entered their modish Western heyday in the mid-1970s. In addition to writers like Doris, musicians were now becoming Sufis, including several members of Mighty Baby, a group nicknamed "The English Grateful Dead," and Richard Thompson of the seminal folk-rock band Fairport Convention.

As prolific as Idries was, even he couldn't keep up with demand, so as a publisher he turned to reissuing works of Victorian Orientalism that were long out of print. One was a translation of Rumi by E. H. Whinfield; another a translation of Sa'di by Edward Backhouse Eastwick, a professor of Hindustani at the East India Company's college.[78] Then came the old rendering of Hafiz by Lieutenant-Colonel Henry Wilberforce Clarke of the Bengal Engineers and the version of Nafasi's *Maqsad-i Aksa* by the Cambridge professor E. H. Palmer.[79] Finally Octagon reissued Hajji Abdu el-Yazdi's *Kasidah*, a pseudonymous poem by Sir Richard Burton that was arguably inspired more by FitzGerald's *Rubaiyat* than by actual Sufi texts.[80] Since these works of sympathetic Orientalism were otherwise available only in rare old editions, Idries put them back into popular circulation.

Another deceased author whom Idries resuscitated via Octagon was Ikbal. Blackballed after his Vietnam book, he now returned posthumously with a treatise on black magic.[81] In the early 1970s, the weekly encyclopedia magazine *Man, Myth and Magic* was selling by the tens of thousands on both sides of the Atlantic, while the existentialist Colin Wilson was back on the bestseller lists with a history of occultism, which he dedicated to Robert Graves.[82] Even patrician novelist Anthony Powell was completing his *Dance to the Music of the Time* sequence with a final installment about a magician called Scorpio Murtlock who leads his middle-class acolytes to mesmerized humiliation. As for Afghanistan, it remained a space for literary play as novelist Simon Gandolfi wrote *The 100 Kilo Club*, in which a character called "Pleasure" gets stoned immaculate on the finest hash on the hippie trail.[83] But this vulgarized East would play no part in Idries's books, whether as author or publisher. His imaginary homeland, with all its romantic detachment from the drought, famine, and coups of early 1970s Afghanistan, was a place of lofty mystic secrets.

In Britain, far from the muddy backwaters of the former empire, the old imperial networks remained quietly useful. Laurence Rushbrook Williams, now of All Souls, Oxford, had supported Ikbal throughout the war years and known Idries since he was a schoolboy in the city.[84] Although well into his eighties, he still wielded enough influence to arrange a conference in Idries's honor, the papers from which would be published as a Festschrift, that accolade of academic standing. Since such events were usually associated with retirement, and Idries had not yet turned fifty, the conference would officially celebrate the seven-hundredth anniversary of the death of Rumi, the most famous Sufi of all. But as all the papers were about Idries, they suggested he was Rumi's modern-day successor.

Digging out his old address book, Rushbrook Williams sent invitation letters far and wide. Many went to former colleagues from the days of empire, others to an odd mix of Muslim liberals and ideologues. (None were specialists on Sufism.) He invited Sir John Glubb, former commander of Transjordan's Arab Legion, and Abdulkerim Julius Germanus, a ninety-year-old Hungarian Orientalist who had converted to Islam in colonial India. He invited I. H. Qureshi, a graduate like Ikbal of the Muhammadan Anglo-Oriental College, who had gone on to a career as a government minister in Pakistan. And he invited Mahmoud Shawarbi, an Egyptian specialist on soil chemistry and supporter of the Nation of Islam, like Malcolm X, who a decade earlier had lectured at the Oxford Union.[85]

Despite the presence of Shawarbi and so many retired officials and diplomats, the conference was not concerned with political matters. Sir Edwin Chapman-Andrews, former ambassador to Lebanon and president of the Royal Central Asian Society, opened the conference with a tale of Mulla Nasrudin, and the other delegates followed his lead. Swiping aside "academic qualifications" with his soldierly hand, Sir John Glubb began and ended his lecture by declaring that everyone owed Idries Shah a great debt.[86] Though Mahmoud Shawarbi held a doctorate in organic chemistry, he chose to celebrate Idries's books on magic, which, he explained, led the way for future researchers, since *Oriental Magic* had received a "scientific welcome" while Idries's other such works were apparently guiding scientists everywhere.[87] Rushbrook Williams eulogized Idries as a man who could have been a great diplomat, or anything he wanted, but had instead decided to fulfill his father's mission to lead the West from uncertainty and materialism.[88] Alas, not knowing Idries's pseudonyms, the delegates could celebrate only half of his writings, but that did allow them to quote his alter egos as testimonials.

For all his achievements, Idries still bore the scars of youthful years spent watching his contemporaries flit in and out of their Oxford colleges from his father's flat on Turl Street. The Festschrift that emerged from Rushbrook Williams's conference in Oxford was a balm for those old wounds. It was also a most curious volume. Like a training manual for semioticians, it was like a book from a Borgesian library, its self-referential citations luring readers into a hermeneutic labyrinth. To make this robust tome appear like an independent scholarly celebration of his work, its first edition bore no editor's or publisher's name though it was republished by Octagon Press and in *Books and Bookmen*, a two-page advert appeared with a photograph of Idries leaning over his typewriter in a checked sports jacket.[89] The caption beneath promised that "Shah's books work away at the mind whether one wants them to do so or not."[90]

This latest book was certainly working away at the mind of Laurence Elwell-Sutton, if perhaps not in the way Idries's publicists intended. Since their last epistolary tussle, the Irish Orientalist had been sharpening his rhetorical stiletto and was probably all too delighted when a review copy turned up in his mailbox. He used his review to address the larger issues he detected behind the popularity of such books. "The rise of Idries Shah as guru to a band of ardent and uncritical disciples is a piece of modern folklore emanating from a social class—the intelligentsia—generally considered (by themselves at least) to be immune from such irrationalities. . . . But perhaps after all the intellectual is more credulous than he would have us think."[91]

A response from Doris wasn't long in coming. Unlike Laurence's review in an obscure folklore journal, Doris's review of the conference volume appeared in *The New York Times*, where in the wake of the 1973 oil crisis, she taunted American capitalists that their country was losing its intellectual as well as its economic hegemony. A shift in the "balance of power from West to East" was something every right-minded person should celebrate, she announced. Earlier that year she had already written a long feature on Idries for *The Guardian*, which recounted his biography exactly as he described it to her, complete with studies in various universities and family palaces in India and Afghanistan.[92]

Responding in an article for *Encounter*, Laurence pledged to piece together all the evidence he had found about Idries and the Sufi lineage he had invented. Laurence distinguished between past and present, between what was written in Arabic and Persian and what was written by Idries Shah.[93] Having explained the known facts about what the historical Sufis had taught, he turned to those he labeled "pseudo-Sufis." Although these contemporaries claimed the authority of past tradition, he explained, their teachings had to be carefully distinguished from the long dead luminaries whose legacy they claimed. It was a more general point, applicable as well to other spokesmen for Muslim tradition, whether Sufi or Salafi. *Encounter* received many letters in response, both in agreement and disagreement.[94] For in 1975 it still seemed possible to hold a reasoned public debate on Islam.

Even so, it wasn't a debate into which Idries wished to be drawn. His books had always been exceedingly careful in their mentions of Islam, so much so that the word rarely appeared. It was with anxiety bordering on horror, then, that one morning in 1974 when his mail arrived at Langton House, he perused the cover blurb for Penguin's forthcoming mass reprint of his *Way of the Sufi*. The jacket copy claimed that the Sufis had "breathed life into the dry bones of Islam." He responded immediately, demanding his editors withdraw the book from sale on the grounds that the phrase might cause offense to millions of Muslims and, in turn, stir up much trouble for author and publisher alike.[95]

Unfortunately, by this point publication was well underway. His editor wrote back to explain that the book had already been printed, and copies shipped to booksellers in Britain and abroad, including the Middle East and India.[96] The best he could offer was that the "offending clause" be "excised" the next time the book was reprinted.[97] Idries responded immediately by threatening Penguin with legal action if the affair—he reached for an infelicitous idiom—blew up in the Middle East.[98] His editor replied that, having discussed potential repercussions with the company's overseas representatives, they would recall from the Middle East and India all copies of the book bearing the "offending phrase."[99] The publisher would also issue in the *Times Literary Supplement* a statement of regret about speaking of "the dry bones of Islam" and lamenting any offense the phrase had given.[100] After Idries consented, a public apology appeared in the letters page of the *TLS* amid innocuous debates about Shakespeare and Chaucer.[101]

Having successfully avoided offending Muslim public opinion, Idries returned to defending himself from Laurence Elwell-Sutton— albeit apparently in the guise of "Bashir M. Dervish," under whose name an article appeared in the journal *Islamic Culture* praising the authentic Sufi wisdom of Idries Shah.[102] Mr. Dervish made many extraordinary claims: Idries's books were being taught at Oxford University; he had the full support of the Muslim World League (despite it being a Saudi-funded sponsor of anti-Sufi Wahhabism); he was an adviser to the RAND Corporation in Los Angeles; his Gurdjieff-derived diagrams were used by physicists at the University of Miami; his translations had received a gold medal at the Cambridge Poetry Festival; and he had lectured to packed halls of fourteen hundred students as a professor of medicine at the University of California.[103] More flush with funds, Stanford had gone further and granted him a prize of $15,000.[104] Perhaps all these claims were true, for nothing was impossible when the intelligentsia was enthralled. In this new great game of competing truth claims, Idries now had the upper hand.

Chapter Twelve

WARRIOR

Religious bodies are liable to strange and
unaccountable fluctuations.

—Edmund Gosse, *Father and Son*

CONTINUING HIS ASCENT FROM THE COUNTERCULTURE TO
the mainstream, in the summer of 1975 Idries agreed to an interview at home for *Psychology Today*.[1] Readers may have thought they
had mistakenly bought a copy of *Country Life* as the interviewer
described the large estate where the founder of the Boy Scouts had
roamed as a lad. Langton House was presented as so luxurious that
the dozens of guests who gathered there on Sundays took luncheon
in a converted stable called the Elephant, before retiring to a conser-
vatory where vines drooped over plantation chairs from which they
could lean back and pick grapes with their teeth.[2] Lest readers get
the wrong impression, the interviewer clarified that these sybarites
comprised highbrow glitterati like the poet Ted Hughes, zoologist
Desmond Morris, and of course Doris Lessing.[3] Even the factory-
floor novelist Alan Sillitoe liked to drop by for tea, having renounced
his blue-collar roots for the discreet charm of the bourgeoisie.[4] As
for Idries himself, apparently he was now also a successful businessman with companies dealing in textiles, electronics, and ceramics.[5]
Partway through the interview, Idries voiced his surprise that when
people met him, they asked the "most disturbing" questions, not
least about "how I get money."[6]

It was meant humorously, for in conversation Idries was often droll, even self-deprecating. In any case, the woman from *Psychology Today* posed no such awkward questions. Still, she did have some clear opinions. When Idries explained that he heard many Indian gurus say, "Let's take the Westerners to the cleaners; they colonized us, now we will get money out of them," she declared this "an understandable human reaction to centuries of Western exploitation."[7] Be that as it may, Idries deflected the political comment: he was neither an Indian nor a guru, he clarified, but a psychologist and a scientist—and Western scientists needed to study his *Oriental Magic*. Never having had time for left-wing shibboleths, he was more interested in supporting capitalism, explaining that following Sufism "makes a person more efficient."[8]

Such an approach meant that Idries was increasingly in demand in America. So much so, he told *Psychology Today*, that he had received threats from Indian gurus in California who acted like Al Capone and told him, "Don't touch the United States, because that's ours."[9] But he was undaunted—America was simply too big to miss out on, with a book market that his father had never truly cracked. Fortunately, Doris Lessing was traipsing around New York's bookstores whenever she visited the city with a suitcase of his works, turning up without appointments, like a book-selling Willy Loman, to persuade storeowners to stock Idries Shah.[10] He was also increasingly invited to speak in the United States. Since his days of watching Ikbal enthrall audiences at the University of Montevideo, Idries had learned to captivate a crowd. By now fifty, as his father had been in their Uruguay days, he held his American audiences in the palm of his hand. He drew on a rich store of anecdotes and leavened them with humor, which was markedly self-deprecatory compared to his publicity material, likening his appearance to a mafioso.[11] (This was the 1970s.) He also responded to academic critics in his lectures, accusing them of pedantry and obscurantism (he could do a funny impression of a nitpicking professor) and of thereby missing the point. For Idries, Sufism was above all a learning system; it was in essence a developmental path that could be adapted to any cultural context, with or without the trappings of religion. Here not only the Orientalists but most of history's Sufis would have disagreed. But it was a position Idries apparently held sincerely.

In the spring of 1976 he was repeatedly at the podium in New York, opening his lectures with lines from the *Rubaiyyat* of Khayyam (who he still insisted was a Sufi), then summing up the essence of Sufism in three neat words: *enjoyment, employment, deployment.*[12] Not everyone found this conscientious take on spirituality appealing. During a lecture in San Francisco, 120 hippies stood up and walked out.[13] But by now Idries was reaching larger audiences in the City by the Bay by radio, featuring on the Saturday evening slot of the local NPR station.[14] He also found an influential enthusiast who was a professor of psychiatry at the University of California. A graduate of Harvard Medical School, Arthur J. Deikman had studied the religious cults that swept across San Francisco in the 1960s, and clinical compassion led him to recognize the therapeutic value of at least some mystical practices. By the time he met Idries, he had already taken lessons in Zen, and now he learned of the Sufi "teaching stories" that Idries recast in psychological terms. After drawing these stories into his own practice as a therapist, Deikman wrote a book on psychotherapy and mysticism that drew extensively on Idries's teachings, not least about self-awareness.[15]

Reaching beyond the partly hippie contingent of his West Coast readers, on the East Coast Idries correspondingly began to focus on self-improvement seminars. Advertising in *The New York Times*, he held them in collaboration with the city's leading institutions under the banner of the Institute for the Study of Human Knowledge, itself based in California. Idries Shah's books, the seminar leaflets assured attendees, "are used in university departments throughout the world."[16] One seminar was a full weekend affair at the Hotel Roosevelt, while New York University hosted other seminars (another took place at the New School for Social Research), presenting his work in scientific terms through titles like "Educating Both Sides of the Brain."[17] Founded for scholars who had escaped the anti-intellectualism of Nazi Germany, the New School was now hosting a newer vintage of émigrés like Peter Brent, the British author of *Godmen of India*, who lectured on the importance of having a guru, and Nasrollah Saifpour Fatemi, an Iranian expert on the oil industry, who explained that Sufism had no necessary link to Islam. For as every social theorist knew, whether in Iran or America, the age of religion was over.

After *Human Nature* featured Idries alongside top scientists from British and American universities, next it was *Human Behavior*'s turn to profile him, sending another interviewer to Langton House.[18] The American visitor was quite taken by the "Oxford-accented English" of his host, who showed him around his "rambling whitewashed, green-shuttered mansion." As though writing for an interior design magazine, the interviewer waxed lyrical about the Persian rugs, Moroccan brass trays, and peacock swing in the garden, which seemed material testaments to his host's authenticity. As Idries poured cups from a "glittering heirloom tea service" and leaned back to light a cigar, the conversation settled on the links between psychology and Sufism.[19] Idries looked back to the start of his career. In the 1950s, he explained, when the Korean War was in full swing, the U.S. military had learned that its captured pilots could be brainwashed, or "conditioned in reverse." As a result, psychologists had begun to appreciate the whole process of conditioning. If before that time he had dared to discuss how a person could be "conditioned away from his origins," he explained, he would simply have been "put into the same box as Pavlov."[20] But Idries was more than a mechanical behavioralist. Though he never spoke as a man of religion, he did seem to believe there was such a thing as a soul, even if he used the scientific psychological term *self*.

When it came to the interview photograph, Idries kept on his sunglasses (no longer wearing Wayfarers, as in earlier publicity shots, but big disco lenses), as if covering the windows to his own secret soul. He finished off his suave 1970s look with "a red turtleneck sweater, glen-plaid slacks, magenta socks and calfskin sandals."[21] Turning to his interviewer, Idries quipped—perhaps with a twinkle behind his shades—that, a spiritual teacher "doesn't need to have a white beard."[22]

For all his growing fame, Idries still came across as an affable hail-fellow-well-met. He agreed to meet a nervous reader of his books, and they sat down together in the Coach and Horses, a bohemian pub in Soho, a short hop from his institute's office.[23] Idries went to the bar and returned with two foaming pints of McEwan's ale. Instead of his interview glad rags, he was wearing simple gray trousers and a tweed jacket and throughout the conversation that followed, he chain-smoked Rothmans King Size. He advised the young aspirant in an avuncular tone. His first question was "Have you a job?" "On and off" came the reply. "Well, make sure it's more on than off," Idries said sharply.[24] Always a hard worker, he had no time for hippies and held that true Sufis respected the norms of society around them, including going to work and dressing normally (hence the tweeds).

The conversation skirted around Sufism, focusing more on the English, whom Idries declared to be an "Oriental race" who originally came from the East, from "a land called Sakasina in what is now Afghanistan."[25] It was one of his father's old theories. From there the topic turned to pubs, which Idries declared to be a "unique creation of the English genius."[26] It was an odd pronouncement for a man who sometimes claimed to be the head of Afghanistan's Naqshbandi Sufis, who insisted on the abstemious norms of Sharia. But then, Idries liked pubs, and in England at least, there was nothing wrong with that.

Over the next months, he met the young man several more times, always in a pub: the Salisbury on London's St. Martin's Lane, a favored haunt of Oscar Wilde; the Eagle and Child in Oxford, where C. S. Lewis and J.R.R. Tolkien formerly held their Anglican tertulia, the Inklings; the Old Tom in front of Oxford's Christchurch, near Friar Roger Bacon's medieval observatory. There the talk turned to the Franciscan philosopher Bacon, who had earlier featured in *The Sufis* and who in his publicity materials Idries claimed as his Oxonian forbear. Then finally their conversations turned to the stories Idries told in his books. What did they all mean? How should a reader make sense of them? Idries spoke quietly in response: "Allow yourself to absorb their inner impact and their meanings will become manifest, rise to the surface, in good time."[27]

During his days in London, Idries was still holding regular seminars for which participants were expected to carefully prepare by working their way through thick folders of photocopied readings. Describing the seminars for *Guardian* readers, Doris Lessing painted a comfortably middle-class picture: attendees included a TV interviewer, an editor, a stockbroker, a lawyer, a radio journalist, a children's writer, and several schoolteachers.[28] (There was not a Muslim immigrant in sight.) Another seminar group included a theater costume designer, a psychology professor, two doctors, and a consultant psychiatrist from a London teaching hospital. They met every other Tuesday evening in a well-appointed West End townhouse where, echoing the university life with which they were familiar, they designated Idries their "director of studies" and themselves his "students."[29] It must have been reassuring to know that they weren't joining a cult.

Participants were given set readings from Idries's books, especially the Mulla Nasrudin stories, on which each student would comment in turn, just as in a university seminar. They listened attentively as Idries lectured about indoctrination, conditioning, and brainwashing, teaching them how to free their minds through his scientific approach to Sufi wisdom.[30] Students were not supposed to speak to each another, only to their director, and were strictly forbidden to meet outside class or to contact members of other seminar groups. Sometimes, though, they were favored with an invitation to Langton Green, where they heard talks at the village hall by an odd mix of guest lecturers such as BBC newsreader Robert McDougall, Crusader historian Sir Steven Runciman, and Nirad Chaudhuri, author of *The Autobiography of an Unknown Indian*.[31] On other occasions, they met Idries in a private cinema in Soho's Wardour Street and once in the operating theater of University College Hospital.[32] If the deconditioning process was sometimes disorienting, then at least it was always respectable.

Back at Langton House, life rolled by in a stately idyll, like a recreation of life in the nawwab's palace at Sardhana. From time to time, a maid would bustle in and serve tea, while the master sat in repose, stroking his Siamese cat.[33] But far more work was done at Langton House than in the old days at Sardhana. Idries had inherited his father's work ethic over his grandfather's preference for patrician debt, so he was often in his study, surrounded by walls of bursting bookcases. With a Moroccan mirror above a Georgian mantelpiece, the scene might have resembled La Mauresque, Somerset Maugham's elegant villa on Cap Ferrat. When the weather turned cold, Idries would write at a desk in the lounge, where he liked to have a fire crackling in the hearth.[34] In this tranquil setting, he wrote more books, far removed from the Muslims in the decaying industrial cities of Britain or in the bursting megacities of the Middle East, where the Sufis were being undermined by oil-funded Salafis and revolutionary Islamists.

From his desk, a window overlooked a formal rose garden arranged in such a way that one felt one was sitting among roses. On the adjacent side of the room, French windows opened onto an immaculate lawn, discreetly enclosed by a screen of rhododendrons that concealed a tennis court and lifted the gaze to the rolling parkland beyond.[35] The former royal gardener, Russell Page, had done his work well.

But a Sufi master for modern times shouldn't feel at home only in a rose garden, so beneath the bookcases of tomes on the East (and a manual on tax law) was a display of electronic gadgets.[36] There was an early version of an air ionizer, a short-wave communication receiver, and two tape recorders with remote control microphones.[37] There were also human helpers—a visiting follower, Lewis Courtland, watched in awe as Idries dictated twenty thousand words of folktales to a waiting stenographer.[38] When the visitor voiced his surprise at the arrangement, Idries replied, "Bertrand Russell, as you may know, had research assistants."[39] If it was a curious comparison, it was also a fair point, and Idries had certainly served his own time as secretary to his father. And he would be remembered as a considerate employer. When his housekeeper fretted over breaking an antique plant stand, he told her to forget about it and appeared far more worried about her than the object.[40]

At weekends, followers stayed in the converted stables, which were comfortable nonetheless, for the expectations of spiritual seekers had gone up considerably since George Harrison gave the Hare Krishnas Piggott's Manor.[41] Followers were sometimes expected to help with chores around the estate, though, particularly in the gardens. As a reward, they would spend evenings in the grand salon Idries called the *durbar*, a term from colonial India for the courts of princes, nawwabs, or British governors. Relaxing on couches beneath hanging carpets and embroideries, guests would be served refreshments on hammered brass coffee tables that might have come from Morocco or Afghanistan.[42] There Idries would hold court, more casually than his forebears, telling stories, not only teaching tales, because those privileged to be allowed into his home were given special insights into his remarkable past as he recounted meeting all manner of royal exiles.[43] One time he had been taken into the confidence of King Zog of Albania; another time he had talked spear-throwing with the king of Dongola; and he had once been party to insider gossip about Rasputin from the Grand Duchess Maria.

Idries's sister Amina was a regular at Langton House, acting as gentle go-between with his younger followers. He rekindled connections with aristocratic relatives too, who had stayed in the subcontinent after Independence.[44] One was his Indian cousin Mirza Aqil Hussain Barlas, the son of Ikbal's only sister, who served in the army before entering the Indian diplomatic service. When he came to spend a month, Idries passed around an article about this "well-known personality of the East" who not only belonged to the Barlas princely house but, like one of John Buchan's imperial heroes, also happened to be a "sportsman, crack shot and linguist."[45]

For all his affability, Idries still occasionally echoed the old ways of his ancestors too, such as by asserting his suzerainty over the village of Langton Green. When the local council tried to claim the green as public space, he successfully asserted ownership over the commons in a dispute he liked to jokingly call the Battle of the Village Green.[46] There were other battles he took very seriously, though. He established a Nuclear Protection Advisory Group, drawing members from his closest followers, to prepare for Armageddon. In practical terms, this meant building on the grounds of Langton House a concrete bunker large enough to have a kitchen, storerooms, toilets, and dormitory.[47] Back when he was sixteen, one of his changing childhood homes had been destroyed in the Blitz while Ikbal, Elizabeth, and the children had been safely in an air raid shelter. Now it was Idries's turn to protect his family.

Nevertheless, he had parted ways with his brother Omar, who seemed happy to tread the road of the guru of which Idries had always been wary. Idries preferred to meet and engage with people on their own spiritual, or psychological, level rather than demand abject discipleship, whereas Omar's teachings began to stress the primacy of obedience as the first rule of Sufism. At one meeting in Spain, where Omar now lived, his followers chanted "Agha! Agha!" ("Master! Master!") so loudly and stamped their feet so fiercely that they trapped a young devotee under their boots and shattered her leg.[48] But that wasn't Idries's way—it was too showy and emotional. He worked more subtly on the imagination and the intellect. So he kept on writing his books, another half-dozen in the late 1970s. Venturing into children's literature, he wrote to Beryl Graves to ask if he could include the version of the Arabian Nights tale of Marrouf the Cobbler that Robert had written years earlier.[49]

The Washington Post and *The New York Times* praised the ensuing storybook, for the hunger for what Idries had to say seemed insatiable.[50] He regularly received hundreds of copies of his books in the mail with requests to autograph and return them. "So far," he dryly observed to a visitor who gaped at a pile of two hundred parcels, "they haven't got around to sending me blank cheques to sign."[51] The best way to satisfy the public, though, was to write even more books. In 1978 he published another based on lectures at a New Jersey university that mixed psychology with homilies from Rumi, since in America readers took to such psychological talk more readily than to references to remote Afghanistan; few of them might even have been able to place it accurately on a map. His key message in these lectures was the problem of self-deception, both individual and institutional. He called the ensuing book *A Perfumed Scorpion*. It was a fitting title, considering what was about to come.[52]

On August 19, 1978, in the Iranian oil city of Abadan, four men barricaded the exits of the Cinema Rex and set the theater alight with 422 people inside, all of whom burned to death. Quickly making his way into world headlines, an obscure cleric called Ayatollah Khomeini placed the blame on the shah's secret police. In fact, it was the work of Islamist activists, but people trusted the Ayatollah because mullahs didn't lie.[53] Protests soon spread, and by January 1979, the autocratic shah of Iran had fled, leaving his country in revolution. From the safety of the Rive Gauche, fashionable theorists like Michel Foucault convinced themselves that political Islam was the voice of a colonized Eastern proletariat. But they were soon proven wrong, as the mullahs outmaneuvered, executed, or exiled Iran's liberals and leftists. Nor was there any place for Sufis in the new Islamic Republic. That Iran's ousted aristocrats had been keen supporters of Sufism hardly helped matters now that Islamists co-opted the language of class war from rival Marxists.[54]

Meanwhile in neighboring Afghanistan, a different kind of revolution was unfolding: in April 1978 local Communists overthrew the corrupt nationalist government in a bloody coup d'état. Brutal and ruthless but divided, in a little over eighteen months the Afghan Marxists carried their country to the edge of civil war. Then on

Christmas Eve 1979, Ikbal's inventions of sixty years earlier finally came true as the Red Army invaded via roads it had quietly built from the north. Although the Soviets tried to prop up the Afghan Communist government, a guerrilla war was soon underway, with fighters who called themselves mujahideen, "those who perform jihad."

No one in the West had seen it coming, for theorists from both the left and the right, whether in the name of capitalist or socialist progress, had consigned religion to the dustbin of history. No one took note of the many who disagreed in Tehran and Kabul, where radical socialism had spawned vanguards of revolutionary Islamism. Three months earlier, director Peter Brook had released his film *Meetings with Remarkable Men*. A fantastical biopic of Gurdjieff filmed in Afghanistan, it confirmed Idries's earlier claims by depicting the Sarmoung Brotherhood as Sufis. But it was not the Sufis who had since come to power. It was the commissars and mullahs, and none of them were called Nasrudin.

Idries was far from the only person caught off guard, for the Orientalists had also been none the wiser. Laurence Elwell-Sutton then reacted with one of the earliest articles to dissect the revolution in Iran.[55] While radical chic theorists like Foucault praised the mullahs' rejection of American imperialism, and more moderate optimists believed the clerics would soon retreat from the front line of politics, the Irish professor predicted otherwise. Yet even though Idries had spent years filling his books with tales from the Persian Sufis, he wrote nothing about the revolution, even as its leaders pushed Iran's Sufi leaders into prison or exile. That the Sufis were no longer the loudest voice of Islam, and had not been for some time, was just too inconvenient a truth.

In any case, Idries refocused his attention from Iran, and even the Sufis, to Afghanistan. In February 1980, he wrote a letter to *The Times* on the headed notepaper of the London Athenaeum, equally condemning the "capitalist West" and "totalitarian East," then ending with a call to arms via the Islamic religious command that "tyranny and oppression must be fought by every Moslem."[56]

It was a most unexpected statement from a man who had spent his career avoiding entanglement in either religion or politics. But times were rapidly changing. As the language of the secular left morphed into the language of radical religion, Idries echoed the rallying cry of revolutionary Islamism. From Shiraz to Peshawar, preachers now declared that Muslims were the *mustaza'fin*, the "oppressed," of Franz Fanon's *Wretched of the Earth*, which the Iranian leftist-turned-Islamist Ali Shariati had helpfully translated into Persian.

Although there were some Afghan Sufis among the early mujahideen, the radical Islamists from Pakistan and Saudi Arabia who sponsored the Afghan jihad did their best to ensure they were sidelined. But the teachings of the Sufis somehow had to be kept alive. In 1979, to bolster Idries's activities, Doris Lessing allegedly donated $100,000 of her royalties to set up the Sufi Trust.[57] A few months later Idries's publishing house issued one of its occasional academic volumes containing recent "research papers" on Sufism, by contributors who included alter egos old and new, several with his trademark blend of curiously European- and Muslim-sounding names.[58] There was a chapter by Abdul-Wahab T. Tiryaqi, the name an unlikely amalgam of the great Arabian puritan Abd al-Wahhab and the Persian word for "opium addict." Another contribution was authored by someone called Gustav Schneck, who may have been the German architect Dr. Adolf Gustav Schneck, who had once lived in Turkey but had died ten years earlier; or he may have been another offspring of Idries's onomastic imagination. There was simply no telling.

In another new book, Idries's alias Bashir M. Dervish made a return with a memoir. Now Mr. Dervish introduced himself as a blacksmith's son from an unspecified town in the Middle East who had spent decades among the region's Sufis. He had been disappointed with all of them till in Cyprus he met Idries Shah, dressed (despite the blistering heat) in an impeccably tailored Savile Row suit.[59] From this point on, the book turned into a two-hundred-page hagiography, for everywhere Mr. Dervish traveled he received reassurances of the seniority of Idries Shah, whose character referees ranged from

British Orientalists to North African geologists.[60] Invented characters, both old and new, made cameo appearances to much the same
effect.[61] After the professorial attacks of Elwell-Sutton, Mr. Dervish
tactfully devoted a whole chapter to Idries's academic honors.[62] Yet
by the time it came out in 1982, *Journeys with a Sufi Master* was
a book from a bygone era; the happy Eastern haunts of the hippie
camper van it described no longer existed. The new world was one
of darker forces that V. S. Naipaul described the previous year in
Among the Believers—a world where playful mullahs and tolerant
Sufis seemed to be all too lacking in influence.

Undeterred, Idries was expanding his teaching groups across the
Atlantic. The Society for Sufi Studies, based in Los Altos, became
a refuge for the Sufism being stamped out in Iran and Afghanistan.
Overseen by Stanford-trained psychologist Robert Ornstein, with
Idries visiting a couple of times a year, the organization promoted
reading circles, study groups that initially clustered around the Bay
Area, and then spread south. Idries published a series of brightly
colored booklets for them with titles ranging from *Theories, Practices and Training System of a Sufi School*, a reprint of an old work
by a Christian missionary in Cairo, to *Twelve Years with the Sufi
Herb Doctors*, which described herbal remedies for rheumatism,
appendicitis, and heart trouble that had purportedly been collected
in Afghanistan. Taken as a whole, the booklets blended Sufi ter-
minology and Western psychology with the occult and Gurdjieff.
Despite the talk of "Sufi Studies," they contained next to nothing on
Islam and made no mention of the Quran, the Prophet Muhammad,
or the moral themes that had been the mainstay of Sufi teachings
for a millennium. For quite different reasons, Californians seemed
to agree with Wahhabis and Salafis that Sufism had nothing to do
with Islam.

Some of the booklets carried Idries's name as author, being collections of anecdotes and aphorisms compiled during his addresses
to different teaching groups.[63] A mix of quips, hectoring, and par-
adoxes, the crux of their content was elusive, for they offered no

doctrine that could be pinned down, repeating the message that students weren't "there" yet. When Idries came out to California, he was sometimes severe with these adult students, delivering stern dressing-downs that contrasted with the agreeable anecdotes of his public seminars.[64] Still, the number of groups continued to grow, perhaps helped by the claim that studying Sufism could benefit professional or plainly financial goals.[65] After all, it was now the 1980s, not the spiritually searching '60s.

But as the calumnies of Communism continued in Afghanistan, and the casualties mounted, Idries began to hear the call of a higher cause. Forty years earlier his father's wartime mission had been to persuade the Muslim public that the British and Americans were on their side. Now Idries decided to persuade the British and American publics that the Afghan mujahideen were their fellow cold warriors. Like the mystic masseur of V. S. Naipaul's eponymous novel, Idries was following the path from mystic to publisher to political activist. By allying himself with Washington and Whitehall he might find his making in the war as a writer. But he would not waste time as his father had with propagandist journalism. Instead, he would write the great novel of the jihad.

Despite the dozens of books under his belt, Idries was entirely new to the art of the novelist. With the aphoristic dervishes who skipped through his works, he had proven himself a master of the very short story, but the majority of his books were collages or compendia, with few sustained narratives among his output. His only cover-to-cover narratives were his early *Destination Mecca* and the pseudonymous travelogues of Messrs. Burke and Dervish, which were technically much simpler than a multicharacter novel with a sustained plot. More typical of his writing were fragmentary books produced in haste, ad hoc, and increasingly via dictation, avoiding the craft and revision required for shaping a long coherent narrative. As Gore Vidal had once quipped, Idries's books were "a great deal harder to read than they were to write."[66] Still, for twenty years that style had served him well: confound readers, and they would return for answers; so confound them again, and again, but never give an answer, only another riddle; and finally the most fortunate or persistent readers would perhaps breakthrough to a new way of thinking. This time his aim was different, for what he wanted to write was not a novel of dizzying introspection like Doris Lessing's recent works, but a rousing tale of adventure, an Afghan *War and Peace*, in heft if not in art. And yet, why not in art? For why should only Europe's wars produce great novels?

As Idries pondered the idea of a novel, Salman Rushdie won the Booker Prize for *Midnight's Children*, a mythopoeic reimagining of India's independence. Born of Muslim parents in Mumbai but educated in England, Rushdie after leaving Cambridge had worked for an advertising agency on Soho Square, where Idries had his London office. By the time Idries was setting to work on the first draft of his own novel, Rushdie published *Shame*, another story about the subcontinent's history, this time set in Pakistan, with a main character called Omar Khayyam. With its withering portrayal of a society debauched by its obsession with defending honor, *Shame* showed just how badly Pakistan had failed to live up to the ideals of its modernizing Muslim founders, whom Idries's father had championed.

Still, Rushdie's success showed that both the critics and the market were receptive to the idea of an Indian and Muslim novelist, especially one willing to tackle difficult topics of contemporary history. Why not, then, an Afghan novel that responded to Rushdie's bleak critique of Pakistani corruption with an uplifting paean to the Afghan resistance? The previous decade had seen many potboiler thrillers on the hackneyed theme of avaricious Arabs defeating America via the petrol pump, including a second spy novel set in Cairo with the dubious name *Nile Green*.[67] By contrast, Idries's take on the jihad would respond to the new international politics in which Muslim fighters were now America's allies.[68]

In those early years of the war in Afghanistan, the Western media and intelligentsia were divided between sympathy for the "freedom fighters" and support for the "progressive" Soviets. Several Labour party members of Parliament accepted Soviet invitations to Kabul, returning to report how progressive they found Communist rule, even as whole Afghan villages were being bombed into dust. *The Guardian* was especially torn between loyalty to the socialist goals of the invaders and increasing evidence of their brutality. So *resistance* became the key word: whether on the right or left, everyone could sympathize with it. On television, the seasoned Scottish journalist Sandy Gall made gripping broadcasts from the front line in three documentaries—*Afghanistan: Behind Russian Lines*; *Allah Against the Gunships*; and *Agony of a Nation*—that popularized the British and U.S. governments' emerging support for the mujahideen. Committed to the same cause were Pakistan and Saudi Arabia. But the war wasn't only about government support and secret shipments of Stinger missiles. The great game of geopolitics had always been about ideas as well. So as the jihad took shape, Idries assumed the guise of wartime propagandist, becoming a warrior of both the cold and holy kind.

Yet he realized his experience with short tales and travelogues was insufficient to transform him into a novelist, especially one who might treat so complex a topic as war. So as soon as he completed his first draft in the summer of 1983, he sent it for comments to Doris Lessing. A skilled and sensitive reader, she gave extensive feedback, advising Idries on structure, sequencing, and plotting, taking particular pains to show he needed to breathe life into his characters (all of whom seemed too stock and wooden). She conceded that conventional romantic heroes of the kind he was creating didn't require the psychological subtlety of a Chekhov play, but for them to at least be credible, he would need to give them some token signs of individuality.[69]

After Idries sent her a revised draft with more developed characters, she realized its biggest weakness was structure: the novel was so long, with so many subplots, it was hard for even as experienced a reader as Doris to keep track of what was happening, even after a second read. Like many first-time novelists, he had constructed a plot that was too entangled for him to control. So Doris's next round of advice boiled down to two options: extensive cuts or a complete rewrite. And it needed a different ending.[70]

As for getting the novel published, she suggested, he would have to pitch it in political rather than commercial (still less, artistic) terms. He should tell potential publishers that the novel was the impassioned cry of an Afghan patriot.[71] Earlier in his career, Doris had introduced him to Tom Maschler; she now helped him with other contacts in the publishing world by bringing in literary agent Jonathan Clowes.[72] A Communist like Doris in his youth, Clowes had seen his first big success with Len Deighton's spy novel, *The Ipcress File*, which had subsequently become a Michael Caine movie, so he was a promising prospective agent for Idries in his latest move in the literary game.[73] During the months of rewriting, Doris ensured that Clowes took on the novel.[74] Up to this point, Idries had planned to adopt another pseudonym for his novelistic adventure and become Amir Adil, "the just commander."[75] But in the end, the book appeared under the more marketable name of Idries Shah, from the same American publisher that issued the memoirs of the last shah of Iran.[76]

Idries's novel was called *Kara Kush* after the nickname of its hero, Adam Durany, aka Kara Kush, the "Black Eagle." A professor of technology at the University of Kabul and the heir to a royal lineage, Adam gives up his life of comfort to fight the Soviets, gathering a band of holy warriors to help him.[77] Fortunately, some of the Pathan tribesmen who support him are six feet seven inches tall. In the course of nearly six hundred pages, Adam's mujahideen skirmish with and sabotage a bevy of Commie villains led by Major Mikhail Bakunin (curiously the namesake of a famous anarchist). There is lots of talk of machine guns and dynamite, of magazines and bayonets, and of course of treasure: the lost gold of Ahmad Shah Durrani, the eighteenth-century adventurer who founded Afghanistan. Because despite the war, it was still Shangri-La, where gold lay buried at the foot of the jihadi rainbow.

Naturally, the Russians don't get their hands on the loot, thanks to Adam's band of merry mujahideen. David Callil, an Anglicized Afghan of the Yusufzai clan, is drawn into the struggle by watching Sandy Gall's reports on British TV.[78] Mullah Azimi, an illiterate preacher from Kandahar, raises the masses to rebellion through fearless attacks on Soviet officials.[79] Jamal, an Arab prince, makes his militant entry by screeching from his palatial driveway in a Ferrari, then tossing the keys to one of his African slaves.[80] Together they ride on horseback to do battle with gunships.

Reality blurred with fantasy as the fictional characters rubbed shoulders with real persons. Some of the invented characters were heroic versions of Idries himself, like the science expert Adam and the cultivated Callil, though others were eerie reflections of real men who weren't yet famous. When Prince Jamal signs over his Arabian fortune to fund the jihad, he mirrored the actions of then little-known Osama Bin Laden, who at the time was transferring millions through his Afghan Services Bureau. And when Mullah Azimi gives a rousing speech at the shrine of the Prophet's Cloak, he foreshadowed the speech that would be given in the same place a decade later by another illiterate preacher from Kandahar, Taliban-founder Mullah Omar. It was all uncannily prescient, as though Idries's years studying magic had paid off.

While over the decades Idries had played the warrior less often than his father or brother Omar, he had always enjoyed telling tales of his bellicose ancestors and similar men he had met on his travels. As one of his followers remarked with pride, Idries had been "the guest of kings and guerilla leaders alike."[81] Even his early *Destination Mecca* had romanticized a "guerrilla state" in the badlands of the Afghan-Pakistan border; there Mirza Ali Khan, the so-called "Fakir of Ipi," surrounded by tribesmen wearing bandoliers stuffed with grenades, had been judged by Idries as no more dangerous than "a dreamer."[82] All those illusions found full expression in *Kara Kush*. For Idries and countless other commentators, the war revived every trope of the imperial great game. Adam Durany and David Callil were all too clearly the fictional Afghan sons of Daniel Dravot and Peachey Carnehan from Rudyard Kipling's *The Man Who Would Be King*. Yet the plot of *Kara Kush* was also part of Idries's own family inheritance, for the hunt for the lost gold of Ahmad Shah Durrani was a reworking of Ikbal's 1934 novel, *Afridi Gold*.

Back in 1919, Ikbal had launched his career as an expert insider, inventing Bolshevik incursions during the Third Anglo-Afghan War. Now as the Soviet Union crumbled and the short twentieth century approached its bloody conclusion, his son had come full circle with a story of gallant heroes on horseback, as though Sir Walter Scott's *Ivanhoe* were transposed to the Hindu Kush. For *Kara Kush* was a distillation of family legends about his ancestor Jan Fishan Khan, the supposed Sufi and soldier whom Idries so often celebrated. Unlike V. S. Naipaul, visiting for the first time his grandfather's village in India, Idries could not be content to remain "a colonial, without a past, without ancestors."[83] He had needed a past; cultivated one; then found it came with consequences. Nearly a century and a half after Jan Fishan left Afghanistan as an ally of the British, Idries's postcolonial search for identity made him feel loyal to the holy warriors of his ancestral homeland.

Still, *Kara Kush* was to all intents and purposes an airport novel, a mass-market paperback to reassure anxious readers that Reagan and Thatcher were backing the right team. In *The Sunday Times*, Doris Lessing declared it to be "unputdownable" and the finest war novel she had ever read.[84] Not every reviewer was so generous: foreign correspondent Cyrus Sulzberger II described it as "addicted to clichés," with a "soggy, amorphous" plot, while another American reviewer called its characters "stick figures in ethnic cloaks."[85] But the reviews were less important than the timing. Just as Idries had captured the spirit of the 1960s with his holy fool Nasrudin, now he channeled the zeitgeist again, transmuting alarming headlines into harmless thrills. As his novel hit the shelves, Sylvester Stallone was filming *Rambo III*, set in Afghanistan but shot (a touch ironically) in Israel, and later in the same year that *Kara Kush* came out,

James Bond got in on the action in Afghanistan when *The Living Daylights* began filming. Full of fantasy and dressing up—the mujahideen were as Moroccan as their surroundings—the film's climax features an Oxford-educated Afghan resistance leader who introduces himself to Bond as Shah—Kamran Shah. In early versions of the script, Kamran Shah had been called Ranjit Khan, so the novel maybe influenced the revisions, lending Idries an unexpected new alter ego.

It wasn't only Bond who was back. As British and American support for the mujahideen moved into full force, all the old imperial clichés were wheeled out too. In the Pakistani border city of Peshawar, where Western spooks, journalists, and aid workers gathered in their hundreds, lingering colonial-era publishers like the London Book Company reprinted old accounts of Afghanistan from the days of the Raj. *The Pathans* by Sir Olaf Caroe, the last governor of the North-West Frontier Province, was repeatedly reissued as an authoritative source on these exotic old allies, while Ikbal's writings were revived as authentic insider accounts of the country, cited in many a new study. Every other reporter seemed to reference Kipling's "great game," as though casting a spell of romance over realpolitik's cold calculus. Three months after adverts for *Kara Kush* appeared in *The New York Times* with bearded fighters flaunting Kalashnikovs, the CIA finally handed Stinger missiles to the mujahideen.[86]

After announcing in the London *Times* that it was every Muslim's duty to fight tyranny, Idries's intensifying feelings for his ancestral homeland urged him to do more than merely write fiction. The brutality of the war, brought home by nightly news reports, made new moral demands on him, calling him from his comfortable study and closed-door seminars to the duty of public action. But unlike the younger Muslims from desolate British factory towns who set off to fight the Soviets, Idries was not about to join the jihad himself. So in July 1984, as the conflict rapidly escalated, he founded a charity called Afghan Relief, starting with a rummage sale at Langton House to raise the initial funds.[87] By collecting money for medicines, food supplies, and clothing for refugees who had fled with nothing more than they could carry, the charity aimed "to relieve poverty and sickness and to promote health and to advance education amongst refugees from Afghanistan."[88]

Idries meant it too. When funds had been raised, he traveled to the Pakistani city of Peshawar, less than thirty miles from the fabled Khyber Pass down which his ancestor Jan Fishan Khan had ridden into exile almost a century and half earlier. In Peshawar, he lodged in the colonial-era Dean's Hotel, where Rudyard Kipling and the young Winston Churchill had purportedly stayed but that was now a favorite of journalists and spooks. As word of his charity spread, people came to meet him at Dean's to suggest ways of distributing the sacks of grain and medicines to the needy, but there was a lot of double-dealing, so he sometimes accompanied the trudging delivery trucks to the refugee camps near the border.[89]

A generation earlier, when Ikbal had briefly found a cause in the Pakistan movement, he had tried to establish a news agency in London. Now his son had found a cause, he established his own little agency from Langton House with regular newsletters for Afghan Relief. He called on Doris Lessing to contribute, which she did through a series of "Tales from the Afghan War." A former Communist, her political and moral journey had been long and courageous, but in September 1986 she showed a different kind of courage by accepting Idries's invitation to visit Peshawar, on behalf of Afghan Relief. Intended as a short informational trip, Doris's journey was filled with visits to refugee camps and interviews with jihadists. She wrote it up in the prose of frontier romance as *The Wind Blows Away Our Words*.[90] For according to Doris, Peshawar was like the "setting for a Bogart movie," filled with the glamour of smugglers, spies, and adventurers, all rubbing shoulders as though in an exotic film.[91] Green's and Dean's, the two best hotels, looked like the sets of "cloak-and-dagger films," while the whole "Peshawar Experience" was like a "seedy, dangerous black comedy."[92] What an exhilarating change it was from Hampstead! Especially the handsome warriors.

"Why," Doris swooned, "are the Afghans so very good-looking, all of them?"[93]

After spending the past two decades discussing Mulla Nasrudin's dervishes, Doris and Idries were both way out of their depth. Far from the world they knew, they had entered a quagmire of jihadist factions, all with their own publicists, like the Afghan Jehad Works Translation Centre (and its rival Afghan Information Centre), as well as their own unwitting fellow travelers in the Western media. After interviewing the jihad's fractious leaders, Doris repeated their reassurances in her book without question. The different factions had no need for unity, she was told; Afghans were independent by nature: they were untamed frontiersmen who didn't want a central government.[94] She felt outraged by Naipaul's *Among the Believers*, which, based on discussions with the angry young men of Pakistan, in her view peddled false fears of Islamist terrorism. As a rejoinder, in *The Wind Blows Away Our Words*, she interviewed in Peshawar a spokesman for what she called "liberal Islam."[95] It was the other side of a propaganda war into which she was being drawn as though blindfolded.

She named the mujahideen faction whose spokesman she interviewed the "Hiriquat Party," explaining to readers that it stood for friendship with the West, liberal Islam, and a future Afghanistan in which various versions of Islam could peacefully coexist.[96] Perhaps the Hiriquat Party did say such things (at least to foreigners). After all, there were plenty of secular Afghans, though they were mainly Communists and nationalists rather than members of the various Islamist parties. But it would have been impossible for Doris to know to whom she was speaking; she had no idea that there were dozens of groups of fighters calling themselves "Hiriquat" this or that, since the word *harakat* merely meant "movement" or "party," making her "Hiriquat Party" an empty tautology. Maybe she had been speaking to the Hizb-i Harakat-i Islami, which had been inspired by the recent Islamic revolution in Iran; or the Harakat al-Mujahidin, which supported strict enforcement of Sharia. Nothing was clear in the smoke and mirrors of romantic Peshawar. But since she named the leader of this "liberal" group as Amir Mohamedi, she was likely championing the Harakat-i Inqilab-i Islami, the "Islamic Revolution Movement."[97] Its members must have been strange kinds of liberals, because most of them later joined the Taliban.

Like so many Western supporters of the mujahideen, Doris was unable to grasp that the struggle was what its participants said it was: a jihad or holy war. Whenever she described the mujahideen, she didn't use the word's literal translation as "holy warrior" but insisted on calling them "the Resistance." She admitted that the people she spoke with used the word *jihad* in every sentence, but this was merely "their word for the Resistance and did not mean 'Holy War.'"[98] No, not at all: it was just like the French Resistance in the Second World War,[99] or the struggle in South Africa, or the liberation of Rhodesia, or any of her other good causes.[100] She even quoted one informant to the effect that being a mullah didn't mean the person was actually religious.[101] Despite renouncing Marxism decades earlier, she still believed that talk of jihad was the false consciousness of an untutored Muslim proletariat, a quaint local idiom for the righteous universal call for liberation. Like the rallying cries of the 1960s, this was a fight for freedom, pure and simple. For once in her life, Doris agreed with Margaret Thatcher.

Still, as a first-wave feminist, Doris abhorred the veiling of women, especially the burqa. In Peshawar, the secular Afghan scholar and poet Dr. Bahauddin Majruh warned her frankly that the rise of the mullahs posed a threat to women's rights.[102] But she didn't take him seriously; it was all too confusingly off message. But within three months of her book being published, Dr. Majruh was murdered for his opposition to the Islamists. Jihad world had no place for brave men who asked the mullahs difficult questions. The winds of holy war would blow away his words.

Back in England, after decades sporting the tweed jackets of a country gentleman, Idries began adopting a more authentically Afghan look, especially for publicity photos for his charity. He posed in a baggy *perahan-tunban* and a *pakol*, the beige flat hat made popular by the holy warriors who followed Ahmad Shah Massoud's faction. By now the look was well known, shown on every news report about the "freedom fighters" and particularly about the handsome Massoud. As the Che Guevara look of the 1960s gave way to the *pakol*-wearing mujahid as the new face of resistance, Idries had changed with the times. This was no longer the innocent Arabian Nights look of the costumes worn that sunny afternoon twenty years earlier in the garden at Coombe Springs. Since then, many other self-appointed Muslim leaders had emerged in Britain, likewise dressed in the apparel of authenticity. Now it was increasingly hard for anyone, Muslim or not, to know whose claims to authority to accept. The quiet teachings of the Sufis, passed on by peaceful immigrant elders from Pakistan, were increasingly drowned out by angry young activists who pushed their way into mosques and onto college campuses.[103]

Still, Idries reassured a group of followers that no lasting harm would come from the jihad, whether to the Afghans or anyone else.[104] Nor was there any danger that Afghanistan would descend into civil war after the Soviets withdrew, he explained. Yes, there would be a bit of "skirmishing" among warlords, but that was the timeless Afghan way. Like the imperial administrators of old, he saw the Afghans as natural egalitarians, for whom inconveniences like government were meaningless.[105] But in the spring of 1988, when the Soviets admitted defeat and finally withdrew, civil war did break out, bringing worse violence to Kabul than nearly a decade of occupation. Idries responded with an essay on Jan Fishan Khan: as the mujahideen went about destroying what was left of their country, he described how his ancestor personified the noble tradition of combining spiritual and military leadership, for there was no contradiction in a religious leader being a warrior, or for that matter running a country.[106] It was curiously fighting talk for a lifelong man of letters. But then fights were about to break out closer to home, since even literary games can have deadly consequences.

In September that year, Salman Rushdie published *The Satanic Verses*, a novel in which an Indian actor called Gibreel Farishta dreams he is in a place called Jahiliyyah many centuries earlier, giving false revelations to a prophet called Mahound. While it won the Whitbread Prize, not everyone outside Hampstead liked the title's allusions to the angel Jibrail's revelations to the Prophet Muhammad in Mecca at the end of the pre-Islamic age of ignorance, the Jahiliyya. At the start of December, seven thousand Muslims—most of whose fathers were born in British India—marched through the Lancashire town of Bolton, then burned the book in a bonfire. To the British government, it at first seemed a mere immigrant affair, not a moment that would redefine the limits of literature.

But the following month the Muslims of nearby Bradford followed suit with another book-burning, and in mid-February the revolutionary leader of Iran's Islamic Republic issued a fatwa calling on Muslims worldwide to take Rushdie's life. From Charing Cross Road, a few minutes' walk from Idries's office, to the former hippie haven of San Francisco, where he had often lectured on the Sufis, bombs exploded in bookstores that dared to stock *The Satanic Verses*. Murders of publishers and translators soon followed. A year later Rushdie beat a tactical retreat to harmless tales of the Arabian Nights that, like a more artful version of Mulla Nasrudin, appeared as *Haroun and the Sea of Stories*. But it was too late; everything had changed. On hearing about the fatwa, V. S. Naipaul coldly quipped that it was "an extreme form of literary criticism."[107] But it was more than that. Writing about other cultures was no longer literary play, and some stories could no longer be told without punishment.

When Idries's followers asked his opinion, he told them Rushdie lacked any understanding of "the East."[108] Instead, he was merely the "token Easterner" of the "chattering classes" and not a "real Easterner" like himself.[109] But now lots of people were claiming to speak with the authoritative voice of authenticity. Too many players were joining this new game, and soon no one would know who to listen to.

Idries, though, had a few more strokes to play, since the rising public interest in radicalism was an opportunity to take on a new disguise. As the book market blossomed with memoirs of hardy travels among the mujahideen, he traded in his pseudonymous yarns of journeys among Sufis for this latest literary fashion. The posh-sounding Englishman Peregrine Hodson published one such book, and the Scottish television reporter Sandy Gall several others, so Idries's new alter ego, Louis Palmer, claimed to have likewise traveled far and wide with holy warriors.[110] But the Afghanistan he saw was altogether different from the one described by journalists.[111] For in Louis Palmer's Afghanistan, the Sufis were still alive and well. They could be found behind every rock and doorway, speaking riddles, working magic, initiating a new generation into their innocent ways. Despite the combined depredations of the Soviets, the CIA, the Pakistani secret service, the Wahhabi Saudis, and the Afghan mujahideen themselves, Afghanistan still appeared as the same Shangri-La that Ikbal had conjured in his articles on magic and folklore nearly seventy years earlier. Better still, the ubiquitous dervishes seemed to know all about Idries Shah, telling Louis how much they admired him.[112] In case some readers didn't get very far into the book, that message was communicated at the start of the first chapter.[113] Far from recounting the horrors of a country that had been wrecked by a decade of war, the book became an outlet for delayed revenge on Major Bowen and Elwell-Sutton. This required some imagination, as the evidence Bowen collected in Kabul seemed incontrovertible. So Louis Palmer was placed into a convoluted counterplot, in which he learned that Bowen's poor Persian had made him fall for a joke by Afghans who knew full well how important Idries Shah really was and so mischievously misinformed Bowen.

Louis Palmer's *Adventures in Afghanistan* was published in 1990 as the civil war among rival factions of mujahideen plunged the Afghan people into ever deeper misery. But now that the Soviets were defeated, everyone in Washington and London looked away. The holy warriors had served their purpose, and a new decade was beginning that famous intellectuals promised would herald the end of history itself.

Yet during travels on behalf of his charity, Idries had seen the suffering in the refugee camps that was the reality of Afghan life. It was a shock that nothing seemed able to ameliorate. As the 1990s progressed, his mind withdrew from those dark faraway places to the cozier world of little England, and for the first time in writing, he looked west. He decided to devote the last stage of his career to a trilogy about the English. Maybe it was an attempt to forget about Afghanistan, about the unending violence, about the whole incomprehensible mess of it all. For empire's orphan had finally found a cause in a distant jihad, only to learn that his home had been England all along.

Like a late confession, that final trilogy was perhaps his truest work. It was about country pubs and gentlemen's clubs, polished manners and prep schools; it was about mortgages and county cricket, teatime and fish fingers; about eccentricity, empire, and of course the English weather.[114] It was about an England where people still called one another "old boy" and "dear fellow." By the 1990s, that was nearly as much a fantasy land as Louis Palmer's Afghanistan. But it was one that Idries, now turning seventy and suffering from heart disease, saw with sardonic if evident affection. Despite his early ambitions of finding the descendants of Alexander in the remote Hindu Kush, he was happy to sit out his last years in England. After spending years in Spain and Portugal, his brother Omar also came home and settled in a village near Langton Green.[115] During their childhoods in the ersatz village of Belmont, they had heard many a tale of the valiant land of their ancestors. Now, in an end to his mental exploring, Idries arrived back where he had started and knew the place for the first time: the homeland he had always denied.

Forgetting Afghanistan wouldn't make it go away, though, and from the refugee camps Idries had visited a few years earlier, a new generation of warriors emerged who called themselves *taliban*, or "students." On September 27, 1996, after two years of fighting rival factions of mujahideen, the young radicals captured Kabul and founded the Islamic Emirate of Afghanistan. That distant land of magical mysteries became a place of compulsory burqas and public stonings. Less than two months after a mullah called Omar declared his victory, Idries died of a heart attack in London.[116]

As the twentieth century came to a close, happy talk of dervishes dissolved in the dust of explosions, for the Taliban had taken over Shangri-La, and soon their friends had eyes on other places too. From the Arabia of Ibn Saud's Wahhabis, whom Ikbal had championed, to the triumph of their Afghan allies, whom Idries had novelized, it had been a long time coming, though none of the intellectuals noticed. The Sufis had undeniably lost, without anyone explaining how. Too complex to comprehend, the Muslim world had been smelted into myths in the furnace of empire and its aftermath. It was as perplexing as a riddle of Mulla Nasrudin. As the Afghan horse dealer Mahbub Ali had told the orphan Kim a century earlier, "The Game is so large that one sees but a little at a time."[117]

ACKNOWLEDGMENTS

The first time I heard the name Idries Shah was during an under-graduate class on Islam. The professor's wild black beard and flash-ing eyes made him look like a dervish, but Julian Baldick was quite insistent that he was an Orientalist. In the decades after Edward Said turned the word into an insult, Baldick may have been the last scholar to wear that label with pride. During his lecture one day, he insisted that none of us should read the books of someone called Idries Shah. Evidently I didn't listen.

Over the years that followed, I wandered around Asia on the trail of the Sufis. Though I dreamed of entering Afghanistan, by the time I skirted its frontiers along the borders of Iran and Pakistan, the Taliban were seizing control of the country and making their views on the Sufis quite clear. Occasionally, in bookshops, I glimpsed the name Idries Shah on a shelf, but by this time I took little interest. I was on the quest for what I saw as more authentic representatives of the Sufi tradition, and as I saw things then, knowing English was an immediate disqualifier. Only when I returned to Britain to start a Ph.D. was I reintroduced to Idries Shah. This time it was by way of an article by the Gurdjieffian James Moore in the academic journal *Religion Today*, which presented him as an out-and-out fraud. I was intrigued. My imagination was captured not by the idea of Idries Shah as an imposter—even then, that seemed a simplistic interpre-tive line—but rather by a man who looked like a master exponent of postmodernism. Under the influence of Umberto Eco, I imagined that one day I would write a book that celebrated Idries as the man with a thousand pseudonyms, as a Sufi semiotician. It was the 1990s, my graduate seminars were filled with French theorists, and in those days, the stakes of literary play seemed so low.

In the years since, my life took different directions, and my concerns moved far from *Foucault's Pendulum*. I met, then married a young Afghan woman, who had fled Afghanistan as a refugee. Through her and her family, I came to learn of an altogether different Afghanistan, a brutal society that had emerged from the competing quest for a Socialist or Islamist utopia. It was all too clearly a place that didn't feature in the writings of Idries Shah. Even so, my late father-in-law maintained a skeptical but bemused interest in the "mystical East"—though for him it was located in India rather than his own country.

By the time I sat down to write my book, the daily news was dominated by the expansion of ISIS, then the triumphal return of the Taliban. A celebration of Derridean play in the lands of Islam seemed morally and intellectually untenable. Yet I came to see that Idries, his father, and perhaps more importantly their promoters and readers had something to tell us about the backstory to these later developments, because they help explain how, enchanted by the lingering myths of empire, so few Westerners noticed the rise of Sufi Islam's enemies. As it turns out, their lives tell us many other things too, wrapped up in the riddle that is every human life.

All biographies are necessarily interpretations, some more so than others. Since Ikbal and Idries laid so many false trails, they sometimes obliged their foolhardy biographer to make further interpretations than more straightforward lives might have required. So as a historian I have attempted to reconstruct the most likely sequence of events and the most plausible interpretations of character, based on the evidence I was able to find on the lives of a fascinating but sometimes exasperating father and son. In telling their story, I tried to treat them with the balance of empathy and factual accuracy due to any biographical subjects.

For their faith in the project and their support through its evolving iterations, I would like to express my deep gratitude to my agent, Don Fehr, of Trident Media Group, and to my editor, Alane Salierno Mason, of W. W. Norton. I much appreciate the work of Mo Crist and Susan Sanfrey who, as assistant editor and project editor at Norton, saw the book through production after the deftly sensitive copyediting of Janet Biehl. Thanks to Darryl Jennings for offering legal advice via the Authors Guild. And *grazie* to Carlo Gallo for taking my cover photo.

Turning to the research behind the book, I would like to record my gratitude to the generous donor of the Ibn Khaldun Endowed Chair in World History, which has funded many of my inquiries. I was initially guided by the writings and bibliographies of James Moore, Mark Sedgwick, and Peter Washington, as well as by the anonymous authors and fact-checkers behind the increasingly copious Wikipedia entries on Ikbal and Idries. In outline at least, my account of father and son coheres to the known facts as established by these earlier researchers, whose work I gladly acknowledge. However, in attempting to write as accurate and detailed a double biography as possible, I have tried to expand on the sources used by these pioneers by tracking down far more archival and published sources.

Here I was blessed by a superb research assistant in my former graduate student Michael O'Sullivan, who compiled a bibliography of the publications of Idries and especially Ikbal, then tracked down copies. Mike also located and scanned the materials on Ikbal from the National Archives of India in Delhi and the Lowell Thomas papers. Together with Henry Gardner and Ellen Lu, Mike also carefully typed up my countless revisions to the manuscript, while my undergraduate assistants Arman Abrishamchian and Sara Eckmann helped with related tasks. I am also indebted to three other former graduate students, Sohaib Baig, Roy Bar Sadeh, and Naveena Naqvi, for scanning documents at my request from the Jeddah British Consulate files, the National Archives of India, and the Aligarh College Directory.

I was helped with insights about Idries's character and seminars by Max Gorman, James Moore, Jeffrey Somers, Terry Westwood, and several other former associates who wish to remain anonymous. Gabriel Escobar talked me through his recollections of Idries Shah reading circles in early 1980s California, and generously gave me his large archive of pamphlets and documents. Robert Abdul Hayy Darr shared his memories of Idries's impact in the Bay Area and later of working with Afghan refugees in Peshawar. During a conference on Doris Lessing, conversations with Robert Twigger provided more anecdotes on Idries's life and helped me appreciate his creative impact on the novelist. Idries's former longtime housekeeper, Margaret Smith, provided unique insight into life at Langton House. Robert Hillenbrand kindly shared recollections of his former colleague Laurence Elwell-Sutton. I am also grateful for helpful advice from Zafar Daqiq, the late Patrick French, Simon Gandolfi, William Graves, Ali Karjoo-Ravary, Jonathan Lee, Afshin Marashi, Jamil Hanifi, Saad Ullah Khan, Arash Khazeni, Mark Sedgwick, D. J. Taylor, Thomas Wide, and Christopher Wyatt.

Like any biographer doing their due diligence, I also turned to the Shah family, writing to inquire about any surviving diaries or papers, particularly concerning the vaguer periods and contested travels of both Ikbal and Idries. Although no primary sources were directly provided to me, I would like to gratefully acknowledge the generosity of Tahir Shah for his helpful emails and, via him, the Estate of Idries Shah for providing permission to access the files on Idries Shah kept in the Random House (Jonathan Cape and Penguin) Archives at the Universities of Reading and Bristol respectively. Reference to the unpublished copyright letters of Doris Lessing regarding *Kara Kush* is featured by kind permission of Jonathan Clowes Ltd, London, on behalf of The Estate of Doris Lessing. On the question of Idries's pseudonyms, I have attempted to either corroborate or disprove the surmising of earlier commentators through bibliographical, archival, and library investigations, as well as by contacting potential real-life authors bearing the names in question. I am particularly grateful to the explorer Louis Palmer of Switzerland for graciously replying (in the negative) to yet another inquiry as to whether he was the author of *Adventures in Afghanistan*.

Treading the archival trail in search of factual foundations for my research also saw me incur many institutional debts of thanks. In alphabetical order, I am most grateful to the American Institute of Afghanistan Studies, Kabul; A.P. Watt Records, Wilson Library, University of North Carolina, Chapel Hill; Archive of the National Liberal Club, London; Archives of Aligarh Muslim University, Aligarh, India; Archives of Radio Afghanistan, Kabul; Archives of the Folklore Society, London; Archives of the Royal Empire Society, University Library, Cambridge; Archives of the Royal Geographical Society, London; Archives of the Royal Overseas League, London; BBC Written Archives, Caversham, Reading; City of Oxford Archives, Oxfordshire History Centre, Oxford; Companies House Records, Companies House, London; Doris Lessing Archive, University of East Anglia, Norwich (particularly Justine Mann); East Sussex Record Office, The Keep, Brighton; Edinburgh University Archives, Edinburgh; Gerald Gardner Collection, Museum of Witchcraft and Magic, Boscastle, Cornwall; Henry W. and Albert A. Berg Collection of English and American Literature, New York Public Library; India Office Collections, British Library; Jonathan Cape Archive, Special Collections, University of Reading; Lincoln College Archives, Oxford; Lowell Thomas Papers, James A. Cannavino Library, Archives and Special Collections, Marist College, University of Sussex Archives; National Archives of Great Britain (incorporating the former Public Record Office), Kew, London; National Archives of India, New Delhi, India; National Archives of Scotland, Edinburgh; National Library of Scotland, Edinburgh; Omar Khayyam Collection, Special Collections, Oregon State University, Corvallis; Oxford University Archives, Oxford; Papers of L. F. Rushbrook Williams, Centre for South Asian Studies, Cambridge; Papers of Sir Evelyn Shuckburgh, Special Collections Department, University of Birmingham; Papers of T. C. Lethbridge, Cambridge Museum of Archaeology and Ethnology, Cambridge;

Reuters Archive, London; Robert Graves Archive, St. John's College, Oxford; St. Catherine's College Archives, Oxford; Surrey County Archives at Kingston-on-Thames (particularly Alex Beard); and the University of Sussex Archives, Special Collections Department, The Keep, Brighton.

My final thanks go to my beloved wife, Nushin, who through decades of courage and encouragement has shown me the richest treasures of Afghan culture.

NOTES

Abbreviated References to Archival Collections Cited in Notes

IAS: Ikbal Ali Shah

IS: Idries Shah

OAS: Omar Ali Shah

AMU: Archives of Aligarh Muslim University, Aligarh, India

APW: A. P. Watt Records, Wilson Library, University of North Carolina, Chapel Hill

ARA: Archives of Radio Afghanistan, Kabul

BBC: BBC Written Archives, Caversham, Reading

   BBC(1): R/cont 1, Shah, Ikbal Ali, Talks (1926–1940), file 1 A

   BBC(2): R/cont 1, Shah, Ikbal Ali, Talks (1941), file 1 B

   BBC(3): R/cont 1, Shah, Ikbal Ali, Talks (1942–1962), file 1 C

BNYPL: Henry W. and Albert A. Berg Collection of English and American Literature, The New York Public Library

CHR: Company House Records, Company House, London

DLA: File: Shah, Idries, 1983–1986 (Comments on the MS of *Kara Kush*), Doris Lessing Archive, University of East Anglia, Norwich

ESRO: East Sussex Record Office, The Keep, Brighton

EUA: Edinburgh University Archives, Edinburgh

FSL: Archives of the Folklore Society, London

GGC: Gerald Gardner Collection, Museum of Witchcraft and Magic, Boscastle, Cornwall

GOA: The Orwell Archive, University College London

IOC: India Office Collections, British Library

   IOC(1): British Library, India Office Records L/PS/10/806

   IOC(2): British Library, India Office Records L/PS/12/216

   IOC(3): British Library, India Office Records L/I/1/1509

JCA: Jonathan Cape Archive, Special Collections, University of Reading

JCA(1): JC 70/1

JCA(2): JC 102/3

JCA(3): JC 102/4

JCA(4): JC 158/6

LCO: Lincoln College Archives, Oxford

LFRW: Papers of L. F. Rushbrook Williams, Centre for South Asian Studies, Cambridge

LON: Archives of the League of Nations, Geneva

LTP: Lowell Thomas Papers, James A. Cannavino Library, Archives and Special Collections, Marist College, Poughkeepsie, N.Y.

NAI: National Archives of India, New Delhi, India

  NAI(1): Frontier Branch, Foreign and Political Records, File No. Progs. 36, Part B (1920)

  NAI(2): Frontier Branch, Foreign and Political Records, File No. Progs. 189–195, Part B (1922)

  NAI(3): Frontier Branch, Foreign and Political Records, File No. Progs. 300-F (1923)

  NAI(4): Frontier Branch, Foreign and Political Records, File No. Progs. 465F (1925)

  NAI(5): Frontier Branch, Foreign and Political Records, File No. 47/-f (1930)

  NAI(6): Frontier Branch, Foreign and Political Records, File No. 168 (1930)

  NAI(7): Home Branch, Political Records, File No. 40/14 Poll. III (1958)

NAS: National Archives of Scotland, Edinburgh

NAUK: National Archives of Great Britain, Kew, London

  NAUK(1): FO 317/61379

  NAUK(2): FO 371/11433

  NAUK(3): FO 371/11446

  NAUK(4): CO 732/35/1/1

  NAUK(5): CO 732/35/1/2

  NAUK(6): CO 732/35/1/3

  NAUK(7): CO 732/35/1/4

  NAUK(8): CO 732/35/1/5

  NAUK(9): CO 732/35/1/6

  NAUK(10): CO 732/35/1/8

NLC: Archive of the National Liberal Club, London

NLS: National Library of Scotland, Edinburgh

OHC: City of Oxford Archives, Oxfordshire History Centre, Oxford

  OHC(1): S211/3/A5/1 (School Register)

OHC(2): S211/3/A13/1 (Visitors' Book)

OHC(3): S211/3/F10/1 (Lawrence Brothers Memorial Scholarship)

OHC(4): S211/3/A10/3 (Pupil Record Cards, 1917–62)

OKC: Omar Khayyam Collection, Special Collections, Oregon State University, Corvallis

OUA: Oxford University Archives, Oxford

PAB: Penguin Editorial File: Idries Shah (DM1952/Box 685), Penguin Archive, University of Bristol

RAL: The Reuters Archive, London

RES: Archives of the Royal Empire Society, University Library, Cambridge

RGA: Papers of Robert Graves, Robert Graves Archive, St John's College, Oxford

RGA (1): Correspondence: RG/J/ShahI/

RGA (2): Correspondence: RG/J/ShahIkbal/

RGA (3): Correspondence: RG/J/ShahK/

RGA (4): Correspondence: RG/J/ShahO/

RGA (5): Correspondence: RG/J/Wasson/

RGA (6): Correspondence: RG/J/Kabraji/

RGA (7): Correspondence: RG/J/ShahAmina/

RGA (8): Correspondence: RG/K/Mus/

RGA (9): Correspondence: RG/J/ShahAnna/

RGS: Archives of the Royal Geographical Society, London

ROSL: Archives of the Royal Overseas League, London

SCA: Surrey County Archives, Kingston-on-Thames

SCC: St. Catherine's College Archives, Oxford

SES: Papers of Sir Evelyn Shuckburgh, Special Collections Department, University of Birmingham

TCL: Papers of T. C. Lethbridge, Cambridge Museum of Archaeology and Ethnology, Cambridge

USA: University of Sussex Archives, Special Collections Department, The Keep, Brighton

Preface

1. Description based on a photograph of Idries Shah and his followers taken at Coombe Springs in 1965. I am grateful to Terry Westwood for providing me with a copy.

2. On Jan Fishan's career, I have relied mainly on the colonial records in IOC(1) and on the detailed family history in Agha Syed Jalal Uddin Shah, *Khans of Paghman* (Quetta, n.d.).

3. Sir John Kaye and Col. George Malleson, *Kaye's and Malleson's History of*

the Indian Mutiny of 1857–8, 6 vols. (London, 1898), 1:355 and 2:137. On Jan Fishan's role in 1857, see also Sir Roper Lethbridge, *The Golden Book of India: A Genealogical and Biographical Dictionary of the Ruling Princes, Chiefs, Nobles and Other Personages, Titled or Decorated, of the Indian Empire* (London, 1893), 13.

4. Kaye and Malleson, *Kaye's and Malleson's History*, 2:145.
5. Kaye and Malleson, *Kaye's and Malleson's History*, 2:145.
6. Ikbal Ali Shah is listed among the ship's passengers in "Arrival of the Mail," *Times of India*, July 19, 1913, 12.

Chapter One: STUDENT

1. Ikbal's arrival in London is recorded in "Arrival of the Mail," *Times of India*, July 19, 1913, 12. His journey to Edinburgh is a reconstruction based on period timetables and walking the route from the station to the association.
2. John C. Cunningham, *The Last Man: The Life and Times of Surgeon Major William Brydon CB* (Oxford, 2003).
3. Ikbal's entry to the school, as pupil no. 470, is recorded in *Muhammadan Kalij Da'iriktri, 1875–1911* (Bada'un, 1914), 2:74.
4. Syed Mahdi Hussain Bilgrami, *Oxford Varsity Life; Being the Substance of a Lecture Delivered Before the Students at Aligarh College* (Aligarh, 1906).
5. A. Logan Turner, *Sir William Turner: A Chapter in Medical History* (Edinburgh, 1919).
6. Turner, *Sir William*, 252.
7. Turner, *Sir William*, table 2, p. 152.
8. Records of Edinburgh University Indian Association, EUA GD25.
9. Circular Letter, February 1903, EUA GD25/1.
10. Indian Fair leaflet, EUA GD25/3.
11. *Constitution, Laws and Regulations of the Edinburgh Indian Association* (Edinburgh, 1911), 3–4, EUA GD25/1.
12. "Indian (Edinburgh) Association," *Edinburgh University Calendar* (Edinburgh, 1919), 903.
13. *Constitution, Laws*, 13, EUA GD25/1.
14. Gosh to Kirkpatrick, April 14, 1908, EUA GD25/1.
15. IAS, *Eastern Moonbeams* (Edinburgh, 1918), 3–5.
16. IAS, "An Address Delivered at Edinburgh," *Islamic Review and Muslim India* 4, no. 1 (January 1916): 421.
17. IAS, "Address Delivered," 422.
18. IAS, "Address Delivered," 422.
19. For the print run, see James Gilham, *Loyal Enemies: British Converts to Islam, 1850–1950* (London, 2014), 136.
20. IAS, "The Garden," *Eastern Moonbeams*, 23–27.
21. Debate topics listed in EUA GD25/1.
22. Anonymous, *The Royal Pavilion as an Indian Military Hospital* (Brighton, n.d.), 5.

23. "Shaikh, Abdul Hamid," in *British School and University Memorial Rolls, 1914–18* (accessed via Family History Library, Salt Lake City, Utah).

24. "Shaikh, Abdul Hamid," 4.

25. *India* [newspaper], January 5, 1917, 11.

26. Unnamed Rajput soldier, letter, January 29, 1915, quoted in Indian Hospital exhibition, Brighton Pavilion.

27. IAS, "A Tear in a Sapphire Vessel," *Eastern Moonbeams*, 15–20.

28. IAS, "Tear in a Sapphire," 19.

29. IAS, "In Fading Rays," *Eastern Moonbeams*, 37–41.

30. IAS, "In Fading Rays," 37.

31. Modern Pythagorean, "The Tear," in Frederic Shoberl, ed., *Forget Me Not* (London, 1832), 223–26.

32. *India*, January 5, 1917, 11; *Lancet* 190, no. 4904 (August 25, 1917): 302–3.

33. "Indian Wounded Soldiers' Flag Day," *Scotsman*, September 25, 1916, 4.

34. Valuation Roll for the Burgh of Edinburgh (1915–16): 21 Thirlestane Road (accessed via www.ScotlandsPeople.gov.uk). The address is given on Ikbal's 1916 marriage certificate, discussed below.

35. IAS, "'Yes,' Came a 'Voice,'" *Eastern Moonbeams*, 9–11.

36. IAS, "Two Phases of the Moon," *Eastern Moonbeams*, 31–33.

37. For the following section, I have taken many details from Elizabeth's pseudonymous autobiography: Morag Murray Abdullah [Elizabeth Mackenzie], *My Khyber Marriage: Experiences of a Scotswoman as the Wife of a Pathan Chieftain's Son* (London, 1934), 9–18.

38. Abdullah, *My Khyber Marriage*, 10–12.

39. Abdullah, *My Khyber Marriage*, 10.

40. Abdullah, *My Khyber Marriage*, 11.

41. Abdullah, *My Khyber Marriage*, 11.

42. Marmaduke Pickthall, "Woman's Rights in Islam," *Islamic Review and Muslim India* 8 (November 1920): 406.

43. Abdullah, *My Khyber Marriage*, 13.

44. The address is given on Elizabeth's subsequent marriage certificate.

45. Valuation Roll for the Burgh of Edinburgh (1915–16), 2 Argyle Park Terrace, (accessed via www.ScotlandsPeople.gov.uk).

46. Valuation Roll for the Burgh of Edinburgh (1915–16), 21 Thirlestane Road (accessed via www.ScotlandsPeople.gov.uk). The address is given on Ikbal's 1916 marriage certificate discussed below.

47. IAS, "Peace of the Soul," *Islamic Review and Muslim India* 5, no. 1 (January 1917): 190.

48. IAS, "Peace of the Soul."

49. Quoted in Gilham, *Loyal Enemies*, 127.

50. IAS, "Influence of the Soul on the Body," *Islamic Review and Muslim India* 6, no. 1 (1918): 125–26.

51. A. C. Jewett, *An American Engineer in Afghanistan* (Minneapolis, 1948), 51, 120–22. Thanks to Rethel Noa Davis for this reference.

52. Abdullah, *My Khyber Marriage*, 14–15.

53. Abdullah, *My Khyber Marriage*, 18.

Chapter Two: JOURNALIST

1. Abdullah, *My Khyber Marriage*, 19.
2. Abdullah, *My Khyber Marriage*, 20.
3. Marriage of IAS and Elizabeth Mackenzie, November 30, 1916, Registration District St. Andrew (685/02), wedding no. 581, accessed via www.ScotlandsPeople.gov.uk.
4. The address is given in Marriage of IAS and Elizabeth Mackenzie and in *Edinburgh and Leith Post Office Annual Directory for 1916* (Edinburgh, 1916), under the listing for Gardiner, David & Co.
5. Marriage of IAS and Elizabeth Mackenzie. I have identified Isabella L. Williams through the 1911 Scottish Census. There were too many women named Margaret Sinclair to reliably identify the second witness.
6. Saira Shah, *The Storyteller's Daughter: Return to a Lost Homeland* (London, 2003), 42.
7. Gilham, *Loyal Enemies*, 171–72.
8. IAS, "Fifteenth August at Dryburgh: A Foreigner's Impression," *Border Magazine* 23, no. 265 (January 1918): 198.
9. IAS, "Fifteenth August."
10. Mackenzie's career is outlined in his obituary: "Death of Edinburgh Author," *Scotsman*, March 3, 1936. I am grateful to his granddaughter, Maggie Goodman, for further information.
11. IAS, "Visions of a Recluse," *Eastern Moonbeams*, 45–56.
12. IAS, "The Hermitage of Sankara," *Eastern Moonbeams*, 59–80.
13. IAS, "Hermitage of Sankara," 77.
14. Donald Mackenzie, foreword to IAS, *Eastern Moonbeams*, ix.
15. Mackenzie foreword to *Eastern Moombeams*, ix. The adoption into Persian of the prose-poem (*shi'r-i manthur*) was a later twentieth-century phenomenon.
16. C. M. Grieve (pseud. for Hugh MacDiarmard), *Northern Numbers: Being Representative Selections from Certain Living Scottish Poets* (Edinburgh, 1920), 111–22 (Donald's poems); Mackenzie foreword to *Eastern Moonbeams*, xiii.
17. Mackenzie foreword to *Eastern Moonbeams*, xiv.
18. "New Books," *Scotsman*, January 13, 1919, 2.
19. IAS, *Eastern Moonbeams*, unpaginated dedication.
20. My thanks to Nancy Chaley (RAS archivist) for checking membership records on my behalf. Ikbal's membership lapsed in 1922.
21. IAS, *The Briton in India: A Pocket Interpreter Containing Phrases and Travel Talk, Etc.* (London, 1918).
22. IAS, *Briton in India*, 32.
23. IAS, "Afghanistan and the War," *Near East* 14 (February 15, 1918), 135–36; IAS, "Afghanistan and the German Threat," *Edinburgh Review* 228, no. 465 (July 1, 1918): 59–72; IAS, "The Indian Frontier and the War," *Asiatic Review* 13 and 14, nos. 37–40 (1918): 341–46; IAS, "Afghanistan and the Great War," *Los Angeles Times*, April 12, 1918, 114.
24. IAS, in *Scotsman*, August 1, 1918, 2, and February 3, 1919, 2.
25. Abdullah, *My Khyber Marriage*, 22; birth registration of Bibi Amina Shah,

October 31, 1918, Registration District Morningside, mother's name Elizabeth Louise Shah, in *Scotland, Birth Index*, p. 273, entry no. 817, accessed via www.ScotlandsPeople.gov.uk. The location of the birth is listed as 2 Argyle Park Terrace.

26. IAS, "The Khanates of the Middle East," *Contemporary Review* 115 (January 1919): 183–87.

27. Stephen Wheeler, *The Ameer Abdur Rahman* (London, 1895), 152.

28. The long friendship between Ikbal and Spence is evidenced retrospectively in Spence to Darling, November 11, 1941, BBC(2), file 1B.

29. I am grateful to Caroline Oates, archivist of the Folklore Society, for checking the membership records. Ikbal remained a member until his subscription dues lapsed in 1923.

30. Ikbal's election to the Folklore Society, and the hearty reception of his speech, are noted in "Minutes of Meetings: June 18th, 1919," *Folk-Lore: Transactions of the Folk-Lore Society* 30, no. 3 (September 1919): 1, 167–68. The speech was published as IAS, "The Folk Life of Afghanistan," *Folk-Lore* 30, no. 4 (December 30, 1919): 249–81.

31. IAS, "Folk Life of Afghanistan," 249–50.

32. IAS, "Folk Life of Afghanistan," 256.

33. IAS, "Folk Life of Afghanistan," 251.

34. "Minutes of Meetings, June 18th, 1919," 168.

35. IAS to Lloyd George, February 3, 1919, IOC(1), with a copy in NAI(1).

36. IAS to Lloyd George, February 3, 1919.

37. Lesley Hall, *A Brief Guide to Sources for the Study of Afghanistan in the India Office Records* (London, 1981), 56.

38. Shuckburgh, internal memo, February 22, 1919, IOC(1).

39. Shuckburgh to Dobbs, January 29, 1920, NAI(1).

40. IAS to Crooke, May 20, 1919, IOC(1).

41. Crooke to Holderness, May 28, 1919, IOC(1).

42. Ewing to Menzies, May 22, 1919, IOC(1).

43. Ikbal, "Notes of Conversation with IAS," May 27, 1919, NAI(1).

44. Sir John Shuckburgh, "Notes of Conversation with IAS."

45. Shuckburgh, "Notes of Conversation with IAS."

46. Subsequent meetings are mentioned in Shuckburgh to Oliphant, May 5, 1928, NAUK(8).

47. IAS to Shuckburgh, July 11, 1919, and attached note, IOC(1).

48. IAS to Shuckburgh, June 23, 1919, IOC(1).

49. IAS to Shuckburgh, June 23, 1919, IOC(1).

50. "Anniversary Meeting," *Journal of the Royal Central Asian Society* [henceforth *JRCAS*] 6 (1919), 139.

51. Reported in "Afghans and Britain: Distrust of Foreigners," *Times of India*, December 3, 1919, 5, and "The Position in Afghanistan," *Tribune* (Lahore), December 7, 1919, 8.

52. Dobbs to Shuckburgh, January 29, 1920, NAI(1).

53. "Afghanistan: A Lecture at York," *Times of India*, November 25, 1920, 10.

54. Aziz-ud-din to Secretary of Political Department, October 28, 1919, IOC(1).

55. IAS to Shuckburgh, November 3, 1919, IOC(1).

56. "Edinburgh Oriental Society," *Scotsman*, March 13, 1920, 8.
57. IAS, "British or Soviet in Afghanistan," *Scotsman*, June 25, 1920.
58. IAS, "Bolshevism in Central Asia," *Edinburgh Review*, July 1921, 136–46; IAS, "Bolshevism in the Khanates," *Herald* (Glasgow), August 6, 1921.
59. IAS, "The Federation of the Central Asian States Under the Kabul Government," *JRCAS* 8, no. 1 (1921): 29–48.
60. Discussion minuted in E. W. Sheppard, "Some Military Aspects of the Mesopotamia Problem," *JRCAS* 8, no. 1 (1921): 13–28, quotation at 26.
61. Sheppard, "Some Military Aspects," 27.
62. IAS, "Federation of Central Asian States," 47.
63. Edinburgh University Archives contain no evidence that Ikbal had been a "Lecturer and Examiner in Oriental Culture." The claim appears in various documents after his move from the city, including his own résumé in IOC(3).
64. Cynicus, "Merry-Go-Round-Flights of Fancy," *Ceylon Observer*, August 11, 1920, 1210.
65. IAS, "The Charms, Spells, and Divinations of Afghanistan," *Occult Review* 30 (July–December 1919): 156–66.
66. IAS, "Sufism in Afghanistan," *Occult Review* 31 (January–June 1920): 38–44.
67. IAS, "Sufism in Afghanistan," 39.
68. H. Travers, "Sufism," *Theosophical Path Illustrated Monthly* 23 (July–December 1922): 33–35. Travers was responding to IAS, "General Principles of Sufism," *Hibbert Journal* 20, no. 3 (April 1922): 524–35.

Chapter Three: INFORMANT

1. Date based on declaration by his friend A. C. Yate that "Sirdar Ikbal Ali Shah left for Kabul very soon after delivering this lecture [on November 10th 1920]." Quoted in an editorial footnote to IAS, "The Federation of the Central Asian States under the Kabul Government," *JRCAS* 8, no. 1 (1921): 48.
2. IAS to Shuckburgh, October 23, 1920, IOC(1).
3. IAS, "A Walk Through Kabul," *Chambers's Journal*, ser. 7, vol. 12 (May 1922): 276. His account of Panjshir was published later as IAS, "Young Afghans on Trek," *Contemporary Review* 132 (July 1927): 368.
4. IAS, "Young Afghans," 371.
5. IAS, "On a Far and Wild Frontier," *Quiver* (January 1922), 204.
6. IAS, "The Bolshevist Menace in the Middle East," *Contemporary Review* 120 (October 1921): 500–6; IAS, "Bolshevism in Central Asia," *Edinburgh Review* 234 (July–October 1921): 136–46.
7. Anonymous, "The Afghan Mission," *Herald* (Glasgow), August 10, 1921.
8. "Bolshevism in the Khanates," *Herald* (Glasgow), August 6, 1921.
9. IAS, "The Bolshevist Menace," *Graphic*, July 23, 1921, and IAS, "Rovings in Mid-Asia," *Field*, September 24, 1921.
10. For background, see Malcolm Yapp, "British Perceptions of the Russian Threat to India," *Modern Asian Studies* 21, no. 4 (1987).
11. Cook to Montagu, August 5, 1921, IOC(1).

12. Abdul Ghani, *A Review of the Political Situation in Central Asia* (Lahore: Khosla Bros. Electric Printing Works, n.d. [1921]).

13. On actual policy, see A. E. Snesarev, Lester W. Grau, and Michael A. Gress, *Afghanistan: Preparing for the Bolshevik Incursion into Afghanistan and Attack on India, 1919–20* (Solihull, 2014).

14. Bray, telegram, August 16, 1921, NAI(2). A later summary of the investigation was compiled as "Notes on Sirdar Ikbal Ali Shah," NAI (5).

15. British Representative, Kabul Mission, telegram, August 25, 1921, NAI(2).

16. Bray, unsigned telegram, August 17, 1921, NAI(2).

17. Viceroy to Secretary of State for India, telegram, September 4, 1921, IOC(1).

18. Viceroy to Secretary of State for India, telegram, September 4, 1921, IOC(1).

19. Lumby, memo, September 19, 1921, NAI(2).

20. Sir Francis Humphreys, report, September 1, 1921, NAI(2).

21. Sir Francis Humphreys, report, September 1, 1921, NAI(2).

22. Report on IAS's application for employment, December 12, 1921, IOC(1).

23. Bray, telegram, September 9, 1921, NAI(2).

24. IAS to Shuckburgh, November 18, 1921, IOC(1).

25. IAS to Shuckburgh, November 18, 1921, IOC(1).

26. IAS to Cook, November 18, 1921, IOC(1).

27. IAS to Montagu, November 24, 1921, IOC(1).

28. IAS to Montagu, November 24, 1921, IOC(1).

29. "Bolshevist Photographs: An Editorial Correction," *Field*, January 1922, 165.

30. Ali Masjid in Khyber Pass, letter to *Field*, January 1922.

31. From Bangalore, letter to *Field*, January 1922.

32. Bray, telegram, August 22, 1921, NAI(2).

33. Report by Deputy Secretary, Foreign, June 27, 1922, filed in "Activities of Sardar Saiyad [*sic*] Iqbal [*sic*] Ali Shah, FRGS," NAI(3).

34. Shaista Wahab and Barry Youngerman, *A Brief History of Afghanistan* (New York, 2007), 105.

35. Viceroy, telegram, September 13, 1921, NAI(2).

36. Secretary of State for India to IAS, December 20, 1921, IOC(1).

37. IAS, "The Occult Lore of Burma," *Occult Review* 24 (July–December 1921): 139–45.

38. "Woman Changed into Tigress," *Evening News*, September 5, 1921.

39. IAS, "A Hidden Race Roaming in Unknown Afghanistan," *Conquest* 3, no. 26 (December 1921): 45–49.

40. Birth registration of Omar Shah [*sic*], April–May–June 1922, Registration District Bristol, mother's maiden name Mackenzie, in *Register of Births (England and Wales)*, 6a:35.

41. IAS, "Travels and Hazards in Central Asia I: In Kafiristan and Kara-kum," and "Travels and Hazards in Central Asia II: In Khiva, Bokhara and Samarkand," *Asia* 22, no. 2 (February–March 1922): 121–26, 173–78.

42. Contents page, *Asia* 22, no. 2 (February 1922).

43. Advertisement for February 1922 issue of *Asia* in *Asia* 22, no. 1 (January 1922): 2.

44. IAS, "Travels and Hazards," *Asia* 22, no. 2 (February 1922): 124.

45. IAS, "Travels and Hazards."
46. "Notes on Ikbal Ali Shah's Articles in the American Magazine *Asia* of February and March 1922," March 8, 1922, IOC(1).
47. "Notes on Ikbal Ali Shah's Articles."
48. "Notes on Ikbal Ali Shah's Articles."
49. Kaye (?), memo, July 6, 1922, NAI(3).
50. Passenger manifest for HMS *Mantola*, London to Bombay, June 30, 1922. See also the indirect date of the journey given in Abdullah, *My Khyber Marriage*, 23.
51. Abdullah, *My Khyber Marriage*, 253–56.
52. The following section is based on the dramatised account of the meeting and wedding in Abdullah (1934), 30–73.
53. Sir William Stevenson Meyer et al., *The Imperial Gazetteer of India* (Oxford, 1908–31), 22:104, 107.
54. Meyer et al., *Imperial Gazetteer*, 22:105, 107.
55. Meyer et al., *Imperial Gazetteer*, 22:105, 107.
56. Michael H. Fisher, *The Inordinately Strange Life of Dyce Sombre: Victorian Anglo-Indian MP and Chancery "Lunatic"* (London, 2010).
57. IAS to Howell, September 20, 1922, NAI(3).
58. "Note by Attaché Regarding Mr. Ikbal Ali Shah, MRAS, FRGS, at Present Secretary to the Afghan Consul-General," NAI(4).
59. "Mirza Shakir Hussain Hussain," Geni.com, January 27, 2017, https://www.geni.com/people/Mirza-Shakir-Hussain/324434083630005520.
60. "Information from D.I.B. Files," September 11, 1922, NAI(3).
61. "Williams, (Laurence Frederic) Rushbrook," in *Oxford Dictionary of National Biography*.
62. "Information from D.I.B. Files," September 11, 1922, NAI(3).
63. IAS to Rushbrook Williams, September 20, 1922, NAI(3).
64. IAS, untitled/undated typescript beginning "In all propaganda . . . ," 3 and 5, NAI(3).
65. General Staff Branch, "Critiques to Offer on Mr. Ikbal Ali Shah's Note on Propaganda in Bukhara," NAI(3).
66. Rushbrook Williams to Howell, October 3, 1922; Howell to Rushbrook Williams, October 4, 1922, NAI(3).
67. IAS to Rushbrook Williams, December 4, 1922, NAI(3).
68. Howell to Rushbrook Williams, December 13, 1922, NAI(3).
69. "Note by Attaché Regarding Mr. Ikbal Ali Shah," NAI(4).
70. "Note by Attaché Regarding Mr. Ikbal Ali Shah," NAI(4).
71. Ikbal's position as editor of *The Spectator* was subsequently recorded in NAUK(3).
72. "Note by Attaché Regarding Mr. Ikbal Ali Shah," NAI(4).
73. "Note by Attaché Regarding Mr. Ikbal Ali Shah," NAI(4).
74. Review of Thomas, *Beyond Khyber Pass*, in *Spectator* (1925).
75. Abdullah, *My Khyber Marriage*, 265.
76. The circumstances of Ikbal's invitation are reported by Vice-Consul S. R. Jordan, NAUK(3).
77. IAS, "Mecca (Part I)," *Times*, July 21, 1926, 15.

78. Vice-Consul Stanley Jordan explicitly acknowledged Ikbal's centrality to his information gathering on the conference, which British officials, as non-Muslims, were banned from attending. In an official dispatch to the Foreign Office in London, Jordan stated: "I am indebted for the greater part of this information to the Indian and Malaysian pilgrimage officers and a certain Mr Ikbal Ali Shah, until recently editor of the 'Spectator' of Delhi . . . [who] was good enough to give me some of the details which figured in my report." See S. R. Jordan, NAUK(3).

79. IAS, "Mecca (Part I)," *Times*, July 21, 1926, 15.

80. IAS, "Mecca (Part I)," 16.

81. IAS, "Mecca (Part I)," 307–8.

82. IAS, "Mecca (Part I)," 307–8.

83. IAS, "A New Prophet Speaks for Fiery Islam," *New York Times*, August 15, 1926, SM10.

84. IAS, "Mecca: Part II," *Times*, July 22, 1926, 15.

85. IAS, "Mecca: Part II," 15.

86. IAS, "Mecca: Part II," 16.

87. IAS, "Mecca (Part III)," *Times*, July 23, 1926, 15–16.

88. The room is described by S. R. Jordan, July 12, 1926, 3, NAUK(2).

89. S. R. Jordan, July 3, 1926, NAUK(3).

90. Printed report (E 4319/1426/91), 1, NAUK(3).

91. IAS, printed report (E 4319/1426/91), 1, in NAUK(3).

92. IAS, "Mecca (Part III)," *Times*, July 23, 1926, 15.

93. S. R. Jordan, July 12, 1926, 2, NAUK(2).

94. S. R. Jordan, handwritten comment on cover page dated August 9, 1926, NAUK(2).

95. S. R. Jordan, handwritten comment on cover page dated July 12, 1926, NAUK(2).

96. S. R. Jordan, handwritten comment on cover page dated July 12, 1926, NAUK(2).

Chapter Four: EXPERT

1. Director of Talks to IAS, September 9, 1926, BBC(1).

2. "Note by Attaché Regarding Mr. Ikbal Ali Shah," NAI(4).

3. Relationship detailed in Shepstone to Stutt, July 31, 1926, BBC(1).

4. I am grateful to Julie Carrington, librarian of the Royal Geographical Society (hereafter RGS), for tracing documentation on Shepstone via the RGS membership records. Shepstone's correspondence with the RGS, mainly concerning his various travels and articles, is filed as CB8 1911–1920-Shepstone, Harold J; CB8 1911–1920-Papers/Shepstone, Harold J; CB9 1921–1930-Shepstone, Harold J.

5. IAS, "The Mecca Conference," *Contemporary Review* 130 (July 1926): 304–11.

6. IAS, "Mecca Conference," 308–9.

7. IAS, "Mecca Conference," 304.

8. IAS, "Mecca Conference," 309.
9. IAS, "Mecca Conference," 309.
10. IAS, "Mecca Conference," 309.
11. Harry St. John Philby, *Arabia of the Wahhabis* (London, 1928).
12. IAS, "The All-World Muslim Conference," *Spectator*, July 24, 1926, 125.
13. IAS, "The Revival of Islam," *Saturday Review*, August 28, 1926, 222.
14. IAS, "Mecca," *Times*, July 21, 1926, 15–16; IAS, "Mecca [ctd]," *Times*, July 22, 1926, 15–16; and IAS, "Mecca [ctd]," *Times*, July 23, 1926, 15–16.
15. IAS, "A New Prophet Speaks for Fiery Islam," *New York Times*, August 15, 1926.
16. IAS, "New Prophet Speaks."
17. Harry St. John Philby, "The Moslem Congress," *Times*, August 11, 1926, 8.
18. Arthur Field, "Asiatic Matters," July 31, 1926, in National Archives of India, File No. 345-N (Serial Nos.1–48).
19. Mahomed Yusuf Asfahani, in "Points from Letters: Moslems and Ibn Saud," *Times of India*, September 9, 1926, 5.
20. Fees reported in Shepstone to Stutt, July 31, 1926, BBC(1).
21. Shepstone to Stutt, July 30 and 31, 1926, BBC(1).
22. Shepstone to Stutt, July 30 and 31, 1926, BBC(1).
23. "Broadcasting," *Times*, August 6, 1926, 10, and "Broadcasting: To-day's Programmes," *Gloucester Citizen*, August 6, 1926, 5.
24. Script filed as "A Pilgrimage to Mecca," BBC(1).
25. Field, "Asiatic Matters."
26. IAS to BBC Secretary, August 28, 1926, BBC(1).
27. Stutt to IAS, September 9, 1926, BBC(1).
28. IAS to Stutt, November 27, 1926, BBC(1).
29. Stutt to IAS, November 29, 1926, BBC(1).
30. IAS to Shuckburgh, November 29, 1926, IOC(1).
31. The address is given in BBC Ltd. to IAS, November 29, 1926, BBC(1).
32. IAS, "Mystic Life of the Holy City," *Blue Peter: A Magazine of Sea-Travel* 7 (1927): 18.
33. IAS, "Ferments in the World of Islam," *JRCAS* 14 (1927): 130–46.
34. IAS, "Ferments," 130.
35. IAS, "Ferments," 131.
36. IAS, "Ferments," 131.
37. *Times Literary Supplement*, September 13, 1928, 646.
38. IAS, *Westward to Mecca* (London, 1928), 37.
39. IAS, *Westward*, 146.
40. "Burn Lawrence in Effigy," *New York Times*, January 22, 1929, 3.
41. Eldon Rutter, *The Holy Cities of Arabia*, 2 vols. (London, 1928).
42. Eldon's biography is reconstructed in William Facey and Sharon Sharpe, introduction to Rutter, *Holy Cities of Arabia* (London, reprint 2015).
43. Eliot to IAS, March 21, 1927, in Valerie Eliot and John Haffenden, eds., *The Letters of T. S. Eliot* (New Haven, Conn., 2012), 3:455–56.
44. George Orwell, "An Age Like This," in Sonia Orwell and Ian Angus, eds., *The Collected Essays, Journalism and Letters of George Orwell* (London, 1968), 1:197.
45. Eliot to IAS, September 5, 1927, in *Letters of Eliot*, 3:686.

46. IAS, "The Meeting of East and West," *New Criterion*, June 1928, 37–53.

47. IAS, "Meeting of East and West," 52.

48. IAS, "Meeting of East and West," 41.

49. McSweeney to Eliot, July 9, 1928, in *Letters of Eliot*, 4:205n1.

50. Eliot to McSweeney, July 10, 1928, in *Letters of Eliot*, 205.

51. IAS, "The Revolt of Asia," *New Statesman*, April 2, 1927, 764–65; IAS, "A Kabul Night," *New Statesman*, January 15, 1927, 417; IAS, "Young Muslims on Trek," *Contemporary Review* 132 (September 1927): 368–72; IAS, "Possibilities of Christianity in India," *New Statesman*, October 29, 1927, 73–74.

52. H. G. [Garrett] to Wakely, April 5, 1927, IOC(1).

53. Reported in Wakely to Shuckburgh, May 8, 1928, NAUK(9).

54. IAS, *The Golden East* (London, 1931), 11.

55. IAS, *Golden East*, 49.

56. IAS, *Golden East*, 12.

57. IAS, *Golden East*, 25.

58. IAS, *Golden East*, 66.

59. IAS, *Golden East*, 67.

60. IAS, *Golden East*, 49.

61. Shah, *Storyteller's Daughter*, 117.

62. Shah, *Storyteller's Daughter*, 99.

63. IAS, *Golden East*, 98.

64. IAS, *Golden East*, 115.

65. IAS, *Golden East*, 162–63.

66. IAS, *Golden East*, 163.

67. IAS, "Gandhi and his Mission," *Saturday Review*, March 15, 1930, 318–19.

68. IAS, *Golden East*, 182f.

69. Passenger manifest for SS *City of London*, Calcutta to London, April 23, 1928.

70. H.A.R. Gibb, review in *Journal of the Royal Institute of International Affairs*, January 1929, 71–72.

71. H.A.R. Gibb, review in *Journal of the Royal Institute of International Affairs*, May 1928, 221–22.

72. Gibb review in *Journal of the Royal Institute of International Affairs*, May 1928, 221.

73. IAS to Shuckburgh, April 28, 1928, NAUK(4).

74. IAS to Shuckburgh, May 5, 1928, NAUK(5).

75. Shuckburgh to IAS, May 5, 1928, NAUK(6).

76. Shuckburgh to Wakely, May 5, 1928, NAUK(7).

77. Wakely to Shuckburgh, May 8, 1928, NAUK(9).

78. Shuckburgh to Oliphant, May 5, 1928, NAUK(8).

79. Shuckburgh to Oliphant and Wakely, May 10, 1928, NAUK(4).

80. Shuckburgh to Oliphant and Wakely, May 10, 1928, NAUK(4).

81. IAS, *Afghanistan of the Afghans* (London, 1928), 79, 87.

82. IAS, *Afghanistan of Afghans*, 272.

83. Lecture described in "Palestine Today a Country of Progress and Endeavour, Says Sirdar Ikbal Ali Shah," *Palestine Bulletin*, February 18, 1929, 3.

84. "Palestine Today."

85. "Palestine Today."

86. IAS to "Respected Brother," sample solicitation letter, c. May 1928, NAUK(8).
87. IAS to "Respected Brother," sample solicitation letter, c. May 1928, NAUK(8).
88. Shuckburgh to IAS, August 17, 1928, NAUK(10).
89. Patrick to Seton, August 30, 1928, IOC(1).
90. Patrick to Seton, August 30, 1928, IOC(1).
91. The quotation (referring back to 1931) is given in Walton to Williams, November 27, 1936, IOC(2).
92. "A Life Dream—Copper Into Gold," *Advocate*, November 19, 1928, 1.
93. "King's Cousin to Lecture," *Sheffield Daily Independent*, February 18, 1929, 6, and "Exhibitions," *Times*, February 18, 1929, 10.
94. Poster for Couéism show, February 18, 1929, IOC(1).
95. Poster for Couéism show, February 18, 1929, IOC(1).
96. IAS, "With the Arab Raiders of Iraq—Captured by Brigands," *Times of India*, December 16, 1929, 14; IAS, "Captured by Brigands—in 1929!," *Derby Daily Telegraph*, December 2, 1929, 6; IAS, "Bandit Kings of the Desert . . . ," *Atlanta Constitution*, February 23, 1930, 7; IAS, "My New Year's Day with a White Brigand," *Derby Daily Telegraph*, January 1, 1930, 4.
97. IAS, "The Fall of the Ottoman Empire," *Straits Times*, April 27, 1931, 10.
98. IAS, "Afghan Beauty Secrets: Women Who Are Trained as Soldiers," *Aberdeen Press and Journal*, December 17, 1929, 2.
99. IAS to Drummond, December 17, 1928, LON.
100. H. R. Cummings, memo, December 20, 1928, LON.
101. IAS to "Secretary," April 28, 1928, BBC(1).
102. "Secretary" to IAS, May 3, 1928, BBC(1).
103. IAS to Fielden, December 29, 1928, BBC(1).
104. IAS to MacDonald, June 7, 1929, IOC(1).
105. "Uppingham—Lecture," *Grantham Journal*, February 23, 1929, 10; "Hull Appointments," *Hull Daily Mail*, March 19, 1929, 4; "Kaleidoscopic Kabul," *Western Daily Press*, January 18, 1929.
106. "Bouverie Society—Programme for Twelfth Session," *Folkestone Herald*, September 13, 1930, 2, and "Bouverie Society—Syllabus of 12th Session," *Folkestone Herald*, September 27, 1930, 8.
107. Birth registration of Osman Ian Ali Shah, January–February–March 1929, Registration District Croydon, mother's maiden surname Mackenzie, in *England and Wales Birth Index, 1916–2005*, 2a:673.
108. IAS, Form of Application and Nomination, October 7, 1930, NLC.
109. Mohamedi, Letter of Recommendation, October 9, 1930, NLC.
110. Ali, Letter of Recommendation, October 26, 1930, NLC.
111. M. A. Sherif, *Searching for Solace: A Biography of Abdullah Yusuf Ali* (Kuala Lumpur, 1994), 130.
112. Achmed Abdullah, ed., *Fifty Enthralling Stories of the Mysterious East* (London, 1930).
113. IAS, *Eastward to Persia* (London, 1930).
114. IAS, *Eastward*, vii.
115. Agha Khan, foreword to IAS, *Eastward*, x; William L. Langer, review of IAS, *Eastward*, in *Foreign Affairs*, July 1931.
116. IAS, *Eastward*, 181.

Chapter Five: AUTHOR

1. IAS, "On Being Presented to the English King," *Saturday Review*, June 14, 1930, 745-46.
2. IAS, "On Being Presented," 746.
3. IAS, "On Being Presented," 746.
4. IAS to India Office, February 3, 1930, NAI(5).
5. IAS to India Office, February 3, 1930, NAI(5).
6. Amjad Ali Shah of Sardhana, statement, March 18, 1930, NAI(5).
7. Amjad Ali Shah of Sardhana, statement, March 18, 1930, NAI(5).
8. Amjad Ali Shah of Sardhana, statement, March 18, 1930, NAI(5).
9. Francis Yeats-Brown, *Bloody Years: A Decade of Plot and Counter-Plot by the Golden Horn* (London, 1932).
10. O.M. Green, "Asia from the Other Side," *Bookman* 80, no. 479 (August 1931): 255.
11. "East and West," *Saturday Review*, July 4, 1931, 24-25.
12. "The Poetry of Robert Graves," *Saturday Review*, July 4, 1931, 25.
13. IAS, *Arabia* (London, 1931).
14. IAS, *Turkey, With Eight Illustrations in Colour* (London, 1932).
15. IAS, *Mohamed: The Prophet* (London, 1932); *Times Literary Supplement*, June 16, 1932, 435.
16. IAS, *Extracts from the Koran* (London, 1933).
17. IAS, *Extracts from Koran.*
18. IAS, *Lights of Asia*, viii.
19. Humayun Ansari, ed., *The Making of the East London Mosque, 1910-1951: Minutes of the London Mosque Fund and East London Mosque Trust Ltd.* (Cambridge, 2011), 19-22.
20. IAS, *Mohamed*, 291.
21. IAS, *Mohamed*, unpaginated dedication, and IAS, "Nadir Shah and After," *Contemporary Review* 145 (January 1, 1934): 337.
22. IAS, *Islamic Sufism* (London, 1933).
23. Margaret Smith, *Studies in Early Mysticism in the Near and Middle East* (London, 1931).
24. IAS, *Islamic Sufism*, 223-27. Compare the translations of Ghazals I, II VII, XIV, XVI, and XVIII in *Teachings of Hafiz*, trans. Gertrude Bell (London, 1897).
25. IAS, *Islamic Sufism*, 14.
26. IAS, *Islamic Sufism*, 14.
27. IAS, *The Oriental Caravan: A Revelation of the Soul and Mind of Asia* (London, 1933).
28. IAS, *Lights of Asia* (London, 1934).
29. IAS, *Lights of Asia*, viii.
30. IAS, *The Tragedy of Amanullah* (London, 1933).
31. IAS, *The Prince Aga Khan: An Authentic Life Story* (London, 1933); IAS, *Kemal: Maker of Modern Turkey* (London, 1934).
32. IAS, *Alone in Arabian Nights* (London, 1933).
33. IAS, *Alone in Arabian Nights*, 20.

34. IAS, *Alone in Arabian Nights*, 50.

35. IAS, *Alone in Arabian Nights*, 175.

36. IAS, *The Golden Pilgrimage* (London, 1933).

37. IAS, "The Simon Commission and After," *Daily Mirror*, June 12, 1930, 7.

38. IAS, "Simon Commission."

39. IAS to Joyce, July 23, 1931, IOC(3).

40. IAS to Joyce, July 23, 1931, IOC(3).

41. IAS to Joyce, July 23, 1931, IOC(3).

42. Walton to Williams, November 27, 1936, IOC(2).

43. India Office to IAS, July 25, 1931, IOC(3).

44. IAS to "Director," December 17, 1930, BBC(1).

45. IAS to "Director," May 12, 1932, BBC(1).

46. Anonymous ["for the Director"] to IAS, May 18, 1932, BBC(1).

47. "South Parade Pier Lecture," *Portsmouth Evening News*, October 11, 1932, 5.

48. "Sirdar Ikbal Ali Shah and His Wonderful Oriental Films," *Portsmouth Evening News*, October 12, 1932, 1.

49. IAS, "The Arab Lady and 'The Pictures'—My Desert Adventure," *Portsmouth Evening News*, October 8, 1932, 8.

50. For example, "The Persian Vogue," *Times of India*, February 17, 1931, 11; "Kemal and Islam," *Times of India*, July 14, 1931, 6; "Mohamed—The Prophet," *Bookman* 82, no. 487 (April 1932): 90; "Life and Letters . . . The Growth of Islamism," *West Australian*, July 9, 1932, 4; "East and West—The Tragedy of Amanullah," *Saturday Review*, January 28, 1933, 97; Kenneth Williams, "Egypt, Arabia, and Afghanistan," *Bookman* 83, no. 498 (March 1933): 498; "Extracts from the Koran," *Bookman* 83, no. 498 (March 1933): 510; "A Pen Picture of the Aga Khan," *Times of India*, May 5, 1933, 5; "Islam in the Modern World," *Times of India*, July 14, 1933, 7; Geoffrey Tillotson, "The Oriental Caravan," *Fortnightly Review*, September 1933, 380; J.V.-T., "The Golden Pilgrimage," *Bookman* 85, no. 507 (December 1933): 265; J.V.-T, "Islamic Sufism," *Bookman* 85, no. 507 (December 1933): 418; "What Religion Can Give," *Times of India*, August 24, 1934, 5; "Islamic Sufism," *Times of India*, August 24, 1934, 5.

51. Anonymous, review of IAS, *Eastward, New Statesman* 36 (1930): 444.

52. O. M. Green, "Some Books on Persia and its Arts," *Bookman* 79, no. 473 (February 1931): 298.

53. Sir Wolseley Haig, "Book of the Day—Not Exactly Persia," *Yorkshire Post*, January 23, 1931, 6.

54. "A Travel Book—'The Golden East,'" *West Australian*, August 8, 1931, 4.

55. IAS, "Tales of Mystic Meaning," *Saturday Review*, August 29, 1931, 272–73.

56. IAS, Letter, *Bookman* 84, no. 504 (September 1933): 302.

57. Court Circular, *Times*, September 10, 1936, 15.

58. 17th Ordinary Session of the Assembly, September 1936, File Reg. 33-46-R5239-R5240/15/25682, LON.

59. IAS to Azcárate, May 31, 1934, LON.

60. "A.P.," memo, June 13, 1934, LON.

61. "A.P.," memo, June 13, 1934, LON.

62. Abraham to Ralph Stevenson, July 31, 1934, IOR.R.12.17.

63. IAS to Pelt, September 3, 1934, LON.

64. IAS to Avenol, September 28, 1934, LON.

65. Aga Khan to Avenol, September 26, 1934, LON.

66. IAS, *Prince Aga Khan.*

67. Pelt, memo, October 16, 1934, LON.

68. List of attendees, in "Le Congrès Musulman d'Europe," *L'Echo de la Presse Musulmane* 4 (November 22, 1935): 4. Also Raja Adal, "Constructing Transnational Islam: The East-West Network of Shakib Arslan," in Stéphane A. Dudoignon et al., eds., *Intellectuals in the Modern Islamic World* (London, 2006), 193. Ikbal's attendance is further attested by the photograph of the congress delegates.

69. IAS, "European Muslim Conference at Geneva," *Great Britain and the East,* September 26, 1935, 396–97.

70. IAS to Pelt, October 27, 1934, LON.

71. On the multiple citizenships, see, e.g., IAS to Walters, March 15, 1935, LON.

72. Houriet to Chef du Bureau, April 8, 1935, LON.

73. Quoted in Houriet to Chef du Bureau, April 8, 1935, LON.

74. "Private File: Not to Be Circulated," undated, LON.

75. Telegram included in file "Article on Afghanistan by Sirdar Ikbal Ali Shah," NAI(6).

76. Sheikh Ahmad Abdullah, *Fighting Through: The Story of a Pathan Chieftain* (New York, 1933), and Abdullah, *Mysteries of Asia* (London, 1935).

77. Abdullah, *My Khyber Marriage.*

78. John Grant, *Through the Garden of Allah* (London, 1938).

79. Grant, *Through the Garden,* 219–20 passim.

80. Grant, *Through the Garden,* chap. 9; "satanic traffic," 256.

81. Grant, *Through the Garden,* 245, 251.

82. IAS, "Confessions of a Bandit King," *The Graphic,* November 23, 1929.

83. Amir Habibullah, *My Life: From Brigand to King* (London, 1936).

84. Hui-min Lo, "The Ching-shan Diary: A Clue to its Forgery," *East Asian History* 1 (1991).

85. My thanks for this information to Prof. R.D. McChesney (New York University), current owner of Howland's copy.

86. Donaldson to Macon, July 6, 1932, IOC(1).

87. Ibn Amjed, "The Food of Paradise," in IAS, *Book of Oriental Literature.*

88. IAS, "English Novels Through Eastern Eyes," *Bookman* 81, no. 481 (October 1931): 7.

89. IAS, "English Novels," 8.

90. *The Evening Standard Book of Best Short Stories* (London, 1934).

91. IAS, "The Sheik, the Sun and the Sack," in *Evening Standard Book,* 180–90.

92. IAS, "The Sheik, the Sun," 182, 185.

93. IAS, "The Sheik, the Sun," 188.

94. IAS, "An Oriental Looks at Films of the East," *Film Weekly,* September 19, 1931, 9.

95. The precise setting of the opening scenes of *Lost Horizon* is deliberately opaque, but Hilton mentioned Peshawar, in British India's North-West Frontier Province, and Baskul, near the Iranian border with Afghanistan.

96. IAS, *Afridi Gold* (London, 1934).

97. George Orwell, "Good Bad Books," *Tribune*, November 2, 1945.

98. "New Novels—An Exciting Tale by a Moslem," *Times of India*, July 13, 1934, 7.

99. Shah to Talks Director, May 6, 1934, BBC(1).

100. The offer was turned down: Talks Director to IAS, May 7, 1934, BBC(1).

101. "Indian Affairs in London," *Times of India*, July 22, 1935, 15.

102. "Indian Affairs in London—Prophet's Birthday Celebrated," *Times of India*, June 17, 1936, 6.

103. Cited in Gilham, *Loyal Enemies*, 173n231.

104. Talks booking form, November 18, 1936, BBC(1).

105. Williams to Walton, November 25, 1936, Walton to Williams, November 27, 1936, and Williams to Walton, December 1, 1936, IOC(2). Director, Empire Service, to Williams, November 25, 1936, BBC(1).

106. Director, Empire Service, to Williams, December 3, 1936, and Director, Empire Service, to IAS, December 4, 1936, BBC(1).

107. Talk booking form, February 3, 1937, BBC(1).

108. Milan Hauner, "Afghanistan Between the Great Powers, 1938–1945," *International Journal of Middle East Studies* 14, no. 4 (1982).

109. Talk booking form, February 3, 1937, BBC(1).

110. IAS to Director, British Council, February 6, 1937, IOC(2).

111. Edward Corse, *A Battle for Neutral Europe: British Cultural Propaganda During the Second World War* (London, 2013), 71–76.

112. Walton to Bridge, February 19, 1937, and Bridge to Walton, February 9, 1937, IOC(2).

113. Leeper to Bridge, March 3, 1937, IOC(2).

114. IAS, *Nepal: Home of the Gods* (London, 1938).

115. IAS, *Modern Afghanistan* (London, 1939).

116. Thanks to Professor Jamil Hanifi for this observation.

117. IAS, *The Controlling Minds of Asia* (London, 1937).

118. IAS, *The Book of Oriental Literature* (New York, 1938); IAS, *The Golden Treasury of Indian Literature* (London, 1938); IAS, *Spirit of the East* (New York, 1939).

119. IAS, *Fu'ad al-Awwal*, trans. Muhammad 'Abd al-Hamid (Cairo, 1939).

120. A. [Amina] A. Shah, *Tiger of the Frontier: Being the Hair-Raising Adventures and Exploits of Shair Khan, the Pathan Chieftain, etc.* (London, 1939).

121. Mallet and IAS, record of conversation, January 2, 1939, IOC(2).

122. Mallet and IAS, record of conversation, January 2, 1939, IOC(2).

123. Thomson (?) to Silver, November 22, 1937, IOC(2).

124. Memo to Secretary of Political (Internal) Department, January 9, 1939, IOC(2).

125. Antonio Gramsci, "La nuova evoluzione dell'Islam," Notebook 2 (1929–1933), in Joseph A. Buttigieg, ed., *Prison Notebooks* (New York, 2011), 1:332–34.

126. "Conferenza di Sirdar Iqbal Ali Shah nel nostro Istituto," *Oriente Moderno* 19 (1939): 231.

127. Christian Tripodi, "Propaganda and Counter-Propaganda on the Frontier, 1937–43," in Greg Kennedy and Christopher Tuck, eds., *British Propaganda*

and *Wars of Empire: Influencing Friend and Foe, 1900–2010* (London, 2016), 59; Hauner, "Afghanistan Between the Great Powers."

Chapter Six: PROPAGANDIST

1. D. J. Taylor, *Orwell: The Life* (New York, 2003), 250.
2. Joyce to Silver, April 25, 1939, IOC(3).
3. Joyce to Silver, April 25, 1939, IOC(3).
4. Joyce to Silver, April 25, 1939, IOC(3).
5. Joyce to Silver, Dibdin, and Walton, report, May 13, 1939, IOC(3).
6. Joyce to Silver, Dibdin, and Walton, report, May 13, 1939, IOC(3).
7. Joyce to Silver, Dibdin, and Walton, report, May 13, 1939, IOC(3).
8. Joyce to Silver, Dibdin, and Walton, report, May 13, 1939, IOC(3).
9. Joyce to Silver, Dibdin, and Walton, report, May 13, 1939, IOC(3).
10. IAS to Perowne, June 12, 1939, BBC(1).
11. Haskell Isaac, "Obituary: E. H. Paxton," *Bulletin of the British Society for Middle Eastern Studies* 4, no. 1 (1977).
12. Paxton to IAS, August 16, 1939, BBC(1).
13. Paxton to IAS, August 16, 1939, BBC(1).
14. IAS to Paxton, August 20, 1939, BBC(1).
15. IAS to Zetland, September 25, 1939, IOC(2).
16. IAS to Zetland, September 25, 1939, IOC(2).
17. IAS to Zetland, September 25, 1939, IOC(2).
18. *England and Wales Register* (1939).
19. *Mitcham Printing Works: Promotional Materials for Sirdar Ikbal Ali Shah* (Mitcham, repr. 1939), held at University of Iowa Libraries.
20. IAS to Wade, November 3, 1939, BBC(1).
21. Wade to IAS, November 7, 1939, BBC(1).
22. IAS to Under Secretary of State for India, December 4, 1939, IOC(2)
23. "Commutation of Political Pensions in the Sardhana and Bulandshahr Families," May 14, 1938; Donaldson to Commissioner, Meerut Division, April 1, 1940, IOC(2).
24. Peel to IAS, May 15, 1940, IOC(2).
25. IAS to Joyce, October 17, 1940, IOC(2).
26. Paxton to IAS, February 21, 1940, BBC(1).
27. IAS to Darling, May 23 and June 5, 1940, BBC(1).
28. IAS to Joyce, February 14, 1940; IAS to Rushbrook Williams, February 8, 1940, IOC(2).
29. Joyce to Silver, October 30, 1942, IOC(2).
30. I am grateful to Lindsay McCormack, archivist of Lincoln College, for information on 4 Turl Street.
31. Idries and Osman's entry to the school is recorded in OHC(1)/1, pupil no. 3093 and pupil no. 3079 and OHC(1)/3 pupil no. 3079.
32. Cited in Mitchell Stephens, *The Voice of America: Lowell Thomas and the Invention of 20th-Century Journalism* (London, 2017), 119. The phrase was reputedly an "old Turkish saying."

33. School registers in OHC(1).

34. OHC(1).

35. "Masud Khaddarposh—Human Rights Activist," Pakistan Prayers (blog), April 9, 2006, http://pakistanprayers.blogspot.com/2006/04/masud-khad darposh-human-rights.html.

36. "Shah, Edris Ali," OHC(4).

37. The hospitalization is referred to in Winser to "John" [Chidell?], December 18, 1942, IOC(2).

38. The anecdote is recorded from Idries's own mouth in Lewis F. Courtland, "A Visit to Idries Shah," in Leonard Lewin, ed., *The Diffusion of Sufi Ideas in the West* (Boulder, 1972), 121.

39. For example, IAS, "The Leaders of Turkey To-Day," *Contemporary Review* 159 (January 1941): 548–53; IAS, "Britain and the Muslims Problems," *Contemporary Review* 162 (July 1942): 346–50; IAS, "Iran and Britain," *Contemporary Review* 166 (July 1944): 91–94.

40. IAS, "Italy Versus Islam," *Free Europe* 6–7 (1942), and IAS, ". . . And They Scorn Nazism," *Bulletins from Britain*, September 10, 1941.

41. Nicholas Lloyd, "Losing the Game: Propaganda and Influence in the British Raj, 1917–47," in Kennedy and Tuck, *British Propaganda*, 48.

42. IAS, "Egypt's Part in the War," *Singapore Free Press and Mercantile Advertiser*, July 19, 1940, 4; IAS, "The Happy Lot of the Average Muslim in Britain," *Straits Times*, February 8, 1940, 12.

43. IAS, "Rights of the Small Nations and Islam," *Singapore Free Press*, March 4, 1940, 4; IAS, "The Spiritual Aspect of the War," *Singapore Free Press*, March 20, 1941, 4.

44. Hauner, "Afghanistan Between the Great Powers," 487.

45. Minutes of meeting, August 14, 1941, in Ansari, *Making*, 193.

46. IAS, "Muslims Under American Flag," *Islamic Review* 29 (1941).

47. Lecture poster filed in IOC(3).

48. Announcement of lecture by IAS, *Singapore Free Press*, October 15, 1941, 3; published version of lecture at the Royal Empire Society on February 5, 1941, IOC(3).

49. IAS to Joyce, April 19, 1941, IOC(2).

50. IAS to Joyce, July 26, 1941, IOC(2).

51. IAS to Joyce, telegram, April 29, 1942, IOC(2).

52. IAS to Secretary of State for India, July 15, 1942, IOC(2).

53. Typescript report on IAS, c. July 1941, IOC(2).

54. Typescript report on IAS, c. July 1941, IOC(2).

55. Typescript report on IAS, c. July 1941, IOC(2).

56. Joyce to Suhrawardy, October 27, 1942, IOC(2).

57. Joyce to Silver, October 30, 1942, IOC(2).

58. Secretary of State for India, memo, undated, IOC(2).

59. IAS to Amery, August 14, 1942, IOC(2).

60. Paxton to Pring, November 5, 1941, BBC(2).

61. Paxton to Pring, November 5, 1941, BBC(2).

62. Unnamed to IAS, May 13, 1941, BBC(2).

63. Darling to IAS, July 31, 1941, BBC(2).

NOTES TO PAGES 146–152   333

64. Talks booking form, July 14, 1941, BBC(2).
65. IAS to Darling, July 29, 1941, BBC(2).
66. Talks booking form, October 17, 1941, BBC(2).
67. MacInnes to Gennings, January 18, 1944, IOC(2); Serjeant to "Sirdar," June 1, 1942, BBC(3); Paxton to Darling, undated note, all BBC(3).
68. Ikbal appears in the *University Calendar* (as "Ali Shah, I.") as a student at St. Catherine's between 1941 and 1951. My thanks to Barbara Costa, Archivist, St. Catherine's College, Oxford. There is no record of his completing the degree.
69. IAS to Joyce, February 14, 1941, IOC(3).
70. IAS to Boswell, October 22, 1941, BBC(2); Contracts Director to Shah, October 29, 1941, BBC(2).
71. Darling, internal memo, November 22, 1941, BBC(2).
72. Proposed schedule of talks, August 20, 1941, BBC(2).
73. Proposed schedule of talks, August 20, 1941, BBC(2).
74. IAS to Paxton, January 9, 1942, BBC(3).
75. Sheikh A. Abdullah, "The Shrine of the Holy Pir," *The Evening Standard Second Book of Strange Stories* (London, 1937), 69–75.
76. Paxton to IAS, January 14, 1942, BBC(3).
77. Paxton to IAS, January 14, 1942, BBC(3).
78. Quoted in Melissa Dinsman, *Modernism at the Microphone: Radio, Propaganda, and Literary Aesthetics During World War II* (London, 2015), 102.
79. "Speakers for Week 51—Eastern Services," December 7, 1942, GOA I/3a/4.
80. Kristin Bluemel, "Casualty of War, Casualty of Empire: Mulk Raj Anand in England," in Shafquat Towheed, ed., *New Readings in the Literature of British India* (Stuttgart, 2007).
81. Quoted in Taylor, *Orwell*, 312.
82. Blair to IAS, January 17, 1942, BBC(3). This and several other letters to Ikbal have also been published in George Orwell, *All Propaganda Is Lies: 1941–1942*, vol. 13 of *The Complete Works of George Orwell*, ed. Peter Davison (London, 2001), 127–28.
83. IAS to Blair, January 21 and 22, 1942, BBC(3).
84. IAS to Amery, August 14, 1942, IOC(3)
85. IAS to Blair, January 29, 1942, BBC(3).
86. Blair to IAS, January 29, 1942, BBC(3). On the British Council's involvement, see Blair to IAS, February 16, 1942, BBC(3).
87. British Council to Suhrawardy, March 10, 1943, in Ansari, *Making*, 231.
88. Blair, memo, February 10, 1942; Blair to Boughen, February 10, 1942, BBC(3).
89. Shah to Boswell, February 15, 1942, BBC(3).
90. Quoted in Dinsman, *Modernism*, 105.
91. Darling, memo on IAS, February 20, 1942, BBC(3).
92. IAS to Darling, March 13, 1942, BBC(3).
93. Bernard Miall, reader's report on "Wartime Britain as an Oriental Sees It" by IAS (1942), University of Reading, Special Collections, AURR 10/2/91.
94. Anne Hocking, *Nile Green* (London, 1943).
95. George Orwell, *Keeping Our Little Corner Clean: 1942–1943*, vol. 14 of *The Complete Works of George Orwell*, ed. Peter Davison (London, 2001), 71, 76.

96. Orwell, *Keeping Our Little Corner*, 358.

97. IAS to Blair, March 8, 1943, BBC(3).

98. Blair to IAS, March 10, 1943, BBC(3).

99. Winser to "John," December 18, 1942, IOC(2).

100. Talk Booking Form, March 26, 1943, BBC(3).

101. IAS to Sawnney [sic], March 12, 1943, and Sahni [sic] to IAS, March 16, 1943, BBC(3).

102. Blair to Salkeld, "Best Books," c. 1946, GOA I/6.

103. IAS to Rushbrook Williams, March 8, 1943, BBC(3).

104. "Some Activities of Sirdar Ikbal Ali Shah" [1944], IOC(3). The archives of the National Liberal Club contain no record of the organization's existence.

105. Ansari, *Making*, 194.

106. Memo, February 15, 1943; "H.M." to Leach, April 13, 1943; "J.F.G." to McInnes, January 21, 1943, all IOC(2).

107. IAS to Foot, May 21, 1942, BBC(3).

108. "H.M." to Leach, April 13, 1943, IOC(2).

109. "H.M." to Leach, January 14, 1943, IOC(2).

110. "H.M." to IAS, February 17, 1943, IOC(2).

111. IAS, "Economic Justification of Pakistan," *Contemporary Review* 164 (July 1943): 231–34, and IAS, *Pakistan: A Plan for India* (London, 1944).

112. "Some Recent Books: The British Record in India," *Times of India*, October 19, 1945, 6; *Times Literary Supplement*, March 3, 1945, 98.

113. IAS to Noon, July 7, 1944, in Arup K. Chatterjee, *Indians in London: From the Birth of the East India Company to Independent India* (London, 2021), 288–89.

114. IAS to Noon, July 7, 1944. For context, see Milton Israel, *Communications and Power: Propaganda and the Press in the Indian Nationalist Struggle, 1920–1947* (Cambridge, 1994), chap. 5.

115. M. Rafique Afzal, *A History of the All-India Muslim League, 1906–1947* (Oxford, 2013), 351.

116. IAS to Joyce, April 1, 1944, IOC(2).

117. IAS to Joyce, October 21, 1944, IOC(2).

118. Watt to MacGregor, February 17, 1943, IOC(2).

119. Watt to MacGregor, February 17, 1943, IOC(2).

120. "Comments on Iqbal [sic] Ali Shah's Letter," November 1, 1944, IOC(2).

121. IAS to Jinnah, November 14, 1944, in Z. H. Zaidi, ed., *Quaid-i-Azam Mohammad Ali Jinnah Papers* (Islamabad, 2005), series 2, 11:2, app. 2, 581–82.

122. Chatterjee, *Indians in London*, 294.

123. IAS to Joyce, April 23, 1945, IOC(2).

124. Report quoted in Chatterjee, *Indians in London*, 295.

Chapter Seven: APPRENTICE

1. In addition to the primary sources cited below, of which I offer a biographical interpretation in light of their historical context, my account of Idries in the following chapters draws on shorter accounts of his life and work: Olav Ham-

mer, "Sufism for Westerners," in David Westerlund, ed., *Sufism in Europe and North America* (London, 2004); James Moore, "Neo-Sufism: The Case of Idries Shah," *Religion Today* 3, no. 3 (1986); "Shah, Idries," in Andrew Rawlinson, *The Book of Enlightened Masters: Western Teachers in Eastern Traditions* (Chicago, 1997); Mark Sedgwick, *Western Sufism: From the Abbasids to the New Age* (Oxford, 2016), chap. 12; and Peter Wilson, "The Strange Fate of Sufism in the New Age," in Peter B. Clarke, ed., *New Trends and Developments in the World of Islam* (London, 1998).

2. Abady to IAS, November 13, 1942, BBC(3).
3. Contract for Idries Ali Shah, November 20, 1942, BBC(3).
4. Contract "on behalf of your son," November 20, 1942, BBC(3).
5. IS, "Pan-Arab Moves," *Spectator* 171 (July 2, 1943).
6. IS, "Turkey To-Day," *Chambers's Journal*, ser. 8 (1944): 13:231–34; IAS, "A Walk Through Kabul," *Chambers's Journal*, ser. 7, vol. 12 (May 1922): 276–78.
7. IS, Letter on "Indian Deadlock," *Spectator* 173 (September 8, 1944): 220, in response to Z. [*sic*], "India: A Suggestion," *Spectator* 172 (August 17, 1944): 6.
8. IS, "Facts Behind the Syria-and-Lebanon Dispute," *War Illustrated* 9, no. 210 (July 6, 1945): 150.
9. For example, cover of issue in which Idries's membership (as Edris Ali Shah) was recorded: *United Empire* 36, no. 6 (1945).
10. "Obituary of Sir Frank Brown," *Journal of the Royal Society of Arts* 107, no. 5033 (1959): 366–67.
11. "Notices to Fellows," *United Empire* 36, no. 6 (1945): 251.
12. Cleary to Wilson-Young, April 2, 1946, IOC(2).
13. Passenger manifest for Royal Mail Lines *Drina* (ship no. 169903), London to Buenos Aires, December 19, 1945. The address given for both Ikbal and Idries is 4 Turl Street, Oxford.
14. Passenger manifest for *Drina*, December 19, 1945.
15. "Arrival of Ikbal Ali Shah," *Standard* (Buenos Aires), January 8, 1946.
16. Millington-Drake to Church, January 14, 1946, IOC(2).
17. Millington-Drake to Church, January 14, 1946, IOC(2).
18. Millington-Drake to Church, January 14, 1946, IOC(2).
19. Millington-Drake to Church, January 14, 1946, IOC(2).
20. "J.F.G." to Tunnard-Moore, March 7, 1946, IOC(2).
21. Wilson-Young to Cleary, March 22, 1946, IOC(2).
22. "El 2° Centenario de la Universidad de Princeton," *Anales de la Universidad [de Montevideo]* 56, no. 161 (1947): 5.
23. Phrase taken from "Releventes Personalidades Honran a Nuestra Universidad," *Annales de la Universidad* 56, no. 159 (1947): 21.
24. Arturo Ardao, *Espiritualismo y positivismo en el Uruguay: Filosofías universitariás de la segunda mitad del siglo XIX* (Montevideo, 1965), 103–5, 257.
25. "Releventes Personalidades," 21.
26. Text of translated lecture subsequently published as IAS, "El Espírutu de la Filosofía Oriental," in "Releventes Personalidades," 93–104.
27. IAS, "El Espírutu de la Filosofía," 96.
28. Varela to IAS, August 21, 1946, IOC(2).

29. Varela to IAS, August 21, 1946, IOC(2).
30. Shuckburgh to "Evelyn," December 17, 1947, IOC(2).
31. Cleary to Wilson-Young, April 2, 1946, IOC(2).
32. Cleary to Wilson-Young, April 2, 1946, IOC(2).
33. Finlay to Cleary, March 28, 1946, IOC(2).
34. Passenger manifest for *Darro* (ship no. 168452), Buenos Aires to London, October 17, 1946.
35. IAS to Joyce, October 21, 1946, IOC(2).
36. IAS to Joyce, October 21, 1946, IOC(2).
37. IS, "The Carpets of Persia," *Chambers's Journal* (1946), 197–98.
38. Vereker to Perowne, January 25, 1947, NAUK(1).
39. Vereker to Perowne, January 25, 1947, NAUK(1).
40. Finlay to Perowne, February 21, 1947, NAUK(1).
41. Finlay to Perowne, February 21, 1947, NAUK(1).
42. Perowne to Vereker, March 8, 1947, NAUK(1).
43. Shuckburgh to Vereker, November 13, 1947, NAUK(1).
44. Shuckburgh to Vereker, November 13, 1947, NAUK(1).
45. Vereker to Shuckburgh, December 17, 1947, NAUK(1).
46. Vereker to Shuckburgh, December 17, 1947, NAUK(1).
47. Vereker to Shuckburgh, December 17, 1947, NAUK(1).
48. IAS to Barnes, July 9, 1947, BBC(3).
49. Barnes to IAS, July 10, 1947, BBC(3).
50. Curran to IAS, August 7, 1947, BBC(3).
51. IAS, "The Future of Indian States," *Fortnightly*, August 1947.
52. Sirdar Muhammad Abdul Kadir Effendi, *Royals and Royal Mendicant: A Tragedy of the Afghan History, 1791–1949* (Lahore, 1947).
53. Booker to Joyce, August 27, 1947, IOC(2).
54. Booker to Joyce, August 27, 1947, IOC(2).
55. Booker to Joyce, August 27, 1947, IOC(2).
56. Carter [Reuters secretary] to Booker, September 1, 1947, IOC(2). I have been unable to find further documentation via the Reuters Archive at Canary Wharf, London, of contact with Idries. Thanks to John Entwisle, manager of the Reuters Archive, for assistance.
57. Booker to Joyce, August 27, 1947, IOC(2).
58. Joyce to Barker, September 7 and 9, 1948, IOC(2).
59. Advertisement for lecture by IAS, *Algemeen Handelsblat*, May 10, 1948, 6.
60. Aldous Huxley, *Ape and Essence* (London, 1948), 8.
61. Sirdar Ikbal Ali Shah, *Occultism: Its Theory and Practice* (London, 1952), 183.
62. Gerald Gardner, *High Magic's Aid* (London, 1949), vi.
63. I have based this overlap on the assertion by Louis Marin in his foreword to Idries's *Oriental Magic* (published in 1956) that Idries had "spent five years studying his subject," which would take his research back to at least 1951 and, publishing timetables being what they are, more likely 1950. See Marin, foreword to IS, *Oriental Magic* (London, 1956), xiv.
64. For "Ju-Ju Land," see the title of chap. 6 in IS, *Oriental Magic*.
65. IAS, "Mecca Revisited," *Times*, July 28, 1951, 7.

66. IAS, "Mecca Revisited." The article, published in July, expressly stated that it was written in Mecca, thus dating Ikbal's journey outside that year's hajj season, which commenced on September 3, 1951 (Dhu'l-Hijja 1, 1370).

67. IAS, "Mecca Revisited."

68. IAS, "Mecca Revisited."

69. IAS, "Modern Movements in the World of Islam," *Contemporary Review* 181 (January 1952): 81.

70. IS, *Destination Mecca* (London, 1957), 15.

71. 1950 Electoral Register for City of London and Westminster, Charing Cross Polling District.

72. IS, *Destination Mecca*, 24.

73. IS, *Destination Mecca*, 35 and chap. 5.

74. IS, *Destination Mecca*, 48.

75. IS, *Destination Mecca*, 52. On Ikbal's meeting with King Farouk, see Abdullah, *Valley*, 1–37.

76. IS, *Destination Mecca*, 53–54.

77. IS, *Destination Mecca*, 140.

78. IS, *Destination Mecca*, 144.

79. IS, *Destination Mecca*, 153.

80. IS, *Destination Mecca*, 157, 160.

81. IS, *Destination Mecca*, chap. 21.

82. IS, *Destination Mecca*, chap. 22; IAS, *Kamal: Maker of Modern Turkey* (London, 1934).

83. IS, "Cyprus Looks to the West," *Tablet*, November 24, 1951, 376–77.

84. IS, "To the Forbidden City," *Wide World Magazine*, April 1952, 18–23.

85. IS, "Forbidden City."

86. IS, "Britain's War Against TB," *Illustrated Weekly of India* 77, no. 3 (1956): 266–67.

87. "Edris Ali Shah" is mentioned as a regular former contributor in *Countryman* 53, no. 3 (1956): 469.

88. IS to Thomas on headed notepaper, June 19, 1953, LFP.

89. The address 134 Fellows Road is given in advertisement for his work in *Electronics World* 49 (1953): 61.

90. The address 19 Winchester Road is given in IS to Thomas, June 19, 1953, LFP, and in *1956 Electoral Register for Borough of Hampstead*, Adelaide No. 2 (F) Polling District.

91. Reported retrospectively in IS, letter to *Times*, March 21, 1986, 13.

92. *Electronics World* 49 (1953): 61: "Reports may be sent to Director of English Programs, Kabul Radio, Post Box 24, Kabul City, Afghanistan, or to *Edris Ali Shah*, London Agent, Kabul Radio, 134 Fellows Road, London, NW 3, England."

93. [Abdul Haq] Waleh, "In and Around Town: Graves' Khayyam: The Final Clue," *Kabul Times*, December 27, 1969, 3–4.

94. IS to Thomas, June 19, 1953, LFP.

95. IS to Thomas, June 19, 1953, LFP.

96. IS to Thomas, June 19, 1953, LFP.

97. IS, letter to *Countryman* 53, no. 3 (1956): 470.

Chapter Eight: OCCULTIST

1. Afzal Iqbal, *Life and Work of Jalal-ud-din Rumi* (London, 1956). I have been unable to inspect an original copy of this Octagon Press edition and so have had to rely on the WorldCat listing.
2. Review of Iqbal, *Life and Work of Rumi*, in *Journal of the Royal Asiatic Society* 1, no. 2 (1958): 78–79.
3. IS, *Oriental Magic* (Philosophical Library, 1957), xiii–xiv.
4. IS, *Oriental Magic*, 194–95.
5. IS, *Oriental Magic*, 1–2, 134–37.
6. Louis Marin, foreword to IS, *Oriental Magic*, xvii.
7. Reviews of *Oriental Magic* in *Journal of Bible and Religion* 26, no. 1 (1958): 59–60, and in *Journal of Asian Studies* 17, no. 2 (1958): 255–56.
8. Reviews of *Oriental Magic* in *Time and Tide* 37 (1956): 690, and in *Folklore* 119 (1956): 256.
9. IS to Lethbridge, November 22, 1956, Add. 9777/26/6/268, TCL.
10. IS, *The Secret Lore of Magic* (New York, 1957).
11. IS, *Secret Lore of Magic*, 309.
12. IS, *Secret Lore of Magic*, 248.
13. IS, *Secret Lore of Magic*, 80, 169.
14. Though both works appeared in 1956, that *Destination Mecca* was published after *Oriental Magic* is made clear by the citation in *Destination Mecca* of *Oriental Magic* as already published. See IS, *Destination Mecca*, 170.
15. IS, *Destination Mecca*, 29, 49, 61, 89–90, 104–6, 139.
16. IS, *Destination Mecca*, 34.
17. IS, *Destination Mecca*, 39, 62, 115.
18. IS, *Destination Mecca*, 49.
19. IS, *Destination Mecca*, 171.
20. IS, *Destination Mecca*, 188.
21. Milan Hauner, "One Man Against the Empire: The Faqir of Ipi and the British in Central Asia on the Eve of and During the Second World War," *Journal of Contemporary History* 16, no. 1 (1981): 183–212.
22. IS, *Destination Mecca*, 34.
23. IS, *Destination Mecca*, 188, 190.
24. *1957 Electoral Register for Borough of Paddington, North Division*, Polling District L, Maida Vale South Ward.
25. *1957 Electoral Register*; David Leeming, *Stephen Spender: A Life in Modernism* (London, 2011), 84.
26. Naipaul's address is given in Patrick French, *The World Is What It Is: The Authorised Biography of V. S. Naipaul* (London, 2008), 130, 173.
27. The Indian citizenship of IAS is listed on the passenger manifest for HMS *Carthage*, Bombay to London, July 7, 1959. The date of 1956 is given in his own declaration in "Commutation of Political Pensions Enjoyed by Syed Ikbal Ali Shah of Sardhana," NAI(7).
28. The lodging address of IAS is given in *1960 Electoral Register for Borough of Paddington, North Division*, Polling District L; and in Carey to IAS, April 5, 1960, BBC(3).

29. Dr. Aref Taner, "Sufism in the Art of Idries Shah," in L. F. Rushbrook Williams, ed., *Sufi Studies: East and West* (London, 1974), 180.

30. The book is discussed, as Ikbal described it, in "Commutation of Political Pensions," NAI(7).

31. "Commutation of Political Pensions," NAI(7).

32. "Commutation of Political Pensions," NAI(7).

33. Frederic Lamond, *Fifty Years of Wicca* (Glastonbury, 2004), 19. Lamond writes as an eyewitness.

34. Dan Carrier, "Refuge and Restaurant: Remembering the Cosmo," *Camden Review*, November 21, 2013.

35. Lamond, *Fifty*, 19. On the Jung portrait, see Norman Lebrecht, "When Swiss Cottage Spoke German," *Slipped Disk*, April 5, 2015.

36. Hunter Davies, "Hallowe'en—and the Witches Gather in Force," *Sunday Times*, October 27, 1963; Gerald Gardner, *Witchcraft Today* (London, 1954).

37. Lamond, *Fifty*, 30–32. Lamond lived at Fiveacres during the late 1950s when Bracelin was manager there.

38. Lamond, *Fifty*, 31.

39. Lamond, *Fifty*, 12.

40. Lamond, *Fifty*, 13, 21, 35–36.

41. Michael Howard, *Modern Wicca: A History From Gerald Gardner to the Present* (Woodbury, Minn., 2009), 145.

42. Gerald Gardner, *A Goddess Arrives* (London, 1939).

43. The many newspaper articles are described in Doreen Valiente, *The Rebirth of Witchcraft* (London, 2007), chap. 5.

44. Valiente, *Rebirth*, 41–42.

45. Philip Heselton, *Witchfather: A Life of Gerald Gardner* (Loughborough, 2012), 1:99–102.

46. Gerald Brosseau Gardner, "British Charms, Amulets and Talismans," *Folklore* 53, no. 2 (1942): 95–103.

47. Quoted in Lamond, *Fifty*, 14.

48. The real Dorothy Clutterbuck was a quiet Christian widow whose cabals were no more esoteric than meetings of the local beekeepers' association. See Ronald Hutton, *The Triumph of the Moon: A History of Modern Pagan Witchcraft* (Oxford, 1999), 208–12.

49. Valiente, *Rebirth*, 54–55.

50. IAS, *Viet-Nam* (London, 1960).

51. Review of IAS, *Viet-Nam*, in *International Affairs* 37, no. 2 (1961): 265–66.

52. Review of IAS, *Viet-Nam*, 266.

53. Review of IAS, *Viet-Nam*.

54. Passenger manifest for P&O Lines *Carthage*, Bombay to London, July 7, 1959.

55. Jack Leon Bracelin [IS], Gerald Gardner, *Witch* (London, 1960).

56. Valiente, *Rebirth*, 66–68.

57. Quoted in Lamond, *Fifty*, 19.

58. IS to Graves, c. 1962, RGA(1).

59. Idries's authorship of the biography, and adoption of Jack Bracelin's name as a pseudonym, is corroborated by multiple witnesses and subsequent researchers. See inter alia Lois Bourne, *Dancing with Witches* (London,

1998), 28–29; Heselton, *Witchfather*, 8–9; Hutton, *Triumph*, 205, 450; and Lamond, *Fifty*, 19.

60. Bracelin, *Gardner*, 166–67.
61. IS, *The Englishman's Handbook: Or, How to Deal with Foreigners* (London, 2000), 209.
62. IS, *Englishman's Handbook*, 209.

Chapter Nine: AMANUENSIS

1. Gardner to Arnold and Patricia Crowther, letter, December 1960, quoted in Heselton, *Witchfather*, 2:619.
2. IS to Graves, January 3, 1961, RGA(1). This and other IS letters to Graves have been published, in full or in excerpt, in Paul O'Prey, ed., *Between Moon and Moon: Selected Letters of Robert Graves, 1946–1972* (London, 1984). However, for accuracy I have also checked the originals in the Robert Graves Archive at Oxford.
3. IS to Graves, January 3, 1961, RGA(1).
4. Bracelin to Graves, July 27, 1960, RGA(8).
5. Bracelin to Graves, July 27, 1960, RGA(8).
6. Bracelin to Graves, December 8, 1960, RGA(8).
7. R. G. Wasson, "Seeking the Magic Mushroom," *Life* 49, no. 19 (1957): 100–2, 109–20.
8. Robert Graves, *Food for Centaurs* (New York, 1960); Bruce King, *Robert Graves: A Biography* (London, 2008), 193.
9. Heselton, *Witchfather*, 2:621.
10. IS to Graves, "Friday," January 1961, RGA(1).
11. IS to Graves, "Monday," January 1961, RGA(1); Heselton, *Witchfather*, 2:622.
12. For Idries's relationship with Graves, I have also relied on Grevel Lindop, "From Witchcraft to the Rubaiyyat: Robert Graves and the Shah Brothers," in Dunstan Ward, ed., *The Art of Collaboration: Essays on Robert Graves and His Contemporaries* (Palma, 2008).
13. IS to Graves, 'Monday," January 1961, RGA(1).
14. IS to Lethbridge, July 4, 1961, Add. 9777/28/5/37, TCL.
15. Offprint filed with IS to Lethbridge, July 4, 1961.
16. Heselton, *Witchfather*, 2:623.
17. Heselton, *Witchfather*, 2:624; Courtland, "Visit," 82.
18. Heselton, *Witchfather*, 2:625.
19. Heselton, *Witchfather*, 2:625–26.
20. Miranda Seymour, *Robert Graves: Life on the Edge* (New York, 1995), 390–91.
21. IS to Graves, March 21, 1961, RGA(1).
22. R. C. Zaehner, *Mysticism Sacred and Profane: An Inquiry into Some Varieties of Praeternatural Experience* (Oxford, 1957), 104.
23. Michel Pharand, "The Mythophile and the Mycophile: Robert Graves and R. Gordon Wasson," *Gravesiana* 1, no. 2 (1996): 204–15.
24. Graves to Wasson, June 16, 1962, RGA(5).

25. Graves to Wasson, June 16, 1962, RGA(5).

26. Graves to Wasson, June 16, 1962, RGA(5).

27. IS to Graves, May 29, 1961, RGA(1).

28. IS to Lethbridge, June 19, 1961, Add. 9777/28/5/35, TLC.

29. IS to Lethbridge, June 19, 1961, Add. 9777/28/5/35, TLC.

30. IS to Lethbridge, June 29, 1961, Add. 9777/28/5/36, TLC.

31. IS to Lethbridge, June 29, 1961, Add. 9777/28/5/36, TLC.

32. IS to Graves, May 29, 1961, RGA(1).

33. IS to Graves, June 9, 1961, RGA(1). The mentally ill member of Graves's household is not named.

34. R. P. Graves, *Robert Graves and the White Goddess* (London, 1995), index listing for Sargant.

35. IS to Graves, June 9, 1961, RGA(1).

36. IS to Graves, June 9, 1961, RGA(1).

37. IS to Graves, August 18, 1961, RGA(1).

38. IS to Graves, August 18 and 24, 1961, RGA(1); King, *Robert Graves*, 195. More fully see Michel Pharand, "'In the Irish-Sufic Tradition': Robert Graves and Idries Shah," *Gravesiana* 1, no. 3 (1997): 305–17.

39. For example, IS to Graves, April 11, 1961, RGA(1).

40. Seymour, *Graves*, 400.

41. Arkon Daraul [IS], *A History of Secret Societies* (New York, 1961).

42. Daraul, *History*, chap. 8, p. 97.

43. Daraul, *History*, chaps. 17, 18, and 23. The lecture was given in 1963. Lindop, "From Witchcraft," 198.

44. Daraul, *History*, chap. 5.

45. Arkon Daraul [pseud. for IS], *Witches and Sorcerers* (New York, 1962).

46. Daraul, *History*, 141.

47. Daraul, *History*, 141.

48. Daraul, *Witches*, 259–61.

49. In fact, Burke is an Irish name of Anglo-Norman origin, derived from the town of Burgh in Suffolk.

50. IS to Graves, January 1, 1962, RGA(1).

51. IS to Graves, January 1, 1962, RGA(1).

52. IS to Graves, February 8, 1962, RGA(1).

53. IS to Graves, February 8, 1962, RGA(1).

54. Omar M. Burke [pseud. for IS], "Solo to Mecca," *Blackwood's Magazine* 290, no. 1754 (1961): 481–95.

55. Burke, "Solo to Mecca," 481–82.

56. Burke, "Solo to Mecca," 487.

57. Burke, "Solo to Mecca," 486.

58. Omar M. Burke [pseud. for IS], "Tunisian Caravan," *Blackwood's Magazine* 291 [1756] (1962): 128.

59. Burke, "Tunisian Caravan," 131.

60. Burke, "Tunisian Caravan," 133.

61. IS to Graves, July 3, 1963, RGA(1).

62. The hotel is evidenced by Idries's use of its headed notepaper for his letter to

Graves of July 3. On the hotel itself, see Rakım Ziyaoğlu, *Tourist's Guide to Istanbul* (Istanbul, 1951), 241.

63. John G. Bennett, *Witness: The Autobiography of John G. Bennett* (Charles Town, 1983), 355; Augy Hayter, preface to Omar Ali-Shah, *Sufism for Today* (New York, 1990), vi.

64. Kathleen Ferrick Rosenblatt, *René Daumal: The Life and Work of a Mystic Guide* (New York, 1999), 15.

65. Bennett, *Witness*, 355.

66. Bennett, *Witness*, 355.

67. Robert Twigger, interview by the author, UEA, September 13, 2019.

68. Bennett, *Witness*, 355.

69. G. I. Gurdjieff, *Meetings with Remarkable Men* (London, 1963), 116–17, 156–60, 219–23, 236–37.

70. Elizabeth Bennett, conversation with James Moore, quoted verbatim in James Moore, email communication, January 12, 2016.

71. Gurdjieff, *Meetings*, 2, 90, 148, 164. Photostats of the English translation were shared among Gurdjieff's followers prior to its publication.

72. Gurdjieff, *Meetings*, 2.

73. Helena Edwards, *All This—and Heaven Too?* (Bath, 2009), 68–75.

74. Coombe Springs is described in Chris Coates, "How Many Arks Does It Take?," in Timothy Miller, ed., *Spiritual and Visionary Communities: Out to Save the World* (Abingdon, 2013); and Edwards, *All This*, 17–31.

75. Many of his talks have been preserved as J. G. Bennett, *Sunday Talks at Coombe Springs* (Santa Fe, N.M., 2002).

76. I have relied for this section on Edwards, *All This*, 117–18.

77. *Declaration of the People of the Tradition* (London, 1966, 1974). The text is also published in full in Bennett, *Witness*, 357–58, bearing the copyright of Octagon Press.

78. Bennett, *Witness*, 358.

79. Ivan Tyrrell, *Listening to Idries Shah: How Understanding Can Grow: A Memoir* (Chalvington, 2016), 55.

80. Tyrrell, *Listening*, 55.

81. Bennett, *Witness*, 358.

82. Bennett, *Witness*, 359.

83. Bennett, *Witness*, 359.

84. Major Desmond R. Martin, "Below the Hindu Kush," *Lady* 162, no. 4210 (December 9, 1965). Idries later had the article republished by his own Octagon Press in Roy Weaver Davidson, ed., *Documents on Contemporary Dervish Communities* (London, 1966). It was claimed that Martin was editor of *The Lady*, though the magazine has no record of this.

85. Letter quoted in Paul Beekman Taylor, *Gurdjieff's America: Mediating the Miraculous* (Chicago, 2004), 219.

86. Taylor, *Gurdjieff's America*, 219–20.

87. Hayter, preface to Ali-Shah, *Sufism for Today*, vi. Note that Hayter writes as an eyewitness participant.

88. Hayter, preface to Ali-Shah, *Sufism for Today*, viii.

89. Hayter, preface to Ali-Shah, *Sufism for Today*, viii, xi.

90. Hayter, preface to Ali-Shah, *Sufism for Today*, x.

91. Hayter, preface to Ali-Shah, *Sufism for Today*, vii.

92. "From a Correspondent," "Elusive Guardians of Ancient Secrets," *Times*, March 9, 1964, 12.

93. Marriage of Cynthia D. G. Kabraji, October–November 1963, in *England and Wales Marriage Index, 1916–2005*, 5d:592.

94. "Fredoon Kabraji," *Making Britain*, Open University, http://www.open.ac .uk/researchprojects/makingbritain/content/fredoon-kabraji.

95. The Kabraji family was still living there after the war: London, England, Electoral Registers, 1832–1965: Camden Hampstead: 1949, 27.

96. Fredoon Kabraji, *A Minor Georgian's Swan Song* (London, 1944).

97. Kabraji, *Minor Georgian's*, 17.

98. Adrian Wright, *Foreign Country: The Life of L. P. Hartley* (London, 2001), 201; Kabraji to Graves, September 5, 1956, RGA(6).

99. King, *Robert Graves*, 196–97; Kashfi Shah to Graves, 1962–66, RGA(3).

100. IS, *Darkest England* (London, 1987), 259.

101. IS to Graves, August 21, 1961, RGA(1).

102. IS to Graves, August 24, 1961, RGA(1).

103. IS to Graves, August 31, 1961, RGA(1).

104. IS to Graves, September 27, 1961, RGA(1).

105. IS to Graves, October 16, 1961, RGA(1).

106. IS to Graves, January 11, 1962, and "Thursday," January 1962, RGA(1).

107. *1963 Electoral Register for Borough of St. Marylebone*, Polling District B (M) Lord's Ward. Idries and Kashfi stayed there for three years, until 1966, when the house was listed for demolition. See IS to Graves, February 14, 1966, RGA(1).

108. Terry Westwood to the author, August 9, 2018.

109. IS to Graves, September 27, 1961, RGA(1).

110. IS to Graves, October 2–3, 1961, RGA(1).

111. IS to Graves, October 2–3, 1961, RGA(1).

112. IS to Graves, October 2–3, 1961, RGA(1).

113. Heselton, *Witchfather*, 2:634.

Chapter Ten: MYSTIC

1. IS, *The Sufis* (New York, 1964).

2. Graves introduction to IS, *Sufis*, ix.

3. IS, *Sufis*, 401–3.

4. IS, *Sufis*, 401–3.

5. IS, *Sufis*, 42, 49.

6. Dag Hammarskjöld, *Markings* (London, 1964), 55.2, 55.3.

7. IS, *Sufis*, 357–65.

8. IS, *Sufis*, 362–64.

9. John A. T. Robinson, *Honest to God* (London, 1963). Its cultural impact is described in Dominic Sandbrook, *White Heat: A History of Britain in the Swinging Sixties* (London, 2006), 460–63.

10. Robinson, *Honest to God*, 140, quotation on 45.

11. Donald S. Lopez, *Prisoners of Shangri-La: Tibetan Buddhism and the West* (Chicago, 1999), 99–100.

12. IS, *Sufis*, 26, 28, 139–40, 295, 354.

13. IS, *Sufis*, 26, 28, 137–63, 354.

14. Review of IS, *Sufis*, in *Islamic Studies* 3, no. 4 (1964): 531–33, quote at 531.

15. Review of IS, *Sufis*, in *Journal of the Royal Asiatic Society* 1, no. 2 (1965): 80; IS to Graves, October 2–3, 1961, RGA(1).

16. Review of IS, *Sufis*, in *New York Times*, September 13, 1964, 24.

17. Review of IS, *Sufis*, in *Listener*, October 29, 1964, 677–78.

18. Review of IS, *Sufis*, in *Spectator*, September 18, 1964, 373.

19. Robert Twigger, interview by the author, UEA, September 13, 2019; Carole Klein, *Doris Lessing: A Biography* (New York, 2000), 219.

20. On Lessing's reading of Lefort, see Nick Holdstock, "Doris Lessing's Library: A Life in 4,000 Books," *Guardian*, February 7, 2017.

21. Klein, *Doris Lessing*, 221.

22. Bennett, *Witness*, 359.

23. Bennett, *Witness*, 359–60.

24. Bennett, *Witness*, 359–60. Also described in Peter Washington, *Madame Blavatsky's Baboon: Theosophy and the Emergence of the Western Guru* (London, 1993), 396–99.

25. Quoted in Bennett, *Witness*, 360.

26. Bennett, *Witness*, 360–61.

27. Bennett, *Witness*, 361; Edwards, *All This*, 14–15, 118.

28. Terry Westwood to the author, August 9, 2018.

29. This description is based on a photograph taken at Coombe Springs soon after Idries took over the property in the summer of 1965. My thanks to Terry Westwood for providing a copy.

30. Bennett, *Witness*, 361.

31. Tyrrell, *Listening*, 58.

32. Tyrrell, *Listening*, 58.

33. IS to Graves, June 9, 1966, RGA(1)/84.

34. Rafael Lefort [pseud. for IS], *The Teachers of Gurdjieff* (London, 1966). On IS as the author, see the first-person testimony in Jessmin Howarth and Dushka Howarth, *It's Up to Ourselves* (New York, 2009), 332.

35. Howarth and Howarth, *It's Up to Ourselves*, 332. I have attempted without success to corroborate Bennett and the Howarths' account of Idries's sale of Coombe Springs by searching for original sale documents in the Surrey County Archives at Kingston-on-Thames.

36. Howarth and Howarth, *It's Up to Ourselves*, 362, and Tyrrell, *Listening*, 63.

37. Howarth and Howarth, *It's Up to Ourselves*, 362, and Tyrrell, *Listening*, 63.

38. Howarth and Howarth, *It's Up to Ourselves*, 362, and Tyrrell, *Listening*, 63.

39. E. Langridge, ed., *Langton Green through the Ages* (Tunbridge Wells, 2009).

40. Langridge, *Langton Green*, 70.

41. Courtland, "Visit," 118–19.

42. Christopher Woodward, "Russell Page: The Most Famous Garden Designer No One's Ever Heard Of," *Telegraph*, March 21, 2015.

43. Tyrrell, *Listening*, 87.
44. Russell Page, *The Education of a Gardener* (1962; reprint New York, 1983), 36–37.
45. OAS to Graves, October 5, 1964, RGA(4).
46. OAS to Graves, March 13, 1964, RGA(4).
47. OAS to Graves, October 3, 1965, RGA(4).
48. OAS to Graves, May 26, 1966, RGA(4). The translation appeared as Sa'di, *Le Jardin de roses (Gulistan)*, traduction et préface de Omar Ali-Shah (Paris, 1966).
49. IS to Graves, February 14, 1966, RGA(1).
50. IS, *Special Problems in the Study of Sufi Ideas* (London, 1966), annotated text of a lecture given at the University of Sussex in 1966.
51. Mary Ann Gillies, "A. P. Watt, Literary Agent," *Publishing Research Quarterly*, February 1993, 20–33.
52. Gillies, "A. P. Watt," 29.
53. Maschler to IS, August 4, 1964, JCA(1); Tom Maschler, *Editor* (Madrid, 2009), 70.
54. Tom Maschler, introduction to Maschler, ed., *Declaration* (London, 1959), 7.
55. IS, *Sufis*, 56–97.
56. Gurdjieff, *Meetings*, 2.
57. IS, *Sufis*, 59.
58. IS to Ketley, April 21, 1965, JCA(1).
59. IS to Maschler, June 12, 1965, JCA(1).
60. Sample publicity postcard, September 23, 1966, JCA(1).
61. IS to Maschler, October 14, 1966, JCA(1).
62. IS, *The Exploits of the Incomparable Mulla Nasrudin* (London, 1966).
63. Graves's feedback is acknowledged in IS to Graves, May 1, 1962, RGA(1).
64. Reviews of *The Exploits of the Incomparable Mulla Nasrudin* in *Birmingham Post*, November 25, 1966, and in *New Statesman*, November 25, 1966.
65. On Williams's role in the Mulla Nasrudin venture, I have relied on Matthew Dessem, "Animation's Lost Masterpiece," *Dissolve*, June 5, 2014, https://thedissolve.com/features/movie-of-the-week/602-animations-lost-masterpiece/, accessed November 2016.
66. IS to Graves, February 14, 1966, RGA(1).
67. IS, *The Pleasantries of the Incredible Mulla Nasrudin* (London, 1968).
68. IS to Maschler on headed notepaper, October 23, 1967, and Williams to Maschler on headed notepaper, April 10, 1968, JCA(3).
69. Sally Johnson (SUFI) to Maschler, February 1, 1968, JCA(2).
70. Courtland, "Visit," 62; IS to Graves, February 14, 1966, RGA(1).
71. IS to Maschler, August 21, 1968, JCA(3).
72. Dessem, "Animination's."
73. Uncatalogued letter filed with Graves to IS, August 2, 1972, RGA(1).
74. IS to Maschler, October 23, 1967, JCA(3).
75. Laura McLaws Helms and Venetia Porter, eds, *Thea Porter: Bohemian Chic* (London, 2015), 69.
76. Helms and Porter, *Thea Porter*, 39, 69.
77. On the hippies at Langton House, see Tahir Shah, untitled essay in Stafford

Cliff, *Home* (New York, 2007), 250. On fans on the village green, Margaret Smith, interview by the author, August 16, 2023.

78. On the Salinger link, see Shah, untitled essay in Cliff, *Home*.

79. Julian Palacios, *Syd Barrett and Pink Floyd: Dark Globe* (London, 2010), 161; John A. Walker, *Cross-Overs: Art into Pop—Pop into Art* (London, 1987), 103.

80. Advertisement, *San Francisco Sunday Examiner*, October 17, 1967, 42.

81. The Sufi doctrine of love was, however, partly discussed in IS, *Sufis*, 317–25.

82. Courtland, "Visit," 71.

83. Courtland, "Visit," 71.

84. IS, *Tales of the Dervishes: Teaching Stories of the Sufi Masters over the Past Thousand Years* (London, 1967).

85. McCormick to Graves, November 20, 1967, RGA(1).

86. Review of IS, *Tales of the Dervishes*, in *Observer*, December 17, 1967, 21.

87. George Bruce, *Retreat from Kabul* (London, 1968) and obituary, *Times*, June 14, 2005.

88. However, a "Sultan Jan Fishar [*sic*]" is mentioned in passing, albeit without detail or identification, in Bruce, *Retreat*, 85.

89. IS, *Problemas especiales para el estudio de las ideas sufis* (Buenos Aires, 1968); *Reflexiones* (Buenos Aires, 1971); *The Pleasantries of the Incredible Mulla Nasrudin* (London, 1968); *Caravan of Dreams* (London, 1968); *The Way of the Sufi* (London, 1968).

90. IS to Ross, May 3, 1968, JCA(2).

91. On the use of Lorimer, see Mark Sedgwick, "The Tradition of Omar Ali-Shah in Latin America," in Marco Pasi and Juan Bubello, eds., *El Esoterismo occidental en Iberoamérica* (La Plata, forthcoming).

92. D.L.R. Lorimer and E. O. Lorimer, *Persian Tales: Written Down for the First Time in the Original Kermānī and Bakhtiārī* (London, 1919), 47n1.

93. Anonymous (IS), *New Research on Current Philosophical Systems* (London, 1968).

94. Anonymous, *New Research*, 3, 5.

95. Anonymous, *New Research*, 17.

96. Anonymous, *New Research*, 6.

97. Anonymous, *New Research*, 5.

98. Anonymous, *New Research*, 13.

99. Anonymous, *New Research*, 20–23.

100. Anonymous, *New Research*, 32.

101. Anonymous, *New Research*, 28.

102. E. H. Palmer, *Oriental Mysticism* (1867; reprint London, 1969); Mahmoud Shabistari, *The Secret Garden*, trans. E. A. Johnson (1887; reprint London, 1969).

103. IS, *The Book of the Book* (London, 1969).

104. The two BBC awards are noted in Doris Lessing, "The Mysterious East," *New York Review of Books*, October 22, 1970. I have been unable to independently corroborate the claim. See also Courtland, "Visit," 79–80.

105. Edwards, *All This*, 16.

106. The address is taken from IAS to Shuckburgh, March 18, 1969, MS191/2/6/1, Folder 1, letter 28, SES.

107. Photograph of the gate in Edwards, *All This*, 100.

108. On the visits, see IS to Lethbridge, October 21, 1961, Add. 9777/28/5/43, TCL; and IS to Graves, August 29, 1961, RGA(1).

109. Robyn L. Coburn, *Dervish Dust: The Life and Words of James Coburn* (Lincoln, 2021), 131, 141; Edwards, *All This*, 16.

110. Tahir Shah, *In Arabian Nights* (New York, 2007), 144; "Hotel Cecil, Tangier, Morocco," https://www.hotelcecil.com/.

111. IAS to Graves, undated and September 1968, RGA(2).

112. IAS to Shuckburgh, March 18, 1969, SES.

113. Coburn, *Dervish Dust*, 130.

114. Coburn, *Dervish Dust*, 130.

115. Coburn, *Dervish Dust*, 132.

116. Coburn, *Dervish Dust*, 140–41.

117. Coburn, *Dervish Dust*, 130–31.

118. Tahir Shah, *Arabian Nights*, 143.

119. "Obituary: Sirdar Ikbal Ali Shah," *Times*, November 8, 1969, 8.

120. Hayter, preface to Ali-Shah, *Sufism for Today*, xiii.

121. Sedgwick, "Tradition of Omar Ali-Shah."

122. Hayter, preface to Ali-Shah, *Sufism for Today*, x–xi, xiv.

123. OAS to Graves, June 17, 1966, RGA(4).

124. OAS to Graves, June 17, 1966, RGA(4).

125. OAS to Graves, August 31, 1966, RGA(4).

126. OAS to Graves, January 9, 1967, RGA(4).

127. OAS to Graves, January 9, 1967, RGA(4).

128. A. J. Arberry, trans., *The Romance of the Rubáiyát* (London, 1959).

129. OAS to Graves, March 4, 1967, RGA(4).

130. OAS to Graves, March 4, 1967, RGA(4).

131. IS to Graves, December 29, 1966, RGA(1).

132. OAS to Graves, April 14, 1967, RGA(1).

133. OAS to Graves, April 14, 1967, RGA(1).

134. OAS to Graves, June 17, 1966, RGA(4).

135. Raphael Patai, *Robert Graves and the Hebrew Myths: A Collaboration* (Detroit, 1992), chap. 6.

136. Patai, *Robert Graves,* 140.

137. Patai, *Robert Graves,* chap. 22, p. 404.

138. Robert Graves and Omar Ali-Shah, *The Original Rubaiyyat of Omar Khayyam: A New Translation with Critical Commentaries* (New York, 1967).

139. Graves and Ali-Shah, *Original Rubaiyyat*, 1, 13.

140. Graves and Ali-Shah, *Original Rubaiyyat*, 26.

141. Graves and Ali-Shah, *Original Rubaiyyat*, 22–23.

142. Review of Graves and Ali-Shah, *Original Rubaiyyat*, in *Sunday Times*, November 27, 1967; IS to Graves, November 27, 1967, RGA(1).

143. Review of Graves and Ali-Shah, *Original Rubaiyyat*, in *Encounter*, January 1968, 77–79; Patai, *Robert Graves*, 382.

144. Review of Graves and Ali-Shah, *Original Rubaiyyat*, in *Times*, November 11, 1967. For Bowen's translations, see John Bowen, *Poems from the Persian* (London, 1948).

145. Doris Lessing, "Omar Khayyam," *New Statesman* 74 (December 15, 1967).
146. L. P. Elwell-Sutton, "The Omar Khayyam Puzzle," *JRCAS* 55, no. 2 (1968): 167–79.
147. Laurence Elwell-Sutton, *In Search of Omar Khayyam* [translation of 'Alī Dashtī, *Dam-ī bā Khayyām]* (New York, 1971).

Chapter Eleven: LUMINARY

1. Elwell-Sutton, "Khayyam Puzzle," 167.
2. The *Rubaiyyat* affair is also described in J.C.E. Bowen, *Translation or Travesty? An Enquiry into Robert Graves's Version of Some Rubaiyat of Omar Khayyam* (Abingdon, 1973), and Lindop, "From Witchcraft."
3. Elwell-Sutton, "Khayyam Puzzle," 174.
4. Elwell-Sutton, "Khayyam Puzzle," 175.
5. Elwell-Sutton, "Khayyam Puzzle," 176.
6. Elwell-Sutton, "Khayyam Puzzle," 179.
7. Robert Graves, "Translating the Rubaiyyat," *Commentary*, July 1, 1968, 66–71.
8. Graves, "Translating," 66.
9. OAS to Graves, c. 1967, RGA(4).
10. OAS, letter to *Times*, November 20, 1967.
11. OAS, letter to *Times*, November 20, 1967. On the absence in "any dictionary," see Bowen, *Translation*, 8.
12. OAS, letter to *Times*, November 20, 1967.
13. OAS to Graves, February 17, 1968, RGA(4).
14. OAS to Graves, March 31, 1968, RGA(4).
15. Graves to *Sunday Times*, March 31, 1968, quoted in Lindop "From Witchcraft," 200.
16. L. P. Elwell-Sutton, "The Rubaiyyat Revisited," *Delos* 3 (1969): 170–91.
17. Elwell-Sutton, "Rubaiyyat Revisited," 177.
18. Cited in Elwell-Sutton, "Rubaiyyat Revisited," 189.
19. Elwell-Sutton, "Rubaiyyat Revisited," 189.
20. OAS to Graves, November 14, 1968, RGA(4).
21. OAS to Graves, December 28, 1967, RGA(4).
22. OAS to Graves, December 28, 1967, RGA(4).
23. Ascoli to OAS, April 1, 1968, RGA(4).
24. Ascoli to OAS, April 1, 1968, RGA(4).
25. "90,000 Tourists Expected Here During 1970," *Kabul Times*, May 1970.
26. Max Pam, *Going East* (Paris, 1992), 14.
27. For "Svengali Shah," see Bowen, *Translation*, 13.
28. Bowen, *Translation*, 4.
29. Bowen, *Translation*, 4.
30. Bowen, *Translation*, 4.
31. Abdul Haq Waleh, "In and Around Town: Graves' Khayyam: The Final Clue," *Kabul Times*, December 27, 1969, 3–4.
32. Waleh, "In and Around Town," 3.

33. Waleh, "In and Around Town," 3.
34. Waleh, "In and Around Town," 3.
35. Waleh, "In and Around Town," 3.
36. Waleh, "In and Around Town," 3.
37. Bowen, *Translation*; John Bowen, "The Rubā'iyyāt of Omar Khayyam: A Critical Assessment of Robert Graves' and Omar Ali-Shah's Translation," *Iran* 11 (1973): 63–73.
38. OAS to Graves, February 2, 1968, RGA(4).
39. OAS to Graves, November 30, 1969, RGA(4).
40. L. P. Elwell-Sutton, "Mystic-Making," *New York Review of Books*, July 2, 1970.
41. IS to Graves, October 30, 1970, RGA(1).
42. Doris Lessing, letter to *New York Review of Books*, October 22, 1970.
43. L. P. Elwell-Sutton, letter to *New York Review of Books*, October 22, 1970.
44. Lessing to Cochrane, June 19, 1972, PAB.
45. IS, *Thinkers of the East: Studies in Experientialism* (London, 1971); IS, *The Magic Monastery: Analogical and Action Philosophy of the Middle East and Central Asia* (London, 1972).
46. IS, *The Dermis Probe* (London, 1970).
47. Review of IS, *Dermis Probe*, in *Guardian*, November 26, 1970.
48. On the RAND claims, see review of IS, *Dermis Probe*; Walter Lang, "The Process of Our Evolution," *London Evening News*, April 5, 1972, 9.
49. The full version of *One Pair of Eyes: Dreamwalkers* is at https://www.youtube.com/watch?v=1v0oGh7mTV0.
50. Alexander Mitchell, "Did Mr. Graves Take a Sheaf Out of the Wrong Book?," *Sunday Times*, March 24, 1968; Alexander Mitchell, "Graves: The Final Clue," *Sunday Times*, December 7, 1969.
51. IS to Maschler, December 29, 1970, JCA(4).
52. IS to Maschler, April 14, 1970, JCA(4).
53. *Dossier: Idries Shah* (Octagon Press, 1970), JCA(4).
54. Quoted from full letter published in O'Prey, *Between Moon*, 282–83.
55. O'Prey, *Between Moon*, 282–83.
56. IS to Graves, December 11, 1972, RGA(1); Hayter, preface to Ali-Shah, *Sufism for Today*, xiv.
57. Hayter, preface to Ali-Shah, *Sufism for Today*, xv.
58. Hayter, preface to Ali-Shah, *Sufism for Today*, xv.
59. On Sufi Sahib, see Pnina Werbner, *Pilgrims of Love: The Anthropology of a Global Sufi Cult* (London, 2003).
60. *Dossier: Idries Shah*, JCA(4).
61. IS to Beryl Graves, September 29, 1972, RGA(1).
62. Rose to Cochrane, June 27, 1972, PAB; Charles Champlin, "Critic at Large: Lucky Encounter with Two Books," *Los Angeles Times*, July 20, 1973, D1.
63. Robert Twigger, interview by the author, September 13, 2019.
64. Robert Twigger, interview by the author, September 13, 2019.
65. My thanks to Robert Twigger for helping me understand this point.
66. Doris Lessing, "An Ancient Way to New Freedom," *Vogue*, September 15, 1971, n.p.

67. Doris Lessing, "In the World Not of It," *Encounter*, August 1972, 61–64.
68. L. P. Elwell-Sutton, letter to *Encounter*, December 1972, 91–92.
69. L. P. Elwell-Sutton, letter to *Encounter*, December 1972, 92.
70. Paul Theroux, *The Great Railway Bazaar: By Train Through Asia* (London, 1975), 67.
71. Court Circular, *Times*, May 18, 1972, 21; "The East's New Dawn," *Books and Bookmen* 29, no. 9 (June 1975): 26–27.
72. "UNESCO International Book Year," *Kabul Times*, February 11, 1973, 3–4; "East's New Dawn," 26–27.
73. IS and Pat Williams, *A Framework for New Knowledge* (1973); IS, *Questions and Answers* (1973); Alexander King, IS, and Aurelio Peccei, *The World and Men* (1972); Alexander King et al., *Technology: The Two-Edged Sword* (1972), all via Seminar Cassettes.
74. IS, *Nasreddin Hoca: The Subtleties of the Inimitable Mulla Nasrudin* (London, 1973); *The Spirit of the East: An Anthology of the Scriptures of the East* (London, 1973); Omar Michael Burke [pseud. for IS], *Among the Dervishes: An Account of Travels in Asia and Africa, and Four Years Studying the Dervishes, Sufis and Fakirs by Living Among Them* (London, 1973).
75. Amina Shah, *Folk Tales of Central Asia* (London, 1970).
76. The Club of Rome, *The New Threshold* (London, 1973); IS, interview by Elizabeth Hall, "The Sufi Tradition," *Psychology Today*, July 1975, 56. An official inquiry to the Club of Rome confirms that IS was a member: Cecile Picard, administrator, Club of Rome, to the author, August 2, 2016.
77. Donella H. Meadows, Dennis L. Meadows, Jørgen Randers, and William W. Behrens III, *The Limits to Growth* (New York, 1972).
78. Jalal al-Din Rumi, *Masnavi-i Ma'navi*, trans. E. H. Whinfield (1887; reprint London, 1973); Sadi, *The Rose-Garden*, trans. E. B. Eastwick (1852; reprint London, 1974).
79. Hafiz, *The Divan*, trans. H. Wilberforce Clarke (1889; reprint London, 1974); E. H. Palmer, *Oriental Mysticism* (1867; reprint London, 1974).
80. Sir Richard Francis Burton, *The Kasîdah of Hâjî Abdû el-Yezdî* (1880; reprint London, 1974).
81. IAS, *Black and White Magic: Its Theory and Practice* (London, 1974); IAS, *The Book of Oriental Literature* (London, 1974).
82. Colin Wilson, *The Occult: A History* (London, 1971).
83. Simon Gandolfi, *The 100 Kilo Club* (London, 1975).
84. L. F. Rushbrook Williams, "Shah in his Eastern Context," in Laurence Rushbrook Williams, ed., *Sufi Studies, East and West: A Symposium in Honour of Idries Shah's Services to Sufi Studies by Twenty-Four Contributors Marking the 700th Anniversary of the Death of Jalaluddin Rumi* (London, 1974), 22.
85. Saladin Ambar, *Malcolm X at Oxford Union: Racial Politics in a Global Era* (Oxford, 2014).
86. Sir John Glubb, "Idries Shah and the Sufis," in Rushbrook Williams, *Sufi Studies*, 139–45.
87. M. Y. Shawarbi, "Shah: Knowledge, Technique and Influence," in Rushbrook Williams, *Sufi Studies*, 231.

88. IS, *Pleasantries of Nasrudin*, 9, cited in L. F. Rushbrook Williams, "Shah in his Eastern Context," in Rushbrook Williams, *Sufi Studies*, 23.

89. The book carried only the minimal legal mention that it was printed in Tonbridge, the town nearest to Langton House, hence the attribution to Idries's publishing house.

90. Ishtiaq Husain Qureshi, "Projecting Sufi Thought in an Appropriate Context," in Rushbrook Williams, *Sufi Studies*, 27; "East's New Dawn."

91. Review of Rushbrook Williams, *Sufi Studies*, in *Folklore* 87, no. 1 (1976): 120–21.

92. Doris Lessing, "If You Knew Sufi . . . ," *Guardian*, January 8, 1975, 12; Lessing, "A Revolution," *New York Times*, August 22, 1975, 31.

93. L. P. Elwell-Sutton, "Sufism and Pseudo-Sufism," *Encounter* 44, no. 5 (May 1975): 9–17.

94. "Letters," *Encounter*, August 1975, 94–96; September 1975, 89–92; October 1975, 94; December 1975, 93.

95. IS to Sulkin, March 11, 1974, PAB.

96. Sulkin to IS, March 14, 1974, PAB.

97. Sulkin to IS, March 14, 1974, PAB.

98. IS to Sulkin, March 15, 1974, PAB.

99. Sulkin to IS, March 21, 1974, PAB.

100. Sulkin to IS, March 21, 1974, PAB.

101. IS to Sulkin, March 22, 1974, PAB, and Sulkin to *TLS*, March 26, 1974, published in *TLS*, April 12, 1974, 365.

102. Bashir M. Dervish (pseud. for IS), "Idris Shah: A Contemporary Promoter of Islamic Ideas in the West," *Islamic Culture* 50, no. 4 (1976).

103. I have attempted without success to verify these claims via the archives of the RAND Corporation, Stanford University and the University of California, San Francisco. My thanks to Cara McCormick, Archivist, RAND Corporation, and David Krah, University Archivist, UCSF Library for their assistance.

104. There is no record of this award in the *Stanford Daily* newspaper. I am grateful to Daniel Hartwig, University Archivist, Stanford University, for consulting the records on my behalf.

Chapter Twelve: WARRIOR

1. Elizabeth Hall, "The Sufi Tradition," *Psychology Today*, July 1975, 53–60.

2. Hall, "Sufi Tradition," 57.

3. Hall, "Sufi Tradition," 57.

4. IS to Graves, May 13, 1969, RGA(1).

5. Hall, "Sufi Tradition," 56.

6. Hall, "Sufi Tradition," 53.

7. Hall, "Sufi Tradition," 53.

8. Hall, "Sufi Tradition," 58.

9. Hall, "Sufi Tradition," 54.

10. Carole Klein, *Doris Lessing: A Biography* (New York, 2000), 222.

11. See, for example, the 1976 lecture and audience response in "On the Nature of Sufi Knowledge part 2 of 2," at https://youtu.be/VTMcqVFk39s.

12. Lectures published as IS, *Neglected Aspects of Sufi Study* (London, 1977), with locations and dates on flyleaf, 7–8, 46.

13. IS quoted in Hall, "Sufi Tradition," 58.

14. "Tonight on FM," *San Francisco Examiner*, November 13, 1976, 32. The station was KQED.

15. Arthur J. Deikman, *The Observing Self: Mysticism and Psychotherapy* (Boston, 1982).

16. "Classified Ad 55" and "Classified Ad 17," *New York Times*, September 1, 1976, November 10, 1976, 25 and 33; ISHK History East and West Seminar, New York, May 1–2, 1976 (Institute for the Study of Human Knowledge).

17. "Classified Ad 55," "Classified Ad 659," *New York Times*, March 7, 1976, E9.

18. "Subscribe to *Human Nature* (Display Ad 762)," *New York Times*, March 19, 1978, BR9; Edwin Kiester, "Grand Sheikh of the Sufis," *Human Behavior* 6, no. 8 (August 1977): 25–30.

19. Kiester, "Grand Sheikh," 26.

20. Kiester, "Grand Sheikh," 27.

21. Kiester, "Grand Sheikh," 26.

22. Kiester, "Grand Sheikh," 29.

23. The description and conversation are from Max Edward Gorman, "A Drink with Idries Shah" (unpublished memoir, copyright Max Gorman, 2016), quoted with permission. I am most grateful to Mr. Gorman for sharing this document with me.

24. Gorman, "Drink," 2.

25. Gorman, "Drink," 5.

26. Gorman, "Drink," 6.

27. Gorman, "Drink," 11.

28. Lessing, "If You Knew."

29. Bruce Main-Smith, "Inside an Idries Shah Group," June 17, 2022, https://groups.google.com/forum/#!topic/alt.sufi/F9aMJ8eITuo.

30. Lessing, "If You Knew."

31. Their lectures were published in Institute for Cultural Research, *East and West: Today and Yesterday* (Tunbridge Wells, 1978).

32. Institute for Cultural Research, *East and West*.

33. Courtland, "Visit," 83.

34. Margaret Smith (Idries's housekeeper), interview by the author, August 16, 2023.

35. Courtland, "Visit," 59, 69.

36. On the tax manual, see Courtland, "Visit," 68.

37. Courtland, "Visit," 59.

38. Courtland, "Visit," 66.

39. Courtland, "Visit," 124.

40. Margaret Smith, interview by the author, August 16, 2023.

41. Courtland, "Visit," 93–94.

42. Description based on Margaret Smith, interview by the author, August 16, 2023.

43. Courtland, "Visit," 93–94, 96.

44. On Amina, Terry Westwood, email communication, August 9, 2018.

45. Unprovenanced article filed with IS to Graves, September 10, 1973, RGA(1). Idries's Octagon Press later published his translation of Sa'di's Persian Sufi classic: Saadi of Shiraz, *The Bostan of Saadi*, trans. Mirza Aqil-Hussein Barlas (London, 1984).

46. IS to Graves, September 13, 1971, RGA(1).

47. Tyrrell, *Listening*, 111–12.

48. Hayter, preface to Ali-Shah, *Sufism for Today*, xvi; Sedgwick, "Tradition of Omar Ali-Shah."

49. IS, *World Tales: The Extraordinary Coincidence of Stories Told in All Times, in All Places* (New York, 1979); IS to Beryl Graves, June 27, 1977, RGA(1).

50. Lisa Alther, "Tales from All Over," *New York Times*, October 21, 1979, 7, 30; Dan Sperling, "Itinerant Coincidence," *Washington Post*, November 17, 1979, B2.

51. Quoted in Courtland, "Visit," 64.

52. IS, *A Perfumed Scorpion* (London, 1978).

53. Ali Ansari, *Modern Iran: The Pahlavis and After* (London, 2007), 259–60.

54. Matthijs van den Bos, *Mystic Regimes: Sufism and the State in Iran, from the Late Qajar Era to the Islamic Republic* (Leiden, 2002).

55. L. P. Elwell-Sutton, "The Iranian Revolution," *International Journal* 34, no. 3 (1979): 391–407.

56. IS, "Invasion of Afghanistan," letter to *Times*, February 6, 1980, 15. Also Amina Shah, letter to *Times*, January 19, 1980.

57. Klein, *Doris Lessing*, 221. I have been unable to verify Klein's claim or to establish precisely what these funds were used for.

58. Various [entirely IS?], *Visits to Sufi Centres: Some Recent Research Papers on Sufis and Sufism* (London, 1980).

59. H.B.M. Dervish [pseud. for IS], *Journeys with a Sufi Master* (London, 1982), 16.

60. Dervish, *Journeys*, 51, 87–88, 104.

61. Dervish, *Journeys*, 89.

62. Dervish, *Journeys*, 97–114.

63. For example, IS, *Observations*, "collected by Lindsi Tarabdar and Zoltan E. Na'lbandev" (London, 1982).

64. Robert Darr, interview by the author, August 29, 2023.

65. For example, Chawan Thurlnas, *Current Sufi Activity* (London, 1980), 4–5.

66. Quoted in Christopher Hitchens, *Arguably* (New York, 2011), 90.

67. David Jordan, *Nile Green* (London, 1973).

68. Simon, *Spies and Holy Wars*, chap. 5.

69. Lessing to IS, September 30, 1983, DLA.

70. Lessing to IS, July 5, 1983, DLA.

71. Lessing to IS, July 5, 1983, DLA.

72. Lessing to IS, September 30, 1983, DLA.

73. Obituary of Jonathan Clowes, *Guardian*, December 1, 2016.

74. Lessing to IS, April 29 and July 11, 1984, DLA.

75. Chapman to Clowes, October 18, 1984, DLA.

76. Mohammad Reza Pahlavi, *Answer to History* (New York, 1980).

77. IS, *Kara Kush* (London, 1986).

78. IS, *Kara Kush*, 101.

79. IS, *Kara Kush*, 482–86.

80. IS, *Kara Kush*, 191–92.

81. Courtland, "Visit," 67.

82. IS, *Destination Mecca*, chap. 23, pp. 188, 190.

83. V. S. Naipaul, *An Area of Darkness* (London, 1964), 266.

84. Review of IS, *Kara Kush*, in *Sunday Times*, February 9, 1986, 43.

85. C. L. Sulzberger, "With the Mujahedeen: Kara Kush by Idries Shah," *New York Times*, June 15, 1986, BR22; review IS, *Kara Kush*, in *Kirkus Reviews*, May 1, 1986.

86. Display advertisements 341 and 251, *New York Times*, June 8 and October 12, 1986, BR31 and BR45.

87. Afghan Relief was registered with the U.K. Charity Commission as charity no. 289910. It ceased activities in 2002. It was distinct from the U.S. charity Afghan Relief Organization. The rummage sale was mentioned in Robert Twigger, interview by the author, September 13, 2019.

88. U.K. Charity Commission records, http://apps.charitycommission.gov.uk/ Showcharity/RegisterOfCharities/RemovedCharityMain.aspx?RegisteredCh arityNumber=289910&SubsidiaryNumber=0.

89. Robert Darr, interview by the author, August 29, 2023.

90. Doris Lessing, *The Wind Blows Away Our Words; and Other Documents Relating to the Afghan Resistance* (New York, 1987).

91. Lessing, *Wind Blows*, 38, 45.

92. Lessing, *Wind Blows*, 48, 93.

93. Lessing, *Wind Blows*, 43.

94. Lessing, *Wind Blows*, 53.

95. Lessing, *Wind Blows*, 63–68.

96. Lessing, *Wind Blows*, 63.

97. Lessing, *Wind Blows*, 63.

98. Lessing, *Wind Blows*, 43.

99. Lessing, *Wind Blows*, 43.

100. Lessing, *Wind Blows*, 71–72.

101. Lessing, *Wind Blows*, 68.

102. Lessing, *Wind Blows*, 102–3, 135–36.

103. These developments are eloquently described in Ed Husain, *The Islamist: Why I Joined Radical Islam in Britain, What I Saw Inside and Why I Left* (London, 2007).

104. Tyrrell, *Listening*, 131–32.

105. Tyrrell, *Listening*, 131–32.

106. IS, "The Jan Fishan Khan," in Safia Shah, ed., *Afghan Caravan* (London, 1990), 190.

107. Quoted in French, *The World Is What It Is*, 434.

108. Tyrrell, *Listening*, 135.

109. Tyrrell, *Listening*, 135.

110. Peregrine Hudson, *Under a Sickle Moon: A Journey through Afghanistan* (London, 1987); Sandy Gall, *Behind Enemy Lines* (London, 1983), and Gall, *Afghanistan: Travels with the Mujahideen* (London, 1989).

111. Louis Palmer [pseud. for IS], *Adventures in Afghanistan* (London, 1990). My deduction of pseudonymity is based on my unsuccessful attempts to verify the independent existence of this Louis Palmer.

112. Palmer, *Adventures*, 59, 114, 228.

113. Palmer, *Adventures*, 10–11.

114. IS, *Adventures, Facts, and Fantasy in Darkest England* (London, 1987); *The Natives Are Restless* (London, 1988); *The Englishman's Handbook: or, How to Deal with Foreigners* (London, 2000).

115. UK Electoral Register for Omar Ali-Shah, NAUK.

116. Omar Ali-Shah outlived his brother by almost a decade. He died in Jerez, Spain, on September 7, 2005. Both brothers were buried near their mother and father in the Muslim cemetery at Brookwood in Surrey.

117. Rudyard Kipling, *Kim* (London, 1901), 241.

INDEX